WRESTLING
WITH
THE MUSE

Melba Joyce Boyd

WRESTLING

DUDLEY RANDALL

WITH

AND THE

BROADSIDE PRESS

THE MUSE

COLUMBIA UNIVERSITY PRESS • NEW YORK

COLUMBIA UNIVERSITY PRESS

Publishers Since 1893

New York   Chichester, West Sussex

Library of Congress Cataloging-in-Publication Data
Boyd, Melba Joyce.
Wrestling with the muse : Dudley Randall and the Broadside Press /
Melba Joyce Boyd.
p.   cm.
Includes bibliographical references (p.) and index.
ISBN 0–231–13026–0 (cloth: alk. paper)
1. Randall, Dudley, 1914–   2. American literature—African American authors—
Publishing—Michigan—Detroit.   3. Literature publishing—Michigan—
Detroit—History—20th Century.   4. Publishers and publishing—United
States—Biography.   5. African American arts—Michigan—Detroit.   6. Poets,
American—20th century—Biography.   7. African American poets—Biography.
8. Broadside Press.   I. Title.

PS3568.A49Z58 2003
811'.54—dc22
[B]
2003055411

Columbia University Press books are printed
on permanent and durable acid-free paper.

Printed in the United States of America
c 10 9 8 7 6 5 4 3 2 1

For Vivian Spencer Randall and my mother, Dorothy Wynn Clore,
two women who suffered immeasurably for this dream called freedom.

CONTENTS

ILLUSTRATIONS

ACKNOWLEDGMENTS

WRITING A BOOK OF THIS NATURE TAKES TIME, patience and a lot of "help from your friends." It was no small thing to ask people to derive time from their demanding schedules and assist me with research, historical accuracy, references, intellectual clarity and stylistic flaws. Indeed, their efforts illustrate their interest in the preservation of the Dudley Randall legacy and the illumination of this particular perspective of the African American experience.

I first want to thank Vivian Randall, Phyllis Randall Sherron, Robert Randall, William Randall, and James A. Randall, who indulged my questions and shared documents and valuable family pictures, stories, and history. I would also like to thank my editor, Jennifer Crewe, and the Columbia University Press staff, especially Michael Haskell and Juree Sondker, for their patience and invaluable support.

I want to thank Naomi Long Madgett and Ron Milner, whose insights and experiences enriched the history recounted here. I am very grateful to Geoffrey Jacques, Kathryne Lindberg, and Arnold Rampersad who graciously read various versions of the manuscript and identified flaws, ellipses, and inconsistencies that escaped my perception and eluded my perspective. I am also indebted to James Hall and Xavier Nicholas, who shared primary research materials and intellectual exchanges regarding the content and context of the work. The librarians who manage special collections, manuscripts and papers at the following libraries deserve a salute: the Detroit Public Library, the Reuther Labor Library at Wayne State University, the Labadie Collection in the Special Collections in the University of Michigan Library, the Ward M. Canaday Center at the University of Toledo, and, especially, Josephus Nelson, in the Manuscripts Division of the Library of Congress. These archivists were gracious, generous, and made me feel that this project was as special to them as it was to me.

Throughout the struggle to compile the research and distill and articulate the critical and historical analyses in the book, my colleagues at Wayne State University and the University of Michigan were supportive and supplied dialogue that was extremely valuable, in particular: Alvin Aubert, Beth T. Bates, Ron Brown, Walter Edwards, Bill Harris, Chris Leland, M. L. Liebler, Anca Vlasopolos, Alan Wald, Geoffrey Ward, Stephen Ward, Katherine Wildfong, and Alma Young. In a similar regard, members of the broader literary community confirmed and supported this project. Terry Blackhawk, Paulette Childress, Robert Chrisman, Gene Cunningham, Maria Diedrich, James A. Emanuel, Geneviève and Michel Fabre, Joan Gartland, Kim Hunter, Tony Medina, James Miller, Kevin Powell, Eugene Redmond, Mark A. Reid, James Smethhurst, Dennis Teichman, Lorenzo Thomas, Quincy Troupe, and George Tysh have contributed in myriad ways to help me advance this project.

I must thank Wayne State University and the College of Liberal Arts for permitting me the time I needed to finish this book. During the sabbatical, I was able to fully concentrate on writing and editing.

I want to thank my family for being so tolerant of my temperament as I "wrestled with the muse": my partner James Kenyon, my daughter Maya, my son John, my sister Sandra (a Broadside Press worker), my brother Siegel, my nephew Stanley, my sister Dorothy, and my brother-in-law Terry, who carted me to and from the Library of Congress.

And finally, this book is for Dudley Felker Randall, who lived it, wrote about it, talked about it, and honored me with the responsibility to represent it on his behalf.

WRESTLING
WITH
THE MUSE

INTRODUCTION

WRESTLING WITH THE MUSE

My motivation for writing poetry, I believe, is something inside me,
some demon, some possession, compels me to write.

—Dudley Randall

HE MUSE RESIDES INSIDE THE IMAGINATION OF THE POET. It is the mysterious force that separates the words of a poet from ordinary encounters with language. It is a madness that dares to venture into the closets and caves of human anxiety to wrestle with the soul, to argue with the wisdom of God, and to fight with deeds of the devil. It is a balancing act on the edge of forbidden conversations with ghosts, or engaging challenges before the power of authority in hostile territory while measuring the weight of unspoken fears crafted into prayers.

Dudley Randall's fascination with the creative power of words enraptured and enveloped his imagination. Before he was old enough to write, he measured the nuances of sound, pondered words as meaning, and contrasted imagery with feelings. It was a symptom of the condition. His introverted personality connected with an internal sensibility, where he listened to whispers hidden beneath our disparate souls, sifted through contorted imagery and conversations, and untangled vocabularies that conspired with complacency and public opinion. His poetry sabotaged our false sense of sanity, challenged arrogance, critiqued casual engagements with language, and exposed foolish and dangerous expressions, devoid of conviction. Poetry was a way of life, a kind of religion for him.

He loved the imagery of sounds pressed into codes, invoked by sight and memory, and so poetry became the purpose behind many of his major decisions. He majored in English as an undergraduate at Wayne State University.

He loved books. He loved to touch them, to examine the leaves of fine paper between leather covers, and so he got a graduate degree in library science at the University of Michigan. He invested his whole being into the world of words.

Perhaps the muse acquires her own consciousness, and perhaps Erato, the muse of lyric and love poetry, was the visitor that possessed Randall, who was a willing host. Otherwise, why would such a congenial personality as Dudley Randall's embark on a mission to cultivate such a disturbance in the library? Perhaps he perceived his muse as a demon because he pursued themes that were sexual and confrontational. His shyness and aspects of his upbringing might have caused him to refrain from expressing some themes aloud. Hence, subliminally, he felt a kind of rebelliousness, and so he elicited "unacceptable" behavior through his poetry. Later in life, he identified his muse as the City of Detroit, and as a character in his poem "My Muse":

> My Zasha,
> She-Devil,
> Who spews forth filth when she is questioned,
> And carries a butchers knife in her purse.
> (In Randall, *A Litany of Friends: New and Selected Poems*, 38)

The characterization of "Zasha" as a "She-Devil" connects with the "demon" image in his first reference to what compelled him to write. This dichotomy perplexed my study of Dudley Randall's personality and his poetry.

"To make a poet black, and bid him sing," as the Harlem Renaissance poet Countee Cullen so aptly phrased it, is indeed a "curious thing," and, I might add, a cruel irony. Because historical circumstances, critical insensitivity, and prejudice in the publishing industry diminish publishing opportunities for black poets, Randall's poetry was infrequently published between 1930 and 1960, the first three decades of his writing career. But as he believed and so often stated:

> Poets write because they must. Because they have an inner drive. Whether or not any one hears of them, whether on not they make a cent, whether or not they affect a single person, poets write and will continue to write.[1]

Many of Dudley Randall's statements about writing were directed toward an audience of aspiring black poets, but these comments are essentially timeless, planetary, and nonracial. Randall's poetry persisted, and, in 1965, he founded Broadside Press. Within a few years, he had resolved the racial publishing paradox. Hundreds of thousands of books flowed from his small office in Detroit into the conversation and conversion of American and world literatures. For a people whose legacy of slavery had inflicted upon them the pangs of poverty and pervasive illiteracy, he lifted his voice and the voices of other poets above the racist, imperialist traditions of critical discrimination and cultural dismissal for everyone to read. A 1974 review of Dudley Randall's *After the Killing* by poet June Jordan in *American Poetry Review* praised Randall's poetry and his publishing venture:

> As the poet-founding-publisher of Broadside Press which, more than any press, rescued the new Black poetry of the sixties from predictable, white rejection and, furthermore, developed an original, highly effective means of getting these poems to the national Black community—a feat of prodigious, pioneer dimensions, and one that white publishers continue to term "impossible"—Dudley Randall bears impeccable, fighter credentials that more than earn him "the right" to criticize and censure the vanities and excesses of the rest of us—if that's what he wants to do: It's not.[2]

From 1945 to 1965, only thirty-five poetry books authored by African Americans were published in the United States, and only nine of those were published by presses with national distribution. (During this same period, four books were published in England, Russia and Germany.)[3] Of that accounting, Russell Atkins, Robert Hayden, Naomi Long Madgett, Gwendolyn Brooks, Ted Joans, Melvin B. Tolson, and Margaret Danner published two, three, or even four books each. Despite the emergence of at least thirty new poets in journals and anthologies during this time (and this number does not include lesser known poets who have fallen by the wayside), this paltry total reflects the dismal publishing terrain for black poets when Randall decided to challenge that record with an alternative press.

By contrast, between 1966 and 1975, Dudley Randall's Broadside Press published eighty-one books, seventy-four of which were poetry, including single collections by forty poets, and of those forty, fifteen authored two or even three titles. Each printing was at least 5,000 copies, and when there was a second or a third printing and a demonstrated demand, there were print runs of 10,000. Some of these were chapbooks (at least sixteen pages), but many were full-length books of eighty or more pages of text, printed in hard and soft covers. In the case of Don L. Lee, for instance, the number of books in print reached 100,000 by 1974. Broadside printed more than 500,000 books. Additionally, there were several anthologies that published poets. These works were extremely popular and often went to three and four printings. *The*

Broadside Series, single poems from which the press derived its name, was another source for poetry publication. They were very popular and were usually printed in lots of 500. Many of the broadsides sold out shortly after they were printed. A total of 192 poets were published by Broadside during this time. Under the auspices of Dudley Randall, Broadside Press published eighty-six books by more than two hundred poets.

But noble intentions are rarely profitable in business. Dudley Randall was a literary caretaker, not a competitive entrepreneur. So, when the press fell into financial collapse, Randall lost his equilibrium. The world had failed him, which to him meant poetry had failed him. His refusal to write trapped his soul. This depression lingered for more than three years and dug a hole so deep that even the words of his psychiatrist were rendered mute by his self-deprecation. He stewed in this misery until he decided to kill himself.

But his wife Vivian caught him and stopped him from pulling the trigger. A few weeks later, he returned to poetry and reversed the downward spiral. In April of 1980, after recovering from a three-year bout with depression, Dudley told me that he had identified me as his literary executor and his official biographer. I never asked him why he selected me, but I assumed it was because he had been my literary mentor since 1972, when I became his assistant editor at Broadside Press. But I also believe he entrusted me with this responsibility because of something he told the audience at the Detroit Institute of Arts for the 1996 premiere of my documentary film *The Black Unicorn: Dudley Randall and the Broadside Press*: "Melba published a book of poetry, finished a doctoral dissertation, and had a baby, all in the same year. When she puts her mind to something, she always finishes it." At the time, I laughed with the rest of the audience, but, in retrospect, I think it was this tenacity, which was also a prominent feature of Dudley's character, that convinced him that I should be assigned the difficult task of writing his biography and preserving his literary legacy. Besides, since 1972, when I first met Dudley, until his death on 5 August 2000, his struggles were as keen and familiar to me as those of any member of my own natural family.

I was Dudley Randall's apprentice poet and editor. As his protégé, we enjoyed a synergy that invigorated Broadside's productivity and fostered a life-long bond. Dudley profoundly influenced my creative style and scholarly assiduity. He recognized that I, too, was driven to write and that I was as possessed by the poetry demon as he was. I had also studied English language and literature in its many facets, forms, and cultural manifestations and had grown up in Detroit, where consciousness is often complicated by progressive politics of class and race converged into a unique intellectual radicalism.

1. Dudley Randall and Melba Joyce Boyd, 1996.
Photo: Hugh Grannum.

I was of a different generation, but we shared a similar middle-class up-bringing by college-educated parents, who valued culture, intelligence, sports, and the arts. I was third-generation college educated. In fact, my grandparents met on the campus of Tennessee State University, through my great-aunt, who was an English professor. But like Dudley, I had attended state universities, including the University of Michigan, where he also attended graduate school. In a broader but related context, both of our mothers were schoolteachers. Many educated blacks, like Dudley and my father, worked at the post office when they were denied professional employment. My father's application to the Ford Motor Company as an automotive engineer was denied because of racial discrimination, as was the case with Dudley's father, who sought a position at Ford in personnel. At the same time, our families were reflective of highly intelligent, educated blacks who, despite the cruelty of racism, advocated racial pride and education as "the one thing that white society could not take away from you." My family anticipated that

I would seek a doctorate or attend law school, and after I decided to return for that additional degree, Dudley encouraged me to go to the University of Michigan.

Dudley influenced me in subtle, even unstated ways. One day, he asked me why I didn't wear a watch. I told him I didn't think I needed one because everywhere I went there were clocks. I then expounded on my philosophical resistance to the repression of artificial time. He simply said, "You need a watch." A week later, I found a new Timex on my desk. I thanked him for the watch, and we didn't discuss the matter further. There was no argument, and eventually, because my life was constrained by teaching, Broadside Press, and a myriad of activities with temporal constraints, I put on the watch.

In similar ways he honed my literary, cultural, and political views through the quiet workings of our shared experiences at Broadside Press, at literary conferences, and at informal gatherings with other writers. He knew how I worked and that my scholarly activities and exposure would prepare me to write a book that would represent his voice and the world that affected and shaped it. Although he had bequeathed the responsibility to me, he was not a very cooperative subject. When I began to organize my work, he announced, "I don't want my biography to be published until I'm dead." After I convinced him that whatever the publication date, I would have to begin work while he was still living, he confessed that, "When I wasn't feeling well, I destroyed my letters and most of my photographs because I didn't think it was worth much." He had, indeed, destroyed his personal papers and letters during his depression.

Before I began writing this book, I wrote a critical biography of a nineteenth-century black poet, whose papers had also been destroyed. Writing *Discarded Legacy: Politics and Poetics in the Life of Frances E. W. Harper, 1825–1911* prepared me for a similar task with Dudley Randall's life work. With persistence as my armor, I conducted several audio interviews over a period of sixteen years, which became the fodder for this book. In 1981, I conducted video interviews of Dudley for the Hasting Street Opera Film Project, which attempted to document the history of black Detroit from the first Great Migration until the election of Coleman A. Young in 1973. Although the project was abandoned because of lack of funding after the Republican administration increased its attack on the minority arts in the 1980s, the six hours of videotapes were transcribed and compiled with the audiotapes to determine any inconsistencies and to clarify Dudley's recollections.

During the in-between years, I wrote, directed, and produced a documentary that was released in 1996 and incorporated tapings for the Hasting Street

Opera Project with the new footage for the documentary, *The Black Unicorn: Dudley Randall and the Broadside Press*. I also published an article on Dudley Randall and small-press publishing for *The Black Scholar*. But as I researched the libraries, my name kept popping up in articles, books, and correspondence. My biography was a critical connection to Dudley Randall and Broadside Press history, and in order to tell his story, I needed to assume my historical position and integrate this perspective into the narrative. It was the authority of my particular authorship. Hence, this work is a memoir within a memoir configured as cultural memory that has been scrutinized, documented, and corroborated with literary and historical materials, interviews, and observations that constituted Dudley Randall's world.

I reconstructed Randall's narrative by relating his biography to his poetry and then intersecting his personal perspective with key historic events or periods or both. His personal voice resonates with information about his conscious self and his perceptions about the world and historical realities. Similarly, affecting a third-person voice obfuscated my proximity to Randall and valuable insights and experiences we had shared, so in these historical moments I write in the first person. And in a few instances, there is dialogue between us, but only when it reinforces the relationship or effects a better reconstruction of history.

Chapter 1 presents our first meeting, and describes the intensity of the times that forged our relationship and some of the unique features of Detroit's black radicalism. It is written in the first person because it is from my point of view, and it establishes the identity and the historical position and perspective of the author, when I was twenty-two years old and thirty-six years younger than Dudley. In fact, I called him Mr. Randall for many years. I do not remember when I began to call him Dudley, but I am sure it was not until I was in my forties, after his bout with depression.

I return to this first-person narrative in chapter 16 because it is the historical point of my entry into Dudley's life. My memoir encircles Dudley's memoir. Similarly, chapters 16 through 20 are primarily written from my perspective, but within a complicated reconstruction of creative and historical experiences, as Dudley's voice is also prominently featured relative to dialogue, voices of other writers, poetry, critical analysis of poetry, and literary and political philosophies.

For the most part, Dudley was not very talkative, and his language is measured and deliberate. Consequently, there is little variance between his spoken and written voice. This enabled me to construct and sustain a fluidity and consistency of voice when integrating the voices of his oral narrative and his written narrative in chapters 2 through 10. His narrative is presented as memory, while the integration of published interviews with him and essays by him extended and confirm the credibility of that memory. In these chapters, my voice occurs as the third person, making historical connections and correlating his poetry to experience in the narrative.

Chapters 11 and 12 focus primarily on the poets of Broadside Press and their relationship to Dudley Randall. I combined his aesthetic opinion of their poetry with specific interactions. In most instances, Randall's opinions about these writers and their work is drawn directly from essays by him and published interviews with him. This provides documentation and his perspective within the historical moment. For the most part, my interviews with Dudley provided comments consistent with these published materials. Sometimes, however, he declined to comment at all, concealing his private anger or disappointment with these personalities. In these instances, it was actually more useful to rely on correspondence and other written documents that preserved his voice.

I also applied my aesthetic assessment of these poets, their work, and documented historical information about the individuality and complexity of the black literary community. I inserted an analysis about the poetry by these Broadside poets relative to their special talents and audience receptivity during the Black Arts Movement. I have not imposed any of my personal opinions about these writers through my experiences with them until I actually enter the historical stage in 1972. But even in those instances, for the most part, it is relative to their impact on Dudley Randall.

Although affecting the voice of the third person would have obfuscated my proximity to Randall and valuable insights and experiences we shared, chapters 5, 9, 13, 14, and 18 focus primarily on Dudley Randall's poetry. In these contexts, the third person accords the intellectual objectivity necessary for critical analysis. At the same time, I regard my literary criticism in theoretical terms as subjective objectivity because I also supply knowledge about Dudley's life to which a stranger would not be privy. In particular, I analyze the mechanics of his poetics and how he mediated these affects, keeping in mind the aim of Dudley Randall's poetry as he explained it: "My happiest moments have been those in which I was writing. Yet writing is something more than therapy, self-gratification. When a poet publishes his work, he expects it to do something for his readers." Therefore, I expanded my criticism by engaging literary criticism of Randall's poetry by other scholars and poets.

Throughout the book, beginning with chapter 2, the merger of Randall's published narrative with my extensive interviews is indistinguishable. The presentation of his voice is critical to the continuation of his memoir, encoding an intimacy with him through the texture, timbre, and aural authenticity of his voice. To assure this, Dudley read the first completed draft of the book and assisted me with punctuation and phrasing. I involved him as much as possible in this process to check details, to confirm historical accuracy, and to assure that I was not misrepresenting the sound and sense of his memoir. But in no instance did Dudley edit my voice, my opinions, my literary criticism, or my perspective, just as he never practiced censorship of content of any of the poets he published.

Chapters 16 through 20 contain some interactions and dialogue between Dudley and me. The dialogue is limited because it is derived from specific conversations in our history that occurred in memorable ways and coincided with the rhythm and the pace of the master narrative. We shared the same office for five years, and he never engaged mindless chitchat, indulged in gossip, or contributed to rumor or innuendo about others. This explains why the word "kind" occurs so often in impressions and remembrances of him.

This abhorrence of excessive talk developed during his childhood and provides insight into his attitude about work and a perspective into his aesthetics, verbal economy and thematic clarity: "In my own case, however, I was a preacher's son, and heard too much preaching at home. I believe that readers instinctively resist a writer who has an obvious design on them, who too obviously tries to manipulate them."

Though he shared some important information and details about his life with me, I discovered some of the more controversial events and activities reported in the literary history through primary materials during research. In actuality, he reflected the view that if he did more and spoke less he was less likely to contradict himself. He was grounded in experience and used language and culture to enhance and enrich his expressions. He then transferred that primal intensity, creative energy, and verbal clarity into the form that he aspired to master—poetry.

This book attempts to elaborate and illuminate the amazing accomplishments of Dudley Randall and his work at Broadside Press, which were the consequences of historical forces and a creative genius inspired by a love of poetry. But at the same time, it provides insight into a background that prepared him to seize the opportunity. Since the abolition of slavery, the Randalls nurtured a strong sense of intellectual and political independence and a steadfast commitment to personal integrity and cultural pride as family identity. Although he is most often associated with the revolutionary period of the 1960s, his personal lifestyle and politics resulted from an interesting combination of a middle-class Christian upbringing within the context of

Democratic Party politics and the class struggle in the United Auto Workers during the 1920s and 1930s in Detroit. Dudley Randall's early development as a scholar and poet was grounded in racial pride and the labor movement.

"Detroit is a unique place," as Mayor Coleman A. Young stated at the "Tribute to Dudley Randall" during the twenty-fifth anniversary of Broadside Press. It is the city where racial and class struggles merged to intensify, articulate, and determine municipal politics. African Americans immigrated to Detroit with the earliest settlers, and, prior to the abolition of slavery, it was a haven for fugitive slaves. The city's Canadian border internationalized that experience and provided an alternative future for African Americans, who crossed the Detroit River into Canada to seek a better life beyond the shadow of slavery. The twentieth century brought some of the most dramatic challenges and opportunities as the rise of the automobile industry accorded better jobs and access to better educational institutions.

But employment discrimination characterized northern racism, and the police enforced organized terrorism. As the population became more sophisticated and politically astute, it acquired more economic and political power. Unlike black communities in other cities, the class struggle in the labor movement elevated racial consciousness in many white people, and racial struggle in the labor movement elevated class consciousness in the black community. This dynamic effectively consolidated the black community during the 1960s and 1970s and altered racial policies in the unions. Socialism, communism, and Black Nationalism were not simply academic or narrow political considerations, but philosophies adapted to a particular brand of radical activism that advanced liberation politics and mediated race relations in Detroit for several decades.

As a young man, Dudley Randall identified scholar and an activist W. E. B. Du Bois as his intellectual model. Randall related the political to the cultural and used this perspective to nurture and complicate his aspirations to become the quintessential Renaissance man. He extended his knowledge of American poetry through the study of languages. He translated poetry from Latin, German, Italian, French, Italian, and Russian into English to enhance his skills: "Study of a foreign literature will broaden you and give you a perspective on poetry written in your own language. In short, you should open yourself to all of life, to all experiences, to all of mankind, to the whole rich bustling wonderful world, which you will transmute into poetry."

His travels throughout Europe, Russia, West Africa, and the Pacific islands (during World War II) embellished his internationalist perspective and balanced his nationalist concerns regarding the racial oppression of black Americans. This cosmic vision encouraged an editorial view of poetry that was critical and yet inclusive. He explored ancient literatures and studied the works of Alexander Pushkin, the black Russian writer, whose style and linguistic range reiterated Randall's internationalism and literary diversity. Conversely, the democratic aspirations of his muse motivated him to explore themes about common people and how their concerns affect humanity in general and African American historical circumstances in particular. This capacity to focus on the subtleties of our essential being and how it affects destiny distinguishes his poetry. He compelled his intellectual and artistic complexity to reach into and beyond literary pretentiousness for a broader purpose. This sensibility is readily reflected in his writing—his poetry, his prose, and his essays:

> You can learn about black poetry not only in books, but by listening to the talk you hear all around you in the street, in the home, in bars, churches, from preachers, old folks, children, adolescents, men in varied trades and professions. All these are sources of living speech, which the poet hears and remembers and turns into poetry.
>
> (Randall, *A Capsule Course*, 36–37)

Because Randall had an introverted personality, he kept his unformed thoughts in the primacy of his inner workings, and his poetry became manifestations of the polished working for these reflections. He believed that "a poet should have intensive knowledge and practice of his art," and in the inner sanctum of his muse, Randall explored radical and progressive change for himself and the world: "If the reader likes and respects the poet, he will unconsciously absorb his attitudes, especially if they are couched in memorable language. Poetry delights, and through delight it moves to wisdom as someone has said before."

Randall's poetry is integrated into the master narrative to illuminate his art as experience, just as my critical readings of his poetry attempt to examine these complications and gain a better understanding of his persona, his poetics, and his imagination. Though there are many parallels and consistencies in his creative patterns, his poetry can also be impulsive and provocative, exploring unanticipated paths to experiment with new ideas, disrupting conventional poetic structures to render provocative statements, or applying a poetic structure from a foreign literature to convey an African American thematic experience. This creative behavior is likewise reflected in his personal behavior; hence, his poetry serves as a barometer, reflecting personal needs, yearnings, and responses to his surroundings, as well as aesthetic frustrations and aspirations.

Fortunately, several of Randall's friends and associates did not discard their papers, and I was able to retrieve this venue of his voice as well as insightful communication from the papers of Robert Hayden, Margaret Danner, James A. Emanuel, and Etheridge Knight. For the most part, interviews with friends, family members, and poets reiterated the public persona of the congenial librarian, but his correspondence to some of the same persons revealed a more contradictory side to his personality, a side that was more in tandem with his radical poetic themes and the sometimes caustic incisiveness of his essays. His letters to Robert Hayden are usually sedate and serious, and their correspondence during the height of literary tension during the 1960s reflects some very somber moments. But Randall's letters to the younger, more raucous Etheridge Knight are more open and reveal Randall's sense of humor, his publishing anxieties, and his artistic vulnerability.

His lifelong friendships with Robert Hayden and Naomi Madgett provided the most stable and broad secondary perspectives on Dudley, but when the circle turned into a triangle, as in the case of Dudley Randall, Margaret Danner, and Robert Hayden, intrigue, deception, and competition affected artistic collaborations and friendships. Letters written by Margaret Danner to Robert Hayden about Randall illustrate the confusion and conflict that affected the three poets and the social fabric of the black literary community. Similarly, in the case of Gwendolyn Brooks, Margaret Danner, and Margaret Burroughs, misunderstandings and personal histories conflicted and rebounded in a flurry that often crossed Randall's path.

As Randall's creative and editorial prominence evolved, various lines of conflict intersected with his path, and another dimension of history emerged. As poets interacted within the vortex of a fiery literary movement, the politics of personalities and aesthetics were played out in the terrain of journals and small-press publishing. When correspondence is juxtaposed with documentation, public testimonies, interviews, and essays about and by some of the writers, interesting insights into personality conflicts are revealed as debates over aesthetics and popularity, which prevailed during the cultural wars of the Black Arts Movement. These insights and queries become even more provocative when juxtaposed with Randall's political and aesthetic stances in his letters, essays, and reflections about himself and other writers. An interesting exploration and critique of the African American literati surfaced via Randall's strategic and concentric position as poet-publisher.

During his lifetime, Dudley Randall published six books of poetry: *Poem Counterpoem* (with Margaret Danner), *Cities Burning*, *Love You*, *More to Remember*, *After the Killing*, and *A Litany of Friends: New and Selected Poems*.

As the founding editor and publisher of Broadside Press, which still exists with a different editorial staff, he produced a poetry industry that helped set the standard for the black poetry movement during the 1960s and 1970s. By 1984, he had published ninety-five titles of poetry and printed more than a half million books, which reflected the art of almost two hundred poets. In addition to the Broadside Press anthologies and *The Broadside Series*, he was co-editor of *For Malcolm: Poems on the Life and Death of Malcolm X*, and editor of *Homage to Hoyt, Black Poetry: A Supplement to Anthologies That Exclude Black Poetry*, and the seminal poetry anthology, *The Black Poets*, which is still in print and widely read. Through Bantam, a mainstream press, he amplified and complemented his efforts at Broadside and brought black poetry to an even larger audience.

Dudley Randall's poetry and publishing accomplishments were heralded by institutional recognition and cultural awards, among them: two Wayne State University Tompkins Awards for poetry and fiction, a Michigan Council of the Arts Individual Artist Award, a Kumba Liberation Award, induction into the National Literary Hall of Fame for Writers of African Descent, a National Endowment for the Arts Individual Artist Award, a Life Achievement Award from the National Endowment for the Arts, a Doctor of Letters from the University of Detroit, a Doctor of Humane Letters from Wayne State University, and a Distinguished Alumni Award from the University of Michigan. Most importantly, in 1981 he was named poet laureate of the city of Detroit. In addition to this widespread recognition, his work has been translated into several languages and included in almost every major anthology of black poetry during the 1960s and 1970s. It continues to be anthologized today.

Shortly after Dudley Randall died on 5 August 2000, Betty De Ramus, columnist for *The Detroit News*, telephoned me for a quotation for a feature article about the city's poet laureate. I quickly devised a succinct statement about Dudley's life's work:

> Broadside Press was bigger in terms of impact than just the specific books. As an independent press that was successful but small compared to mainstream publishers, it opened up the literary canon, and mainstream publishers began publishing poetry and black writers and other minority writers. It changed the whole character of American literature.[4]

I do not believe this statement is an exaggeration. The cultural segregation that limited the perception and production of American literature directly affected the publishing opportunities for writers and thereby thwarted the growth of literary culture.

As a poet and pioneer publisher, Dudley Randall made a historic and indelible imprint in our libraries. What began as a modest venture in accord with the Civil Rights Movement and its cultural offshoot, the Black Arts Movement, Broadside Press quickly grew into a vehicle for change and unparalleled success within and without the African American literary culture. While working inconspicuously and assiduously, Randall published poetry as broadsides and as small chapbooks that became so popular and prominent with audiences that they broadsided mainstream publishers. The dominant Anglo-American cultural gatekeepers had to reassess preconceived notions and prejudices about the genre.

Randall's poetry was collected in both the *Norton Anthology of Poetry* and the *Norton Anthology of Modern Poetry*, but it is conspicuously absent from Henry Louis Gates's *Norton Anthology of African American Literature*. Moreover, Randall's publishing activity was relegated to a mere mention in Houston Baker's introduction to the section on the black literature of the 1960s; Dudley Randall was excluded from the book now considered to be the definitive canon of African American literature. Indeed, a "curious thing" or a cruel irony that makes this biography all the more necessary. As poet and editor Tony Medina stated:

> My generation must be responsible for making sure that the name of Dudley Randall remains alive for our generation and the generations to come. Dudley Randall's importance is invaluable. This is why I felt compelled to pay tribute to Dudley's legacy by including his poem, "A Poet Is Not a Jukebox," among the works of giants like Margaret Walker and Gwendolyn Brooks in the invocation to the anthology *Bum Rush the Page: A Def Poetry Jam*, a cross-generational anthology of diverse contemporary American poetry. I wanted to make sure the younger generation of poets and readers knew who Dudley Randall was through his poetry.
>
> What I have learned (and continue to learn) from Dudley Randall is to be dedicated to the art of poetry; to be dedicated to literature; not to be narrow-minded or extremist in my political views; to be a gentleman; to be an astute editor committed to good, well-written work with integrity; to be inclusive; and to be independent as a thinker and an institution builder. As a cultural worker and institution builder, Dudley Randall's example is clear: when you control your institutions, you control your ideas. Dudley Randall must not

only be remembered, he must be emulated. Dudley Randall was a cultural force whose work continues to resonate throughout American society and beyond.[5]

The librarians, who were some of the first to assist Randall in his endeavors, were also the first to commemorate his legacy after his death. Joan Gartland, also a poet and a librarian at the Detroit Public Library, organized a tribute with poet and publisher M. L. Liebler on 24 January 2001. This program foreshadowed a grander ceremony at the University of Detroit—Mercy on 22 May 2001, at which the Friends of the Library of Congress deemed the university library a literary landmark in honor of Randall because he had worked there as reference librarian and poet-in-residence. The ceremony also included the dedication of the Dudley Randall Center for Print Culture and the revitalization of the University of Detroit Press in recognition of his work as a publisher.

Al Ward, Broadside poet and lecturer at the university, was a key instigator of this honor. He had served on the staff of the previous Governor of Michigan, James Blanchard, and he knew how to effectively move things forward. I was invited to speak at the ceremony on "The Man, The Poet." In addition to readings of his poetry and the showing of my film, university dignitaries and organizational representatives spoke about the kind and quiet librarian who ordered and organized books while spearheading a revolution by composing and publishing poetry. When the bronze dedication plaque was unveiled, I thought that it was both symbolic and appropriate to engrave Dudley Randall's image as a library landmark, into a historical space in the world of books.

In the introduction to *Abandon Automobile: Detroit City Poetry 2001*, which I co-edited with M. L. Liebler, we focus on what distinguishes Detroit poets, and in that analysis, Dudley Randall's earliest instincts characterized that identity and foreshadowed his literary destiny:

Literary relationships of historic note, such as the friendship between Dudley Randall and Robert Hayden, demonstrated how the automobile industry and the labor struggle stimulated artistic expression and aesthetic exchange in the working-class and the African American community.

During the Great Depression in 1937, Randall and Hayden met and provided aesthetic sustenance for each other and their artistic pursuits. By day, Randall labored in the Ford foundry, while Hayden worked for the WPA. By night, Randall and Hayden met at the YMCA to discuss literary techniques and their own writings. In fact, Randall typed Hayden's first manuscript, *Heart-Shape in the Dust*, for submission to a poetry contest. Although it did not win the prize, Falcon Press, founded by a group of union organizers, published the manuscript.[6]

That character was reiterated and that destiny extended when it was decided that lines from his poem "George" would be engraved in bronze as part of the Labor Legacy Landmark, a complex series of sculptures in granite surrounding a massive metal arc in Downtown Detroit's Hart Plaza. For this same structure, lines from my poem, "We Want Our City Back" were also selected. In metal and stone, the imprints of our poetry bond us and our struggles as poets to that greater voice that reaches beyond the page and the politics of critical acclaim and publication.

As the daughter poet, I traced the high points and low points and ventured into the black light glimmering in the backdrop of imaginative, poetic spaces. I wrestled with Clio, the muse of history, the demons that haunted Dudley Randall's life, and the muse that enchanted his poetry. Two years after his death, almost as if he had planned it, I completed the circle and the task.

Melba Joyce Boyd
13 April 2002
Detroit

Musing on roses and revolutions,
I saw night close down on the earth like a great dark wing,
and the lighted cities were like tapers in the night,
and I heard the lamentations of a million hearts
regretting life and crying for the grave,
and I saw the Negro lying in the swamp with his face
    blown off,
and in northern cities with his manhood maligned and felt
    the writhing
of his viscera like that of the hare hunted down or the
    bear at bay,
and I saw men working and taking no joy in their work
and embracing the hard-eyed whore with joyless excitement
and lying with wives and virgins in impotence.

And as I groped in darkness
and felt the pain of millions,
gradually, like day driving night across the continent,
I saw dawn upon them like the sun a vision
of a time when all men walk proudly through the earth
and the bombs and missiles lie at the bottom of the ocean
like the bones of dinosaurs buried under the shale of eras,
and men strive with each other not for power or the
    accumulation of paper
but in joy create for others the house, the poem, the game
    of athletic beauty.

Then washed in the brightness of this vision,
I saw how in its radiance would grow and be nourished
    and suddenly
burst into terrible and splendid bloom
the blood-red flower of revolution.

Dudley Randall, "Roses and Revolutions,"
in Cities Burning (Detroit: Broadside Press, 1968), 5

1

BEGINNINGS AND ENDINGS

I MET DUDLEY RANDALL IN THE SUMMER OF 1972. I was 22 years old and had just completed my course work for a master's degree in English at Western Michigan University. During my research in black American poetry, I discovered that the major publisher of this literature at that time was Broadside Press in Detroit. So, that summer, when I returned home to find a shortage of teaching jobs, circumstances led me to another career possibility. I consulted the copyright page of Dudley Randall's book *Poem Counterpoem*, which located Broadside Press at an address on Old Mill Place, a poetic name suggestive of a distinguished location. I envisioned an office in an imposing building located in the heart of the city, juxtaposed with the towering bulwarks of international capitalism, somewhere near the General Motors headquarters and the Fisher Building, overlooking the looping intersections of the automobile freeways.

This romantic image of the press was dispelled when I found 15200 Livernois Avenue registered as the current address of the press in the yellow pages. In fact, such imaginings dissipated as I drove past the address painted over the door of what was once a corner hamburger joint. It sat at the end of an aggregate of small neighborhood businesses and a Sunoco gas station. Livernois Avenue was a busy thoroughfare that extended from Eight Mile Road, the northern boundary of the city, to the Detroit River, the border between the United States and Canada.

I parked my Volkswagen on a side street under the shade of the building and a large tree of heaven growing next to the curb. When I entered the door,

2. Melba Joyce Boyd, the author and assistant editor of Broadside Press, 1972–77.

a young, moon-faced woman greeted me and offered her assistance. I explained I wanted to apply for a job. She excused herself and disappeared through a narrow passageway. Almost instantly, she returned and said, "Mr. Randall will help you." At first, I was stunned. At that point, all my illusions about the business setting had vanished. But the mundane setting had not diminished the awe associated with meeting a famous author. In fact, it enhanced the moment.

I adjusted my composure and clumsily explained my interest in working for the press. Mr. Randall said in a very polite and soft voice that he could not afford to employ a person with my education. I protested that I was not doing anything with all this education and if he could not pay me, I would work for free and the opportunity to learn the trade of editing. But he declined my offer and said, "I believe a person should be paid for her labor." I left my name, address, and phone number with the young woman and returned to my car simmering in the smoldering sun. But having met a literary icon reactivated my imagination and an elated sense of satisfaction claimed the day.

No sooner had I reached home than a telephone call from Mr. Randall turned illusion, bewilderment, and awe into opportunity. He asked me if I was serious about working for free. When I said yes, he said, "I would like for you to start work as my editorial assistant. I can't pay much, but I can pay you three dollars an hour."

The next morning I passed through the same narrow passageway. On one side, stacks of large cardboard boxes full of books scaled the wall from the floor to the ceiling. On the other side, two cubicles composed of thin plasterboard separated the stock from the editors. The first office was where Bill Whitsitt, the office manager, worked after his full time accounting job at Ford Motor Company. His association with the press came through his sister, Ruth Fondren, who had worked as an office assistant for Randall when the press was still housed in his home on Old Mill Place. Whitsitt's dream was to build Broadside into a viable company.

Dudley Randall worked in the second office. Stacks of books, manuscripts, and incoming and outgoing piles of papers in various stages of editorial consideration completely covered his desktop. Across from his workspace, a small table with a surface of about four feet by eighteen inches held mounds of manuscripts contained in manila and white envelopes, tilting toward the table's edge. My task was to cipher these poetry submissions into respective categories, either for consideration as a book manuscript, for individual poems for *The Broadside Series*, or for rejection. My other charge was to identify possible submissions for *The Broadside Annual*, edited by Jill Witherspoon Boyer. I also edited galleys and prepared proof sheets for book publications, and corresponded with the poets about their work.

Initially, I was overwhelmed by the backlog of work, but when I considered that Dudley Randall had been doing all of this and more during his lunch breaks and after his full time job as a reference librarian at the University of Detroit, I sucked in my breath and readjusted my attitude. He instructed me to give him all manuscripts that contained cover letters addressed to him. I was not to return these submissions with a standard rejection form. More often then not, they were requests from young, aspiring, and inexperienced poets asking for critiques of their writing. Responding to these requests, which he always wrote in longhand, was to a large extent why he was so far behind in his editorial work.

This generous accommodation of others and his dedication to the press were characteristic of those in his generation who believed in serving the "race," a dutiful commitment ingrained in the inner workings of their social consciousness. In turn, the Broadside Press staff related to his leadership and was more dedicated to him than to poetry. A dignified and genteel man, Randall was also relentless. He generated a pleasant environment, which made the press an unusual workplace. We felt like a part of something significant and historic. The office staff, who were not writers and worked from nine to five to make a living, especially appreciated his gracious manner and sensitivity. During breaks, they would pick up copies of books and critically compare the styles and personalities of the authors who sometimes interfered with the serenity of their workspace.

I was comfortable working in close proximity to Dudley Randall in the editorial office. It reminded me of my childhood, when I would sit with my father in the living room, and we would read or study crossword puzzles. My father was also a quiet worker, who taught me to read and do mathematics when I was four years old, before I started school. He also taught me to think carefully and to value silence as a resource.

In July, I had to make my oral presentation before the committee as the last requirement for my M.A. in English. I submitted the topic, "Pan African Consciousness in Nikki Giovanni's Poem, 'Ego Trippin.'" In preparation, I consulted Mr. Randall. Of course, he knew things about the poem and the poet that were not available in literary criticism, and I appeared before the committee empowered by this inside information. What I did not realize at the time was that I was in the middle of a new era in literary history—a time that would change the conventional values of poetics and aesthetics.

When we moved into the new office in September, I was promoted from editorial assistant to assistant editor, and my name appeared on company stationery. This new status included more decision-making responsibilities and editorial influence on new selections for publication. My personal relationship with Dudley Randall and his wife Vivian was also elevated. They embraced me as part of their family, and I was invited to their home regularly, where we shared meals and celebrated holidays. As time unfolded and personal tragedies invaded our lives and the future of the press, no pretenses and few barriers separated us.

One afternoon when my car was in the shop and Dudley drove me home so I would not have to wait on the bus, we talked about writing, American literature, racial discrimination—a collage of topics. When he asked me, "What do you think about whites teaching black literature?" I paused because I suspected he was trying to figure out my cultural politics. I told him,

"I went to university when the subject wasn't even offered until we, the students protested and demonstrated to get courses in black studies. There wasn't a single black professor in the English department, and if it hadn't been for Professor Murphy, a white man who had studied black literature on his own, the course wouldn't have happened, at least not while I was a student. I'd been reading black literature on my own, but when he offered to teach the course, I got the chance to study it in the classroom, as an English major, and I was thankful for the opportunity."

"I agree, but you know a lot of blacks don't feel that way," Dudley said quietly.

"I know, but I also wanted to know how the literature worked, and that meant more than just talking about the problem of racism. I wanted to figure out how the words worked, which most of the other black students in the class weren't interested in. They took the course because they mistakenly though it would be easy, and the lectures on symbolism, metaphors, literary style, and vocabulary weren't that interesting to them."

A few weeks later, Dudley asked me, "Do you write poetry?" I admitted that I did, but I said it reluctantly because I kept my poems in notebooks, only to be read by the uncritical eyes of family and close friends. My poetry professor, Robert Stallman, at Western Michigan University encouraged me to write poetry, but as a student of literature, I held poetry in such reverence that I never thought that I could ever publish any of my own. But I was complimented by Dudley's inquiry and both curious and anxious to get his appraisal. I showed him the poem "1965," and he made one comment about developing parallelism to enhance the form. I realized at once that the key to his editorial judgment was that he could read a poem and determine how to strengthen it without infringing on its originality or thematic intentions.

After I reworked the poem and showed it to him, he said, "I'm going to publish this in the *Broadside Series*." I shared more poems with him, and he further encouraged me by inviting me to read poetry with him and Naomi Long Madgett at the Highland Park Public Library. Dudley told Detroit literary scholar, A. X. Nicholas, "It's a thrill to read one manuscript out of many and say to yourself, 'This is good.' I think that my biggest reason for publishing is not to make money, which I haven't done, but to find new and good poets and have them published. There's a feeling of discovery and pride in publishing those poets whom you think are good."[1]

After securing a teaching position in English at Cass Technical High School, I continued working at Broadside. I valued the challenge and the excitement of making books, and I assumed a nonstop work schedule similar to Dudley's. But I did not realize was that the stress was adversely affecting his health until one autumn afternoon in November 1972. After loading his car's trunk with a cargo of books in preparation for the Paul Lawrence Dunbar Celebration in Dayton, Ohio, he noticed that the right, rear tire was flat. While he was changing it, a sharp pain pierced his chest, but he did not go to the hospital until later that evening. The doctor told Dudley that he had suffered a minor heart attack and that he had to stay home for several weeks.

When he initially decided to pursue the idea of the press as an alternative for poetry publishing, he had determined that four books a year would be his limit. But as the books appeared, the number of manuscripts and requests for publication multiplied tenfold. As the poets wrote more books, he felt obliged as their editor to service their prolific output. Ironically, the national publishing houses had denied that there was a demand and an audience for this literature, this black poetry. But the response to Broadside publications reflected the exact opposite. The popularity of the poetry spread and became even more successful. First, Broadside outgrew Dudley's home library and then the small former burger building. Although the doctor deemed Dudley's attack minor, it was a sign that the double duty of holding down a full-time job and running the press was too much for him. And a history of heart disease in the Randall family intensified the severity of that warning. But Dudley Randall was a driven man. He was possessed by this publishing dream, and I hoped that I could help lighten the load.

THE STRESS INCIDENT

Randall's heart attack in November foreshadowed a tragedy in my personal life that I could not have imagined in my worst nightmare. I knew my brother was intensely involved with a group of militant young men who were frustrated by the havoc that the heroin dope trade was creating in the black community. But I thought the meetings he attended were like most other gatherings infused with youthful zeal and enthusiastic political rhetoric. What I did not know was that these meetings were strategic, and he was a part of an underground cadre that harassed and threatened dope dealers until they moved out of neighborhoods. This inevitably led to a clash with undercover police activity.

The broader issue may have been police corruption and oppression, but the specific case in Detroit in the 1970s was a police decoy operation called "STRESS," or "Stop The Robberies Enjoy Safe Streets," which was responsible for the unwarranted deaths of more than twenty-two black citizens. The night of 4 December 1972, three young black men retaliated when a STRESS unit blasted a hole in the rear window of their Volkswagen. All four police-men were seriously wounded, but their intended victims escaped unscathed. Three weeks later, a second shoot-out on 27 December left one officer dead and a second critically injured.

The three men were John Percy Boyd Jr., Hayward Brown, and Mark Bethune. John was my brother, and Hayward was my first cousin. In retali-ation, the police department lashed out at the black community and target-ed the families and friends of Boyd, Brown, and Bethune. The evening fol-lowing the shoot-out, a battalion of police (at least twenty) broke down the front door of my parent's house with a battering ram and held me, my moth-er, my step-brother, and my two-year-old baby brother at gunpoint. As they ransacked the house, I tried to calm my screaming baby brother and a nerv-ous policeman with a carbine rifle aimed at us yelling, "Freeze! Or I'll shoot!"

In a calm and deliberate tone, I kept repeating, "Can't you see, I'm hold-ing a baby. Can't you see, I'm holding a baby?" After they were satisfied that my brother John was not hiding up the chimney or underneath freshly fold-ed linen in the laundry room, they arrested me and my step-brother, John Clore, and took us downtown to be grilled for hours under their heated frus-tration and anger.

A couple of days later, I told the series of events to Dudley at the Broad-side Press office, who listened patiently and sympathetically. The main-stream media had reported the official police explanation of the shoot out as "drug related," without any information or interest in the mistreatment of the family or the black community at large. Dudley advised me to call Na-dine Brown at *The Michigan Chronicle*, the black Detroit newspaper. His ad-vice to involve the black press proved immensely effective. After a series of articles, we managed to counter the criminal characterization of Boyd, Brown, and Bethune and to publicize the police department's mass-scale ha-rassment of the blacks in the city, especially young, black males and anyone perceived to be sympathetic to their cause. The policeman actually threat-ened, "We'll blow up your damn house," because we wouldn't help them find John. As it was later reported,

> Hundreds of black families had their doors literally broken down and their lives threatened by groups of white men in plain clothes who had no search warrants and often did not bother to identify themselves as police. Eventu-ally, 56 fully documented cases of illegal procedure were brought against the department. One totally innocent man, Durwood Foshee, could make no complaint because he was dead. . . . This 57-year-old unemployed security guard was killed when he fired his shotgun at STRESS invaders whom he believed to be a gang of robbers.[2]

A group of activists formed Families Under STRESS with the families of Boyd, Brown, and Bethune to devise strategies to inform the public about the true nature of the incident and the young men's engagement in an underground war against dope pushers. The newspaper headlines quoted Police Chief John Nichols's portrayal of them as "Mad Dog Killers" and drug addicts who robbed dope houses to support their habit. As a result of our efforts, it was soon confirmed and reported that my brother was a Vietnam veteran and a student at Wayne State University; Mark Bethune was a former member of the Student Nonviolent Coordinating Committee (SNCC) and the Black Panther Party; and Hayward Brown was an eighteen-year-old kid on a political mission.[3]

After citywide rallies, a number of interviews on local black and mainstream television programs, articles in Wayne State University's student newspaper *The Southend* and in other alternative publications, the perspectives represented in *The Detroit Free Press* and *The Detroit News* shifted from the official Police Department line, as the dailies began to engage some actual investigative reporting. The editor of the *Southend*, Gene Cunningham, deployed a team of writers to investigate the Boyd, Brown, and Bethune story, including Tom Williams, Arthur Bowman Jr., Paul Curtis, Conrad Mallet Jr., Bonita Burton, Chris Booker, and Sumi Ali Ber.[4] Because of their coverage, the police consistently harassed these young college students.

The consciousness of the city was considerably altered and many citizens of the black community became insulted when some black leaders blamed Boyd, Brown, and Bethune for the repressive behavior of the police. Instead, the community continued to resist the retaliatory actions of the police department and came to share the sentiment that not only were the police responsible for their own actions, but they were also irresponsible because they had done nothing to rid the community of drugs. Families Under STRESS joined other community organizations to mount a more effective counterattack. These new allies included Councilwoman Erma Henderson and the young, Marxist attorney Kenneth V. Cockrel (who was a candidate for mayor) and his cohorts, including the newly elected Marxist Judge Justin Ravitz (who had initially refused to display the U.S. flag in his courtroom). We generated a highly visible and critical campaign against STRESS. Cockrel stormed into the STRESS Hearing organized by the City Council, and in a dramatic gesture he dumped thousands of petitions on the table calling for the abolishment of the police unit. The statistics were frightening:

The 1970s began with Detroit's police killing more civilians than any other police force in the nation—seven civilian deaths for every 1,000 police officers on the force in 1971; Houston was second with a rate of five per 1,000.

The 100-man "STRESS" unit formed that year (STRESS stood for "Stop The Robberies, Enjoy Safe Streets") added 22 more civilians to the death toll—21 of them black—while conducting over 500 provocative and frequently illegal raids in black neighborhoods. Far from stopping crime, STRESS added to the growing violence. In 1973, the number of homicide victims in Detroit was three times higher than the death toll in Northern Ireland's civil war.[5]

Hayward Brown was the only survivor of the three. My brother, John Boyd, and Mark Bethune were tracked to Atlanta and killed by police in two separate shooting incidents. My brother was with our brother Darnell Winfield, and they were assassinated in the dark of night by a black cop who was feared and hated by blacks in Atlanta. I got the news of my brothers' deaths after returning to Detroit from a poetry festival at Central Michigan University, where I read with Dudley, Quincy Troupe, Etheridge Knight, Herbert Martin, and Alice Walker. After Alice heard the report on the national news, she sent a condolence letter and signed a copy of her broadside of "Revolutionary Petunias," "For Melba, may your petals grow like blades of steel to protect you."

The family buried our dead and prepared for a series of trials for Hayward, who had been captured on 12 January 1973 in Detroit, during daylight hours and, fortunately, in front of several witnesses. He told me that he wanted Kenneth Cockrel to defend him. Cockrel withdrew his bid for mayor and devoted himself full-time to Brown's defense. Cockrel, Ted Spearman, and Jeff Taft, an interracial legal team, masterminded a political defense that put the police on trial. The law firm did not charge Hayward for his defense, but there were court costs and expenditures. The family donated money, members of Local 600 at the Ford Rouge Foundry (where Hayward's father, Peter Brown, worked) donated money. There were fund-raisers including one on Wayne State's campus, where Hayward Brown and Kenneth Cockrel spoke, Don L. Lee read poetry, and jazz musicians lifted our spirits.

Cockrel had been the former spokesman for the League of Revolutionary Black Workers, an organizational expansion of the Revolutionary Union Movement in the automobile plants, which was formed after a wildcat strike at a Dodge factory in May 1968. "4,000 Dodge Main workers—whites as well as blacks—walked off the job without the UAW's strike authorization. Out of that unexpected, largely unplanned protest over working conditions, activists associated with the Inner City Voice forged a new organization—the Dodge Revolutionary Union Movement, or DRUM."[6] General Baker, "the soul of DRUM," as described by the authors of *Detroit: I Do Mind Dying, A Study in Urban Revolution*, Dan Georgakas and Mavin Surkin, was fired from his job for leading the strike. It was this meeting of forces that took black militancy to the heart of the fight for social change, where "the black revolution of the 1960s had finally arrived at one of the most vulnerable links of the American economic system—the point of mass production, the assembly line." And "DRUM's anger was the anger of the Great Rebellion [The 1967 Detroit Riot] and its vision was that of a new society."[7]

Mike Hamlin, a DRUM leader, advocated a broader membership base, involving students and the community at large. This led to the establishment of the League of Revolutionary Black Workers, a Marxist or revolutionary nationalist organization that included personalities like John Watson, Gene Cunningham, and Kenneth Cockrel, who had by this time graduated from the Wayne State University Law School. In addition to his legal work in defense of members of the League, in 1971 he successfully defended James Johnson, a worker who was unjustly fired by his foreman at a Chrysler plant. Johnson snapped and killed four men with a M1 carbine rifle. Cockrel turned the tables and "put Chrysler on trial for damages to this man caused by these working conditions."[8]

The first of Hayward Brown's three trials took place in the courtroom of Judge George Crockett, a progressive, black judge who had served on Paul Robeson's defense team and who defied the Detroit Police Department after their attack on people attending a conference at Rev. C. L. Franklin's New Bethel Baptist Church on 29 March, 1968. Crockett set up court inside the jail, conducted hearings and released fifty of one hundred fifty members and associates of the Republic of New Africa before the county prosecutor intervened with police.[9]

A mural by artist Leroy Foster depicting the conspirators at Harpers Ferry dramatized the left wall of Crockett's courtroom. Images of John Brown, Frederick Douglass, and Hariett Tubman set the scene for the people's courtroom and the jury's acquittal of Hayward with a verdict of self-defense. Hayward was acquitted of all charges in three separate trials, and this victory invigorated and radicalized the mayoral election. Cockrel had endorsed Coleman A. Young's candidacy for mayor, and the fervor of the moment mobilized a record voting turnout to take over the city government and to get the police under control.

THE ELECTION OF COLEMAN A. YOUNG

The shift in political consciousness after the 1967 Race Rebellion characterized new beginnings arising from the smoldering ashes of discontent and social upheaval. Although the construction of the Chrysler Freeway had bulldozed the remains of the legendary "Black Bottom," this neighborhood became a metaphor for strength and fortification in black history, and one of its progenies, Coleman A. Young, became the figure that led the city into its next life. Initially, Young was not regarded as a leading contender in the 1973 mayoral race. In fact, when he filed an application to run for the office, it was rejected, and the argument was not resolved until the court ruled that a Michigan state senator did not have to resign in order to run for mayor. It was not until May of 1973 that his candidacy was officially recognized and duly recorded. And the timing was just right because it came in the middle of the momentous struggle between Hayward Brown and the Detroit Police Department, and the people claimed victory.

Young's political history was daring and flamboyant. He was famous for "decking one of Bennett's goons" during a confrontation at the Ford Rouge Foundry when he was a laborer,[10] for his incarceration when he refused to leave the whites-only officers club when he was a Tuskegee Airman during World War II, and for his standoff with the House UnAmerican Affairs Committee in 1952 when he was indicted for "subversive activities" because he was a labor and civil-rights activist. Young acquired a legendary reputation for standing up to injustice, and in turn, he gained an unimpeachable allegiance from the black masses and progressives alike, especially in Detroit.

But during the Black Power Movement, Young's socialist views collided with the black nationalist zeal and political agenda of poet Imamu Amiri Baraka in Gary, Indiana, at the 1972 Black Political Caucus organized by U.S. Representative Charles Diggs of Detroit. When Baraka insisted that the delegates review his black agenda within two hours and then vote on it, Young contested that a text of such size and consequence should be studied and discussed over a more reasonable length of time. Young felt it was a separatist document and that the platform "was completely off target and unacceptable." In his autobiography, he graphically recounts what nearly turned into a violent confrontation:

> Baraka wanted to impose his will on every black person in America, and I, for one, wasn't buying it. I refused to surrender the belief that any black solution will derive from unity between the races, and maintained, then as now, that separatism is asinine and suicidal. You don't have to be too damn good at arithmetic to figure out that a party with a small percentage of the population and even less of the money is not well advised to strike out on its own in pursuit of equality. Besides that, I didn't have much use for Baraka. I made him mad when I told him that behind that fancy-ass name he was still LeRoi Jones to me, a half-assed poet in a flowing gown and patent-leather shoes.

That more or less marked the time for me and my 245-member Michigan delegation to leave the premises. Baraka's henchmen tried to prevent us from going, but we were strapped down pretty well and showed them enough artillery to make it out of there. We closed ourselves off in our section of the hotel, and I contacted some trade union guys from Chicago who brought us some additional firepower under the cover of darkness. It was a tense and volatile situation—Baraka's followers were zealots, and he had brought a lot of muscle from New Jersey—but violence never broke out.[11]

Young had not been intimidated by the political persecution of the federal government or by the goons at the Ford factory. He certainly was not afraid to challenge the ill-fated directives of black nationalists. With the exception of Cockrel, Young was the only candidate who took an unequivocal position against police brutality and STRESS. He said, "When asked by the press what I would do first, I said I'd fire John Nichols as police chief." The second thing he said he would do would be to disband STRESS. His supporters included U.S. Representatives John Conyers and Charles Diggs and the Rev. Albert Cleague of the Shrine of the Black Madonna, a black nationalist and Christian organization that engaged in political, cultural, and economic development. On the broader level, Young stood on the strength of the black working class, the rank and file of the UAW that rejected the Walter Reuther's slate during the primary. "When Young narrowly defeated [Police Chief] Nichols, STRESS's violent mandate came to an end. So too did decades of racial discrimination and anti-black violence in the city's police department."[12]

REFLECTIONS AND RESOLUTIONS

An articulate, educated, and expanding African American population steeped in the legacy of the labor movement came to characterize the complexion and direction of politics and culture in Detroit. The development of a viable, black middle class and alternative institutions such as Broadside Press demonstrated the capacity of the community to produce talent, retain identity, and overcome antagonistic and sometimes deadly adversity.

When I left Detroit for Kalamazoo, Michigan, in the simmering autumn following the July 1967 Race Rebellion, I was a naive freshman pursuing the secrets of the muse and the excitement of student activism on the opposite end of the state. Five years later, I returned to Detroit at a critical historical moment that alerted my senses, commanded my attention, and devastated my young life. To a large extent, the herculean tasks that Coleman A. Young

3. The second location of Broadside Press, 15205 Livernois, Detroit, Mich. (The building has since returned to its original architectural purpose as a corner hamburger restaurant.)

and Dudley Randall undertook were beyond human capacities, and Randall's heart attack in the autumn of 1972 was a sign, a signal, a warning about the other side of success, the heart-breaking consequences of unanticipated despair, like the sacrificial deaths of my brothers.

Dudley had said, "In any age of poetry there is a certain ambiance, which influences all poets whether they are black or white." It was a time for revolution and a time for poets. I grieved, he comforted me and published my funeral poem, "For Darnell and Johnny," as a broadside. Something was pulling us into the whirlwind. The sky was gray, and the river was black.

2

THE FERTILE BLACK BOTTOM
OF PARADISE VALLEY

I came to Detroit New Year's Day 1920. I remember the date because when the train pulled into the station and we got off, you could hear the whistles blowing and the bells ringing. It was New Year's. I remember standing by the big locomotive. The wheels were just about as tall as I was. Two weeks later, on my birthday, I was six years old.

UDLEY RANDALL GAZED WISTFULLY into the fading cigarette smoke. A middle child, Randall was born in Washington, D.C., on 14 January 1914, but he spent almost all of his life in the automobile capital of the world, a time that nearly spanned the twentieth century.

Spurred by Henry Ford's five-dollar-a-day labor campaign throughout the South, a major migration of African Americans to Detroit, Michigan, began in 1914. It was also the beginning of World War I and the year Dudley Felker Randall was born. But when his father, Arthur Randall, initially set his sights on Detroit, he was not interested in a factory job. He was in search of job opportunities and a better life for his wife, Ada, and their five children—James, Arthur, Dudley, Philip, and Esther. Originally from Macon, Georgia, Arthur Randall was from a family of five brothers and two sisters. The Randalls were ambitious, industrious, and tenacious.

I only remember Uncle Philip, who was an attorney from Pittsburgh, because he once came to visit us in Detroit while attending a political convention. He was involved with politics like my father. I never met my grandparents, but I remember my father saying that his father had a large farmhouse and made his living as a vegetable farmer. He would put his crops in a wagon and take them to market in Macon. My father was born after 1863 and hadn't been a slave, but his mother and father were born in slavery. My grandparents encouraged their sons to get an education, and they did.

The first Arthur Clyde Randall, who was part Indian, was freed from slavery at the age of sixteen. His wife, Missouri, outlived him, and her daughter Coreen, by a second marriage, reported that Missouri was twelve years old when slavery ended. "When freedom came" Missouri was living on the Lucius Lamar Plantation in Pulaski County, Georgia. Her father had been sold to another plantation when she was very young, but she was allowed to remain with her mother.

As a slave, Missouri was responsible for the babies and toddlers of slave women who had to pick cotton and harvest corn in the fields. On the Lamar Plantation, small children and farm animals were fed in the same manner—from a trough "hewed out of logs." In a newspaper interview around her ninety-fifth birthday, Missouri said, "Into the trough vegetables, pot liquor, and meal and bread was poured. When dinner was served, they called the children much as you would call puppies or hogs and from every direction they came running."[1] Missouri said she remembered the day they captured Jefferson Davis and brought him through the Lamar plantation on his way to Macon. The Northern soldiers asked the old black overseer to cuss him out. She said, "Old Granddaddy stood flat-footed and cussed that man for thirty minutes without repeating himself. Not one time."[2]

After slavery, Missouri learned to read and write, and she was quite the speller. In 1871, she moved to Bibb County with the Willingham family, where she met her first husband, Arthur Randall. Their marriage was registered in the Bibb County courthouse on 28 September 1976. The couple had four sons: Philip James Clyde, Arthur George Clyde, Robert, and Harry. Robert died during childhood, when he fell out of a tree at the age of eight or nine.

Arthur Clyde Randall had a cab company, which comprised a horse and a carriage that he used to taxi patrons of the Brown Hotel. The farm was actually a family enterprise, and Missouri Randall was the architect of its success. Initially, it was a vegetable farm, and the crops were marketed in Macon. The land was fertile and near the river, and, as the couple prospered, they acquired more acreage and expanded the farm into a wholesale vegetable business. Missouri would sell the crops to peddlers instead of selling them at retail rates in the market.

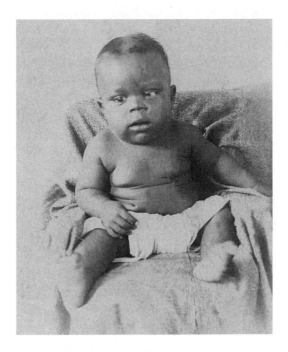

4. Dudley Felker Randall, 1914.

Arthur Clyde Randall died at the age of twenty-six in a freak accident when he was kicked in the head by his horse. Missouri Randall married Adrian Hawkins, and they had one son, Adrian, and two daughters, Mary and Coreen. But unlike her first husband, Hawkins was mean and drank too much and too often. The marriage lacked the mutual respect and cooperative spirit Missouri enjoyed as Mrs. Randall. Hawkins would often beat his industrious wife when he returned home after one of his drunken bouts. The marriage came to an end on the night Hawkins returned home in a drunken rage. That night, he was especially brutal, and Missouri thought he was going to kill her. She called out to God and her dead husband for help. She said the spirit of Arthur Randall appeared and frightened Hawkins out of his wits. Hawkins was not the same after that, and a few days later he left their home and was never heard of or from again.[3]

In addition to being a businesswoman, Missouri Randall Hawkins was also a community leader. She was one of the founding members of the First Baptist Church, the first black church in Macon. After the Civil War, the black Baptists worshipped in "nigger heaven," or rather, the balcony of the white-run Baptist Church. Disgruntled and disrespected, they decided to build their own church on a lot right around the corner. But in 1896, Missouri Randall Hawkins converted to the Church of God because it had a progressive doctrine that advocated equality among the races and between the sexes. She became a minister and sometimes delivered sermons and taught Sunday school, but she never pastored her own church.

During the 1890s, when Dudley Randall's father was coming of age, Georgia accounted for more than two hundred lynchings, making it the worst state in the South for these kinds of atrocities. Almost all blacks worked for dire monthly wages or as sharecroppers.[4] To own one's farm was a rarity, and this situation benefited the Randall family in practical and pragmatic ways. In 1894, Philip and Arthur Clyde Randall left Macon and literally walked over three hundred miles to the Talledega College in Alabama. It took them several days to make the trip. While attending school, they worked in a coal mine to support themselves and their studies:

> While my father was a student at Talledega College in Alabama he got suspended because he organized a student strike against the professors. He said the professors didn't treat the students with enough dignity. So, he protested. He was suspended, and that same year, 1898, he volunteered for the Tenth Calvary to fight in the Spanish American War in Cuba.

After returning from the war, the two brothers graduated despite their involvement in the protest. Philip Randall then completed a law degree at Howard University in Washington, D.C. He passed the Georgia State bar examination in 1909 and set up his first legal practice in Macon.[5] Subsequently, he left the South to establish himself and his practice in Pittsburgh. Harry Randall, the brother, remained in Macon and ran the family business. He studied the insurance business in Valdosta, Georgia, where he became the district manager for the Afro-American Insurance Company. After three years, he returned to Macon and became a minister at the Church of God. Arthur Randall continued to travel and to seek his future. In Columbus, Georgia, he met Ada Viola Bradley, a fellow schoolteacher. They fell in love and got married. "He was like Mr. McCawber in David Copperfield. He had big ideas. He told my mother he would build her a big house with a swimming pool, and teach the children Latin and Greek."

Born in Boston and a graduate of Buffalo Normal College, Ada Viola was beautiful, intelligent, and refined and was one of the first women in the United States to teach in higher education, at Hampton Institute in Virginia. But after she married Arthur Randall and began to have children, she abandoned the classroom and became a full-time housewife. She named her third son, Dudley Felker, after the husband of a friend. Her own husband was a good provider, but he was impulsive, outspoken and defiant.

My father was educated to be a minister and at first was a part of the African Methodist Episcopal Church. But he could never get a church of his own because he was always fighting with the bishops, criticizing them for womanizing and not respecting the scriptures. They considered him a "bishop buster." We moved from city to city. First, we lived in Washington, D.C., where I was born, then Towson, Maryland, then East St. Louis, Illinois. He came to Detroit from a job in East St. Louis as a YMCA secretary. When we moved to Detroit, he applied for an office position in personnel at Ford Motor Company, which he didn't get. He first worked as a salesman for Absopure and sometimes preached at the Congregational Church and would incorporate poetry into his sermons. After a while he sold stock for the Gray Motors Company. Being a preacher and able to talk, he must have been a pretty good salesman because I remember him telling my mother that he won prizes for most sales. And afterward, when I became a young man, people would tell me that they knew my father and they had bought stock from him. They were still drawing dividends on the stocks. Finally, he worked at the Ford Foundry as a laborer because the automobile companies paid better wages.

First we lived on the west side on Williams Street, and I went to the Columbian School. But soon we moved to the east side on Joseph Campau near Monroe, and I went to Duffield School. One of my classmates was Marion Carter, the daughter of Dr. Carter. I think she's a librarian, if she has not retired. She was one of my earliest loves, even though she didn't know I was in love with her. She was one of these unusual looking people with hazel eyes.

The schools were not racially segregated. Duffield School, I remember, was mixed and so was Barstow. I had my first black teacher at Barstow, Miss Poindexter. She was a very good teacher and students would come back to visit her. I had weak eyes and she made me get glasses and wear them. The other teachers hadn't paid that much attention to me.

The Randalls lived in Black Bottom, but their children attended integrated schools. The area had gotten its name from farmers in the nineteenth century because of its fertile soil, but during the Great Migration, that name acquired additional symbolic meaning as black southerners crowded into a neighborhood situated on the bottom of the city's social strata. Despite discrimination, the accomplishments of black Detroiters were impressive, including two hospitals, a pharmacy, music studios, an NAACP branch, an

Urban League office, and many other small businesses within the perimeters of their community. Located on the lower east side of the city in close proximity to Italian, Slavic, and Jewish communities, Black Bottom housed most of the expanding black citizenry. The 1910 U.S. census reported Detroit's black population as 5,741, but by 1920, the year the Randalls arrived, that number had reached 40,838. At that time, African Americans still regarded the northern states as the "Promised Land," and Detroit, one of the key havens during slavery and a gateway to Canada and unretractable freedom, was a focal point for a different kind of future with better wages in the burgeoning automobile industry.

The Randalls arrived in East St. Louis about a year after the worst race riot in U.S. history. Violence erupted on 28 May 1917 after meat packing companies that held government contracts hired African American workers to replace striking white workers. This and other social tensions aggravated a racial conflict that resulted in forty-eight deaths: eight whites and forty blacks. Similar racial problems beset the automobile industry and race relations in Detroit, which contributed to its 1919 race riot. Though blacks had been recruited from the South to work in the automobile factories, unlike whites they were rarely paid the five-dollars-a-day standard and were relegated to the worst jobs in the most deplorable working conditions—work whites shunned or refused to do.

The Ford Motor Company restricted African Americans, Latinos, Arabs, and other dark-skinned workers to the sweltering foundry, and this employment policy contributed to racial animosity between workers. This divisiveness weakened "Whites-only" labor unions and reinforced defensive reactions of black strikebreakers. At the same time, corporate financial contributions to African American churches and community organizations influenced conservative leadership and encouraged black compliance.

The "Red Summer of 1919" reflected the contradictions and the ironies of a segregated democracy. Returning black veterans from World War I were simultaneously welcomed in parades, harassed on the streets, and murdered in the backwoods. Headlines in the black press describing riots in the big cities were underscored by reports of lynchings and mob violence against blacks. Armed and determined, blacks fought back despite overwhelming odds. The 1925 "Ossian Sweet Incident" in Detroit shocked the nation, when Dr. Ossian Sweet, an African American dentist, defended his home in a white neighborhood from an armed white mob. After Sweet's brother fired a shotgun blast into the raging mass of four hundred and killed a man, murder charges were filed against Sweet, his wife, two brothers, and seven of their friends. The famous radical attorney Clarence Darrow and the integrated legal staff of the NAACP engineered their defense. They were acquitted, but this case was only the tip of the iceberg, as Detroit police readily dispensed organized violence against blacks: "Between January, 1925, and June, 1926, the police killed 25 blacks [in Detroit]; in New York City, with a black population three times greater, police killed three black citizens during the same period."[6] This deadly force was fueled by the power of the Ku Klux Klan, which numbered more than 32,000 in Detroit and was so influential that Charles Bowles, the Klan's write-in candidate in the 1929 mayoral race, won the election by approximately 7,000 votes. Fortunately, "17,000 of his write-in ballots were disqualified for misspellings, and John Smith became mayor." [7]

The Randalls could not have anticipated these eruptions of racial violence, but they somehow managed to stay either outside of it or just beyond its reach. Clearly, terror was the monster hiding beneath the sheets of racial hatred, but its means were often as vicious as incidents of mass murder. In contrast to the Jim Crow South, where racism was marked and measured openly, the civilized indiscretions of northern discrimination affirmed white supremacy through the controls of uniformed police and unwritten socioeconomic practices. There was greater social mobility and more educational opportunities for blacks, which gave the appearance or the illusion of social freedom, but there were barriers that deterred African American professional, political, and economic equality. Despite these obstacles, the Randalls bought a home and nestled into possibilities of their own making.

We moved to our house on Russell, in Black Bottom, near Hastings Street, and it was while I lived in that house on Russell that I really grew up. I became twenty-one there. It was a fairly big house with eleven rooms. There was a window that opened onto the porch and there was a chestnut tree and a tree of heaven that overshadowed the porch and made a cool private spot. I would sit on the roof of the porch underneath the shade of the trees and read the poetry of Keats and Shelley. I liked to read, and I could read undisturbed in the summertime.

We had roomers in the house to subsidize the family income, and the roomers liked to talk about the kids. One of them said that I sat on the roof of the house and read books. But it wasn't the roof, it was just the cover over the porch. Because I was shy I didn't like to go into the kitchen because there would be so many people. My mother would tell me to come in for dinner, and I would say, "No, there are too many people." The roomers were very frank, they would talk about the children in their presence, and would say, "Dudley is mean."

We used to call my sister Esther "Bunnie." I don't remember why exactly. In personality, she was the opposite of myself. She was very outgoing and could charm people, while I was shy and private. One day, when we were sitting on

5. Dudley's godmother,
Mrs. Dudley Felker, ca. 1890–1900.

6. Ada Bradley Randall, Dudley's
mother, 15 May 1935.

7. Arthur Randall, with son Dudley
peeking from behind, ca. 1922–1924.

8. Dudley, Arthur, and
James Randall, 1925.

the porch and the paperboy was coming up the street, she said, "Watch this." When he reached the house she started smiling and talking to the guy and he responded immediately. I was jealous of her personality because I couldn't do that. But she was pretty and sweet and wasn't afraid to talk to others.

Mostly in my childhood I remember being a Boy Scout. That was a big thing in my life. I had two older brothers, James and Arthur, and we were boy scouts in Troop 238. We would drill in the street and go to camp every summer in Vandalia, Michigan, where there were many black farmers. Runaway slaves settled in southwestern Michigan near Cassopolis where there were Quakers living and where there had been an Underground Railroad station. Blacks have lived there since before the Civil War.

Plymouth United Church of Christ sponsored the troop. Reverend Hood III, who is also a city councilman, is the present minister at the church, but at that time it was a little church on Antietam Street near St. Aubin. There was a Reverend Brooks and a Reverend Lavescount, and then after Reverend Lavescount there was the Reverend Horace White, the famous labor union supporter. Reverend Nicholas Hood II, succeeded him and he served on the Detroit City Council for several years during the 1960s and 1970s.

My father was what was called a race man. He was active in politics and was the campaign manager for black candidates who ran for city council. He envisioned black councilmen and worked for that dream. My mother would criticize him and say he was butting his head against a brick wall because several men ran for council but were not elected. I don't remember the names of the candidates that he backed because they were never elected. I know that he was a friend of Sammy Davis, the singer, and perhaps his candidates were also members of the Michigan Federated Democratic Clubs. When I was a young man, I was also a member of the Young Democrats. One of the posters presented the candidates in a tuxedo, black tie and, black coat, with the question: "Can anything good come out of Georgia?" That wasn't very persuasive, but that's a quote derived from the Bible, 'Can anything good come out of Galilee?'"

I think that the black people voted for black candidates, but not in numbers sufficient for these people to be elected. The council was elected citywide, not in wards as in Chicago. And although there were solid black areas of the city, the total population [at that time] was not large enough to elect a candidate. It was not until Bill Patrick ran that we got a black member on the council. Bill Patrick stayed at our house when he was a kid. When he and his father first came to Detroit, his father boarded Billy at our house until the rest of their family arrived. Billy was about the age of my kid brother, Philip, and he was like a younger brother to me. [8] After he grew up, he went to college, gained skill as a debater, and he became the first black to be elected to the Detroit City

Council in the late 1950s. So what seemed impossible in the 1920s, and 1930s was eventually realized in the 1950s. If you have a dream, you just have to work it out, and it will come to pass. But my father didn't work on that campaign. He died beforehand in his home in Macon, Georgia, in 1952.

My father was a big supporter of the NAACP. Whenever W. E. B. Du Bois came to Detroit, he would take us to hear him as well as other great men of that era, like James Weldon Johnson, the poet and author of "Lift Every Voice and Sing," the Negro National Anthem. We owned books by black authors such as Du Bois's Dark Water and The Souls of Black Folk. He bought all the novels by Jessie Fauset and whatever black books were available. My father would walk through the house, reciting poetry from memory, especially Tennyson and Browning.

I got my first job during the summer of 1925. My father would get us out of bed because he wanted us to work. He would tear off the covers and say, "Get out of bed! Go out in the street and find a job." One day I wandered downtown looking for work and saw a man giving out cards. He said, "You want a job shining shoes?" I said yeah. So he gave me the card and I went to the shoeshine stand, but I didn't know how to shine shoes. I shined my own, but I didn't know how to pop the rag or make a syncopated rhythm like professional shoe shiners did. After a few minutes, a man came in and he took a seat. I started to shine his shoes.

Apparently I didn't shine them right because the proprietor took me by the shoulder and said, "Here, take your hat and get out." That was the shortest job span I ever had. I guess I lasted about ten minutes. But I did get a job when I was eleven, delivering papers. A guy I knew had a route that he was giving up, so he asked me if I wanted to deliver papers. He had about 243 customers. I delivered papers until I was about fourteen. Then I thought I was too old and felt embarrassed to deliver newspapers.

In 1929, there came the big crash and the Great Depression. Everybody was out of work, but in a way it was a happy time because folks were more together then. There were no robberies because there was nothing to rob. You could leave your doors unlocked. I don't remember locking our front door. And you could visit your neighbors. When you sat on the porch, you knew everybody passing down the street. At first, all you had for music in the home was a piano or maybe a player piano or a gramophone, which you would wind up by hand. It would run down and the records would run too slow and then you would have to wind it up again.

But then, radios came. My brother, Arthur, got a job cleaning up a radio company, and he was able to buy one. People would go to other people's houses and listen to the music or to the ball game. Everyone listened to Joe Louis's *fights. Not everybody had a radio, so some people would go and stand outside of a store or go to a neighbor's house to hear his fights. Joe Louis would say, "Hello Ma, I'm glad I win." Then, after the fight, everybody would rush out into the street and go up and down Russell Street and on Hastings and Adams Street. The cars would form parades and people would make confetti out of rolls of toilet paper and throw it in the air. It was a big celebration.*

Since I delivered papers, I saw different things. Once, I went to a house and saw a man who had a gleaming, gold tooth, playing away on the piano. He could really bang the ivories. He was one of those musicians who played at rent parties. Because of the Depression, things were very cheap. Milk was thirteen cents a quart, and men sold apples downtown on Woodward Avenue in front of Hudson's Department Store. You could go to a drugstore and buy a cigarette for a penny or two pennies. Then, cigarettes were about thirteen cents or fifteen cents cents a pack. At two cents per cigarette, the peddler could make a good profit.

But then again there was evidence of being black. There was a little restaurant downtown, The Penny Kitchen on Monroe. You could get a dish for a penny or two cents or three cents. My brother Arthur and I were downtown and wanted to get some food. We went in this Penny Kitchen and the proprietor said, "We'll serve you, but you will have to eat in the kitchen." My brother said, "This is the cheapest damn place in town and you expect us to eat in the kitchen?" We walked out. We didn't eat.

The 1920s was the decade of the Harlem Renaissance, which generated parallel responses in cities like Detroit and Chicago. It was the time of the "New Negro," when people like the Randalls were motivated by progressive pronouncements and an assertiveness in the culture that affirmed them. *The Crisis*, the official publication of the NAACP, encouraged black pride and a sense of cultural identity, and this enthusiasm permeated the Randall home and the family's community activities. Moreover, Arthur Randall was an advocate of labor, and at that time this political radicalism conflicted with middle class propriety, even in Detroit. Joining the Democratic Party distanced progressive blacks from the accommodationist politics of black Republicans, and this shift in political parties helped to redefine the importance of class in terms of racial identity and the struggle for racial parity.

Dudley Randall read the literature and listened to the lectures and was drawn to the new politics and the new aesthetics, especially the poetry of Jean Toomer, Countee Cullen, Claude McKay, and Langston Hughes. His mother's pliant and sensitive demeanor balanced his father's sternness and strict child-rearing practices. While Arthur Randall recited literature and preached the gospel, Ada read stories to the children and spoke in a kindhearted voice.

Their son, who was destined to be a poet, was more attuned to his mother's reflective and sensitive tones. His father's booming voice grated against Dudley's shy personality and his temperament, which aspired for subtler, meditative engagements with language. And yet there was a creative bond between father and son.

The most tragic and significant event in Dudley Randall's otherwise contented childhood occurred when his younger brother Philip died of spinal meningitis on the eve of Dudley's fifteenth birthday. Their father's response foreshadowed Dudley's adult life. He wrote a poem.

3

POETS OF BLACK BOTTOM:
DUDLEY RANDALL MEETS ROBERT HAYDEN

We left Washington when I was four years old, before I could read or write. However, I remember that my mother took us to a band concert in Towson, Maryland, where the band played "Maryland, My Maryland." I was so impressed by the big bass drums and the big brass horns that I composed words about them to the melody of "Maryland, My Maryland." This is the earliest instance I can remember of my composing a poem. I think, however, that I write because I have an urge to write and because I enjoy writing. Some of my happiest hours have been spent writing.[1]

I grew up reading books. Since my mother was a schoolteacher and my father was a preacher, the house was always full of books. My family read books written by writers of every nation. We knew that there were good people in every nation and good people of every race, that there are bad people of every race and bad people in every nation. So we were always taught, not so much by precepts, but by example, that people are just people, and I think that was the philosophy of my parents.

I read poetry at an early age because we had it in the home. I can remember the books not only for the contents but also for the surface, the color and the feel of the books. My father had a two-volume edition of Browning's Lyrics *in white covers trimmed with gold, and he had a cowhide-bound volume of Tennyson's* Complete Poems. *My mother resented that book because his girlfriend gave it to him when he was in college. I liked the feel and the heft of the books. I liked the look of those books,*

My mother had a book called Favorite Poems, *and a lot of the poems in that book were my favorite. A child doesn't have good taste in poetry. Just as children go to the movies now and like horror pictures, I liked the horror poems in that book. My favorite poems were Longfellow's "The Skeleton in Armor," Edgar Allen Poe's "The Raven," "The Wreck of the Hesperus," and "Binger on the Rhine," about a German soldier dying. It's all very sentimental and scary and not very good poetry, but that's what a kid likes. As you develop your literary taste, you grow up from Edgar Allen Poe and Longfellow to better poets. I would read poetry in class, and once, when I was in the fourth grade, Miss Piondexter caught me reading* Macbeth. *That was something that I wasn't supposed to do, but I liked it.*

I was about nine years old when I started writing poetry to influence a girl who lived upstairs—Willie Mae. But it was while I was delivering papers, when I was thirteen and attending Eastern High School, that I finally decided to be a poet. At that time I earned my first money writing poetry by sending a poem to the Detroit Free Press. *There was a young people's section every Sunday, and there was a poet's page. The column was first edited by Sylvester Dorian and then by Elsie Beck. One poem would be selected the prize poem for the week. You could win a dollar, which was big back then. The first poem I sent to them was a sonnet about one of these icy mornings when the trees were covered with ice and they glittered in the street lights.*

The Sunday paper came out on Saturday night. The truck would throw them on the corner, and I would pick up my papers. Then, I'd go to St. Joseph's Catholic School and sit down on one of the windowsills and turn to the section to see whether or not my poem had been published. During the 1930s and the 1940s, when I became a young man, The Detroit News *published poems every Sunday in the "Random Shots" column. It was a humorous column during the week, but on Sunday it was poetry, and my poems were also published there.*

The lyrical elements of sound and romance were Randall's earliest inspirations for writing poetry. His affection for books was also a response to this interest in poetry, an instinct that was nurtured by the family library. He excelled academically, graduating from Eastern High School in 1930 at the age of sixteen. His membership in the pro-labor Plymouth Congregational Church and in the Young Democrats dovetailed with his intellectual alignment with W. E. B. Du Bois and the political shift of the black community in Detroit. About this same time, African American labor leaders began to gain prominence in the community, and coalitions between black and white union organizers contributed to a stronger labor movement. In 1932, Dudley began working in the Ford foundry.

Two years after I graduated from Eastern High School, I worked for fifty cents an hour in the blast furnace unit at Ford Motor Company's Rouge foundry. The poem "George" is about a man that broke me into the job. I was eighteen years old when I first started working in the foundry. Years later, when I was a librarian, I found him in a hospital ward and remembered how once he had been strong and vigorous, but he had a stroke and all he could do all day was just sit tied to a chair so that he wouldn't fall out. I wrote this poem contrasting his youth and strength to his old age.

I was a labor supporter but was laid off before the UAW was recognized by Ford Motor Company. I remember I reached work just after the "Battle at the Gates," when the company police beat Walter Reuther and the labor advocates.

Labor historian Steve Babson relays the incident and Walter Reuther's account of it in *Working Detroit*:

The afternoon of May 26, [1937,] some 60 UAW members and officers set out from the union's Ford organizing office in Detroit to leaflet the Rouge plant two miles away. Most of the group, about 50 women, went by trolley, but Walter Reuther, Richard Frankensteen and several others went ahead with the sound truck to survey the scene at Gate 4, the plant's principal entrance (site 57). While waiting for the main group of leafleters, they walked onto the overpass across Miller Road and posed for photographers.

They were immediately set upon by a group of 35 Service Department men. . . . "The men picked me up," Reuther later remembered, "about eight different times and threw me down on my back on the concrete . . . kick[ing] me in the face, head, and other parts of my body. . . . Finally, they threw me down the stairs . . . [and] drove me to the outside of the fence, about a block of slugging and beating and hurling me before them."[2]

After I was laid off from Ford's, I went to work for the post office and was a member of the United Postal Workers. The UPW supported Henry Wallace (who had been the secretary of agriculture) when he ran for president of the United States for the Progressive Party, which had communist influence. But I voted for Roosevelt because he had proven himself to be a good man.

Dudley Randall's two older brothers, James and Arthur, attended the University of Michigan during the 1930s, and James won the Hopwood Award for his essay, "Sleepy St. Louis, the City of the River" in 1933. He received a bachelor's and a master's degree in sociology. James taught sociology and criminology at Prairie View College in Texas, and he later became the first black social worker for the Southern Michigan State Prison System. Arthur took a degree in journalism from the University of Michigan and shortly thereafter left for Baltimore, where he wrote for the *Baltimore Afro-American* and developed a national reputation as a journalist. His writings brought him into contact with black intellectuals in Chicago, the Communist Party, and the editors of the progressive New York magazine, *New Challenge*.

Their sister Esther attended Talledega College, their father's alma mater. She later completed a master's degree in social work and a jurist doctorate in law from the University of Detroit. The Great Depression and marriage deferred Dudley's aspirations to attend college:

> *I got married in 1935 to Ruby Hands. I thought her name, Ruby Hands, was very poetic. We eloped. We went to Mt. Clemens, Michigan, to get married on May 27. The taxi fare from Detroit to Mt. Clemens [a town about twenty-five miles northeast of Detroit] was thirty dollars then. She was very pretty, slender, with a light brown complexion, and long, dark hair. She liked music and sang in the Miller High School Girls Quartet. She had a lovely voice.*

Ruby Hands was actually Ruby Hudson, according to the marriage certificate. Her maternal aunt and uncle, whose last name was Hands, raised her. They lived across the street from the Randall home on Russell Street. Since she was only sixteen years old at the time, they decided to elope because they knew her guardians would not approve of the marriage. Dudley was twenty-one at the time, and he did not think a wife should work. He felt it was the responsibility of the husband to support the family. Moreover, the choices of jobs for black women without a college degree were limited in the 1930s. They were rarely employed in clerical positions, and the depression intensified the competition for employment, as black women were usually hired as maids and nannies.

Despite his domestic responsibilities and grueling work in the Ford Foundry, Dudley continued to study and write poetry. The same year he married Ruby, he submitted "Hastings Street Girls" to *Opportunity Magazine*, a national publication that gained prominence during the Harlem Renaissance:

> With ivory, saffron, cinnamon, chocolate faces,
> Glowing with all the hues of all the races;
> Lips laughing, generous-curved, vermilion-tinted,
> Lips of a child, but, like a woman's, painted;
> Eyes where the morning stars yet glimmer on;
> Feet swift to dance through juke-box nights till dawn:

9. Dudley and Ruby Hands (Hudson) Randall, 18 September 1937.

> O little girls, so young, so foolish-wise,
> Flaunting such knowledge in your ignorant eyes.
> You are like flowers that bud, then droop away,
> Or like the bright, quick-darkened tropic day.
> Lovers and kisses, cruel, careless, light,
> Will you remember down the long, deep night?

Randall's poem about young girls in search of the nightlife on one of the main streets in Black Bottom resembles Claude McKay's "Harlem Shadows," a poem about Harlem prostitutes. Both poets unveil the eroticism associated with false romance and the sexual exploitation of women by using the sonnet form, and, in both instances, the language is aurally feminine, with a lyrical lilt that complements the movements of the young women who appear on urban streets in black communities. While "Hastings Street Girls" praises the physical beauty of the "girls," there is a foreboding undertone in the ambiguous contrast between their physical maturity and their actual youth. The imagery contains racial complexity and historical contradiction, as the "Hastings Street Girls" live in a segregated region in Detroit, but are described as reflecting *all the hues of all the races.* The perspective of poem shifts from description to introspection as the poet addresses the girls with a warning about the dangers of "sporting life" and fading beauty into "the long, deep night."

Though "Hastings Street Girls" was accepted for publication, in 1937 *Opportunity* folded and the editors returned the poem.[3] There was a dire lack of publishing opportunities for black poetry, and this delayed Randall's publishing debut. But missed chances did not deter his enthusiasm for writing. That same year, Randall met Robert Hayden.

Hayden's early poetry was deeply influenced by black life in Detroit, which was reconfigured in many of his poems. In his memoirs, he recalls the vitality and complexity of this primary imagery: "At night in the summertime the children would play hide and seek with the lamppost as base, wait for the crab man, and the waffle wagon with its tinkling bell or watch a small crowd gathered around a street-corner preacher, interested more in the Baptist hymns that two fat women with tambourines would sing than in what the preacher had to say."[4] Down Hastings Street or other thoroughfares that defined the boundaries of Black Bottom and Paradise Valley, "there might be parades for the followers of Marcus Garvey and his 'Back to Africa' movement, or on special occasions, like Halloween, grownups and kids alike would watch masqueraders make their surreal progress along St. Antoine. Clowns, red devils with curling tails, Zulus, men in evening gowns, women in tuxedos, each sex a parody of the other."[5]

In the documentary, *Robert Hayden, America's Poet Laureate,* Hayden recalls his younger days in Black Bottom and how he and Dudley "hung out" and shared poetry, philosophical perspectives, and the cultural wealth of the community. Hayden grew up in poverty with foster guardians, while Dudley Randall lived a more comfortable "middle-class" lifestyle overseen by college-educated parents. Despite this difference in their backgrounds, there were similarities. Both poets used poetry as an escape from strict fathers who were also ministers. Similarly, both poets could be withdrawn and introverted. Another possible parallel between Randall and Hayden was their emotional attachment to their mothers, which might have contributed to their sensitive and genteel demeanors.[6] But it was their mutual interest in poetry that brought them together. They became friends, and Dudley Randall valued this camaraderie and Hayden's influence on his poetics.

I met Robert Hayden in 1937. A fellow who worked at the YMCA who knew that both of us were interested in poetry introduced us. We got together and showed each other our poetry, and criticized each other's poetry. He would always say, why don't we collaborate and do a book together. But we never did. We would sometimes go to the local clubs to hear the music, and once, I remember, we went to hear Billie Holiday sing. But I wasn't very sophisticated, and I didn't feel very comfortable in nightclub settings.

Dudley related to D. H. Melhem that

I made a study of versification, and was very interested in it by the time I met Bob Hayden. He was interested in diction, in metaphors, and I was interested in sound. So he would tell people, Dudley knows more about how to write verse than I do. But he introduced me to something, or anyway he got me interested in images, so then I started studying images, too, as well as the sound. One time I wrote some hendecasyllablics, that Catullus wrote in. And I wrote something in the Sapphic stanza, translated a couple of poems in the Sapphic stanza. And I translated some of Catullus into hendecasyllables: "To Lesbia and Her Sparrow."[7]

I learned something from him, but I don't know whether he learned anything from me. But, I was interested in his career and admired him. I had been published in The Detroit News *and* The Detroit Free Press, *but not in any of the serious magazines. He was also eager to get published, like all young poets, I suppose. He would send out his poems and they would be rejected. Finally, one of his best poems, "Frederick Douglass" was finally published in* The Atlantic. *He inscribed a copy and sent it to Alice Hanson, the poetry librarian at the Detroit Main Library. She displayed it in a lobby showcase. At that time there was a separate poetry room in the main library filled with books of poetry and books of criticism of poetry, and black people would frequent that room.*

I remember once there was a poetry contest for the best manuscript, and Bob was complaining about all the trouble it would take to type his poems, so I volunteered to type them for him. I typed his poems and he sent the book in, but it didn't win the prize. It was difficult for him to be published, though he was eventually published in the early 1940s. His first book Heart-Shape in the Dust *wasn't published by a regular publisher. His friends, some of whom were in the labor union, donated money and published it. They made up a fictitious name for the publisher, Falcon Press.*[8]

Those were his earliest poems, and later he disavowed that book and decades later when (as editor of Broadside Press) I asked to reprint some of the poems from it, he said, "No! No! No! No! No! I wrote those poems when I was an apprentice." He would refuse to allow those poems to be reprinted. Here's a lesson for beginning poets who are too eager to rush into print. It's all right to be published in magazines because your work there is temporary, and it disappears when the periodical ends. But if you put it in book form, it's there to haunt you.

However, I really didn't agree with him. Some of those poems are very beautiful. When the book was reviewed in The Detroit News, *they praised many of the poems, and some of these early poems you can find in* The Negro Caravan *because the poems reprinted there are from his first book. He was called by the editors, Ulysses Lee and Sterling Brown, the most promising of the younger poets.*

In the essay "The Black Aesthetic in the Thirties, Forties, and Fifties," Dudley Randall wrote about Hayden's first book and their generation of writers: "The horizons of poets were widened beyond their own Negro struggle to include world events. In his first book, *Heart-Shape in the Dust*, Hayden wrote of youths dying in the Spanish Civil War in 'Spring Campaign,' and in that 'Speech,' he urged Black and white workers to cooperate."[9]

Even if black writers did not join the Communist Party, as did Richard Wright, they were sympathetic toward it and its policy of nondescrimination. Black writers did not give up their struggle for Negro rights, but regarded it as the struggle for the rights of man everywhere. A popular union-organizing slogan was, "Black and white, unite and fight."[10]

In 1936, Hayden left Detroit City College (now Wayne State University) for a job with the Federal Writers Project. During this period, Hayden wrote poetry, plays, and a history of the Underground Railroad in Michigan. He "took part in anti-war rallies, read his poetry for the John Reed Club and at a rally of the United Auto Workers in Detroit, and he demonstrated with his fellow WPA workers for higher pay."[11] Hayden's poetry found favor with black union organizers for the CIO. They often read his poetry at meetings and used Hayden's poetry as a source of inspiration.[12]

Eclectic and introspective, Dudley Randall and Robert Hayden delved into various forms and subjects, never seeming to lose sight of their aim to master their skills and knowledge of poetry. Both were politically aware and creatively motivated by historical and social events affecting black life. Randall and Hayden sharpened each other's intellectual and aesthetic acumen during this developmental phase. Although there are distinct differences between their styles, there are considerable similarities, especially with regard to their humanist and internationalist perspectives. Their poetry displays an appreciation for black cultural roots and the folk experience. The people of Black Bottom live in Randall's poetic portraits, just as Hayden's "Elegies for Paradise Valley" retrieves scenes and personalities that characterize this age, this community, and a resilient people.

ENDINGS AND BEGINNINGS

> Baby, born only yesterday—
> Name yet to choose,
> We wish your tiny lips could say
> What name to use
>
> Shall we name you after a flower, sweet girl,—
> Violet or Rose?
> Or after a jewel—Ruby, Pearl,
> For your skin that glows?
>
> Shall we call you Constance, Prudence, Faith?
> From the storied dead
> Select a name like a laurel wreath
> For your little head?
>
> Barbara, Ardis, Ruth, Germaine
> Are a singing few.
> In years to come may you not complain
> Of our name for you.
>
> (Dudley Randall, "Our Name for You (For My Daughter),"
> in *More to Remember*, 27)

"Our Name for You" was composed on 21 May 1940, when Dudley and Ruby Randall had their first and only child, Phyllis. That same year, Robert Hayden married Erma Morris, and Hayden's first book, *Heart-Shape in the Dust*, was published. The following year, Robert and Erma moved to Ann Arbor, Michigan, and Hayden began his studies for a M.A. degree in English under the tutelage of W. H. Auden. In 1942, Hayden was awarded the Hopwood Major Award for Poetry for a collection of works focused on the African American historical struggle. Some of the poems included were "The Ballad of Nat Turner" and "Frederick Douglass." He worked as a teaching assistant at the University of Michigan, and upon completion of his degree in 1942, took a professorial position at Fisk University in Nashville, Tennessee.

In Black Bottom, Dudley Randall had grown up in a home imbued with poetry and in a family determined to transcend unfair racial barriers. In this allegedly "disadvantaged" neighborhood during the Great Depression, Randall forged a literary friendship with Robert Hayden through their mutual love of poetry that lasted a lifetime. Hayden's departure from the Detroit area for Nashville benefited his creative and professional advancement, but it separated the two poets during a difficult time for Randall.

In 1940, Dudley Randall separated from his wife and daughter. He moved into a small room in a house on the west side of the city. His job as a postman delivered him from the brutal toil of factory labor, but it was poetry that salvaged him from the inner turmoil and the throes of divorce. In "Separation" he wrote:

> She's going away
> Without telling where.
> She refuses to stay,
> She's going away.
>
> (In *More to Remember*, 26)

And in "Rx":

> Love's a disease that's difficult to cure;
> but purgatives of tears may have some power,
> with regimen of loneliness, denial,
> deceitfulness and falsehood and betrayal.
> Injections of contempt may hasten health,
> or daily immersions in a bath of filth.
>
> (In *A Litany of Friends*, 27)

After Dudley's marriage to Ruby ended, poetry became the balm that eased the anger and the bitter pangs of divorce. In "Happiness"[13] he wrote about those lonely days in his room and decided:

Happiness
is a capricious girl.
Woo her, she flees.
Ignore her, she follows.

When I was young and alone,
Sundays I stayed in my room all day
making poetry on the card table and Tottie,
hearing no sound, would tap on the door and ask,
"Are you all right?" And when I answered,
she'd go down to the kitchen and bring me
sandwiches and milk.

I never thought that I was happy then.
But now when I look back, I know
I was very happy.

4

WAR AT HOME AND ABROAD

There are days in our times people remember, like the assassination of President Kennedy or the death of President Roosevelt. Everybody remembers December 7, 1941, because of the bombing of Pearl Harbor. I was at my brother's house having breakfast when the announcement came on the radio. All the people sitting around that table were affected. My brother's wife worked in the tank arsenal and wore a military uniform during the war. Her brother, Kenneth, who was sitting at the table, joined the infantry and was killed in action in Italy. My brother, James, joined the army and was sent to Europe. Everybody was affected, and everybody remembers where they were December 7, 1941.

DUDLEY RANDALL MET MILDRED PINCKNEY the same year that the United States entered World War II and he and Ruby Randall were divorced. He made this acquaintance through a mutual friend. Mildred was also a divorcée, but, unlike his first wife, Mildred was a working woman employed as a secretary for the United Auto Workers (UAW). Such positions for black women became available as a result of the more liberal employment practices of the UAW and the increased labor demands generated by the war. Mildred was an attractive, intelligent woman with a quick wit and a temper to match. On a very fundamental level, she and Dudley were as much opposites as Mildred was the opposite of Ruby's quiet, demure personality. While Randall was introverted and shy, Mildred was extroverted and outgoing.

What they had in common, however, was that they were both children of ministers. They had been reared in strict Christian homes, but as adults neither of them was very religious.

Dudley Randall and Mildred Pinckney were married on 20 December 1942. Later, Dudley could not recall the exact date; in fact, in most recollections of his life, she was edited out, no doubt because of the arguments and anger that beset the relationship. They advanced into a marriage that would be disrupted by domestic and foreign wars, literally and figuratively. With World War II looming above it, the summer of 1943 exploded in Detroit's most critical race riot up to that time. These historical events converged and intervened into Dudley's otherwise mild-mannered existence. In metaphorical terms, his second marriage foreshadowed and underscored the 1940s as a time of conflict, change, and discontinuity.

The decade opened in the midst of employment opportunities and racist resistance. Union pressure improved the pay and positions of black workers, but the growing dissatisfaction of whites with the transfers and upgrading of blacks and women in wartime production jobs resulted in the "Hate Strikes" of 1941 at various factories. In contrast, the majority of the 10,000 black workers at Ford Motor Company participated in the final organizing strike which began in April of that same year, and on 19 May Paul Robeson sang "Ballad for Americans" at the UAW-Ford organizing rally in Cadillac Square in downtown Detroit.

Many of the factories had been transformed to build tanks and jeeps for the war, and massive hiring resulted in more minorities and women in the workplace. There was also an increase in the number of blacks migrating to Detroit for these jobs, which put pressure on the housing situation as the physical limitations of Black Bottom and similar segregated neighborhoods were unable to accommodate the influx of newcomers. Constructed adjacent to a predominantly white neighborhood, the opening of the Sojourner Truth Homes in February 1942, a federal housing project, resulted in conflict when white residents from nearby blocked the moving vans. Despite progress made in race relations in the labor unions, there was considerable resistance to black advancement in the plants and into newer neighborhoods. This opposition was often instigated and led by the Ku Klux Klan.

On Sunday, 20 June 1943, a race riot broke out on the Belle Isle Bridge after a rumor spread about a black woman being murdered and her baby being thrown off the bridge by a white mob. The same rumor was inverted when it was passed on to white communities, with a white woman and child being murdered by a black mob. Dudley Randall remembered not only the

10. Dudley and Mildred Pinckney Randall, 1943.

catastrophic impact of the violence, but also instances of human kindness and resistance to the mob mentality gripping the city:

> *The riot started on a Sunday, around Belle Isle and around the Naval Armory on Jefferson at the foot of the bridge to Belle Isle. I didn't know anything about what happened Sunday, but Monday morning when I was delivering mail, a woman at a lunch stand told me there had been fighting. At this time I was a mailman, and I delivered mail in a Polish neighborhood, and it was peaceful on my route. But when I returned to the post office and the other mailmen came in for lunch, they arrived with tales about Hastings Street being littered with glass from people breaking windows and looting.*

One white mailman who delivered mail in a black neighborhood said people followed him around and said, "We are not going to let anybody bother you." There wasn't any tension in the post office between the white letter carriers and the black letter carriers either. But when the inspectors arrived at the station, the mailmen were reassigned to different routes.

I was assigned to a route in a black neighborhood. I went to Hastings Street, and I saw that it was covered with shattered glass. When I entered a jewelry store where the windowpanes were broken out, there were some cops inside. They raised their guns and said, "What do you want?" I said I want to get out. No, I didn't say that. I said, "I'm delivering the mail." So, they took the mail. Then, when I was going home and I was on Milwaukee Street waiting for a streetcar, a police cruiser drove by. The policemen did a double take and then whirled around the block and drove by again. But they saw that I was safe, that nobody was bothering me.

After I got on the street car and it turned onto Oakland Avenue into the black neighborhood, black people started stoning the street car and we pulled down the shades to protect ourselves from the bricks, rocks, and hurling concrete. I got out of the streetcar on the corner of Oakland and Holbrook Avenues, and watched the people in the crowds. If there were whites in the car, they would stone the motorists. The black people put white handkerchiefs on their cars to distinguish them. I had witnessed a gang fight a few weeks earlier between fellows from the Northend and the Southend, and I recognized some of the same boys that had been in the gang fight. They took the lead in the stoning. As I watched them stone the streetcar, a girl threw a hunk of concrete and missed the streetcar entirely. It went over the top and almost hit me, so I decided it was time for me to get out of the street and get home.

At home everybody had a story to tell. I was living in a rooming house with a young couple from Lincoln University in Missouri. A friend of theirs had just arrived in Detroit. As he was coming to their house on the Woodward Avenue streetcar, whites were stoning the streetcar and dragging blacks out into the street and beating them. The conductor told him to hide under the seat so the mob wouldn't get him. He got to our house unharmed, but he was so terrified by the violence in the North, that he said he was going right back down South where he could be safe.

We told our neighbor, a white lady who lived next door, that if there was any trouble come to our house. She said she did not anticipate any problems, so she stayed where she was. When I returned to my regular route, which was in a Polish neighborhood, nothing happened to me. There were some kids sitting on a porch and talking about me, one kid said, "What is he doing in our neighborhood?" But another said, "Well, he's a mailman and he has just as much

*right to be here as anybody else." The uniform of a letter carrier was respected.
People respected the federal government in the 1940s.*

*There was also tension on the streetcars. Unlike today, not everybody had a
car. People depended on the streetcars and the crowded streetcars created tension and sometimes fights broke out. Later on, race relations got better in the
factories. Blacks and whites that worked together and knew each other didn't
have such conflicts.*

Businesses were demolished and people were attacked. More than one
hundred fires were set and five thousand U.S. soldiers, initially trained for
foreign battlefields, infiltrated the city to quell the riot and their fellow citizens. In the end, twenty-five blacks and nine whites had been killed. "The
major cause of the racially lopsided death toll was Detroit's police. In contrast to their open tolerance of white rioters, the city's patrolmen fired indis-
criminately into buildings and crowds around Hastings Street, killing 17 of
the 25 blacks who died in the rioting."[1] Naomi Long Madgett related an incident that occurred during the riot that reflected this contempt of and dis-
regard for black life:

In the summer of 1943 I was home in New Rochelle, New York, from Virginia State College, and my brother was home from Lincoln University in
Missouri, where he was a roommate of Julian Fields Witherspoon from Detroit. We read in the local paper, the *New Rochelle Standard Star*, about a
riot in Detroit. My brother, Clarence M. Long Jr., said "You know, I think
Spoon is in the riot." And as an afterthought he said, "If he's in Detroit, he's
in the riot." The next day we read an account of Spoon being shot by a state
trooper on the steps of the St. Antoine YMCA [in Black Bottom]. What I
later learned was that he was living there at the YMCA, and, as many young
men did, he would go across the street to the YWCA for a meal. He was
crossing the street, returning to the YMCA when he saw a state trooper
chasing a black boy down the street. He yelled, "Heil Hitler," and the trooper turned and shot Witherspoon in the back.

They left him lying there, bleeding on the steps for quite a long time and
kept some of the other fellows lined up at gun point, delayed for no particular reason. I believe the future judge, Charles Farmer, as well as Alfred
Williams, were there. I don't know how many more young black men were
detained, but it was some time before they sent for help. Fortunately, it
turned out to be only a flesh wound, but they had no way of knowing that
at the time. Julian Witherspoon was an activist and very outspoken and not
likely to pass up an incident without saying something.[2]

Some time later, Witherspoon expressed regret in having not filed a lawsuit over the incident. However, the Michigan State Troopers did pay for his medical bills, indicating some responsibility, even though no inquiry or investigation into such blatant infractions against or shootings of civilians during the riot was implemented. The irony of Julian Witherspoon's allusion to Hitler relates to the timing of the riot and the unfortunate consequences of American race relations. The war against fascism abroad had not diminished fascism at home.

The government's response to civil unrest was to send young black men to war, including Dudley Randall. But he considered traveling throughout the United States and the Pacific Islands as opportunities to enrich his poetic eye. This was his first extended time outside of Detroit, and these national and international experiences altered his perspective on blackness and expanded his creative vision.

I wanted to go to the Atlantic, so they sent me to the Pacific, naturally. That's the way they do in the army. It wasn't like the Vietnam War. We felt we were fighting for something. We were fighting against Hitler, we were fighting against fascism. We were fighting against the government that had launched the sneak attack on Pearl Harbor. People were patriotic then. Nobody objected to the war, except the German-Americans. They put the Japanese-Americans in concentration camps, but not the Germans. Not even the Germans who objected to the war.

When I went into the army, I looked on it as an adventure, possibly helping my poetry, because there would be different images that I could use, a different vocabulary. Also, both my brothers had gone away to college, so basic training was fun to me. I would imagine myself being on a track team when we worked out. Living in the barracks was like living in the dormitory. Those were experiences that my brothers had had and that I had missed. In addition, there were different cities we visited, as well as being in Greensboro, North Carolina, and seeing the various towns traveling throughout the South. Since my parents didn't have much money, we didn't travel much, so seeing different parts of the country as we traveled west to California really opened my eyes to the world.

During World War II, the troops were in different outfits by race. I remember when I took the train to go to basic training in Greensboro, North Carolina. We were from the North. We didn't know the South, and we feared it. When we reached the Mason-Dixon Line, the conductor told us we had to transfer to a Jim Crow car. We objected. So he sent for the transportation officer. He said he was from Pennsylvania, and he didn't believe in discrimination, but that's the way it was, so he wanted us to go along. We finally went on. But

11. Dudley Randall in U.S. Army uniform, 1943.

I think he had us transferred to a Pullman sleeper car. But that wasn't the army, that was the United States. In the dinning car for instance, they had a black drape dividing the diner, and blacks had to eat behind the black cloth so they wouldn't upset the digestion of the white people. My poem, "The Southern Road," is about that experience:

> There the black river, boundary to hell.
> And here the iron bridge, the ancient car,
> And grim conductor, who with surly yell
> Forbids white soldiers where the Black ones are.
> And I re-live the enforced avatar

Of desperate journey to a dark abode
Made by my sires before another war;
And I set forth upon the southern road.

To a land where shadowed songs like flowers swell
And where the earth is scarlet as a scar
Friezed by the bleeding lash that fell (O fell)
Upon my fathers' flesh. O far, far, far
And deep my blood has drenched it. None can bar
My birthright to the loveliness bestowed
Upon this country haughty as a star.
And I set forth upon the southern road.

This darkness and these mountains loom a spell
Of peak-roofed town where yearning steeples soar
And the holy holy chanting of a bell
Shakes human incense on the throbbing air
Where bonfires blaze and quivering bodies char.
Whose is the hair that crisped, and fiercely glowed?
I know it; and my entrails melt like tar
And I set forth upon the southern road.

O fertile hillsides where my fathers are,
From which my griefs like troubled streams have flowed,
Love you I must, though they may sweep me far,
And I set forth upon the southern road.

    (Dudley Randall, "Southern Road," in *Poem Counterpoem*, 13)

Whereas "The Southern Road" intertwines the irony of fighting a war against fascism in a segregated army for a nation where Jim Crow laws were tolerated, "Legacy: My South" extends that dilemma by reflecting the conflicted consciousness of being black in a land haunted by the memory of slavery and drenched in the blood of lynching:

What desperate nightmare rapts me to this land
Lit by a bloody moon, red on the hills,
Red in the valleys? Why am I compelled
To tread again where buried men have trod,
To shed my tears where blood and tears have flowed?
Compulsion of the blood and of the moon

Transports me. I was molded from this clay.
My blood must ransom all the blood shed here,
My tears redeem the tears. Cripples and monsters
Are here. My flesh must make them whole and hale.
I am the sacrifice.

See where the halt
Attempt again and again to cross a line
Their minds have drawn, but fear snatches them back
Though health and joy wait on the other side.
And there another locks himself in a room
And throws away the key. A ragged scarecrow
Cackles an antique lay, and cries himself
Lord of the world. A naked plowman falls
Famished upon the plow, and overhead
A lean bird circles.

(Dudley Randall, "Legacy: My South," in *Poem Counterpoem*, 14)

Dudley's letters to his daughter Phyllis always included a drawing to illustrate his words and to make them memorable. The story about the train ride does not convey the darkness of segregation draped between passengers. Instead, he wrote about the wonders of his travels with pictures of cows, pigs and farmhouses along the passing landscape. In a letter from the Pacific Islands, he wrote, "I saw fish that leap out of the water and fly like airplanes." Nor did he forget to remember the life his daughter was leading back home:

December 5, 1943

My Darling Phyllis,

Daddy has gone away on a choo choo again. But he'll be coming back to see you again before long. I was so glad to see my little daughter. You are such a pretty little girl, but remember you cannot continue to be pretty unless you are good too.
Obey mama and teacher and drink all your milk and Santa will bring you a nice present. Are you still wearing the wings Daddy gave you?
Did you go to Jimmy's birthday party?

Love, Daddy[5]

12. Phyllis Randall (Dudley's daughter), ca. 1946.

In the army in basic training, we were in separate outfits, but I didn't mind that. I was in the air corps. The air corps was part of the army then, it wasn't separate and people that got the highest scores in the tests could be sent to the Air Force. Those of us who scored high were usually from the North, mostly Boston, New York, Detroit, Chicago, and California. We had high morale because we were bright and confident people. I wanted to be an officer and applied for officer's training school and tried to follow up on it, but I never got there. Everybody in our outfit had scored high enough to be officers. Then, later on when things got tough in Europe, they wanted blacks to go to officer school; but I didn't volunteer. I said to hell with it. I finished out as a T-4.

When I went overseas, I went as a replacement, not with a unit. I was in a signal corps, and I worked in the headquarters detachment. Since I was one of the new recruits, they had me doing things like digging up trees. We went to different camps on different Pacific Islands, and we would have to set up camps. When we were digging on the side of a hill to prepare for the building of the officers quarters, they called me Jungle Jim because I cut off my fatigues and wore just boots and these cutoffs with nothing above the waist but a sun helmet. But where we were digging was full of scorpions. As soon as I saw the scorpions, I dashed to the tent and changed into coveralls that could be laced tight around the ankles and around the wrists.

Like many black soldiers, Randall was assigned to preparing and maintaining supplies for the military base. He did not engage in combat, but the irony in his short poems grouped under the title, "Pacific Epitaphs," captures the various forms of death that ensnared the soldiers. Each title marks a grave:

> "New Georgia"
> I loved to talk of home.
> Now I lie silent here.
>
> "Palawan"
> Always the peacemaker,
> I stepped between
> One buddy armed with an automatic
> And another with a submachine gun.
>
> "New Guinea"
> A mosquito's tiny tongue
> Told me a bedtime story.
>
> "Treasury Islands"
> I mastered the cards,
> The dice obeyed me.
> But I could not palm
> The number on the bullet.
>
> "Coral Sea"
> In fluid element
> The airman lies.
>
> (Dudley Randall, "Pacific Epitaphs," in *More to Remember*, 36–38)

My sergeant, who was bright and had a strong personality, was at odds with the sergeant major. For some reason, the sergeant major didn't like me either. Because of this politics of personalities, Sergeant Hart requested that I work with him in supply. In supply, we had to keep records of all of our machinery on the different islands in the Pacific. When we were signaled heavy construction detail, we had to put up telephone lines to the airfields. Then, we had to fill out reports in quadruplet and triplet. Whenever we moved to another island, we would have to record every item, including which box it was in. I had everything itemized in alphabetical order. When the officers would come and ask, "Randall, where are the spoons?" I would look under "s" and say, "The spoons are in box number 427." They liked that because they were able to find everything. Sergeant Hart had more seniority, and when he was released, I was made the supply sergeant.

I saw a tremendous waste of money and resources during the war. For instance, in the Philippine Islands the army had a mountain of fatigues in storage. The Filipinos didn't have much clothing, and the army could have given those clothes to them. Instead, the army burned the fatigues. I had a buddy from Detroit, and he was one of those slick guys. He told me that he knew how we could make a lot of money. I told him I wasn't interested because I was an honest supply man. But I guess there was a lot of crooked dealing going on. The army rationed cigarettes and everybody liked Camels. They were the most popular. But you couldn't get a Camel cigarette. You could get some off-brand that gave coupons—Old Gold. However, you could go to town and these little Filipinos kiosk shacks would be full of Camels. So it seemed somebody had a hustle going.

My brother was stationed in Europe, and he was a supply sergeant as well. Once a truck came and the guys asked for a load of cheese, but they didn't have authentic documents so he told them no. Later, he got a telephone call from some officer who asked him how soon could he pack his things to be moved to another unit. My brother told him one hour. The officer told him to do it in a half. "This is for your own safety," the officer told him. So my brother packed his things and got out. He was too honest. If he had stayed as the sergeant there and refused these "black" marketers, he could have been killed because they were making thousands of dollars by selling American army supplies on the side.

The only hustle I did was not for me. It was near the end of the war, when there was no fighting, and we were just keeping camp. Filipino teenagers would come and clean out the tents and make up the beds. They didn't have shoes, so as the supply sergeant, I ordered shoes for them. But we had a very sharp supply lieutenant. He said, "Randall, why is it we are getting so many new shoes for small feet?" (Filipinos had very small feet. Whenever the Filipino women would try to sell me sandals as souvenirs for my wife, I would tell them, "These sandals are too small. American women have big feet.") The sergeant said, "Randall, you are probably giving these to the houseboys. Don't order any more." So I quit ordering them. But we didn't sell them to the teenagers. We gave them the shoes because they needed them.

Dudley Randall's talent for classifying and cataloguing foreshadowed his future career as a librarian, and his literary vision soared. In "The Ascent," a transcendent view mocks the divisions between the races and the conflict between nations by juxtaposing them against the wonder of the planet's magnificence:

Into the air like dandelion seed
Or like the spiral of lark into the light
Or fountain into sun. All former sight
From hill or mountain was a mere hint of this.
We gain a new dimension. What had been
Our prison, where we crawled and clung like ants,
We spurn, and vision lying far beneath us.

O naked shape of earth! What green mammelles,
Arteries of gold and silver, turquoise flanks,
Plush jungles now are patterned! As we bank,
The earth tilts; we are level and aloof,
And it spins on and on among the stars.
We poise in air, hang motionless, and see
The planet turns with slow grace of a dancer.

I remember going on a ship across the Pacific Ocean and seeing flying fish. I remember seeing the islands and seeing New Caledonia with houses pink and white and green against the hillside, and butterflies as big as brightly colored birds, flying over the palm trees. And I marveled at the wonderful variety in nature. I visited a French colony where everybody spoke French, and I went to see the Catholic church there. I remember the Caledonians with their naturals. Those were the first Afros I had seen. They wore their hair long and nappy. Some of them had red hair. I met the people who lived there, and it opened my eyes to the wonder and the beauty and the variety of the world.

"The Ascent" and "Coral Atoll" are intricate, abstract portraits of land and sea and earthy things viewed from afar. These poems provide another perspective of the planet and challenge our earthbound vision. From "The Ascent":

All former sight
From hill or mountain was a mere hint of this.
We gain a new dimension.

The poems focus on the power of Earth as a living force, with lines such as "birth pangs of an earthquake" or "green plateau that's sentient with warm life" ("Coral Atoll"), "and O naked shape of earth!" (The Ascent"). More than many others, these poems reflect the impact of the Pacific experience on Randall's vocabulary, the broadening of perspective from the urban social setting to the vast, natural wonders of the greater expanse of the planet and its largest ocean. It is an expansive view from an airplane, from above and beyond his cosmic obscurity on earth as human and as a socially circumspect person of race.

> Our prison, where we crawled and clung like ants,
> We spurn, and vision lying far beneath us.

These poems convey both a sense of insignificance relative to the grandeur of the planet and an awareness that empowers and enlightens humanity:

> We poise in air, hang motionless, and see
> The planet turn with slow grace of a dancer.
>
> ("The Ascent," in *More to Remember*, 40)

In "Coral Atoll," Randall ponders these infinite possibilities and revels in the imagery despite the horrors of Georgia lynchings, race riots in Detroit, or the tragedy of a planet at war:

> No wedding ring of doges, this white cirque that lies
> dazzling, immaculate, upon the blue
> of wide Pacific. High the airman sees
> small ships crawl past it, and the surf exclaim
> upon that O in foam less shining white.
> No spiny island hurled out of the deep
> by birthpangs of an earthquake is this round,
> or green plateau that's sentient with warm life.
> Things without thought, unvisioned and undreamed,
> through mute numb years under the swaying tides
> have died into a perfect form that sings.
>
> ("Coral Atoll," in *More to Remember*, 41)

5

THE RETURN: POETRY AND PROPHECY

When I returned to the United States, I was eager to go to college. The GI Bill of Rights was a wonderful thing because it helped a whole class of people who would not have had the chance to get a college education. I believe the teachers liked that generation because we were older and more mature. We wanted to study. The previous generations of college students had done pranks like panty raids or swallowing goldfish, but the soldiers that came back had seen the world. We had seen war. We had seen death, and we were serious. We wanted to learn.

FTER DUDLEY RANDALL RETURNED FROM THE WAR, his primary goal was to go to college, and the campus setting provided a reprieve from a difficult marriage and a conflicted country. Many black veterans faced renewed terrorism, especially in the South. As Martin Duberman's biography of Paul Robeson relates: "The latest tide of violence seemed aimed at 'uppity' black veterans who had returned from the 'struggle for democracy' overseas determined to struggle for it at home as well."[1] In Detroit, the second wave of black migration to the city after World War II significantly impacted its demographics. By the end of the decade, the black population approached 500,000. But despite the economic gains made through labor union struggles, social conditions remained dismal: "In the middle and late 1940s, thousands of newly arrived black migrants squeezed into Detroit's segregated neighborhoods, filling the dilapidated ghetto homes to the bursting point. Acute overcrowding in these already depressed areas caused a steady decline in living

13. Wayne University, post-WWII, view of Cass Avenue.

conditions."[2] Even when blacks found homes in other neighborhoods, it was nearly impossible to secure mortgages from the banks. New black neighborhoods were developed on the edges of the city to avert integration into white neighborhoods and racial confrontation over housing. Veterans were often able to secure mortgages through the Veteran's Administration.

But Dudley Randall focused his sights on securing his long-awaited degree and took advantage of the GI Bill to pay his college tuition. He and Mildred settled into a modest apartment at 14 E. Hancock, within walking distance of the campus:

I started my college education at Wayne University in 1946. It was called Wayne University then because it was a municipal school, not yet a state university. I majored in English literature and graduated in 1949. Even though both of my brothers had pledged Alpha Phi Alpha at the University of Michigan, I pledged Kappa Alpha Psi to be different. I didn't want to be the same as them. My brothers were out of college in 1948, so they didn't care that I pledged Kappa instead of Alpha.

I also pledged Kappa because I had met Ernie Marshall, who was a Kappa, and he helped me when I was out of work. I had taken the post office test and had gotten a 98.7 on the test, fourteenth on the list. It was during the depression, when everybody, even college graduates tried to get a work at the post office because it was a secure job. Time went by and people were called to work, but I wasn't called. So, I went down to the Detroit Board of Education, where there was a placement office to help young people get jobs. There, I told Ernie Marshall about how I took this test and never got called. At that time there was the "rule of three," names would come up in three. They wouldn't have to take the top person, but could choose one of the three. He said, you mean to tell me you got 98.7 on the test and you haven't been called yet? So, he took the rest of the day off and took me down to the post office to see one of the officials who gave the test. I was given a letter of recommendation, and, shortly thereafter, I was called to work.

I worked full time at the post office while taking a full course schedule at the university. It was just something that had to be done. If you have something to do, you just do it. Many of the fellows who worked with me at the post office went to college and became supervisors and were promoted up the hierarchy. When you worked on the line throwing general mail, you could sit by anybody. I worked at night as a clerk and some of us would sit together and talk about books and ideas and politics. One fellow joked and called us the brain trust. Robert Millender, for instance, became a lawyer and a force in city politics. He engineered the campaign of Mayor Coleman Young and many other politicians.[3] Many of us left the post office, but those who stayed became supervisors.

While I was a student at Wayne, I was a member of the Miles Modern Poetry Group. I like different poets for different reasons. Of the early English poets I favor Shakespeare, William Blake, John Keats, and Milton. Of the American poets, I prefer Whitman and especially Jean Toomer. I also became interested in Alexander Pushkin, the Russian poet, and in Russian culture because of the Cold War. In addition, I studied the Russian language. We first met to study contemporary poetry, but then we started bringing our own poems to discuss. I was interested in sound and the structure of verse. Chester Cable was the faculty advisor for the Miles Poetry Workshop. Whenever I used to come to his office, he never once looked at his wristwatch, meaning I could stay as long as I liked.

The workshop decided to publish a magazine, so we published Milestone 1, 2, 3, and 4. A lot of fine poets came out of that group. Robert Huff, Phil Levine, and Henrietta Epstein. In fact, Phil Levine won the National Book Award for poetry. Wayne produced some good poets.

Dudley Randall met Hoyt Fuller, the future editor of *Negro Digest* and *Black World* magazines at Wayne. Fuller was born in Atlanta, but he grew up

14. Dudley Randall at Wayne University, 1948.

in Detroit. He and Dudley became friends because they took three English courses together. After graduation, Hoyt Fuller worked for the *Michigan Chronicle* and the *Detroit Tribune*, both black newspapers. They reconnected after Fuller became editor of *Negro Digest* in the 1960s. Broadside Press poet Murray Jackson, who became a professor at the University of Michigan and served on the Board of Governors for Wayne State University, was also a student at Wayne during this period. He first met Randall when Jackson was a Boy Scout, and Dudley and Arthur Randall were the scoutmasters for Troop 166 at the Bethel Church on St. Antoine Street in Black Bottom. His next encounter with Dudley Randall was at Wayne State University when he went to hear a nationally renowned poet sponsored by the Miles Poetry Workshop:

Most of us came to the university on the street car, that's what they called Wayne, "the street car university." There were a variety of people who came to this place, and I remember talking with Dudley at the student union. A group of us would get together at Mackenzie Hall and sit around with a ten-cent cup of coffee and solve the problems of the world. We were a great melting pot of intellectual interests and different ways of viewing the world. Not that it mattered to anybody else, but it mattered to us. It was one of my most gratifying experiences at Wayne, and Dudley was a part of that. Dudley was the kind of person to help bring awareness to people.[4]

While Dudley was involved with the Miles Poetry Workshop, he perfected his craft and was encouraged to finish drafts of poems that were conceived in notebooks during the 1930s and the war years: "Every poet is molded by his age, by the great events or Great Event that took place during his impressionable years. In the thirties it was the Great Depression and the Spanish Civil War. In the forties it was World War II."[5] Some of his most impressive poems about the thirties, "For Pharish Pinckney, Bindle-Stiff During the Depression," "Vacant Lot," and "Laughter in the Slums" deal with the ramifications of the Great Depression, the black migration to the city, and demonstrate an adherence to classic forms adapted to a black perspective. However, Randall's poems about his experiences in the army during World War II—"Spring Before a War," "Helmeted Boy," "Football Season," "Coral Atoll," "The Ascent," "Lost in the Mails," and "Pacific Epitaphs"—do not conform to any traditional form, nor do they necessarily contain racial themes or tones: "'Helmeted Boy' (about Pee Wee, a baby-faced high-school boy in basic training) is only four lines long, but it takes up four pages in my notebook, as I tried to concentrate all my thoughts and feelings about war into four lines."[6]

By contrast, "Legacy: My South," which was also conceived during his tour of duty, demonstrates his skill with blank verse. Randall considered the full range of his linguistic and literary options both as he ventured into universal reflections and into the especial dilemma of race and class:

There was a world depression, and a world war. In their outlook, black poets saw race as one problem among the world problems of poverty and fascism, and appealed to all men of good will to help solve the problem. As for their style, they no longer considered it sufficient to pour new wine of content into old bottles of form, but absorbed the techniques of the experimental poets Hart Crane, Pound, and Eliot. In this group were Tolson, Hayden and Brooks. Another group—Brown, Walker, Davis and Fenton Johnson—were influenced in varying degrees by Negro folk poetry and by

Sandburg and Masters. Race was central to their poetry. Langston Hughes, growing beyond the Renaissance attraction to the more superficial and merely picturesque aspects of Negro life, wrote of its more serious aspects in the speech of the urban working man and in blues and jazz cadences.[7]

Although Randall's poetic flexibility evolved as an outgrowth of his improvisational approach to aesthetics, this flexibility determined radical alternatives in form as well as content. As African American poets evoked independent stances in their poetics, Randall combined his discipline of craft, his extensive linguistic resources, his internationalist literary framework, and his appreciation of African American cultural roots to nurture his own creative demands. Often concerned with common themes and common people, his poetry illustrates how unjust social conditions affect historical outcomes. His poetic strategy was derived from John Keats's concept of "negative capability," the denial of ego in order to enter into the consciousness of the poetic subject. But the consciousness of his poetic subjects resides in a black cultural gestatlt considered through a working class perspective infused with a wealth of literary knowledge. His poetry brings notice to the elemental truths that thrive in blackness and how that insight is inextricably bound to America's spiritual destiny. To accomplish this aesthetic goal, Randall grounded his imagery in commonplace settings and evaded the pitfalls of obscurity and elitism.

His concern for negated humanity determined the forms of "For Pharish Pinckney, Bindle-Stiff During the Depression" and "Old Witherington." In accessible language, these poems reflect Randall's class sensitivity and the tragic dilemmas of these characters. "Pharish Pinckney" was completed 1949, but the experience was conceived during the depression era of the 1930s. Though the poem opens with Pinckney rising in the morning from a hard night's sleep in a boxcar, the past tense foreshadows his death, "Bindle Stiff." The country is developed into a metaphor of birth and death, as earth and as nation. Randall used the dialectical tension of opposites and contrast in the poem to present society and nature as contentious and contradictory forces in the hobo's life and death:

> Now, in the land you loved and cursed, you sleep.
> Summer and winter lave you with their tears.
> Fruitless to ask now, Do you smile or weep?
> Your bitter laugh no longer rives our ears.
> In the womb you left to suffer and to die,
> Find peace at last, while you in silence lie.

(In *More to Remember*, 15)

"Old Witherington," on the other hand, is free verse, but in a related sense, Randall used dialogue to incorporate voice and the perspective of the character. The incorporation of voice is an especial characteristic of African American poetry. It is an aesthetic aspect derived from the oral tradition that can be traced to the nineteenth-century abolitionist poetry of Frances E. W. Harper and further evidenced in the folk poetry of Paul Laurence Dunbar, James Weldon Johnson, and Sterling Brown, to cite a few. The poem's scene is a typical brawl between two drunken buddies, and the poem attempts to penetrate the core of the raucous disorder to expose the horrible glee the neighbors extract from this alcoholic catastrophe and to reveal the agonizing loneliness that incites the violence.

> "And I'll baptize these bricks with bloody kindling.
> I may be old and drunk, but not afraid
> To die. I've died before. A million times
> I've died and gone to hell. I live in hell.
> If I die now I die, and put an end
> To all this loneliness. Nobody cares
> Enough to even fight me now, except
> This crazy bastard here."[8]

"Memorial Wreath" commemorates the "200,000 Negroes who fought for freedom in the Union Army during the Civil War," to acknowledge the heroism of black soldiers. The imagery bemoans the lost of history and the anonymous soldiers, who are reframed relative to famous figures like Frederick Douglass, John Brown, Nat Turner, Sojourner Truth, and Harriet Tubman. Likewise, "Legacy: My South" contours a somber portrait of a land haunted by death, suffering, and a bloody history, which leave an indelible imprint on racial memory. Although his northern upbringing protected him from blatant racist assaults and insults, Randall's military assignments in the South, and especially in Georgia, reconnected him to this past. The haunting imagery and blank-verse form expressed in melancholic, lyrical, repetitive patterns are reminiscent of Jean Toomer's Georgia in *Cane*. Both foreboding and enticing, the sound of the poem appeals while the grotesque imagery repulses. The poet enters the land, which once held his ancestors in bondage and still binds him to a memory and heritage that must be reconciled.

> What desperate nightmare rapts me to this land
> Lit by a bloody moon, red on the hills,
> Red in the valleys? Why am I compelled

To tread again where buried men have trod,
To shed my tears where blood and tears have flowed?

Compulsion of the blood and of the moon
Transports me. I was molded from this clay.
My blood must ransom all the blood shed here,
My tears redeem the tears. Cripples and monsters
Are here. My flesh must make them whole and hale.
I am the sacrifice.

(In *Poem Counterpoem*, 14)

The bloody history, hideous atrocities, and persistent injustices constitute a paradox that is intensified by the indignity of serving in a segregated unit to wage war against fascism on foreign shores. "The Southern Road" reiterates this stylistic interest in contradiction and ambiguity as the poet assumes the "I" and contemplates inner conflicts relative to military duty against the failed expectations of American democracy. "The Southern Road," "grim through classical allusions to Hades, and mixing love, hatred, beauty, and bestiality, is Randall's best expression of ancestral and racial devotion, conveyed almost hypnotically in the refrain"[9]:

And I re-live the enforced avatar
Of shuddering journey to a strange abode
Made by my sires before another war;
And I set forth upon the southern road.

O fertile hillsides where my fathers are,
From which my griefs like troubled streams have flowed,
Love you I must, though they may sweep me far,
And I set forth upon the southern road.

(In *Poem Counterpoem*, 13)

I conceived "The Southern Road" while traveling to a basic training center in the South in 1943, but I didn't write the poem until after the war, in 1948. I enjoyed writing "The Southern Road" because of problems of craftsmanship. I admired the poems of François Villon. Villon was a fourteenth-century Frenchman who was a vagabond, a thief, and a murderer. But his "Ballade of the Dead Queens," his "Ballade of His Mother to the Virgin Mary," and his "Ballade Written the Night Before He Was To Be Hanged" are some of the most powerful poems ever written.

His ballade form has been adapted into English poetry, but poets have diminished it into a trivial thing—light verse, vers de société. I wanted to restore its gravity, its power. At the same time I had read a book called *Hypnotic Poetry*. The author said that some poetry, like that of Edgar Allen Poe, by its melody and repetition induced in the reader a hypnotic, dream-like state. I wanted to use the ballade form with its repeated rhyme sounds and refrain, to induce in the reader a hypnotic state, but more like one of nightmare than of dream, as I told of the bestial South. I also wanted to introduce tension and complexity into the poem by mingling love and repulsion, and by extending the bestiality into other times and places, like the Middle Ages, when people were burned at the stake for slight differences of doctrine. These technical problems made the poem fascinating to write.[10]

Written as a French ballade, "The Southern Road" requires an interlinking and repeated rhyme pattern in each stanza, *ababbcbc, ababbcac, ababbcac, bcbc*, which demands a skill for lyrical variance and balance while maintaining a regular meter conforming to the constraints of the rhyme scheme. The poem cynically contrasts the presence of churches on the landscape with the horror of lynching (which echoes being burned at the stake). This atrocity is conveyed through imagery of human fragments. Mutilated and burned bodies evince and answer the poet's internal voice, as he converges and descends "upon the southern road":

> This darkness and these mountains loom a spell
> Of peak-roofed town where yearning steeples soar
> And the holy holy chanting of a bell
> Shakes human incense on the throbbing air
> Where bonfires blaze and quivering bodies char.
> Whose is the hair that crisped, and fiercely glowed?
> I know it; and my entrails melt like tar
> And I set forth upon the southern road.

Although "The Southern Road" and "Legacy: My South" are similar in subject and perspective, they diverge in form and poetic vocabulary. The formal definitions imposed on "The Southern Road" constrain the poem and its focus on the transference of graphic details, while the blank verse contours more allusive and abstract impressions in "Legacy: My South." But in both poems, the poet assumes a space inside the poem and claims consciousness and an agonizing association with the experience.

"Laughter in the Slums," which is reflective of Randall's earliest style in "Hastings Street Girls" was initially drafted in 1935. Again, the poet penetrated appearances to reveal the nature of experience. The dismal impression of the slums is countered by the uplifting laughter of the people who live there. Randall characterized their warm and hopeful voices with southern associations, a historical view of urban migration that was not defeated by the hardships of northern poverty or hazardous winter weather. The poem is historically grounded in the contemporary setting of Detroit, as it imprints an abstract impression of a landscape and a cityscape. He employed free verse to intermesh the effects of environment and attitude:

> In crippled streets where happiness seems buried
> under the sooty snow of northern winter,
> sudden as bells at twilight,
> bright as the moon, full as the sun, there blossoms
> in southern throats rich flower of flush fields
> hot with the furnace sun of Georgia Junes,
> laughter that cold and blizzards cannot kill.
>
> (In *More to Remember*, 18)

Similarly, "Vacant Lot" is a reflection on a boyhood spent in poor kids' playgrounds, the vacant lot. Randall intertwines the free play with the free developments of unattended gardens of wild flowers as nature reclaims space in the city:

> It was the wilderness to city kid,
> And paradise to each pariah weed.

It is a light poem that enters the universal kingdom of childhood imagination and community resources as seasons change and the vacant lot is reconfigured to serve their needs. Despite the common theme, the obscure vocabulary reflects Randall's internal voice:

> While April set us sprinting round the bases,
> October chasing the eccentric ball,
> December sculpturing farcical forms and faces,
> It was chameleon stage containing all.
>
> (In *More to Remember*, 16)

THE RUSSIAN POEMS

Because there was so much emphasis placed on Soviet politics during the Cold War Era, I became interested in Russian culture.

The Great Depression of the 1930s generated interest in socialism and communism in many writers, especially those active in the labor movement. But when poet and critic D. H. Melhem said to Randall, "I think of you as a political person. I was wondering whether you considered yourself a socialist or socialistic?" His response was, "No, I'm not a socialist."[11] Dudley Randall was a Democrat, but he was definitely and indelibly influenced by socialist ideals. While the U.S. government was reeling with its anticommunist crusade against the Soviet Union and conducting a "Red Witch Hunt" against American citizens, Randall was translating Russian poetry. As a student at Wayne University, Dudley studied the Russian language and enhanced his skills by translating Russian poetry into English. His thematic choices in Russian poetry paralleled his interests in poetics. Moreover, his inquiry into Russian culture is suggestive of a kind of cultural resistance to U.S. politics.

He studied the poetry of Konstantin Simonov, who was known for his wartime poetry and his novel, *Days and Nights*, about the Soviet struggle against Nazi aggression. As a writer, Dudley's literary concerns converged with writers who wrote against fascism and who engaged in romantic lyricism. Randall explained that the poetry of K. M. Simonov was very popular during World War II because "Russian soldiers would send copies of the poems to their girl friends or wives."[12] Simonov's poetry does not glorify war but reflects the yearnings of a young man to return home to his lover. Randall relied on his skill with sound to translate Simonov's "Wait for Me" ("Zhdi Myenya"):

> There are different theories about translation. My own is that I try to translate in the meter of the original. I believe that the music of the poem is very important, and I try to recapture some of that music in English, or to find an English equivalent.[13]

Written on the front line of battle, the beauty of the poem resides in its tender approach to the subject of death. The poem is an appeal to high romantic idealism—eternal devotion:

> Son and mother may believe
> That I am no more,
> Friends may give me up and grieve,

And may sit before
The fire, drinking bitter wine
To my memory.
Wait. And with them gathered there
Do not drink to me.

(Randall, *A Litany of Friends*, 67)

Simonov's "My Native Land" ("Rodina"), manages to explain patriotism in personal, earthy terms, undoubtedly in contrast to the lofty rhetoric of power, imperialism, kings, queens, or political primacy. The poem challenges the notion of patriotism because "you do not remember the wide land / which you traversed and which you came to know," but rather, "A precious handful of the simple earth / To be for us a sign of all the rest." The poem focuses on the childhood bonding with the trees and rivers and roads that define a particular space and identity, and the desire and determination to defend that humble life.

In order to enhance his own poetic range, he connected with other poetic experiences, and his translations of Russian poetry contributed to that. However, there are distinct differences between a Russian soldier's relationship to land or space and identity compared to the unrest and conflict the poet must face in "Legacy: My South" or "The Southern Road." Randall's internationalist perspective did not suffer when he reiterated his cultural commitment to his national heritage, and yet he refused to deny his creative freedom to engage an internationalist view or a cosmic consciousness.

This is most clearly shown in his translation of "Ya Vas Lyubil," ("I Loved You Once") by Alexander Pushkin, a task he did not undertake until some years later. The depth, desperation, and passion of "I Loved You Once" commands an assertive and yet somber tone. The same number of lines and a parallel syllabic configuration convey an effective facsimile of the rhythmic language in the original.

I loved you once; love even yet, it may be,
within my soul has not quite died away.
But let that cause you no anxiety;
I would not give you pain in any way.
I loved you wordlessly, and hopelessly,
with jealousy, timidity brought low,
I loved you so sincerely, tenderly
I pray to God some other love you so.

(In *After the Killing*, 16)

The choice of "Ya Vas Lyubil" reiterated Randall's attraction to love poems and to a poet of African descent. Connecting with Pushkin as an inspirational source affirmed Randall's internationalism and his broader racial identity as well. These contextual concerns are relevant but are not incremental. The black Russian poet's expansive knowledge of the Russian language, from formal diction and literary tradition to peasant dialect and folk poetry, is likewise reflected in Randall's relationship to English language and literatures and African American culture. This is what ostensibly attracted him to Pushkin's oeuvre:

> It's hard for people who are not Russian to really get the most out of Pushkin's poetry because he writes so subtly. His poems are classically simple and clear. But in the connotative realms of the language, he uses regular, standard, or literary Russian. He also uses the old religious Slavic, or slang out of the streets, or rural peasant language. Unlike the foreigner, the Russians understand the undertones and the different levels of in his vocabulary.

THE CREATIVE VISION: "ROSES AND REVOLUTIONS"

Originally published in 1948 in *Milestones* 3 (a student publication), Randall's "Roses and Revolutions" would become one of his most famous poems and the poem that identified his political courage and creative vision as a force in the Black Arts Movement of the 1960s. Balanced by a more mature muse, Randall's poetic center serviced the creative energy of new writers in more profound and enduring terms than the rhetoric of their own pronouncements. Ironically, unbeknownst to those writers who read the poem in the 1960s, "Roses and Revolutions" reflects the expansive perspective of the previous generation.[14] At the same time, it is probably the most misdated of all of his poems. Because the poem became prominent during the 1960s, the imagery is associated with the many race riots of that decade, and the publication date is misinterpreted as the time when the poem was composed. A more accurate historical association would be the 1943 Detroit race riot and the lynchings that occurred in the South after WWII. Moreover, Randall's break with conventional forms occurred during the 1940s, but this break became more pronounced during the 1950s and 1960s.

"Roses and Revolutions" provides a grand poetic example of Randall's merging of politics and art and a perspective for reading the deepest reaches of his creative purpose. The poem not only addresses the tragic consequences of racism, but also envisions a society that alters its decadent values and evolves beyond selfish, competitive greed. But, inasmuch as the poem reflects revolution, its purpose is to inspire a love of life. The poem operates on several levels and angles of perspective, moving from the macro to the micro, demonstrating the interconnectedness of humanity's fate while positing an alternative collective consciousness.

The poem opens with the word, "Musing, on roses and revolutions," which is the dialectical dilemma of the black writer's position in literature. In the first stanza of this prophetic poem, his muse reflects the oppressive circumstances that threaten, haunt, murder, and maim his people. The fusion of clear, precise images and incisive statements empowers the poem as a poignant portrayal of racial oppression.

> Musing on roses and revolutions,
> I saw night close down on the earth like a great dark wing,
> and the lighted cities were like tapers in the night,
> and I heard the lamentations of a million hearts
> regretting life and crying for the grave,
> and I saw the Negro lying in the swamp with his face blown off,
> and in northern cities with his manhood maligned and felt the writhing
> of his viscera like that of the hare hunted down or the bear at bay,
> and I saw men working and taking no joy in their work
> and embracing the hard-eyed whore with joyless excitement
> and lying with wives and virgins in impotence.
>
> And as I groped in darkness
> and felt the pain of millions,
> gradually, like day driving night across the continent,
> I saw dawn upon them like the sun a vision
> of a time when all men walk proudly through the earth
> and the bombs and missiles lie at the bottom of the ocean
> like the bones of dinosaurs buried under the shale of eras,
> and men strive with each other not for power or the accumulation
>   of paper
> but in joy create for others the house, the poem, the game of
>   athletic beauty.
>
> Then washed in the brightness of this vision,
> I saw how in its radiance would grow and be nourished and suddenly
> burst into terrible and splendid bloom
> the blood-red flower of revolution.

(In Cities Burning, 5)

Characteristic of Randall's poetry, "Roses and Revolutions" exhibits geometric thematic constructions: opposition, contrast, and counterpoint. It is both a love poem and a war poem, a poem about horror and about peace, about the past and about the future. Randall's poetry is reflexive, revealing elements and areas of intersection while providing a broader perspective for introspection. It engages conflicting associations to reveal a dialectic and its resolution in a peaceful terror. "Roses and Revolutions," as a theme, possibly presents an overview of Randall's poetic vision. He devoted much of his poetry to themes of love and war. In the broader sense, the wars of his lifetime were World War II, the Korean War, and the Vietnam War, and he wrote about them or on related issues with these wars as settings. Within this context, we often find love poems. Concurrently, the civil wars and the struggle to achieve rights and parity in the United States instigate the African American poet to assume an activist position. Therefore, many of Randall's poems assess conflicting loyalties and contradictory circumstances with the passion and temperament of "Roses and Revolutions."

THE UNIVERSITY OF MICHIGAN AND ANN ARBOR

After Randall graduated from Wayne University in June 1949, he attended the University of Michigan (1949–1951) to pursue a master's degree in library science:

> I got a second hand car and drove to Ann Arbor, but I had a lot of trouble with the car, so I sold it and took the bus to Ann Arbor instead. I worked afternoons at the post office from 4:00 P.M. until 12:30 A.M. In the morning, I'd go to Ann Arbor and study in the library either before or after class. I would go to work as soon as I'd return from Ann Arbor, and I studied on my lunch hour. I also studied on the weekends at the main library in Detroit.
>
> I thought about applying to the University of Chicago Library School, but I decided on the University of Michigan because it was close. I didn't have much fun going to graduate school because it was all rush and work. Hurry to school. Hurry to work. Study whenever I had time. It wasn't too difficult, but it kept me busy.

I have good powers of concentration, and can write anywhere or any time. My wife said the house could be on fire and I wouldn't notice it, if I were reading or writing. I carry a notebook in my pocket so I can jot down ideas or transcribe a poem. I like to let a poem grow in my mind before I set it down on paper. I want every line, every word to be inevitable, so I let the poem grow and shape itself in my unconscious mind inevitably.[15]

15. Dudley Randall at the University of Michigan, 1949.

Shifting between Detroit and Ann Arbor affected Randall's muse, but the lack of time and the intensity of his schedule did not afford him opportunities for the kind of intellectual and creative activities that he engaged in at Wayne University. His relationship to the University of Michigan campus was academic and distant. Wayne was situated in his backyard and comprised a more diverse, intense, and socially complex student population. In Ann Arbor, his muse became impassive, and the verse he elicited was more reflective of the imagist poets.

"Shape of the Invisible" is characteristic of his impressionistic attempts in Ann Arbor to capture the imprint of nature as a living force. The capitalization of the first word of each line and the absence of punctuation at the end of each line direct the reading of the poem in a sweeping motion to the right. The movement of the words emulates the sway of the wind, and the shape of the invisible:

> At dawn
> Upon the snow
> The delicate imprint
> Left by the sleeping body of
> The wind.
>
> (In *More to Remember*, 20)

"Winter Campus: Ann Arbor" conveys an objective, abstract negotiation between the poet and the poem as it contemplates seasonal shifts, natural sounds, and noiselessness:

> April took flesh in clear September air
> when one girl paused upon the colonnade,
> turned, and for a heartbeat hovered there
> while yellow elm leaves drifted past her hair.
>
> (In *More to Remember*, 19)

The comparison of student voices with the hum of bees is a numb contrast to the more intense Detroit poems that engage social conflict. From this reposed position, the emotional perspective of the Ann Arbor poem illuminates how the poet intercepts subject matter and contemplates it:

> Here, now, the same soft youngness is conveyed
> as these bareheaded throngs stream to and fro
> with footfalls noiseless in the sudden snow,
> while treble voices tremble in the air
> and rime with chiming of the carillon.

After graduation in 1951, Dudley Randall was offered and accepted a librarian position at Lincoln University in Missouri. He left Detroit with an abundance of poems and the skills to make a living in libraries. From then on, he would spend his life among books—arranging them, organizing them, cataloguing them, and exploring them—in communion with one of his earliest and true passions. As a student, Dudley Randall pursued his intellectual thirst and indulged his creative urges. He abided by his aesthetic creed: that a writer "must serve only the truth as he sees it,"[16] as he wrote, revised, and rewrote poetry about the 1930s and 1940s for an audience in the 1960s and 1970s and for a literary prominence yet to come.

6

SOJOURN AND RETURN

N THE AUTUMN OF 1951, Dudley and Mildred Randall left Detroit for Lincoln, Missouri, for Dudley's first librarian position at Lincoln University, a historically black college. Dudley Randall had hoped that his position at Lincoln would be intensely cultural and intellectually exciting, but Missouri was as Southern as it was Midwestern. Therefore, it was socially segregated and culturally limited. The move was a dramatic shift in lifestyle for the Randalls. Disappointed by the lack of literary activity at the Lincoln University and burdened by a troubled marriage, Randall missed the diversity and sophistication of the big city:

> I had been in touch with poets at Wayne with the Miles Writers Workshop, but when I was at Lincoln University there weren't many people interested in literature there. However, I did publish two book reviews in Negro Digest during this time, and one of my more famous poems, "Booker T. and W. E. B.," first appeared in print in Midwest Journal, which was published by Lincoln University, and I wrote one article for The Missouri Library Journal. A. P. Marshall was the head librarian at Lincoln. He was a very good administrator. He encouraged the librarians to go to professional meetings, to join professional organizations, and to publish. Someone had asked him to write an article, but he referred the request to me. It was a survey, a mechanical discussion about some aspect of the profession and didn't contain much creativity.

I remember when Ulysses Lee came down to Lincoln University to teach when I was a librarian there. He and Sterling Brown always talked about reprinting Negro Caravan, *a new edition with later poets, but they never got around to doing it. Lee was a big fan of Henry James, and he had the library order Henry James novels, and after he left, nobody read them. He was the only Henry James enthusiast at Lincoln University.*

While Dudley was a librarian at Lincoln University, the library staff published a *Staff Manual*, and he was the chairman for the project. "Booker T. and W. E. B." (Booker T. Washington and W. E. B. Du Bois) was written on the eve of the Civil Rights Movement. In the poem, the voice of Du Bois supports the struggle for desegregation and equal rights, while Washington's retorts represent conformity and acquiescence to conventional racial roles. In a terse debate intensified by the restraint of rhyme, Randall captures the essence of the ideological differences between Du Bois and Washington:

> "It seems to me," said Booker T.,
> "It shows a mighty lot of cheek
> To study chemistry and Greek
> When Mister Charlie needs a hand
> To hoe the cotton on his land,
> And when Miss Anne looks for a cook,
> Why stick your nose inside a book?"
>
> "I don't agree," said W. E. B.,
> "If I should have the drive to seek
> Knowledge of chemistry or Greek,
> I'll do it. Charles and Miss can look
> Another place for hand or cook.
> Some men rejoice in skill of hand,
> And some in cultivating land,
> But there are others who maintain
> The right to cultivate the brain."
>
> "It seems to me," said Booker T.,
> "That all you folks have missed the boat
> Who shout about the right to vote,
> And spend vain days and sleepless nights
> In uproar over civil rights.

Just keep your mouths shut, do not grouse,
But work, and save, and buy a house."

"I don't agree," said W. E. B.,
"For what can property avail
If dignity and justice fail.
Unless you help to make the laws,
They'll steal your house with trumped-up clause.
A rope's as tight, a fire as hot,
No matter how much cash you've got.
Speak soft, and try your little plan,
But as for me, I'll be a man."

"It seems to me," said Booker T.—

"I don't agree,"
Said W. E. B.[1]

As the ending suggests, the argument continues, but in this poem Du Bois gets the last word, which indicates the poet's agreement. The poem was later interpreted into a visual work of art by Shirley Woodson Reid, which contains the last two stanzas written in Randall's handwriting. Unfortunately, the differences between Dudley and Mildred Randall were as irreconcilable as the debate between Du Bois and Washington.

I left Lincoln University in 1954 when I got a job at Morgan State College [another black college] in Baltimore, Maryland, but Mildred left for Detroit, where she filed for a divorce. I didn't have many cultural contacts in Baltimore or with the faculty at the university, because I stayed in a suburb with my brother Arthur and his wife. They had a son, Phillip, and a daughter, Shirley. As soon as I finished my work, I would drive home or take the streetcar to Day Village, where they lived.

Arthur was an associate editor at The Baltimore Afro-American. *He was a night editor and would go to work in the evening and come home in the morning. He majored in journalism at the University of Michigan and finished school in the 1930s. It was hard for black journalists during that time. He was unhappy with his job, because the newspaper was family owned, and if there was a promotion, it was usually given to someone in the family. He didn't want to take a chance by going to Chicago and trying to get on with*

16. Dudley Randall with Phillip and Shirley Randall in Day Village, ca. 1955.

Ebony [Magazine], *which at that time was the largest of the very few black-owned publications. He couldn't get hired by white, mainstream newspapers because of racial discrimination at the time.*

By the mid-1950s, the Civil Rights Movement was picking up momentum in the South. Rosa Parks's refusal to surrender to Jim Crow inspired the Montgomery bus boycott, and the Supreme Court decision in *Brown vs. the Board of Education* indicated that desegregation was indeed a national issue. Conversely, Senator McCarthy's "Red Hunt" reflected the antithesis to the Civil Rights Movement, an anticommunist crusade that had particular consequences for black Detroiters. Because the Red Hunt was often focused on people who advocated the rights of workers and blacks, certain personalities were immediately suspects. Paul Robeson was branded a national traitor, and labor and civil rights advocates and leaders, like Coleman A. Young, were attacked and indicted by the UnAmerican Affairs Committee.

At this time, the Reuther brothers of the United Auto Workers (UAW) and Jimmy Hoffa of the Brotherhood of Teamsters dominated the leadership of organized labor in Detroit. Both assumed that an anticommunist stance would lend an American "character" to their organizations and distance their union struggles from their historical affiliation with socialism. They feared the growing anticommunist sentiments espoused by the federal government as the Cold War with the Soviet Union advanced. According to Coleman Young, when Walter Reuther publicly disassociated his union from "communist affiliations" and distinguished his brand of "social unionism" as truly American, he betrayed many of his previous allies and left them twisting in the wind.[2]

In 1953, large areas of Black Bottom were bulldozed. It had been condemned as a slum area and cleared for a new highway and real estate development. 700 buildings were demolished and approximately 2,000 families were displaced.[3] Advances had been made in race relations in the unions, but there was still resistance to integration in housing. "Despite assaults, window breakings, and cross burnings by white neighbors, the relentless pressure of Detroit's growing black population gradually broke down the barriers surrounding all-white neighborhoods."[4] In many instances, blacks bought homes from Jewish owners, and movement into better and more attractive homes followed this pattern.

But despite the difficult political situation in his hometown, Randall's return to Detroit was the beginning of a better life for him on personal, professional, and literary levels.

When I left Baltimore in 1956 and returned to Detroit, I got a job with the Wayne County Federated Library System and worked at the Eloise Branch, which provided services for hospital patients. I would take books to the hospital wards and the mental wards. I didn't write the poem, "George," when I was working in the Ford foundry, but the experience reflected in the poem is derived from my encounter with a man I knew when I worked in the factory in the 1930s, and who was now a patient in that hospital.

The poem "George" marks not only Randall's return to Detroit, but also a reclamation of his past. The poem demonstrates an appreciation of his labor roots and his capacity to embrace that experience in the identity of the working everyman, his friend George. The dramatic tension within the lines and within the stanzas of the poem "George" is accomplished by juxtaposing hard and soft sounds, employing alliteration and assonance, and constructing subtle, syllabic configurations. In a careful arrangement of word spacing, Randall declines any punctuation within the first two lines. This estranges the thoughts and suspends them in a pause for reflection before the memory takes form. Whereas the transitional lines are punctuated with many pauses and short phrases during the retelling of the foundry episode, lines and commas build and accelerate the image and then stop it with a short simple statement.

Images of masculinity are symbolically melded into metal and muscle, flesh and sweat. Randall's characteristic use of contrast complicates this imagery of maleness and physical challenge by enveloping it in tenderness and in a bonding sealed in the face of danger and hardship in the workplace—the confidence and assurance of brotherhood:[4]

When I was a boy desiring the title of man
And toiling to earn it
In the inferno of the foundry knockout,
I watched and admired you working by my side,
As, goggled, with mask on your mouth and shoulders bright with sweat,
You mastered the monstrous, lumpish cylinder blocks,
And when they clotted the line and plunged to the floor
With force enough to tear your foot in two,
You calmly stepped aside.

One day when the line broke down and the blocks reared up
Groaning, grinding, and mounted like an ocean wave
And then rushed thundering down like an avalanche,
And we frantically dodged, then braced our heads together
To form an arch to lift and stack them,
You gave me your highest accolade:
You said, "You not afraid of sweat. You strong as a mule."

Now, here, in the hospital,
In a ward where old men wait to die,
You sit, and watch time go by.

You cannot read the books I bring, not even
Those that are only picture books,

As you sit among the senile wrecks,
The psychopaths, the incontinent.
One day when you fell from your chair and stared at the air
With the look of fright which sight of death inspires,
I lifted you like a cylinder block, and said,
"Don't be afraid
Of a little fall, for you'll be here
Along time yet, because you're strong as a mule."

(In *Poem Counterpoem*, 18)

The Miles Poetry Series was still active when I returned to Detroit, even though it was comprised of different poets. When I was a student at Wayne, our committee invited poets like Stephen Spender to read. We looked up to the more experienced poets. But during these times things were changing and the poets at Wayne were more political. One of these younger poets said to me, Karl Shapiro isn't very good. Because he felt Shapiro's poetics weren't very political, this young white poet rejected Shapiro's poetry.

These politically motivated poets came to the meetings and disrupted them because they didn't want any of the established poets to be invited to read. The committee would agree to let their preferred poet read in place of its original choice. This kind of disruption occurred at every meeting. It became too confusing, so I decided to quit. This was during the "beat period," and the younger poets were attracted to a particular kind of writing. At this time, my contemporaries had all graduated. Robert Huff was teaching and was still around, and the up-and-coming poet, John Sinclair, who had been a student of my brother James Randall at the University of Michigan—Flint, was at Wayne State University. My poem "Poet" reflects my impressions of their perspective.

Patron of pawn shops,
Sloppily dressed,
Bearded, shoeless and graceless,
Reading when you should be working,
Fingering a poem in your mind
When you should be figuring a profit,
Consorter with Negroes and Jews
And other troublesome elements
Who are always disturbing the peace
About something or other,
Friend of revolutionaries

And foe of the established order,
When will you slough off
This preposterous posture
And behave like a normal
Solid responsible
White Anglo Saxon Protestant?

(In *More to Remember*, 55)

The poem engages the rebelliousness of beat poets as reflected in their lifestyle, their demeanor, and their poetic themes. Similar to Randall's poems about black cultural figures or characters from Black Bottom, this poem is a composite portrait of a beat poet. With pithy irony, Randall posits himself on the perimeter of the poem, and yet he identifies this white poet as an ally of "Negroes and Jews," at a time when such associations could have been politically costly. The Beat movement in poetry was an artistic response to the Civil Rights Movement and a precursor to the literary radicalism of the 1960s. Randall's avoidance of the disruptions that occurred at the Miles Modern Poetry meetings was consistent with his dislike of confrontation. Although he avoided arguments during the meetings, his creative response to this generation of poets was receptive and he agreed with their progressive politics.

VIVIAN BARNETT SPENCER RANDALL

Shortly after Randall returned to Detroit, he met his third wife, Vivian Spencer, on the tennis court at the Northwestern High School athletic field. Two previous marriages had ended in divorce. His first marriage to Ruby Hands in 1935 had not ended bitterly. They maintained a mutual respect and friendship, and he kept a close relationship with his daughter and met his paternal responsibilities. In his poem "A Litany of Friends," he wrote: "For Phyllis and Ruby who called when they needed help or advice." Although his second and more difficult marriage to Mildred Pinckney also ended in divorce, his even temperament ultimately resolved that fissure into friendship. In "A Litany of Friends" he also wrote: "For Mildred who listened and talked to me when I was alone and afraid to go home to an empty house." About her father's parenting, Phyllis Randall Sherron said: "My father was very soft-spoken. He was not aggressive. But when he said something, he meant it. Whenever I would ask him for something, he would either say yes, no, or he'd think about it."[5] During the war, he wrote to her: "I am glad you like music, books and concerts too. I like the 'Merry Widow,' too. I'm looking for

17. Vivian Spencer Randall, ca. 1958.

your picture. I'm sure it will be very lovely. Who is this little girl wearing her mother's hat and dress?"[6]

Although her name was derived from poetry, a country maiden in Virgil's *Eclogues*, Phyllis's interests and ambitions differed from her father's: "I wanted to go to Dillard University in New Orleans in 1958, but my father didn't want me to go there. He wanted me to stay in Detroit and go to Wayne State University. But he said he would pay for the first year, then I would have to return to Detroit to finish. But I got a scholarship and was able to complete my degree in nursing there. My father didn't really understand my interest in the sciences because he was involved with literature. But after I got the scholarship, he accepted that accomplishment, and I was allowed to stay."

She later received a master's degree in nursing with a specialization in obstetrics and a second master's degree in vocational education. More importantly, Phyllis said, "My father never broke a promise. If he said he was coming to see me, he would be there. Even if he was a few minutes late, I knew he was coming."[7] Promises are made with words, and Randall, who was careful and deliberate with his writing, was as measured with meanings in his speech. Phyllis married William Sherron III, and they had two children, William IV and Venita. When Venita was born, Dudley wrote "Augury For An Infant (For Venita Sherron)." In it, Randall makes allusions to famous Africans and African Americans. He poses questions that she will in turn ask about the names that appear in the poem written for her. This form encourages an inquiry into black history and the rhyme further invites the interest of a youngster.

> Venita, you have come to us.
> What will you be?
> Proud as Du Bois, humble as Booker T.?
> A poet with the humor of Dunbar,
> Or with fiery feelings of Antar?
> Classic as Pushkin, romantic as Dumas?
>
> There's so much wealth to mine,
> So much to do.
> Will you be a Carver, Banneker, or Drew,
> Or learn the lore of the Ethiopian queen?
> Sing sweet as Marian or Leontyne?
> Or be an artist, skilled, sophisticated
> As those by whom the African bronzes were created?
>
> In you, little babe, I see
> Infinite possibility.
>
> (In *Cities Burning*, 16)

Unlike the first two marriages, Randall's union with Vivian Barnett Spencer not only lasted, it endured and prospered. Born in Louisville, Kentucky, and raised in Lexington, she received a scholarship awarded by the Lexington Public School System to any college of her choice. "It was a competitive scholarship," Vivian explained. "I had to take an examination and from the results two students, one white and one black (because of "separate but equal"), were awarded scholarships. I selected Wayne University because I had an aunt living in Detroit who had said I could live with her if I wanted to go to university in Detroit."[8] Vivian enrolled at Wayne in 1941, and she completed a bachelor's and a master's degree in social work. Vivian and Dudley did not meet on campus during the 1940s, though, but more than a decade later on the tennis courts. Vivian invited Dudley to a dance. "I snatched him right up," she said gleefully. After a short courtship, they were married on 4 May 1957, and they lived in a corner house on Longfellow at Savory Street, on Detroit's west side. In "A Plea," dedicated "To Vivian," Dudley expresses his trust and faith in his wife:

> I place my heart in your hands
> To hold and keep,
> To cherish and understand
> The light and the deep.
>
> I place my life in your hands,
> In perfect faith
> That innocence and trust
> Will be ours until death.
>
> Take care of these frail treasures;
> Neither break nor betray.
> I have only one heart and one life
> to give away.
>
> (Unpublished; from the personal collection of Vivian Randall)

In 1959, Missouri Randall Hawkins died at the age of 96 in Macon, Georgia. That same year, Dudley's brother, Arthur Randall, died of a heart attack. Three years later, Arthur's wife died from cancer. Their daughter, Shirley, moved in with her mother's friend, Hortense Fitzgerald, while their son, Phillip (named after Dudley's younger brother who died in his youth) moved in with another relative. But when Phillip did not get along with that family, he moved in with Dudley and Vivian Randall in 1964. They raised him as their own until he joined the army in 1971.

Returning to Detroit also brought Dudley closer to his brother, James, who became the first black professor at the University of Michigan—Flint. His sister Esther became involved with politics in the Democratic Party, and her career was crowned by her appointments as deputy administrator for the Veterans Administration during President Lyndon B. Johnson's Great Society of the 1960s. Institutional power and political organizations were shifting, and the Randalls were trained and ready to assume positions of influence.

In 1966, Dudley and Vivian built a new brick home in Russell Woods, an established black middle-class neighborhood in northwest Detroit. This modern, quad-level architectural design has large picture windows, sliding glass doors, and a serene view of grass and trees in Russell Woods Park. An openness flows from room to room, from floor to floor, from inside onto the patio or into the greenhouse where Vivian nurtured her array of garden plants and flowers. Hardwood floors and a stone fireplace in the den underscores a classic simplicity. Miniature brass statues from Benin occupy glass shelves that divide the living and dining rooms. African carvings stand like the sentinels of history. African American paintings are juxtaposed with broadsides. "On Getting A Natural," the poem dedicated to Gwendolyn Brooks, which was matted and framed in muted gold, hangs above the piano. Contemporary leather furniture contrasts with the sedate, warm autumn tones in the oriental carpets. Negro spirituals or Chopin sonatas often fill the air.

Books appear and disappear in uneven stacks, crowding end tables or ledges, resisting the confines of bookshelves. They generate in piles next to easy chairs or dominate a glass-top coffee table. Titles resurface as they are shuffled and reshuffled from room to room until they are remanded to one of the many wooden shelves that line the walls and hallways.

Vivian is also a lapidarian and has traveled to China, Japan, and throughout Europe collecting semiprecious stones to be polished until smooth and glossy. Centered and calm, she complemented and balanced her husband's lofty romanticism and artistic exuberance. She was confident when he was uncertain. She was focused when he was scattered. Her smooth steadiness anchored the intensity of his shifting moods. She was mindful and supportive of his poetry, but leveled him with everyday, mundane considerations: "My wife's on my back for neglecting the household, & I told her I resolved to be a mechanic even tho clumsy & inept at such."[9]

Randall's return to Detroit was anchored to a woman who was his intellectual equal and his psychological complement. In the prime of his life, he returned home to a professional future as a librarian and a marriage that would last. In this relationship, he attained clarity about himself. In "Anniversary Words," Randall rebelled against the conventional love sonnet and captured the ambiguity of their marriage as entangled personalities greeting the challenges of partnership with honesty and sincerity:

> You who have shared my scanty bread with me
> and borne my carelessness and forgetfulness
> with only occasional lack of tenderness,
> who have long patiently endured my faculty

18. The home of Dudley and Vivian Randall,
12651 Old Mill Place in Russell Woods in Detroit.

for genial neglect of practicality,
for forgetting the morning and the parting caress
and for leaving rooms in a great disorderliness
which when I entered were as neat as they could be,

despite the absent-mindedness of my ways
and the not seldom acerbity of your tone,
I sometimes catch a softness in your gaze
which tells me after all I am your own
and that you love me in no little way.
But I know it best by the things you never say.

(In *A Litany of Friends*, 29)

7

THE EMERGENCE OF THE SECOND RENAISSANCE IN DETROIT

I write because I have an urge to write and because I enjoy writing. Some of my happiest hours have been spent in writing. I wrote for years before I was published.

DUDLEY RANDALL'S POETRY BEGAN TO APPEAR nationally in the early 1960s during the emergence of the second renaissance in African American culture. As a number of progressive political and cultural periodicals appeared, Randall's earlier poems, written during the 1930s, 1940s. and 1950s, as well as poetry written in response to current events and social issues, reached a larger audience.[1] When activist and educator Edward Simpkins was invited to be the guest editor of a special Detroit issue of *The Negro History Bulletin* (October 1962), the official publication of the Association of the Study of Negro Life and History (ASNLH), several of Dudley Randall's works were included. Symbolic of the racially integrated radicalism that emanated from the intellectual community at the time, the cover for the issue was a photograph of the historical marker of the meeting place of Frederick Douglass and John Brown in Detroit on 12 March 1859. The uniqueness of the Detroit cultural constituency resided in the interchange between civil-rights activities and labor-based organizations. Simpkins, a labor and civil-rights activist, concluded that this consciousness invigorated the aims and aspirations of the community:

You can recall the fervor of that period. Those of us who were entering their professional careers as teachers or librarians or whatever, were pulled by the dynamism of the times. The SCLC [Southern Christian Leadership Conference] and its marches and the frustration and anger of people like Malcolm and the Muslims put a different spin on how we should deal with all of this. It had a radicalizing effect on all of us. We were revolutionary thinkers and doers, and it was those thoughts that germinated and contributed to the times.[2]

The Detroit issue of *The Negro History Bulletin* represented a broad spectrum of the city's black intelligentsia: Henry D. Brown, Director, Detroit Historical Museum; Wade H. McCree Jr., Federal District Judge of Eastern Michigan; Dr. Broadus N. Butler, Wayne State University; Charles C. Diggs Jr., U.S. Congressman; Edward N. Hodges, Executive Director, Michigan Fair Employment Commission; Dr. Arthur L. Johnson, Executive Secretary, Detroit Chapter, NAACP; John Chavis, Curator, Detroit Historical Museum; Dr. Reginald Wilson, the editor of *Correspondence*; and Hoyt Fuller, the editor of *Negro Digest*. In addition to Dudley Randall, other creative contributors were Harold G. Lawrence (aka Kofi Wangara), Margaret Danner, Harrison Bwire Muyia, Edward H. Anderson, Mary Jones, Alma Parks, Woodie King, Naomi Long Madgett, Powell Lindsay, James E. McCall, Margaret Ford, Leroy E. Mitchell Jr., James W. Thompson, Edward Simpkins, and Oliver LaGrone.

In this collection of creative and historical writings, several pieces of Randall's poetry and a short story appeared. At this time, Randall was enrolled in a master's degree program in the humanities at Wayne State University, and that year he won a Thompkins Awards for poetry, including some of the selections in the ASNLH journal. Randall's poetry selections included "Booker T. and W. E. B.," "Memorial Wreath," "The Southern Road," "Legacy," "My Native Land," and "Hymn," and his first published short story, "A Cup for the Loser." While the majority of Randall's works in this collection are related to racial history and memory and were written during the 1940s and 1950s, "Hymn" (first published in *The Negro History Bulletin* 24, no. 1 [October 1962]: 80) offers a broader scope of concerns. This poem laments the detonation of the nuclear bomb and the threat of planetary annihilation looming in the aftermath of Hiroshima and Nagasaki:

> O squat and ugly in thy form,
> But fierce as Moloch in thy power,
> Accept our worship and our warm
> Dependence in this anxious hour.

19. Dudley Randall, ca. 1962.

> While problems of the world and state
> Twist up our minds with knotty choice,
> Thine is the power to extirpate
> All evil with thy deafening voice.
>
> And then no more of wrong or right,
> Or whose shrewd counsels we should keep,
> One flash of solar-blinding light
> And then the sweet eternal sleep.
>
> (In *More to Remember*, 57)

This antiwar poem reflects the national anxiety in a time when routine air-raid drills and bomb shelters dramatized the Cold War between the United States and the Soviet Union. Contrary to this paranoiac mood, a national peace movement emerged, and when the poems "Hymn" and "My Native Land" are juxtaposed, the combination is suggestive of this shift in political consciousness. Randall's translation of K. M. Simonov's poetry was not a procommunist gesture, but a cultural act of resistance and an overture that was certainly incongruent with U.S. politics.

In addition to poetry, Randall published one of four short stories in the Detroit issue of the *Negro History Bulletin*. The other three appeared in *Negro Digest* (1964–1966). Randall said that these works were not very good, and he abandoned this genre after these initial publications. Actually, they are quite good; moreover, they reflect his acute sense of verbal economy, his tendency towards understatement, and his capacity to infuse symbolic complexity into simple formats.

In "A Cup for the Loser," the setting is the Prohibition era, a time when Randall was a young man coming of age. The characters are clearly working class, and the narrator is a young man whose tone is mildly mocking of a rather self-righteous and overbearing father who argues all the time. The story contains autobiographical features that are suggestive of Randall's childhood when he "heard too many sermons" from his strict father and his family took in boarders to supplement mortgage payments. In a disapproving tone the narrator shares his opinion about his father's confrontational debate style: "What Papa liked to do most of all was to argue. He never called it arguing, but always discussing, but anyway to me it sounded like plain arguing." Moreover, young Dave never speaks aloud in the story and serves more as a silent observer, which is also similar to Randall's shy manner and his habit of observing rather than engaging in argument. The argument in the story is over the "evils" of drinking alcohol. Despite Dave's disapproval of his father's passion for debate, he does recognize the practicality of his father's position:

> Sometimes a roomer would come in drunk and Mama would have to put him to bed. Or sometimes a couple would be drinking and suddenly change from playing and lovey-doveying to quarreling and breaking up the furniture on each other's heads, and Papa would have to stop the fight and counsel them about drinking. So he was constantly discussing the drinking habit with them, since it was hard on his own property as well as on their health.

The argument is between Papa, who is a factory worker, a perfect physical specimen, and a devout temperance advocate, and Mr. Goodlow, who is a janitor, but distinguishes himself as a custodian. Dave introduces Mr. Goodlow as an inventor. Mr. Goodlow has a charming, good-hearted nature and an enthusiastic optimism as he labors in a humble job awaiting the big break from one of his inventions that will make him rich. Both men are well-read and verbally adept, but the disagreement is settled by a foot race with a surprise finish that does not prove a point but does resolve the issue and the futility of any argument between two men who are determined not to change. "A Cup for the Loser" is a double entendre as the cup is not a trophy, but a drink of liquor and the bitter aftertaste of defeat lingering in a shut mouth.

It is a clever and entertaining story about human nature, which is the focus of the other short stories as well. A subtle shift in the plot alters the advantage of one character by representing certain assumptions that could have shown a lack of total compassion with the ways of others. Randall's short story themes are consistent in this regard, as they delve beneath the assumptions of dialogue and character projections to determine unspoken meanings. Randall's wisdom appears as the voice of an innocent child, listening behind all the loud talk.

Hoyt Fuller's *Negro Digest* was especially important to Randall's literary visibility. After graduating from Wayne State University, Fuller became a journalist for the *Michigan Chronicle* and the *Detroit Tribune*. But in 1957, he became discouraged by the pervasive racism in the United States, and he expatriated to live in Europe and then in Africa. In 1960 he returned and for a brief period wrote for *Ebony Magazine*. When Johnson Publications revived *Negro Digest*, Fuller became the editor and changed the journal's chronicle format into a forum for creative expression and political dialogue. Fuller reconnected with Randall and frequently consulted with him for editorial advice and book reviews. Randall's poetry and prose appeared regularly in the magazine.

20. Hoyt Fuller, ca. 1972.

Randall published his second short story, "The Cut Throat," in *Negro Digest* in July 1964. The setting is a timeless space described by the inner voice of a barber, as he reveals his accumulated rage and desire to kill someone that he has shaved for years. The second paragraph demonstrates how Randall's minimalist descriptions effectively develop setting and characterization:

> While you relax in the soft chair, soothed with our hypnotic hands and the suave smell of balms and oils, you unwittingly confess things to us and expose the secret nooks and crannies of your souls. We know what goes on in your mind, but do you know what goes on in ours, as you lie helpless under our hands wielding the razor?
>
> (Randall, "The Cut Throat," *Negro Digest* 13, no. 9 [July 1954]: 53)

The story emulates the suspense of Edgar Allen Poe's "The Tell-Tale Heart." The barber becomes fixated on the man's neck, and his compulsion to kill increases as time passes and his contempt for the man amplifies:

At last I began to loathe him. It was then that I felt the temptation. Often, as I scraped the keen steel over his chin, I reflected that a little slip, a little pressure of the wrist, would cut his throat, and end his miserable existence. As I looked into his puffed features, I imagined how they would look with a wide red gash in his throat. (54)

When the barber finally decides to cut the man's throat, the twist in the ending is like an O. Henry story:

One morning when this wretched creature was under my hands, I could resist the temptation no longer. With a quick, deft motion, I drew the razor across his throat. Some last-fraction-of-a-second feeling of pity, or of fear, perhaps, made me lighten the stroke. The wound was wide, but not deep, and did not prove fatal. (56)

For the doctors tell me I will live.

On the surface, this story appears to have no particular racial dimensions, as the barbershop is a common scene for male bonding and socializing in most American ethnic communities. In the African American community, the barbershop was and is a place where politics are debated, philosophies developed, and personal histories and vulnerabilities revealed. Moreover, in the vernacular, "cutthroat" means engaged in ruthless tactics. In this regard, the story has a cultural appeal because it is a familiar setting and the symbolism of the cut throat could subtextually allude to interactions with others and oneself that could be metaphorically fatal or at least injurious. But the key to the meaning appears in the word "the" in the title, making "cut" a participle. In Randall's case, the theme foreshadows his own attempted suicide, two decades later.

In "The Cut Throat," the violence is inflicted as an act of self-hatred, but in "Incident on a Bus" (*Negro Digest* 14, no. 10 [August 1965]: 64–66), the violence is directed at a white passenger expressing his racial hatred on a bus in a northern city. In this short story, "a nondescript Negro" kills the white racist because the other refuses to sit next to him. The bus, a symbolic locus for racial integration, provides an appropriate setting to demonstrate the intense racial hatred some whites still harbor against blacks. It also posits angry frustration as a possible motivation for urban race riots during the summers of 1965 to 1968. The change from a black character's suicide attempt in "The Cut Throat" to the murder of the white chracter in "Incident on a Bus" represents a shift from internalized racism to violent revenge against white sciety.

BOONE HOUSE

Boone House poets grew out of the same group of Detroit poets and writers who contributed to the special October 1962 issue of the Negro History Bulletin. *When the issue came out, Margaret Danner, a Chicago poet and visiting professor at Wayne State University, invited us to read at Boone House. Subsequently, we held readings at Boone House, which occurred once a month. It was very stimulating to meet them and to get to know the writers. Danner founded Boone House to create a cultural center where musicians would play, artists could exhibit their work, and poets could read their poems. With donations, membership dues, and a stipend she got from her husband in Chicago, she operated the cultural center from 1962 to 1964. At the Boone House poetry meetings we didn't criticize each other's work. It wasn't a workshop. Instead, we created a poetry community to inspire each other. We generally had an audience of other people from around the city who came to hear us read. At the time, I didn't know there were so many other black poets writing in Detroit.*

Randall met with this group on a regular basis at an old parson's house donated by Dr. Theodore S. Boone, pastor of the historic King Solomon Baptist Church, where Malcolm X spoke in Detroit on 9 November 1963. Hoyt Fuller suggested to Margaret Danner that she contact Dudley Randall when she left Chicago for Detroit, but before she followed Fuller's suggestion, Randall and Danner met at a party, a social gathering of Detroit writers. Boone House centered Randall's most important cultural activity upon his return to Detroit, and Danner, who had been born in Detroit, is often credited for organizing Detroit poets. But according to Naomi Madgett, the historical progression was quite different. Naomi Madgett reported in her memoirs that Detroit writers were meeting in each other's homes before the establishment of Boone House, and that Danner provided a specific location that congealed their collective interests. Some of their literary production was subsequently collected in the Detroit issue of *The Negro History Bulletin.*

Naomi Long Madgett moved to Detroit after she married Julius Witherspoon on 31 March 1946. In her memoirs, she describes Boone House as an "old house [that] was beautiful in its details but in poor repair. It lacked central heat, some of the lights did not work, and the toilet lacked a seat, but we were glad to have this meeting place and to huddle together good-naturedly in front of the fireplace in cold weather."[3] Randall concurred with Madgett's recollections about the conditions of the house:

21. Margaret Danner, ca. 1966.

In the winter, the place would be insufficiently heated, and we would come early to the meetings in order to break up pieces of wood to make a fire in the fireplace. It was quite hard on Margaret.

During the writing of the poem "Ballad of Birmingham," I was also involved with the Boone House poets, where I first met Naomi Long Madgett. I had known about her before, and was very impressed that she was a published poet. She had published a book of poetry, and I wanted a copy. When I asked her if she had any copies left, she said, "Well, I have one for you." Since then, we've always been friends.

When the four black girls were killed in the bombing of the Sixteenth Street Baptist Church in Birmingham, Alabama, the coeditor of Correspondence, Reginald Wilson, asked me if I would write a poem about it. I told him I didn't know, but I would see. Finally, I got an idea for the poem about the Birmingham tragedy while I was at work, and luckily it was during break time. I was working at the Wayne County Library. I showed drafts of "Ballad of Birmingham" to Naomi, and she told me what she thought of it and gave me some advice on particular words I might use.

"Ballad of Birmingham" demonstrates intracultural developments and Randall's interest in folk forms, such as the spirituals and ballads that influenced the poetry of Sterling Brown and Margaret Walker and were emerging in the songs of the Civil Rights and peace movements. Like Langston Hughes, Randall often wrote about black urban folk and "about racial themes but in the broader context of democracy for all." While pondering how to write the poem about the church bombing, he decided to evoke the voice of a mother and child in a ballad. In form and perspective, the poem intersects with Joan Baez's ballad, "Birmingham Sunday.[4] The poem's domestic setting creates a more intimate proximity with the death of the child and thereby avoids political overstatement.[5] The feminine nature of the opening scene, as the mother prepares her child to go to church, is juxtaposed with the violent images in the mother's warning and reason for refusing to let her child join the other children protesting in the civil rights march. This contrast underscores the brutality of tragedy against the tenderness of maternal love and youthful innocence:

> "Mother dear, may I go downtown
> Instead of out to play,
> And march the streets of Birmingham
> In a freedom march today?"

> "No, baby, no, you may not go,
> For the dogs are fierce and wild,
> And clubs and hoses, guns and jails
> Aren't good for a little child."

> "But mother, I won't be alone.
> More children will go with me,
> And march the streets of Birmingham
> To make our country free."

"No, baby, no, you may not go,
For I fear those guns will fire.
But you may go to church instead
And sing in the children's choir."

She has combed and brushed her night-dark hair,
And bathed rose petal sweet,
And drawn white gloves on her small brown hands,
And white shoes on her feet.

The mother smiled to know her child
Was in the sacred place,
But that smile was the last smile
To come upon her face.

For when she heard the explosion,
Her eyes grew wet and wild.
She raced through the streets of Birmingham
Calling for her child.

She clawed through bits of glass and brick,
Then lifted out a shoe.
"O, here's the shoe, my baby wore,
But, baby, where are you?"[6]

On 23 June 1963, the eve of The March on Washington, Reverend C. L. Franklin of New Bethel Baptist Church (a civil-rights leader and the father of the famous singer Aretha Franklin) was joined by Martin Luther King in the Walk to Freedom March in Detroit. The purpose of the march was to commemorate the 1943 race riot. Approximately 125,000 walked, with at least that many more lining Woodward Avenue to cheer the marchers on. At Cobo Hall, King gave the original version of his "I Have a Dream" speech. It was considered the largest civil rights demonstration until the March on Washington.[7]

The March on Washington was the highlight of the summer, but the assassination of President John F. Kennedy in Dallas, Texas, on 22 November marked 1963 as a year of tragic surprise. It was a year of catharsis marred by murders in Birmingham and Dallas. Hopeful activists seeking governmental support for the freedom struggle viewed the assassination of Kennedy as a major setback. Randall responded to this second historic tragedy with another ballad, "Dressed All in Pink," which parallels "Ballad of Birmingham" in form and in meaning. The romanticism of "Camelot," derived from allusions to the Kennedy presidency, is contrasted against the horror of assassination and the pink, bloodstained suit of the first lady, Jacqueline Kennedy. In 1965, when both poems were set to music by the folk singer Jerry Moore on Blue Note Records, Randall published them as Broadsides Nos. 1 and 2. These became the first Broadside Press publications.

> The Boone House Poets were also invited to join another workshop organized by a white woman from Kentucky, Ethel Guy Seine. There were five white poets and five black poets in total. We would meet and workshop our poems, and out of this experience we published a book entitled Ten. We pooled our money and hired a printer to make the book. The cover had a black hand and a white hand shaking, symbolic of the Civil Rights Movement. Boone House also held readings by poets in Rosey Pool's anthology, Beyond the Blues. The Dutch poet, Rosey Pool, who was visiting the Detroit area and was interested in black poetry, edited Beyond the Blues (1963). When I was introduced to her, she asked me to send her some poems. It was encouraging to be published in an anthology.

On 10 May 1963, the poets in *Beyond the Blues*[8] convened at Boone House to celebrate the publication. More so than Margaret Danner, Madgett names Pool as "the catalyst for a significant period of literary activity." Her series of lectures and readings on educational television, entitled "Black and Unknown Bards," brought together other local, black poets who had not known each other before." Moreover, *Beyond the Blues*, published by the Hand and Flower Press in Kent, England, and *Ik Ben de Nieuwe Neger* (I am the new Negro), a bilingual volume published in the Netherlands in 1965, included the work of several of the Detroit poets."[9]

Rosey Pool, who was originally from Amsterdam, became interested in black poetry when she was a university student. During the Nazi occupation, she was imprisoned for being Jewish, but she survived and joined the Resistance. Pool told Robert Hayden "that in the Nazi concentration camp where she had been a prisoner, 'she and her fellow prisoners, wishing to pray together in secret yet lacking a common faith used lines from Negro spirituals instead, because these old songs expressed what they all felt most deeply.'"[10]

"After the war she attained some notoriety as the former teacher of Anne Frank, whose diary she originally translated into English. Pool settled in London, and as an acknowledged authority on Black poetry she later taught at Negro universities in the United States and lectured on radio and television."[11] Pool promoted and collected the works of black poets in Detroit and was Randall's connection to Paul Bremen and his Heritage Series publishing project in London. Subsequently, Bremen published Dudley Randall's *Love You* (1970) as well as the poetry of Robert Hayden, James A. Emanuel, Audre Lorde, and others.

Playwright Ron Milner remembers this period in Detroit's writing community from the perspective of a young writer who had just received a John Hay Whitney Award (1962–1963) and was the first artist-in-residence at Boone House:

> Margaret Danner had a fondness for Beethoven, which would often boom throughout Boone House while I was trying to write. She loved to talk and would come into my room and say, "I'll only be a minute. I know you're being visited by the muse." The Whitney Fellowship provided me with an income, and Margaret's Boone House provided me a place to work.[12]

Milner had an office, attended the many meetings, and became acquainted with Dudley Randall, Naomi Madgett, Robert Hayden, and Langston Hughes. He remembers Danner as a fine writer with an eccentric and paranoid personality: "She designed her bed so she wouldn't have to get up. She'd swing around to one side to the typewriter, swing around to the other side to the desk." Milner observed that Danner was especially obsessed with Gwendolyn Brooks. This rivalry affected much of her thoughts about her own work and ultimately affected her relationships with others. She was also a fan of Dudley Randall, and during meetings insisted that the shy and reticent Randall read drafts of his poetry. Milner also suspected that Danner was romantically attracted to Randall. Her poem "Belle Isle" suggests such leanings, although Milner witnessed no indications or evidence that this feeling was reciprocated on Randall's part.

> Dudley was a quiet man, he was a librarian, and that all seemed to fit with his persona as the poet. But there was this other side. He had broad shoulders and a muscular build. He was a man of the people. He had worked in the factory. And if you met him on the street, you could have had a different impression of him, as a man who maybe owned a construction company. Maybe he was a deacon in the church. At the Boone House meetings others would say, we need to do this or we need to do that. Dudley's comments were always, "I'll do this," or "I have done that," or "I have contacted so and so." He was so quiet, that whenever he spoke, all the loudmouth people would listen. He was the least talkative of all the poets, and so there was always the mystery of Dudley.

This mystery instigated Milner's mischievous curiosity. Randall was not a debater, and during Boone House meetings, Milner sometimes chided Randall in order to disrupt his reserved posture: "I would purposely mess with him. I would tease him, contradict him. He would say a writer could do this or that, and I would disagree with him to see if I could break down that steel wall, to see if I could get a rise out of him. He would become angry and frustrated. In private, Margaret advised me to leave Dudley alone. She said she admired the quiet strength of Dudley Randall."

Like the character Dave in the short story "A Cup for the Loser," Randall did not like arguments, nor did he have the emotional capacity to engage in them without becoming angry. Perhaps this was a conditioned response to his father's aggressive verbosity, and, as the dutiful son, he developed the habit of repressing his emotions and avoiding direct confrontations.

THE SECOND RENAISSANCE

Between 1952 and 1964, Randall's poetry appeared in *Free Lance*, *Midwest Journal*, *Negro History Bulletin*, *Beloit Poetry Journal*, *Umbra*, and it was anthologized in *Ten*, Arna Bontemps's *American Negro Poetry*, and two collections edited by Rosey Pool, *Beyond the Blues* and *Ik ben de Nieuwe Neger*. As the number of alternative periodicals increased, his poetry was published frequently, and with few exceptions, in every major black poetry anthology published during the 1960s and 1970s. His work figured prominently in the evolving cultural activity during the 1960s. These journals and anthologies provided a platform for the burgeoning literature of activist and minority-arts communities. *Free Lance*, founded by Russell Atkins, Helen Collins, and Casper Leroy Jordan,[13] appeared in 1950 at the beginning of a decade plagued and scarred by McCarthyism and conservative resistance to the Civil Rights Movement; however, it foreshadowed the 1960s and energized the Beat movement. This publication also helped to usher in the Second Renaissance. About *Free Lance*, black poet and literary scholar Eugene Redmond explained that "this Cleveland-based little magazine played an as-yet-unsung role in the development of a multiethnic American literary underground, specifically the 'Beat' movement in poetry, which prevailed between 1955 and 1965."[14]

Especially influenced by the jazz-based rhythms of African American culture, the Beat Movement demonstrated the most explicit example of intercultural exchange between black and white writers, which constituted a direct aesthetic influence on the broadening of American literary culture. Moreover, as one of the most important periodicals during this period, *Free*

Lance derived its purpose from Langston Hughes, whose reputation and prolific career began during the Harlem Renaissance and extended into the Second Renaissance of the 1960s:

> Words are the paper and string to package experience, to wrap up from the inside out the poet's concentric waves of contact with the living world. Each poet makes of words his own highly individualized wrapping for life segments he wishes to present. Sometimes the paper and strings are more arresting than the contents of the package. Sometimes the poet creates a transparent wrapping revealing with great clarity and from all angles what is inside. Sometimes the word wrapping is clumsy and inept, and neither the inside nor the outside of the package is interesting. Sometimes the word wrapping contains nothing. But, regardless of quality or content, a poem reveals always the poet as a person. Skilled or unskilled, wise or foolish, nobody can write a poem without revealing something of himself. Here are people. Here are poems. Here is revolution.[15]

Redmond concluded that "in addition to printing the works of Black poets (such as Hughes, Dudley Randall, and LeRoi Jones), *Free Lance* also opened its pages to white bards: Robert Seward, the Canadian Irving Layton, Don Silberger, and Robert Creeley (also critic and editor of *Black Mountain Review*)," and "during the 1960's *Free Lance* would increase its review space, introduce some exciting new Black poets to the public, and play an important role in the Midwestern Black arts scene."[16] Whereas the publication of Langston Hughes's premier poem "A Negro Speaks of Rivers" (1919) in *The Crisis* marked the beginning of his influence during the Harlem Renaissance, his anthology *New Negro Poets: U.S.A.* (1964) identified his leadership at the onset of the Second Renaissance.

Randall first met Hughes when Hughes gave a poetry reading at Wayne State University in 1962, and Randall's first correspondence with Hughes involved the submission of his poetry for *New Negro Poets: U. S. A*[17]:

> I have heard that you are editing a new anthology of poetry by American Negroes, to be published by Indiana University Press. Because possibly you may not have come across any of my poems in your research for the book, I am being so bold as to send you some of my poems for your consideration.
>
> I met you last winter at your reading at Wayne State University, when you autographed my copy of *BEYOND THE BLUES* and said you would look up my poems included in the anthology. At the party afterwards, I was one of the local poets introduced to the group.

Please forgive this intrusion on your privacy, and thanks for any time you may give for considering my poems.[18]

In a letter dated, 22 January 1964, Randall invited Hughes to visit Boone House during his upcoming trip to Detroit. Information about a political lecture on southern Africa presented at Boone House illustrates the political scope of the group, and his reference to Hughes's engagement with the Umbra poets in New York demonstrates the national fervor of writing communities and the leadership role Hughes played in the cultural resurgence:

> Margaret Danner has asked me to invite you to a program at Boone House, 6126 Fourteenth, while you are in Detroit for your talk at the banquet in behalf of the African Room in the Detroit Institute of Arts. Margaret tells me that you are coming here on the 9th instead of the 16th, so we are considering having the program on the 7th or 8th of February. At that time we are having a graduate student from Wayne State University talk on "Don't You Dare!," an account of her experiences during four years of teaching in Southern Rhodesia.
>
> These programs at Boone House are free to the public, are usually on poetry or literature, and attract an audience of about 20 or 25 people. Attending them fairly regularly are some of the poets who will appear in your new book, *NEW NEGRO POETS: U.S.A.* They would be very glad to have an opportunity to meet you, to hear you talk about your new book, and, perhaps, to question you about it. At the banquet, they would not have the opportunity for this informal exchange. Carolyn Reese, who wrote her thesis on your poetry, is a member of the Arts Committee in charge of these programs, and will almost certainly be there. I read in the July issue of *Mainstream* about your visits to the Umbra poets in New York, and I am sure that we Detroit poets would also enjoy an opportunity to meet and talk with you.[19]

Hughes agreed to meet with the Boone House poets, but because he wanted privacy to write, Randall assured him that "there would be no introduction to the group, no talk, and no publicity, but that you would only chat informally after the program with the poets who are in your book and with other poets and persons who would like to talk with you." [20] But Hughes' schedule during his 1964 (7–9 February) visit to Detroit would not allow much time for writing, and the time he spent at Boone House was probably the only reprieve he had from the whirlwind of affairs. The Association for the Study of Negro Life and History (ASNLH) invited Hughes to Detroit for two major fund-raising events for the opening of the African Art Gallery in the Detroit Institute of the Arts, a testimonial banquet and a gala, at which more than 1,500 patrons attended. Received by Mayor Jerome Cavanaugh as soon as he arrived in the city, Hughes was given a ceremonial "key to the city." The poet asked the mayor: "What will this open that won't cost me anything?"

"I met Langston Hughes through Margaret, and I was the one that engineered the idea for Hughes and Danner to record their poetry," Ron Milner explained. "I was trying to get to New York, to see some plays. But on the other hand, how could you go wrong with those two poets?"

Hughes was doing a play on Broadway, *Tambourines to Glory*, and during the play he moved into a hotel downtown. Margaret Danner and I rode to New York in a station wagon. That's what Motown thought about the written word. A ride in a station wagon. When we got there, we had to record the reading in Hughes's hotel room. They sat on the bed, and I sat on the chair. After Langston heard how prepared Margaret was, he returned the next day with a richer catalogue of pieces. His reading was amazing. He even added lines that weren't in the printed poem to accompany the flow of the trumpet . . . "dreams come back and tumble down the street." Margaret nodded her head, and said, "Yes. Yes. That was very nice." But I could tell she was furious.

After the session she was angry and in tears. "You've forsaken me. You gave him more time to read. You sabotaged me." She didn't believe me when I told her I hadn't intentionally done anything, and that when we got back to Detroit, we could fix her reading, add to it, whatever. But she insisted that she didn't know anything about recording machines. I finally got her to calm down, assuring her that things would be better after we got to Detroit and edited the tape.

But when we got back to Detroit neither one of us got into the editing room. The Motown staff added some organ music and destroyed the aesthetics of the reading. Ruined it. The recording, "Poets of the Revolution," was not released until years after Langston's death in 1967. I thought Margaret was a wonderful writer, and that her work could stand on its own, and that her idea to do the book with Dudley was a great idea.[21]

POET COUNTERS POET

The first time I visited Margaret it was a warm, autumn day. She was living on Edward's Place Avenue. She suggested we go to a nearby cemetery [Elmwood Cemetery][22] and read our poems. She said it was a place where people go to have picnics, like in a park. But when we went there, but couldn't get in, I suggested we go to Belle Isle, an island park in the middle of the Detroit River. We sat on the bank, watched the boats cruising down the river, and read each other's poems. Afterwards, she thought we should write about our Belle Isle experience.

The two poems about Belle Isle marked the beginning of our literary experience, and when Margaret further suggested we publish a co-authored book, I suggested why not do like we did in "Belle Isle" and either write poems on similar subjects or go through our work and find poems on similar subjects and put them together. In the body of the book you'll find two love poems or two poems about old age or two poems about workers juxtaposed. It's a very unique book, and we got the title from that arrangement. At the end of the book are the two poems, "Belle Isle." The poems, "Belle Isle," were really the beginning of our relationship, and those poems were placed at the end of our book. We'd meet at her house before the Boone House meetings to work on the manuscript. I thought very highly of her because she had been the assistant editor of Poetry Magazine *in Chicago with Karl Shapiro, the editor. It was very unusual for a black person to be in such a position during that time.*

Danner's "Belle Isle" celebrates the coming together of the two poets and affirms the inspirational power of the muse. Likewise, the epigraph to Randall's "Belle Isle" poem is "Joy and delight, joy and delight, like bells / Or bell-like flowers pealing in memory." His poem recounts that day the two poets spent together discussing and reading their poetry. It appraises Danner's romantic response to the scenic view of boats passing down the Detroit River and the beautiful blossoms flourishing in the conservatory:

> When leaves were the color of sun,
> And the island floated toward winter,
> You exclaimed at the freighters surging past,
> And reached for words to express their masterful glide.
> You laughed at the insolent motorboats
> Hurling their foaming wake upon the shore,
> Delighted in a blue-sailed vessel, and in the flower house
> You reveled in the bright-leaved plants,
> Grew ecstatic at a firmament of bell-like flowers,
> Reached on tiptoe to steal a blossom
> And pinched a stem to grow "by love" you said.
>
> (In *Poem Counterpoem*, 23)

Danner's poem conveys the sensuality of nature and moment, while Randall's poem responds to this creative spirit. Danner's first stanza asks:

> Are these millions of white velvety petalled bells
> even now crushing and tanning to brown?
> Or will they like the Belgium bells
> or bells of Benin
> continue to ring eternally,
> continue to resound?
>
> (In *Poem Counterpoem*, 22)

In sharp contrast to the more stringent aesthetic attitude that would dominate the upcoming Black Arts Movement, the creative belief expressed by Randall in "Belle Isle" is that "joy and delight" are the true nature of poets and "the inner principle of their art." He later said that "this delight is one of the most important, though often unconscious, aims of poetry. We live on earth not knowing why we are here, where we came from or where we are going. In our brief stay we feel joy, sorrow, pain, hope and fear. The poet takes this mystery, these varied emotions and puts them into a form which gives us

> joy and delight, joy and delight, poems
> conceived in joy, endowing the world and time
> with joy and delight, joy and delight, for ever."
>
> (Randall et al., *A Capsule Course in Black Poetry Writing*, 38–39)

Randall's writing flourished during the Boone House period, but his personal relationship with Margaret Danner became complicated as he observed difficulties in her personality.

> *Margaret was rather secretive, almost paranoid, because she said people were always jealous when they realized something good was happening for her. For example, Arna Bontemp was organizing The American Negro Anthology [1962], and Margaret said she would recommend that Bontemp publish some of my poems. She quickly added, "Don't tell anybody that I told you because they'll get angry."*

Despite her strange behavior, Randall admired her skills: "One virtue of poetry is that it makes us more alive, more perceptive, wakes up our sleeping senses. Reading Margaret Danner's poetry, for instance, with its discrimination of different textures, awakes us to keener sensitivity to the world around us. She wrote a poem comparing carnations to gardenias, calling one masculine and the other feminine because of their texture. We had formerly confused, confounded the two flowers as just white and round, but her subtle discrimination makes us look more closely at these flowers and see their differences. She makes us more alive to the world around us."[23]

The two met frequently and revised their poems and the contents of the book. Sometimes they agreed and sometimes not: "In 'The Southern Road' I began a line with 'Love you I must.' Margaret Danner objected to the inversion. I explained that I wanted to emphasize the love, but she insisted that I keep the natural word order. So I changed it to 'I have to love you.' I don't know whether I gained or lost by the change. One must weigh surprise, expressiveness, and force against being natural" (*A Capsule Course*, 43) Randall conceded to Danner's opinion, and "The Southern Road" was published with this change in their book and in the anthology, *Dark Symphony: Negro Literature in America* (1968). But Randall remained ambivalent and returned to his original phrasing in his 1981 publication, *A Litany of Friends: New and Selected Poems*.

The title of their co-authored book, *Poem Counterpoem*, became prophetic and assumed ironic proportions as the project endured unanticipated encounters and counters. When Robert Hayden presented Danner with the opportunity to publish *To Flower*, a solo collection of poetry, in his Counterpoise Series, she became disenchanted with the joint venture with Randall. Danner and Hayden were both Baha'i, and Danner reiterated this spiritual affinity in her letters to him as a distinction she maintained between them and Randall. But despite her change of heart about *Poem Counterpoem*, Danner explained to Hayden how helpful Randall was to her with promotional plans for *To Flower*. In a letter, she refers to a group of photographs apparently taken while they were working on the book project during what appears to have been pleasant associations: "Bob, I took your pictures out to send to you but I cannot part with them. They are delightful. Dudley was here all morning trying to help me and I showed them to him and he used the same word I had used in the letter to you. He said these pictures are of a pixie nature."[24] However, this amiable triangle between Danner, Randall, and Hayden became strained. In a letter to Hayden, Danner relates: "Dear Dudley was just here. He tries so hard to be a true friend but his own ambitions are so prevalent & his work is not ready. I think he is beginning to worry about the plans we made for *To Flower*."[25] The drama became even more pronounced when Hayden visited Detroit and did not contact Randall while he was in town. When Randall finally saw Danner's new book, he wrote Hayden and relayed his dismay at Hayden's secrecy and hurt feelings about the inclusion of poems initially intended for *Poem Counterpoem*:

> So the cat is out of the bag for me too. I did think it was curious that when you were in Detroit you could neither call me nor come to see me (knowing I work but was home in the evening), and I could not see you until after

you had agreed to publish Margaret's poems. But don't say anything about it. After all, a volume of good poetry was published, & that's all that matters. I was a bit put out temporarily, as the book used some of her poems planned for my book, but she had enough good poems to replace some of those you used, & others I just kept in our book regardless. The book is still in existence, resting on my desk temporarily, while I revise some poems afflicted, according to Robert Bly, with "nineteenth century literary language," Rosey Pool has a copy of the book, which she is trying to peddle in England. I think it's a wonderful idea, and I haven't given up on it.

Saw and liked your poem in the Sept. [Negro] Digest, although it doesn't have the traditional earmarks of a ballad, as taught to me in my course in the ballad. But I like it anyway, never mind its genre.

Why don't you send another poem to the Digest? Hoyt would like some good poems, in his absence.

Have been looking for reviews of your book in Kirkus' Booksellers & Library Service, but haven't seen one yet. Anyway, I have it on order through my library, & am looking forward to reading it.

Thanks for your offer to mention me to your publisher. Just might take you up on that. Love to Erma.[26]

After an argument with Randall about their project, Danner wrote a letter to Hayden that disclosed her aggravation and anger with Randall and her refusal to grant permission for him to seek a publisher for *Poem Counterpoem*. In contrasting emotions and type, she exclaimed her love for her new book and her resentment of Randall:

People love the books they only needed to see them. At least people other than Dudley Randall love the books. He immediately began to publish the book he and I have been working on to be announced on December 7th. I had a big fight with him and refused to release my poems to him for his book UNTIL MY BOOK GOT OFF THE GROUND.

He finally agreed to wait a month before publishing his own book, which he is using my reputation and poems to gain notice by in the first place. The book called his book which is made up of our poems together is NOT READY, BUT HE GOT EXCITED AND DECIDED TO CASH IN ON THE PUBLICITY THAT MY BOOK IS GETTING TO PUBLISH THIS AWFUL CLICHE THING HE AND I WERE DOING JUST FOR FUN AS FAR AS I WAS CONCERNED TO PASS THE TIME WHILE I WAS SO MISERABLE.

PEOPLE CAN BE SO DOG EAT DOG. BUT I FOUGHT FOR TO FLOWER LIKE A MOTHER FIGHTING FOR HER [I]MBICILE CHILD. AND TO ME TO FLOWER IS A BEAUTIFUL BOOK.

Dudley says he would have lots in his book that *To Flower* does not have but if he had gold print on platinum paper the book would still be a turkey and if *To Flower* was printed in mud on wrapping paper it would still have more style and form and tone. It is stark and uncluttered and stands on the poems only. It is beautiful, Bob, and I love it very, very much and will fight for it till death.[27]

Initially, Randall was quite angry about the whole affair, but shortly thereafter, he sent two query letters to Hayden about *Poem Counterpoem*. The first one, dated 16 March 1964, explains the concept of the book's format and posits that Hayden might consider publishing *Poem Counterpoem* in the Counterpoise Series as well:

I haven't written you about Margaret Danner's and my book before because Margaret wanted to make the inquiries as she knows the poetry world better than I. She was also afraid that our idea might be used before our book could be published, as there's no copyright on ideas. However, she has said that now I may make inquiries and I know we can trust our idea with you, and inasmuch as you have expressed interest in the book, I am asking you first whether you would be interested in publishing it.

As far as I know, the format has never been used before, except in isolated instances by Keats, Hunt, Shelley and their group in poems about the cricket and the grasshopper and the Nile. There would be poems by Margaret and by me on alternate pages (facing each other) on the same subject or in related moods or tones, or even contrasting moods or tones. This arrangement would give resonance and reverberation to each poem much more so than if our poems were printed in a separate group. The book could be called POEM COUNTERPOEM. Even by its novel arrangement the book would be unique and an attraction for the COUNTERPOISE series, to say nothing of the quality of the poetry.

I know that you are primarily interested in the quality of the poetry, so I'll leave that up to your own judgment. If you think that our poetry is good enough to be published together in this manner, we can send you a copy of the manuscript.

Although I know that you are not so much interested in the commercial aspects, I think that we could sell an edition or 500 or 1,000 hard-bound copies. I could push it with all my energy in the library and college field and locally. Margaret has sold 200 of TO FLOWER chiefly through readings here.

But I know that you are chiefly interested in good poetry. If you think it's worth looking at, we can send you the book.

Regards to Erma. Showed TO FLOWER to our order librarian. When I looked at the order slip, I saw that Reference (my dept.), Eloise (where I used to work), Inkster and Dearborn Heights had ordered the book.[28]

Randall reiterated his book proposal in another letter the following month, and in a letter dated 22 March 1964, Danner made an about face:

Sometimes, I wonder why people are born. Me, especially. I have made another mistake. Dear Dudley, who has been so loyal and so helpful and is trying to so hard with my books and is so ambitious for a book we are doing together; told me that he wrote to you asking you to publish our book. HE THINKS MY BOOK IS A SUCCESS. I DO NOT HAVE THE HEART TO TELL HIM THAT IT IS NOT. I CANNOT FACE SUCH A FACT MYSELF. I STILL BELIEVE THAT IN TIME IT WILL BE O.K. I told him the book was selling. He spends all of his little money trying to help me and is so loyal and so good. But I could not tell him the book is so slow. I do not want you to take any more chances on any books that might be bad, or might not sell or something.[29]

In the absence of Hayden's responses to these letters (because Randall destroyed most of his correspondence) one can only speculate that Hayden was conflicted about the matter. However, Danner's refusal to allow Randall to pursue the publication of *Poem Counterpoem* had more to do with her guilt and her own insecurities than her opinion about the quality of Randall's writing. Indeed, neither Randall nor Hayden, nor Danner for that matter, was ever fully cognizant of her motivations or her conflicted ambivalence. However, *Poem Counterpoem* was not published until 1966, as a Broadside Press book.

THE TRANSITION

In Detroit and elsewhere, the Second Renaissance was an outgrowth of the Civil Rights Movement. It was the beginning of social and cultural change, and the dynamics of this shift affected opportunity and interest in African American poetry. Randall's Detroit-based affiliations placed his writings in strategic publications, especially through Hoyt Fuller's *Negro Digest*. The prominence of *Negro Digest* can be measured by the fact that by 1971 the circulation of the magazine (which became *Black World* in 1970) had reached 54,174; this was an unprecedented accomplishment for a black literary magazine.[30] Between 1960 and 1970, twenty-one poems, four short stories, three essays, and twelve book reviews by Dudley Randall, as well as cultural and political commentaries by and interviews of Randall, appeared in the magazine. On an editorial level, Randall's influence grew as Fuller consulted him to recommend and review poetry submissions for the *Negro Digest*. In a letter to poet Etheridge Knight, Randall revealed that:

> In part, your "Apology for Apostasy?" was selected by me. Fuller asked me to help Mr. Darius select poetry for the magazine while he was on leave of absence, & of course I chose your poem. No credit for that, as Dave would probably have picked it anyway. All the poetry in the June issue was chosen by me, except the Julia Field poem, which I never saw.[31]

In the essay "Melvin B. Tolson: Portrait of a Poet Raconteur" (*Negro Digest* 15, no. 3 [January 1966]: 54–57), Randall describes his first meeting with Tolson in Detroit:

> One night poet sculptor Oliver LaGrone telephoned me that Tolson was in town and invited me to come and meet him. I found him to be, as Langston Hughes has described him, a man who can talk to students, cotton-pickers and cowpunchers, a great talker—a very warm and human person.
>
> With his bald head fringed by gray tufts over his ears and his seamed, smiling face, he looked like an old-fashioned preacher. When he settled back in his chair, took a cigar in right hand and a glass in his left and remarked that tonight he would forget about Jim Crow and concentrate on Old Crow, we knew that we were in for a good night of talk. (54)

Randall's essay continues by retelling a delightful story by Tolson. In this piece, Randall not only elaborates on the poet's wit and expansive intellect, but also records the interaction of black writers and cultural history as it unfolds.

Although Randall's writing appeared on the national scene during the 1960s, most of this poetry was written during previous decades. Hence, the historical and political circumstances that influenced him during the 1930s, 1940s, and 1950s conversely and invariably had their impact upon the aesthetic values and cultural directions of the 1960s and 1970s. Moreover, the time and the attention his writing received invigorated his work and confirmed his confidence, but Randall did not limit his writing to racial themes and issues. The publication of "Hymn"(1962) demonstrated his concern with the threat of a nuclear holocaust and his translation of K M. Simonov's "Rodina" as "My Native Land" (1962) illustrated his internationalist appreciation of world literature.

These and other more obscure poems reveal interesting currents in Randall's oeuvre.

"Early in 1964, the group [Boone House] began to disperse. Margaret Danner suddenly dropped out of sight, James Thompson moved to New York, and Harold Lawrence changed his name to Kofi Wangara and moved to Africa."[32] As the black cultural movement gained momentum, perspectives and identities were dramatically reassessed. In Detroit, as in other big cities, African American artists began to coalesce in theaters and to participate in political conferences, developing and promoting their cultural interests and expressions. It was a time of transitions, and Dudley Randll's mother, Ada Randall, passed away.

Despite Dudley Randall's difficult relationship with Margaret Danner, the Boone House experience was productive and inspiring. However, in 1966, the generation of poets that Danner, Randall, and Hayden represented collided with a poetry revolution that was less interested in endowing the world with "joy and delight" than in destroying the stranglehold of political oppression and cultural imperialism. Hence, it was not the "bell-like flowers of Belle Isle" that attracted the next generation to Randall's muse, but rather the political courage and prophetic vision expressed in "Roses and Revolutions" and his ability to produce books. The difficulties that beset the book project with Danner prepared him for the politics of personalities and the editorial challenges awaiting him with Broadside Press, which in a very short time would become "the hub of black poetry production."[33]

After Rosey Pool left Detroit to become a guest professor at Alabama A and M, she organized two writers conferences at this small, black college. At the 1966 conference, the "writers on hand this time around were mostly poets—Samuel Allen (Paul Vesey), Margaret Burroughs, Dudley Randall and Mari Evans (who was a repeater). Poet Margaret Danner also appeared as a special guest of the three-day sessions."[34] It was Randall's first national reading. Interest in black poetry and in Randall continued to grow with the historical momentum. Unbeknownst to him, the poem "Ballad of Birmingham" would change his life and have profound impact on the poetry revolution that was about to explode as the Black Arts Movement. As Ed Simpkins explained: "It was Rosey Pool's *Beyond the Blues* that first brought us together, but it was Dudley Randall's Broadside Press that took that energy to another generation."[35]

8

"BALLAD OF BIRMINGHAM":
THE FOUNDING OF BROADSIDE PRESS
AND THE BLACK ARTS MOVEMENT

I N 1965, TWO YEARS AFTER "Ballad of Birmingham" was first published, folk singer Jerry Moore asked Dudley Randall for permission to set the poem to music. To preserve his rights as the author, Randall printed the poem as a broadside and copyrighted it as a Broadside Press publication. This marked the beginning of Randall's publishing career.

Although initially printed to protect his creative interests, the poem became famous in this format. Public demand inspired Randall to print more copies and to publish broadsides by other poets. However, Randall's interest in publishing expanded as a response to the developing Black Arts Movement, a period that cannot be defined by any singular occasion, though the founding of Broadside Press is a major indicator.

Simplifications of the 1960s often dislocate the movement, assigning it exclusively to that decade. Blurred by the broader dynamics of the Civil Rights Movement, this era cannot be separated from the influences of the early 1960s. The Second Renaissance was a response to the Civil Rights Movement and was the primary historical force that instigated the Black Arts Movement, but the latter is a more diffuse period that overlaps both the 1960s and 1970s, approximately 1965–1977. The most significant historical event that influenced the formation of the Black Arts Movement was the assassination of Malcolm X, who spoke in Detroit at King Solomon's Baptist Church one week before his death on 21 February 1965. His life and his death infused the political attitude of black nationalism and inspired a deluge of poetry that was collected in the first book planned by Broadside Press. The assassination of Malcolm X also inspired LeRoi Jones's final decision to move from Greenwich Village to Harlem. Jones was at the Eighth Street Bookstore when he got the news of the assassination:

> Suddenly, Leroy McLucas came in. He was weeping. "Malcolm is dead! Malcolm is dead! Malcolm's been killed!" He wept, repeating it over and over. I was stunned. I felt stupid, ugly, useless. Downtown in my mismatched family and my maximum leader/teacher shot dead while we bullshitted and pretended. . . . In a few days I had gotten my stuff out and gone uptown. We had seen a brownstone on West 130th Street and this was to be the home of the Black Arts Repertory Theatre School. . . . I was gone. A bunch of us, really, had gone, up to Harlem. Seeking revolution![1]

Jones's relocation was a demarcation in his personal, political, and literary identity and a signifier for an upcoming generation of writers across the country to ground aesthetic values in neighborhoods and institutions housed in black communities. LeRoi Jones originated the term "Black Arts," relative to the formation of the Black Arts Repertory Theatre School. But by the end of the year, he had moved from Harlem to his hometown, Newark. This move was more in tandem with the kind of grassroots activity that preceded Jones.

In Detroit, Woody King, Ron Milner, David Rambeau, Clifford Fraquois, "and a white guy, Dick Smith, had already founded The Concept East Theatre in 1962," Milner said. "Smith was a product of the labor movement, and he had the hands-on technology that we needed for running the theater. He and Woody knew how to do the stage production and the lighting." Milner elaborated further on the coincidental and yet collective consciousness that emerged in Detroit and elsewhere:

> What we didn't know at the time was that this was happening all across the country. All we knew was we wanted to write our own stories. We saw the power of theater and what it could do. Norman Jordan was doing it in Cleveland. Ted Ward was doing it in Chicago. We didn't know each other at this point. New York playwrights were still focused on Broadway. They were still interested in those critics. We didn't care about that. But Baraka's impact was felt at the Concept East Theatre in Detroit when we did his play *The Toilet*. It put us on the map because the police closed us down. They came up with every violation, real and imaginary, to shut down the theater, but the real reason was because there is a scene in the play where the black charac-

ters put the white character's head in the toilet. The shock, the violence, and the hostile dialogue in the beginning of the play offended many whites in the audience. The closing of the theatre attracted attention and people crowded into the tiny theatre that could only seat about forty=five people. People wanted to buy tickets in advance, but we didn't even have tickets![2]

In 1965, Ron Milner received a Rockefeller Foundation Grant, and through Langston Hughes's connections, Milner became writer-in-residence at Lincoln University in Pennsylvania for two years. Milner returned to Detroit and the Concept East Theatre, but Woody King had left for New York in 1964 and established residency there. On the West Coast, the Watts Poetry Workshop (formed after the 1965 Race Rebellion in Watts) was in full swing in Los Angeles. Within a few years, poetry activity popularized by the Black Arts Movement characterized cultural and political scenes in most major urban centers, and writers moved back and forth across the country. This development was enhanced by Stokely Carmichael's outcry for "Black Power" in 1966. The Black Arts Movement intersected with rhetorical fervor, and literary responses became the cultural manifestation of the concept. Detroit writer and journalist Betty De Ramus encapsulated the moment for *Negro Digest*:

> Malcolm X had whipped some into a frenzy of bitterness but spurred no action. And then came Stokely Carmichael with his black power in a year when Congress reversed itself; the dream of integration died during Martin Luther King's march in Chicago; Africa, its customs and hair styles became palatable, and the momentum of the civil rights movement screeched to a halt.[3]

As the Black Arts Movement gained momentum, Dudley Randall's presence and prominence in national journals placed him near the center of cultural expression and debate. Specifically, "Black Power" was the subject of discussion by a select group of writers in the November 1966 issue of *Negro Digest*. In his statement, Randall considered Black Power in relation to the diverging political strategies that indicated a critical juncture in the Civil Rights Movement. He did not necessarily view this division as a digression, but he did voice disapproval of the bitter arguments and dispersions between political camps. His response, which inadvertently reflected the characteristic maleness of the movement's language, defends the idea of Black Power:

> In my opinion, Black Power means organizing black people so that they can have power commensurate with their numbers in their communities, states

and in the nation. This will mean that they may dominate some communities politically, will be a strong force in some states, and will wield power in the national government. This is similar to what other groups have done.

So far, there is no prominent black leader advocating such violence, although some have advocated protecting one's self when attacked, as is every man's legal and God-given *right*. All men are not saints (incidentally, the only way you can become a saint is through martyrdom), and they do not have Martin Luther King, Jr.'s saintly qualities and find it hard to look with compassion upon some policeman who is beating their women, or shooting a child, or calling them black sons-of-bitches.

Black Power does not mean violence, but it will give black men a sense of pride and of solidarity and will make them unwilling to continue to bear exploitation.

The direction which Black Power will take depends upon White Power. If White Power acts wisely and with all speedy urgency in making this a livable country for every man, then there will be no reason to fear Black Power.[4]

Most certainly, the Black Power Movement had direct bearing on the Black Arts Movement, and, by the very consequence of the times, it was this convergence of politics and arts that generated this synergy. Subsumed by the heightened political climate, poetry assumed the symbolic character of the radicalized period in all its variegated utterances. As Ron Milner explained, "the Black Power conferences brought people together from across the country. The first really big conference was in Chicago, and Hoyt Fuller illuminated this in *The Negro Digest*. The networking that occurred at these conferences brought writers to different campuses and events. The poet would sell poetry on mimeographed paper and circulate them." By 1966, cultural conferences became as commonplace as political rallies, as institutions were founded and alternative theaters were organized to garner political and artistic energy. At the Black Arts Convention held in Detroit on 24–26 June 1966, at the Central United Church of Christ of Rev. Albert Cleage, Randall directly addressed the need to organize writers by developing literature and publishing institutions free of the corruptive influences of mainstream culture:

The seeming disadvantages of Black writers were in reality opportunities. Because they had less chance of being corrupted or distracted by "success" they could devote themselves to the solitary labor of writing. They should develop their own media publishing houses.[5]

He viewed institution building as a pragmatic and productive response to political rhetoric. A few months earlier, Randall had presented this same message at the 1966 Writers Conference at Fisk University. This was also the site where he decided to take on the challenge of his own words and publish a book:

> As I was walking to one of the sessions, I saw Margaret Walker, the poet, and Margaret Burroughs, the painter, sitting in front of their dormitory. Mrs. Burroughs was sketching, and Miss Walker was rehearsing her reading, for she was to read her poems that afternoon. I sat down to watch and to listen, and when Miss Walker read a poem on Malcolm X, I said, "Everybody's writing about Malcolm X. I know several people who've written poems about him."
>
> "That's right," Margaret Burroughs said, "why don't you collect the poems and put out a book on Malcolm?" I thought it over for a few seconds, snapped my fingers, and said, "I'll do it. And you can be my coeditor." The writers had complained about not having any outlets for their work, so this publication provided one."[6]

The 1966 Writers Conference at Fisk University set the stage for intense ideological debate within the black writing community, as a focus on race identified "Black" as the watchword for the hour. Novelist John Oliver Killens, the conference organizer, and poet Melvin B. Tolson were the primary advocates for this "race-first" argument, and the question was posed publicly to the conference presenters. "Are you Black first, or a writer first?" was the litmus test, and when Robert Hayden rebuked the imposition and insisted on using the word "Negro," he became the "sacrificial lamb" at the nationalist altar. Their personal history and philosophical similarities complicated Randall's reaction to Hayden's predicament at the conference:

> *I'd never been to a writer's conference, so it was a bold move on my part to go. While I was there, I stayed at Robert Hayden's home. He was teaching at Fisk University as a professor of English. For a while, Bob and I had lost touch with each other.*
>
> *Bob was on a writer's panel, and he made his usual statement that he believed poetry should be judged by its merits as poetry, and not for its political utterances. He was strongly attacked from the floor by many of the students at Fisk. They gave him a hard time. The gist of what they said was that he was not black enough, not militant enough. They asked the question which everybody was asking at that time: What are you? Are you black first, or are you a*

poet first? Robert said he was a poet first. There was a very heated debate. I don't remember all the exact words, but it was clear they were against him. But he stood up for what he believed.

That night, he read his poems of the black experience. He read "Runagate" and "Middle Passage" and other powerful pieces. Everybody was moved, even those who had attacked him. The whole audience spontaneously gave him a standing ovation. Offstage, he leaned against the wall exhausted. There were tears in his eyes. I said, "They like your poetry." He said, "It was wonderful." I told him it was a good reading and he replied, "Yes, it was very moving." It was a moving experience for him too.

But the audience was not moved enough to expand their definition of the "Black aesthetic" or their racial essentialism. Biographer John Hatcher explained that "Hayden's fate was sealed by the clear dominance of the angry and defiant mood, and his fine sentiments were rebuked by [modernist poet Melvin] Tolson, who denounced capitalism, by another speaker, who denounced Hayden as having a bad influence on his students at Fisk by not stressing their particular role as 'black poets, black teachers.'"[7] In a similar, but less traumatic experience, Gwendolyn Brooks encountered what she called the "New Black" at that conference: "Here, I was coldly Respected." In her autobiography, she related the discomfort felt at this event, feelings she said were shared by Danner: "All that day and night, Margaret Danner Cunningham—another Old Girl, another coldly Respected old Has-been—and an almost hysterical Gwendolyn B. walked about in amazement, listening, looking, learning. *What was going on!*"[8]

Dudley Randall, on the other hand, accepted identification as "race first." At the same time, he expressed a more complex view of his aesthetic identity in a subsequent interview with Hoyt Fuller that appeared in *Negro Digest* in 1968:

How else can a black writer write than out of his black experience? Yet, what we tend to overlook is that our common humanity makes it possible to write a love poem, for instance, without a word of race, or to write a nationalistic poem that will be valid for all humanity, such as "By the Waters of Babylon, there we sat down, yea, we wept, when we remembered Zion."[9]

But in the heat of the moment, elaboration was neither solicited nor interesting to a volatile and didactic debate. In the same way that neither Randall nor Hayden accepted the racist definitions imposed on them or their historical circumstances, they did not restrict their poetry to the aesthetic tyranny of white cultural imperialism. They wrote freely on a range of subjects, including racial struggle. In his essay about writers of their generation, Randall praises Hayden's poetics and observes cultural density in his imagery:

> The surrealistic "A Ballad of Remembrance" is chilling with its whirling, glittering images and rhythms and its feeling of nightmare and irrationality. It captures the Black experience, but filtered through the poet's sensitive subjectivity, and in "Middle Passage" and "Runagate Runagate," Hayden incorporates all the innovations of the experimental poets of the 1920's: varied and expressive rhythms; anti-poetic materials such as quotations from handbills, legal documents, ship's logs; scraps of poetry, hymns, spirituals; fusing all these together to make two exciting narratives of the beginning and of the escape from slavery.[10]

Even a scant comparison of their poetry reveals some interesting patterns and intersections between these Detroit poets. While Hayden commemorates valor with "The Ballad of Nat Turner," Randall eulogizes tragedy in "Ballad of Birmingham." Whereas Randall's "Roses and Revolution" captures the agonizing depths of racial oppression and resurrection, Hayden's "Middle Passage" portrays the epic terror from the slave trade to the slave rebellions. Randall retraces the bloodstained soil of lynchings in "The Southern Road," while Hayden's "Runagate Runagate" evokes images of heroic escapes via the Underground Railroad.

Randall, who was energized by the political climate, still maintained his friendship with Hayden, who channeled his previous political energy into his belief in the Baha'i faith and a spiritual path for universal brotherhood. In a short thank-you note to Erma and Bob Hayden for housing and hosting him during the Fisk Writers' Conference, Randall wrote, "I'll never forget those crisp shrimps or that breakfast formidable, or our talks in the evening over coffee."[11] In a second, more elaborate letter to Hayden about the conference on 29 April 1966, in which Randall enclosed two of his poems, "Winter Campus" and "Laughter in the Slums," Randall implores Hayden to assist him in the search for submissions to the *For Malcolm* anthology, and he reflects on his personal reaction to the intensity of the writers conference:

> I'm enclosing the poem you asked for the *Fisk Herald*, and I'm including another in case you don't like the first one, so that you can have a choice. Let me remind you to send me your new poem for the Broadside Series, so that I can choose between it and "Gabriel." Perhaps you've heard on the campus that Broadside Press is publishing a volume of poems in memory

of Malcolm X. If you have written one or if you write one in the near future, why not send it to Broadside Press, 12651 Old Mill Place, Detroit,
Michigan 48238. And will you tell other poets on campus and the students
in your Writers' Workshop about it? I'll send a printed notice to the English department about it later, but in the meantime you can pass the word
along, and if you have the names and addresses of any other poets that
would be interested in contributing to the anthology, would you send them
to me, please.

I got some work done at the Writers' Conference. I got promises of
poems for the Broadside Series from [Melvin] Tolson, [Robert] Hayden
and [Margaret] Walker. I got the idea for the Malcolm X anthology, and
Tolson consented to write an introduction for *Ten: An Anthology of Poetry
from Detroit*, a book which some Detroit poets are putting together. The
conference was very interesting, but a little too strenuous for me. I think I'll
sit the next one out, and, as Ossie Davis suggested in his speech, stay at
home like a writer and write.

Thanks again for your and Erma's hospitality. Best regards to Erma and
Maia, and don't forget to send me your poem soon, as I'd like to send in my
list soon for Books in Print, which Bowker is putting together about now.[12]

In retrospect, Randall's reflections on the conference provided additional
insight into the historical confusion and aesthetic naiveté of the students at
the conference:

*Maybe the students didn't know what good poetry was. Maybe they just want-
ed the feelings of anger, but not the art. Many of the poems I wrote were not
published until the 1960s or 70s. For instance, the first poem in one of my books,
"Roses and Revolutions" was written about 1948 and people used to think it
was written in the 1960s. There was an interesting incident Gwendolyn Brooks
tells in her autobiography, about going to Fisk University [Writers Conference]
and the polite but cold way in which the students received the poets. The students thought of her and Margaret Danner as old and conservative poets. The
students said, "Why don't you write like Dudley Randall," and Margaret Danner said, "Dudley Randall. He's older than I am!" Many of the poems that
were published in the sixties had been written in the forties.*

But at the time, Randall stated an opinion that coincided with the popular position of the nationalist agenda, and in his usual noncombative manner avoided the debate, networked with as many writers as possible, and
channeled his passion into poetry production. Ron Milner, who attended the

1967 Writers Conference at Fisk University, felt that the conferences brought writers together on a national level and enabled them to make connections for future readings and lectures. However, he identified Hoyt Fuller, John Oliver Killens, and Dudley Randall as "the ones who held the movement together." He said that "Hoyt Fuller and Dudley Randall could do the detail work, they could also deal with all the weird personalities."[13]

Randall published two stories, "Victoria" and "Shoe Shine Boy," in *Negro Digest* in 1966, and both these stories contain vestiges of the social and cultural values of a previous era.[14] The stories' publication at this moment illustrates how Randall felt caught between the past and the future. In a letter dated 29 August 1966, Randall wrote to Robert Hayden, "Did you read my story in the May Digest? Will take you back to Black Bottom, in spite of the false illustration."[15]

"Vitoria" is a coming-of-age story about David, the young man who was first introduced in the short story "A Cup for the Loser." This charactter, like Randall, studied Italian in order to read Dante in the original. He is a bookworm who loses the girl he desires to a boxer:

> The book of poetry which he had been clutching slipped from his hand. He picked up the book. Through the window came a peal of laughter from Victoria. He flung the book down on the blanket with a sob. It was black dark now, too dark to read. (72)

"Shoe Shine Boy" seems to be a response to the disdain that defiant youths of the movement felt for the acquiescence of the older generation. Its appearance in the September 1966 issue of *Negro Digest* reflects a more tolerant view than those expressed at the writers conference at Fisk. In the story, the shoe-shine boy "toms" and performs for a white, racist soldier in order to get a good tip. A young civil-rights activist observes this but learns that the man is undeucated and has struggled to provide for his family. However, the shoe-shine "boy" refuses to take money from the younger black man and says, "No. No charge. It's for the movement" (55).

The leftist influence of the 1930s and 1940s oriented the older generation of writers into leadership roles in a cultural revolution that primarily benefited the upcoming generation. Specifically, Randall recruited Margaret Burroughs, who was affiliated with leftist politics in Chicago since the 1940s, to be the co-editor of the *For Malcolm* anthology, and he contacted other established writers to publish their more famous poems in *The Broadside Series*. Hence, the earliest broadsides brought prominence to the press and standards grounded in years of creative credibility.

Randall placed an announcement in *Negro Digest* and sent solicitation letters to poets, politics notwithstanding. A letter to Hayden reveals Randall's strategies and some of the responses:

Perhaps you've read about my *Broadside Series* (March *Digest*). Would you be willing to let me re-print one of your poems for $10.00 in the series (one poem re-printed as a broad sheet)? I'd like to use either Gabriel or Obituary or Frederick Douglass. Melvin Tolson is letting me use one of his, and Gwen Brooks may let me re-print one of her poems.[16]

The series for 1966 will include Hayden, Walker, Tolson, and Brooks. I asked LeRoi Jones for a poem for the series but he didn't reply, but forwarded my request to his agent who asked me how much I'd pay for the poem for the Malcolm anthology & who was publishing the anthology. I answered her, but haven't received her answer, and don't know whether I can include Jones or not.[17]

Outside the confines of nationalism, Randall collaborated with nonblack poet-publishers. Dan Georgakas, co-author of *Detroit: I Do Mind Dying*, explains in "Young Detroit Radicals, 1955–1965," how the cross-fertilization of radical politics and culture in Detroit resulted in collaborative publishing projects during the 1960s:

There was a strong self-publishing movement among Black writers in the city, as Black writers were then virtually excluded from literary anthologies of major publishing houses. Dudley Randall began the influential Broadside Press in the 1960's. His press and mine had one joint venture, a wall poster by M. B. Tolson. This kind of interaction between the Black artistic community and radicals was considerable but totally unstructured.[18]

In 1964, an interracial group of poets and musicians founded the legendary Artists Workshop on Forest Avenue near Wayne State University. Poets Robin Eicheles, John Semark, John Sinclair, George Tysh, and Jerry Younkins and musicians John Dana, Charles Moore, Ron English, and Lyman Woodard created a vortex for a unique mix of avant-garde poetry and experimental music, which captured the progressive cultural scene. Like the names of their poetry publications, *Change* and *Work*, this new workshop believed that the consciousness of one's art was as provocative as jazz, poetry readings, and performances. The workshop recorded music, published city poets, and brought in national names for the billboard, such as Allen Ginsberg, Ed Sanders, and Robert Creeley.

The Artists Workshop was the stimulus for starting the Alternative Press in 1969. Editors Ken and Ann Mikolowski created a press that brought national recognition for Detroit-based poets Jim Gustafson, Mick Vranich, John Sinclair, Donna Brooks, Faye Kicknosway, and George and Chris Tysh. Like Broadside Press, Alternative Press extended its identity beyond city borders by publishing noted national poets Robert Creeley, Allen Ginsberg, Anne Waldman, Gary Snyder, and others. Their publishing format was as varied as Randall's press, which included broadsides, postcards, and bumper stickers. The goal of the Alternative Press was to create an eclectic, accessible, and inclusive mix of writing for audiences, and an alternative community of artists.[19]

In the 1960s, broadsides commanded attention for poetry and the political movement. By combining a literary format symbolic of American political poetry of the eighteenth and nineteenth centuries (including the Revolutionary War) with classic poems thematically representative of the black aesthetic, Randall further radicalized these publications by calling the first set (six broadsides) "Poetry of the Negro Revolt." Randall's "Ballad of Birmingham" and "Dressed All in Pink" initiated the series, which showcased a lineup of notable poets who had attended the Fisk Conferences: Broadside No. 3, "Gabriel" by Robert Hayden; Broadside No. 4, "Ballad of the Free" by Margaret Walker; Broadside No. 5, "The Sea Turtle and The Shark" by Melvin B. Tolson; Broadside No. 6, "We Real Cool" by Gwendolyn Brooks.

Randall explained to Xavier Nicholas, who was living and writing in Detroit at the time, that he knew many people kept favorite poems in their wallets and that at thirty-five cents people would purchase a poem for whatever reason. "I noticed how people would carry tattered clippings of their favorite poems in their billfolds, and I thought it would be a good idea to publish them in an attractive form as broadsides."[20]

The next set of poems extended the activist aesthetics of the series: Broadside No. 7, "A Poem For Black Hearts" by LeRoi Jones; Broadside No. 8, "Booker T. and W. E. B." by Dudley Randall; Broadside No. 9, "A Child's Nightmare" by Bobb Hamilton; Broadside No. 11, "Sunny" by Naomi Long Madgett; Broadside No. 12, "Letter from a Wife" by Carolyn Reese; Broadside No. 13, "Backlash Blues" by Langston Hughes; Broadside No. 14, "Race Results, U. S. A., 1966" by Sarah Webster Fabio; and Broadside No. 15, "Song of The Son" by Jean Toomer.

Culture and politics boldly and openly converged, and poetry became a public art to be heard and displayed. *Broadside Series* poetry hung next to the larger-than-life figure of Huey Newton posing in a high-back wicker chair like an African king with a spear in his hand. The poems were framed between posters of Che Guevera in military fatigues smoking a cigar and Malcolm X looking out

the window with a rifle at his side. They reiterated the raised fists of John Carlos and Tommy Smith at the 1968 Olympics. Broadside No. 25, "The Nigger
Cycle: for angela davis kidnapped by the f.b.i. on oct. 13, 1970," by Kuweka
Amiri Mwandishe, illustrated Angels Davis's tremendous Afro and raised contributions for the Angela Davis Defense Fund (all proceeds from the sale of the
broadside were donated to the fund). Broadside No. 69, "For Darnell and Johnny," by Melba Joyce Boyd, was printed during the court hearings for Hayward
Brown and sold out in a few weeks. Most of them were purchased at Vaughn's
Bookstore in Detroit. These words interacted with the imagery they referenced,
the emotions they evoked, and the historical space they shared. Poets attempted to divest language of all pretenses and to explore regions of legitimate anger
embedded in protestations for "Black Power" and to "Stop the War."

"Production for use instead of for profit" was what Randall called his approach to business, and via this creed he created a publishing house free of
aesthetic repression or profit constraints. This profoundly altered the perspective on and the motive for building an alternative to a capitalist model;
but the larger challenge loomed in the distance. Could such a noble philosophy of self-determination in the form of cultural activism survive the material realities that affected the moods of cultural interests and the external
economic forces that determined institutional longevity?

"My strongest motivations have been to get good black poets published, to
produce beautiful books, help create and define the soul of black folk, and to
know the joy of discovering new poets."[21] Inspired and impassioned by the
Black Arts Movement, publishing became Randall's mission. On 30 April 1965,
Dudley Randall included a handwritten copy of his poem "Black Poet, White
Critic" in a letter to poet Melvin Tolson. The last line in this draft of the poem,
later deleted from the published version, posed a query, a literary possibility.[22]

> A critic advises
> not to write on controversial
> subjects
> like freedom or murder
> but to treat universal themes
> and timeless symbols
> like the white unicorn.
>
> A *white* unicorn?
> And why not a *black* unicorn?

Over the next ten years, Broadside Press would answer that question
emphatically.

9

"YA VAS LYUBIL": ALEXANDER PUSHKIN, DUDLEY RANDALL, AND THE BLACK RUSSIAN CONNECTION

> When I think of Russia, she will be
> Not just two syllables to me,
> But Anna Maslova and Igor,
> Sonia, and Fikrat, and many more
> With whom I've laughed and sung and talked,
> Who gave to me their bread and salt,
> the soft-eyed girl who took my hand
> And led me through a red-scarfed band
> While every smiling Pioneer
> Cried, "Mir i druzhba, druzhba i mir"
> And I'll remember many another
> Who clasped my hand and called me, "Brother!"

Dudley Randall composed "When I Think of Russia" shortly after his visit to the Soviet Union in the summer of 1966, and Hoyt Fuller published it in *Negro Digest* (16, no. 8 [June 1967]: 74). In the midst of the Black Nationalist fervor, Margaret Burroughs invited Randall to join a delegation of "Negro American artists" on a tour sponsored by the Council for American-Soviet Friendship. This trip was Randall's first opportunity to see the native land of Russian poets Alexander Pushkin and K. M. Simonov and to experience the Russian language within its cultural context. The delegation toured Leningrad, Baku, and Alma Ata.

Unlike the United States, where business and wealth too often determined cultural values and outcomes, in the Soviet Union a political dictatorship influenced and controlled creative production. At the same time, Dudley Randall observed that the Russian literary tradition was more revered by Russians than American literature was by Americans. Although the political values of the country profoundly affected its writers, he heard that the publication of a book of poetry by a well-known poet could sell out in a matter of hours after it appeared in the bookstores. Randall was more interested in culture than in politics, and he was especially impressed by the popularity of literature in the Soviet Union.

It was luck that got me to the Soviet Union. After meeting Margaret Burroughs at Fisk University during the writers conference, we got to know each other better. She asked me to get in touch with Oliver LaGrone, a Boone House poet and a sculptor, and ask him if he wanted to go to the Soviet Union on a tour with other black artists. But when I spoke with him there was illness in his family, and he was not able to go. She then suggested that I go in his place. But I was afraid to fly, and told her so. She responded by asking me, "How old are you?" I told her I was fifty-two. She said, "You've done about everything you can, so it doesn't matter if the plane crashes." That wasn't very encouraging but the Detroit artist, Cleatie Taylor, said, "You shouldn't miss it."

Russian was very popular after World War II, because of the Cold War and anticommunist mood in the U.S. I became interested in the culture and wanted to learn about the people rather than the government. So, I studied the Russian language when I was a student at Wayne. Because I was especially impressed with Russian poetry, I translated a couple of poems by Simonov in my textbooks into English.

I think the main reason I became interested in Russian literature was Pushkin. Every Russian knows that Pushkin was part black, the descendant of a black slave of Peter the Great. I translated one of his poems when I worked at the Wayne County Library. One of the patrons who came to the library was Russian. He showed me a translation of a love poem of Pushkin, "Ya Vas Lyubil," and I didn't like the translation very much. I thought I could do better, so I translated that poem.

In August 1966, I flew with the artists delegation to Paris. We were late getting our visas, so we were delayed in Paris for two weeks before we were permitted to continue on to Russia. The delay was not good, because we had not anticipated the added expense of a stay in Paris. I had to move out of a good hotel and into an old fleabag with a shared toilet down the hall. Prostitutes living there were recruiting customers right outside the entrance. I restricted my-

self to one meal of a bottle of beer and a ham sandwich until we left for Russia. But when we arrived in Russia, we had caviar.

I conceived "The Old Women of Paris" and composed one line—"their backs curved like bridges across the Seine"—in 1966, when I was down and out in Paris and walked down the Boulevard Raspail morning and evening because I couldn't afford a bus or taxi fare. But I didn't write the poem until 1974, one night when I couldn't sleep. I have my own method of composition, and every writer has to find the method which best suits him.[1]

While waiting to depart, Randall also wrote Robert Hayden. In a postcard, he shared his excitement in anticipation of the literary culture in the Soviet Union: "Hope to meet some poets & writers while I am here, & to hear some poetry readings. They say the readings fill stadiums of 16,000."[2]

We arrived in Moscow and traveled north to Leningrad. Then we went to another country in the Soviet Union, Azerbaijan, and visited the city of Baku. We saw the Black Sea and then we continued on to a country located near China. The people there were Mongolian and were yellow in complexion. On our return to Paris, we visited Czechoslovakia and toured the city of Prague and saw the palaces there. In Paris, we separated. Margaret Burroughs and her husband went to Holland. Others went to England. I had to go back to the United States and back to work in Detroit.

Charlie Burroughs [Margaret Burroughs's husband] had lived in Russia when he was a child, from the age of nine. His mother had been a communist in the 1930s, when it wasn't comfortable for communists living in New York. She left the U.S. and took him with her to Russia where he went to school and grew up living near the Black Sea. He learned to speak Russian like a native and could swear in Russian and talk in the local slang. So, when we were in Russia, we were not like ordinary tourists. We visited the homes of his childhood friends and were able to interact with the people without the interference of a translator or a guide.

One day, he took a few of us to an apartment in Moscow, where we met a couple; both the husband and wife were Ph.Ds. The man had been a major in the Soviet army, and had spent twelve years in a concentration camp because he had surrendered his post during the Great War of Liberation. But after his release when he had been "rehabilitated," he became an established professor at the University of Moscow.

While they were talking and arguing and cursing in Russian, I read a translation of a poem by Alexander Pushkin, "Ya Vas Lyubil" (I loved you once), and also a poem of by Simonov, "Zhdi Myenya" (Wait for me and I'll return). This ex-major said he had a book of Simonov's poems, and that Simonov was very popular during the Great War of Liberation. He gave me the book, and everyone who was there that day signed their names in different colors of ink. They spelled my name the way you would pronounce it in Russian, Doolee Rendall.

Alexander Pushkin was a big force in the Russian literature. Like many of the Russians of the noble families, he grew up speaking and learning French before Russian. But when he learned Russian, he also learned the peasant language and peasant folklore from his nurse, and he wrote a famous poem about his nurse. All the Russians know Alexander Pushkin, and they said to us, "Do you know our great black poet Alexander Pushkin?" They know poetry, and they appreciate it. For instance, when the Russian poet Evtushenko was interviewed in the Paris Review, he said that a poet may read to an audience of 30,000 people in a sports stadium, and then the poet goes to somebody's house and drinks and recites poetry until 3:00 A.M. When a book of poetry is published it's often printed in an edition of 100,000, and if it's the work of a popular poet, the book is often sold out one hour after the bookstore opens.

When we were in Russia, we went to an art camp outside Moscow where they exhibited paintings from all the different regions of the Soviet Union. We had seminars, and we talked about the way art is in the Soviet Union or current artistic trends in the United States. After dinner, we made toasts, which was one of the most enjoyable times of the day. We would drink, and everybody had to get up and make a toast. Some of these toasts were regular speeches. Everybody would be partying, and somebody else would say, "Hey, it's your turn." Someone said to Margaret Burroughs, "You're the leader of the delegation. You make the first toast." Margaret Burroughs was a good speaker, and she made the first toast from the delegation.

But finally it was my turn, and by then we had talked about everything that you could think of: how nice the Russian people were, how we enjoyed being there, solidarity, friendship, and all that. So I read Pushkin's, "Ya Vas Lyubil" in the original Russian. As soon as I started reading, the Russians recognized it, and you could see their lips move in synchronization with mine. That's how well the Russians know poetry, how they enjoy it, and love it.

Russian poets are a great influence. They are powerful and that power reached the czars, the premiers, and the dictators, who all recognized that power. That's why they put poets in jail and in concentration camps in Russia. They've killed them because they realize that poets are powerful people in their country. One of the Russian painters said, "We're social engineers." And they're well paid. Another said, "We make a lot of money, so we stay drunk." That's what many of them do with their money—buy vodka.

22. Dudley Randall in the Soviet Union, 1966.

All our expenses were paid from Paris (for a week) and for a month of tour-
ing in the Soviet Union. It was a very interesting visit. I didn't know exactly
what to look for; I didn't try to analyze the people, like a sociologist or a polit-
ical economist. I just tried to experience the Russians as people. And what I
found was that in spite of a different ideology, in spite of the different econom-
ic system, the Russians behave just like people in America. They may talk about
a classless society, about equality, but whenever people get together, there is a

pecking order. Some people are dominant and some are dominated. Like our guide, who probably had a higher rank than our interpreter, Igor. She would scold him, and even though I wasn't always sure what she was saying to him in Russian, I could tell what was meant just from the tone of her voice. She was either giving him orders or bawling him out. For example, when we would go to a new city and leave luggage, she would bark orders saying something like, "See that these bags are taken care of," and scolded him for being slow. Igor was on the lower scale as far as those two were concerned, but then he was on a higher scale than the waitresses at the hotel. He would order the waitresses around saying, "Bring me some mineral water," or "Give me another piece of chicken." When he wasn't looking, one of the waitresses pointed to him, and then looked at us and drew a knife across the front of her throat. People are just people, no matter where you are.

The people in our delegation were primarily artists, and we weren't that much interested in politics. We were rather ignorant when it came to politics as compared to the Russians. In one of the seminars, the Russians criticized us about the Vietnam War and said that the United States should withdraw from Vietnam. Since we didn't know much about international politics, or about the history of the war, or about the former French government in Vietnam, or about Vietnam, we couldn't say much in response. Although we might have wanted to defend our country, they seemed to know more about United States politics than we did.

One curious and impressive thing that I noticed when I was there was we were 6,000 miles from home, and yet, when we went into the State Library in Moscow, they had copies of Negro Digest. *But the Wayne County Library where I worked, which is only about 280 miles from Chicago, did not subscribe to* Negro Digest. *So the people living in Moscow had access to something American that the patrons of our library system in Detroit didn't. When I returned and my librarian asked me about my trip to Russia, I mentioned that irony. He said, "Well, this library will subscribe to* Negro Digest.*"*

The Russians are very clever. They made itinerary for us, and one of the places we visited was a summer camp where they had kids from about the age of nine to sixteen. They were young pioneers, and they wore the white shirts and red neckerchiefs. When we went to the camp, they had the children line up on both sides of the road and a little child greeted each one of us, took us by the hand, led us down the road, and gave us each a flower. I suppose they did that to all the visitors. While we walked down the road, they chanted, "i druzhba, druzba i mir," (peace and friendship, peace and friendship). That was a part of their propaganda.

Humans are complex and everything is not always what it seems. Maybe they didn't mean it. At the camp, for instance, they had the bulletin boards with the drawings that the children made, and there were pictures of white Russians and dark Cubans or Africans with their hands together as signs of friendship. Yet on the other hand, the son of Margaret and Charlie Burroughs, who was about thirteen, was sent to a summer camp during some portion of our tours, where he would be with the children his own age. He said at the camp they would practice with wooden guns and the children would say to him, "We're gonna shoot you with these guns. We are going to shoot you Americans." So you have things on both sides, nothing is ever as simple as it seems.

BROADSIDE PRESS AND THE RUSSIAN CONNECTIONS

Although For Malcolm *was the first Broadside book planned, the first book published was* Poem Counterpoem [1966]. *Since I knew Hoyt Fuller, editor of* Negro Digest, *I asked him to announce the anthology,* For Malcolm, *in his magazine. I wrote other magazines and asked them to announce it as well. The poems started coming in, but it took a long time to get the book together. After we [Randall and Burroughs] selected a poem, we had to write the poet and ask him or her to send a biographical sketch and a photograph, and they were slow in doing that.*

In the meantime, I decided to publish the book by Margaret Danner and me, Poem, Counterpoem. *I had sent it to the big publishers. I remember definitely I sent it to Harcourt Brace and they sent it back. I was feeling a little more independent, so I decided since they wouldn't publish it, I'd publish it myself. So, I published my first book with Margaret Danner in 1966. And that was the first Broadside Press book. As they say in the army, if you work KP and don't get enough to eat, shame on you.*

What's interesting about Poem, Counterpoem *is just before it was published, I had been to the Soviet Union where I saw a copies of little books about four inches high, a Russian poetry series entitled* The Young Guard. *They sold for about twenty-five kopek, that's about twenty-five cents, cheaply priced. So I published* Poem, Counterpoem *in the same format, a tiny book with tiny print. I thought it would be very convenient for women to put it in their pocketbooks, and for men to put it in their pockets. But, it didn't sell well in that format. So the second edition was published in the regular eight-by-five format, and it sold better. I guess American people like to buy books like cabbages, by the weight or by the size instead of by the content.*

"I found out about a black Russian poet, Jim Patterson, whose book I have, and whose poetry was published in the *For Malcolm* anthology."[3] Randall also befriended Yuri Shkolenko, who translated *Poem Counterpoem* and other poems by Randall into Russian. "Of course there's no pay, even if there was, the law forbids currency payments. You'd have to go to Russia to collect.[4] For the next few years, Dudley maintained contact with Shkolenko, sending him more books to be translated for a Russian audience. These kinds of occurrences during the trip to the Soviet Union inspired Randall's confidence in his poetry and in his publishing efforts.

The enthusiasm with which the Soviet artistic community received Dudley Randall and the 1966 delegation of black artists and the internationalist spirit that transcended national and racial borders made an indelible impression on him. At the same time, this delegation of was largely comprised of a generation of black artists that had been influenced by the politics of the labor movement and Communist Party activities during the 1930s in the United States. Therefore, they were more receptive to the Soviets. The Great Revolution that established the Soviet Union also had broader ramifications that influenced progressive politics in the United States. These historical influences intersected with the black American intellectual community in oblique, yet distinct, ways, especially in terms of racial equality.

Dudley Randall was decidedly not a socialist, but on the other hand, he did not support capitalist ideals either. His experiences as a laborer, union activist, and poet placed him within favorable political proximity with socialists and communists. As was often-evidenced in African American experience, he embraced certain tenets of these political philosophies but resisted sole allegiance to any of them. Paradoxically, Dudley Randall's awareness of Pushkin and his trip to the Soviet Union illuminated and reinforced the value of internationalism in poetry and poetics, which, in turn, provided a buffer to the essentialism of cultural nationalism and the ideological limitations that dominated the Black Arts Movement.

10

CULTURAL WARS AND CIVIL WARS

All you gambling sons and hooked children and bowery bums
Hating white devils and black bourgeoisie.
Thumbing your noses at your burning red suns,
Gather round this coffin and mourn your dying swan.

—From "Malcolm X," by Margaret Walker

N THE ANTHOLOGY'S INTRODUCTION, Dudley Randall and Margaret Burroughs explain how Margaret Walker's poem "For Malcolm X" inspired the publication of *For Malcolm: Poems on the Life and the Death of Malcolm X* (1967), one year after the 1966 Fisk University Writers Conference. The introduction does not elaborate on the politics of aesthetics that fueled so much debate at that conference, but in tandem and in contrast to the generation gap and ideological rift that split that event, the book combines the insight and skill of the older generation of poets with the militant momentum of the burgeoning Black Arts Movement. It also includes white poets and black poets who were not ideologically aligned with either side of the aesthetic argument. Despite his steadfast objection to the blatant merger of poetry and propaganda by many of the younger poets, Robert Hayden responded to Dudley Randall's call for poetry with "El Hajj Malik El-Shabazz":

> He'd X'd his name, became his people's anger,
> Exhorted them to vengeance for their past;
> Rebuked, admonished them,
> Their scourger who
> Would shame them, drive them
> From the lush ice gardens of their servitude.
>
> (*For Malcolm*, 14)

Although they were in opposing camps in the literati, Hayden's poignant presentation of Malcolm's impact on millions intersects with LeRoi Jones's powerful "A Poem For Black Hearts," which epitomizes the new black aesthetic. Jones invokes Malcolm X's cutting, angry vocabulary in a manner that simulates Malcolm's speeches. His words simultaneously chastise and appeal to the black male audience to seek redemption for their weakness and to pledge a spiritual vengeance on a society that assassinated Malcolm and their manhood:

> For Great Malcolm a prince of the earth, let nothing in us rest
> until we avenge ourselves for his death, stupid animals
> that killed him, let us never breathe a pure breath if
> we fail, and white men call us faggots till the end of
> the earth.
>
> (*For Malcolm*, 62)

Actor Ossie Davis, who attended the Fisk Writers Conference, wrote the preface "Why I Eulogized Malcolm" for the book and "The Eulogy of Malcolm X: Our Black Manhood . . . Our Black Shining Prince!" that appears in the appendix. A brief historical essay about Malcolm X's life and a bibliography for "Further Reading" about Malcolm X follows the photos and biographical sketches of the poets. Therefore, the book is more than a collection of poems written in tribute to the man. It is also a useful cultural, historical, and educational guide for readers. Although the eulogy was published in *The Autobiography of Malcolm X*, the reprinting and circulation of it with this book of poetry connects Malcolm's life and death to the collective consciousness of the poets and the impetus for this project.

The thematic range of the poems collected determined the four sections: "The Life," "The Death," "The Rage," and "The Aftermath." Gwendolyn Brooks, LeRoi Jones, Robert Hayden and Margaret Walker, and "prolific and much published poets like Clarence Major, John Sinclair, James Worley, and Ted Joans sent in poems. Talented young poets like Mari Evans, Julia Fields, Sonia Sanchez, David Henderson, Raymond Patterson, Helen Quigless, Bobb Hamilton, and Larry Neal contributed."[1] The divergent political perspectives and broad range of literary styles that characterized the anthology foreshadowed the profiles of future Broadside Press authors.

Etheridge Knight, for example, who was an inmate at Indiana State Prison at the time, contributed three poems while preparing his own poetry manuscript, which was published in 1968. Knight's range of poetic forms and diversity of vocabulary are expressed in three very different compositions. "For

Malcolm, A Year After," a sonnet, signifies on the structural conformity straining against his subject:

> Compose for Red a proper verse;
> Adhere to foot and strict iamb;
> Control the burst of angry words
> Or they might boil and break the dam.
> Or they might boil and overflow
> And drench me, drown me, drive me mad.
>
> (*For Malcolm*, 43)

"It Was A Funky Deal" references LeRoi Jones and Charlie Parker in a jazz rhythm and vocabulary encased in a refrain that borders on the blues:

> It was a funky deal.
>
> You rocked too many boats, man.
> Pulled too many coats, man.
> Saw through the jive.
> You reached the wild guys
> Like me. You and Bird. (And that
> Lil LeRoi cat.)
> It was a funky deal.
>
> (*For Malcolm*, 21)

Dedicated to Gwendolyn Brooks upon the death of Malcolm, the strength of "When the Sun Came" resides in the emotional depth conveyed through the prison setting of the poem and poet mourning inside his cell:

> And now the Sun has gone, has bled red,
> Weeping behind the hills.
> Again the night year shadows form.
> But beneath the placid faces a storm rages.
> The rays of Red have pierced the deep, have struck
> The core. We cannot sleep.
> The shadows sing: Malcolm, Malcolm, Malcolm.
>
> (*For Malcolm*, 73–74)

Sonia Sanchez's "Malcolm" laments in subdued tones the deadly life of a racist society that murdered a truth sayer:

Do not speak to me of martyrdom
of men who die to be remembered
on some parish day.
I don't believe in dying
though I too shall die
and violets like castanets
will echo me.

(*For Malcolm*, 66)

To demonstrate the geographical reach of the book, the introduction identifies some of the poets by their cities, such as Patricia McIlnay, Jay Wright, Carmin Auld Goulbourne, Theodore Horne, Willie Kgositsile (a South African poet), and Edward Spriggs in New York; Kent Foreman, Conrad Kent Rivers, and Zack Gilbert of Chicago; and in Detroit the list includes Oliver La-Grone, Joyce Whitsitt/Malaika Wangara, Le Graham, George Norman, and Reginald Wilson, the editor of *Correspondence*. Other poets include Nanina Alba, Marcella Caine, Bill Frederick, James Lucas, Christine Johnson, and James Patterson, "an Afro-Russian poet whose great grandfather was an American slave. Patterson sent a Russian and an English version of a poem from Moscow."[2] Randall and Burroughs emphasized the similarities in symbolism and allusions and the differences in the individuality of expression:

> The styles vary from the clipped syllables of Gwendolyn Brooks and the glittering phrases of Robert Hayden, from the dense-packed images of Carmin Auld Goulbourne and Oliver LaGrone, to the experimental punctuation and phrasing of LeRoi Jones, John Sinclair, and Le Graham, and the hip dialect of Ted Joans and Etheridge Knight. There are many Semitic words, because of Malcolm's Semitic religion. The figures apostrophized by the poets are not the slave-holding Washington or Jefferson, but freedom fighters Toussaint L'Ouverture, Gabriel Prosser, Denmark Vesey, Nat Turner, and leaders in our own time Marcus Garvey, W. E. B. Du Bois, Robert Williams, Patrice Lumumba, and LeRoi Jones.[3]

Of the four white poets in the collection, the poetry of John Sinclair, who was a member of the White Panther Party and a well-known artist and activist in the Detroit–Ann Arbor area, is especially relevant because of his aesthetic identification with black culture and black struggle. The epigraph for his poem, "The Destruction of America," references LeRoi Jones's *The System of Dante's Hell*, and his biographical statement confirms a political radicalism profoundly influenced by Malcolm X: "Like Archie Shepp said about his music, all my work is for Malcolm."[4]

(hate,

so fast, thru my brain,
smashing cold reservoirs
of feeling. intelligence. Broken streets
of the imagination. Go,
dumb killers, keep them turned
against themselves, stolen niggers,
slaves of luxury, dead puppets
of desire, cadillacs. guns. leather
coats. The obscene repetition
of history, in politicians' bloody dreams.
power. Greedheads. Pimps
for the whore they've made a-

merica

(*For Malcolm*, 58)

At Detroit's Second Annual Black Arts Convention, 29 June–2 July 1967, sponsored by Edward Vaughn's Forum 66, Randall presented a copy of *For Malcolm* to Malcolm X's widow, Betty Shabazz, who was the keynote speaker and to whom the book was dedicated. Poets in attendance from Detroit, Chicago, and New York read their poems. Other featured speakers were the chairman of SNCC, H. Rap Brown; Daniel Watts, editor of *Liberator*; and Reverend Albert L. Cleage, the founder of the Shrine of the Black Madonna. Randall reported in an article for *Negro Digest* that Rap Brown stated: "We didn't make the laws. Why should we obey them?" And "Change your color, and then your power will change."[5] Although not yet published by Broadside, poets Nikki Giovanni and Don L. Lee were both at the conference, and it was the *For Malcolm* anthology that attracted them to Broadside Press. In a letter to Etheridge Knight, Randall revealed his personal impression of LeRoi Jones, who was supposed to attend the conference:

I'm scared to meet the guy, he's such a dragon. He'll probably say I'm not militant enough & a bourgeois. Actually, he came from a schoolteacher mother and a post-office father & had his way paid through college, graduating at 18. My dad was a factory worker often laid off, & I didn't get to college until V. A. paid my way after WWII.[6]

In his autobiography, Jones acknowledges this monstrous image of himself:

I guess, during this period, I got the reputation of being a snarling, white-hating madman. There was some truth to it, because I was struggling to be born, to break out from the shell I could instinctively sense surrounded my own dash for freedom. I was in a frenzy, trying to get my feet solidly on the ground, of reality.[7]

Actually, the backgrounds of Randall and Jones converge as much as they diverge. Like Jones, Randall's mother was also a schoolteacher, and while he was a student at Wayne State and the University of Michigan, he worked at the post office like Jones's father. Class-consciousness for Randall evolved experientially rather than theoretically because of his particular historical context. He had the distinct advantage of being raised in a pro-labor environment and was personally invested in the union movement while he worked in the foundry during the Great Depression.

But such variables were rarely a consideration during rhetorical debates about the identity or the role of the black writer in the heat of the Black Arts Movement. Statements were often prescriptive, definitive, and absolute. For example, Francis Ward, associate editor of *Ebony Magazine*, stated at the conference that "the responsibilities of the black writer were to devote himself to the struggle for equality and freedom, to give leadership through his writing, to discover and promulgate black history, and to interpret the condition of the people."[8] Bobb Hamilton, poet and editor of *Soulbook*, said that literature that does its job "communicates emotions and analyzes and criticizes events."[9] Randall's report to *Negro Digest* also included his summary of such conference dialogues: "The themes of writers' conferences had been, first the role of the black writer, then the black audience; and the trend of opinions was that the writer should write as a black man and to and for the black audience."[10] The opinion Randall expressed at the conference was in support of his previous statement at the 1966 conference about institution building: "We are a nation of twenty million, and could support a flourishing literature."[11] He proposed that a national book council be organized to sponsor a national book week to promote the creation and distribution of literature and to disseminate information about literature. ("Later, a group of writers and editors met and listed what each wanted and what each could provide"[12]).

THE 1967 DETROIT REBELLION

Less than two weeks after the cultural convention, the summer of 1967 witnessed the worst "race riot" in U.S. history. In the same article that Randall reported the Second Black Arts Convention, he stated that "weeks before the rebellion erupted in the 'city of motors,' the simmering mood of disgust and outrage which characterized the feelings of many black people was in open evidence in the city." [13] In a letter to Knight, Randall relays his concerns about the rebellion, as a Detroiter and as a writer:

I've owed you a letter for a long time. Partly my delay was because of this publishing project. There's so much clerical work that I don't have time for writing. And partly it was because of the recent events, when I too stayed by the radio & television, & read current newspapers & magazines. There was no harm done to me or my family, although there were a few anxious nights when there were rumors that they would get the "rich black folks." I never thought it was a crime to have a job.

I don't know how this will turn out. The uprisings have focused attention on the ghettos. I hope that efforts will be made to eradicate the roots of the problem. On the other hand, many whites have been polarized to advocate repression, blind & brutal. I hope the sensible ones prevail. All little people like you and me can do is to support the sensible ones. And write sincerely what we feel. One wants to write with assurance that he knows all the answers, but one can write out of uncertainty and it'll be more sincere.[14]

But in the succinct, three line poem "Sniper," the response of Randall's muse to the '67 Rebellion was more in tandem with the Black Arts perspective:

Somewhere
On a rooftop
You fight for me.
(*More to Remember*, 75)

In her article "Black Power, Black Rebellion" (*Negro Digest*), Detroiter Betty De Ramus opens with a similar image:

Slick Campbell is an actor at Detroit's Concept East Theater, a bushy-haired barrel of a black man who likes to strut on stage and trumpet a poem he composed entitled, "Let Freedom Ring." "Ka-ping, ka-ping," he mocks a rifle at its conclusion. Then, after a pause, comes the cruel irony: "Damn fool, don't you know that's freedom's ring?"

De Ramus explains that the "snipers came to symbolize avenging assassins and in the explosion of their rage completed the birth of a breed of black man who is unafraid."[15]

In *Working Detroit*, labor historian and activist Steve Babson explains that "unlike 1943, the violence in July 1967, was not a race riot," and "with few exceptions, there was no fighting between black and white citizens—in several sections of the city, whites even joined in the looting."[16] The violent exchange was between angry young men and the National Guard. "Police and store owners killed all but a handful of the 39 others who died that week. Many of those killed were innocent bystanders felled by the panicked and random gunfire of the National Guard."[17]

Ron Scott, who had been a member of the Detroit chapter of the Black Panther Party in 1968 and then a member of the League of Revolutionary Black Workers, reiterates Babson's analysis of discontented youth: "We did not feel that the civil rights movement had a particular focus on issues that we faced. In Detroit that was the police. Seven years before the disturbance Mayor Miriani had a crackdown in the Black community. I was 12 years old and a cop put a shotgun in my face and told me not to breathe."[18] Scott considers the destruction of Black Bottom as a contributing factor in the destabilization of other black communities, such as Twelfth Street, where the violence erupted:

> Twelfth Street [now renamed Rosa Parks Blvd.] was interesting because it was in transition. Many people had moved there from the old Hastings Street, which was a viable black economic strip that was taken to make way for I-75. So many of the people including the street element of pimps, prostitutes and others moved onto 12th Street along with the business owners.

The economic advantages for blacks in Detroit were in direct contrast to the social repression and abuse they otherwise endured. Scott explained this dichotomy: "There was money being made through small business and in the plants [automobile factories] etc. We had the economics but no power, no ability to control the phenomena that dictated our daily living."[19]

The mainstream press and politicians called it "a senseless riot," while politically aware folks called it "a rebellion." Ed Vaughn, who was a community leader and owner of a black bookstore during the 1967 Rebellion and later served in the cabinet of Coleman Young's administration and as a representative in the Michigan State Legislature, blamed police aggression and brutality as the primary causes for the civil disruption: "The undercurrent of discontent was always there. We [the grassroots community leaders] were trying to tell them [the white power structure] that the police department was an army of occupation. People were being beaten, even killed."[20] Prior to the rebellion, Vaughn and the membership of the Group on Advanced Leadership (GOAL), a nationalist/pan-Africanist organization, set up forums at various sites in the community in an attempt to address critical issues of conflict with the police. In addition to these forums, GOAL also sponsored the Black Arts Conventions in Detroit. Although Ed Vaughn mis-dates the founding of the press, he does recognize the significance of Randall's presence at the conference and the connection between culture and politics: "Dudley Randall was there. He founded Broadside Press after the Convention. We brought in H. Rap Brown, Stokely Carmichael and Don L. Lee."[21] Vaughn's activities were reflective of the political power the nationalists gained after the 1967 Rebellion. In her 1967 article for *Negro Digest*, Betty De Ramus analyzed the dynamics that contributed to a changing of the guard in the black community, contradicting the notion that New York was the center of black nationalism at the time:

> As a result, in the days of endless dialogue and search that have followed the Detroit riot, the mantle of leadership has been resting more and more on the shoulders of what had been virtually an underground movement, the motley group who call themselves "black nationalists." For several years, Detroit had been considered the center of black nationalism, overshadowing even New York, but the ferment of its fiery activists had drawn little public note. Now it is inescapable.[22]

This analysis was evinced in the founding of the City Wide Citizens Action Committee (CCAC) by Reverend Albert Cleage, of the Central United Church of Christ. The CCAC became "known as the new black establishment," supplanting the previous, more moderate, middle-class leadership. In 1972, *We Don't Need No Music*, a book of poetry by Pearl Cleage Lomax, a daughter of Revered Cleage's, was published by Broadside Press, and the Shrine of the Black Madonna, an institutional affiliate of Cleague's church, became a major retailer for Broadside books.

Despite the prevalence of nationalism, another dimension of radicalism, grounded in the militancy of labor struggles, emerged and also redefined the new black politics sweeping the city. The formation of the Dodge Revolutionary Union Movement (DRUM) was the result of disenchantment with the racist conditions in the automobile plants and a politically compromised UAW. By 1969, the League of Revolutionary Workers, a city-wide organization and a spin-off of DRUM, became symbolic of radical politics particular to Detroit, as young blacks adopted Marxism to their own ideological needs and historical circumstances to "wage a fight against racism, capitalism, and imperialism."[23] The fiery radical attorney Kenneth Cockrel became the primary personality to emerge from this movement, and his reputation as a litigator resulted from his representation of workers and young radical activists. A graduate of Wayne State University's Law School, his Marxist politics were

aligned with the black consciousness that permeated the times, which resulted in his election to the Detroit City Council in 1976.

Violent eruptions in cities intensified the urgency of the political climate
within and without the black community, as the call for racial unity resounded throughout the country. The intensity of nationalist activism and
political radicalism attracted an audience for black literature. In this regard,
the success of Broadside Press, as Randall often stated, was "largely the result
of historical timing."[24] The quality and the activist aesthetic that characterized the literature captured the imagination of an audience eager to understand these circumstances, and Randall's editorial vision and political tolerance recognized the need for a complex range of perspectives that
encompassed the fervor and contemplated the uncertainty of the times.

The ongoing activities at the Concept East Theater produced the works of
nationally prominent, Detroit-based playwrights Ron Milner and Bill Harris,
as well as works by LeRoi Jones, Ed Bullins, and other Black Arts playwrights.
Poets and playwrights alike turned inward to decipher this agitation, to garner institutional sustenance, and to suggest constructive directions. Political
and cultural activity in Detroit positioned Broadside Press at the center of
progressive expression and reflection. Detroit had been a point of origin and
a vital touchstone in the life of Malcolm X, and the publication of the *For
Malcolm* anthology represented both the ideological and symbolic significance of Malcolm X to the city and to a cultural and political movement.

Although the black authors energized a course of activist urgency that was
viewed as part of the Black Liberation Movement sweeping the country, the
Black Arts Movement was primarily literary, and more specifically it generated poetry that needed to be printed. Oddly enough, Randall did not write
a poem for the Malcolm X anthology. In fact, he said he felt Martin Luther
King had done more than Malcolm X for the liberation of blacks. But as an
editor, he acknowledged Malcolm X as a cultural icon and knew that there
was an audience in the factories, in the prisons, and in the nonliterary quarters of the community, spaces where Malcolm X lived and spoke:

> There is a growing market for black books, not only among the young black
> high school and college students, but also among older, less educated persons.
> A neighbor told me that he saw a worker on the production line of an auto-
> mobile factory with a copy of the anthology *For Malcolm* in his hip pocket. I
> often got orders for poetry books, which are scrawled on part of a brown
> paper bag. I was more pleased to receive such individual orders than to re-
> ceive a large order from a bookstore or a jobber, for this showed that black
> people were reading poetry and finding it a meaningful, not an esoteric, art.[25]

11

"PROPHETS FOR A NEW DAY": DIVERSITY AND HERITAGE

And the dark faces of the sufferers
Gleam in the new morning
The complaining faces glow
And the winds of freedom begin to blow
While the Word descends on the waiting World below.

—From "Prophets for a New Day" by Margaret Walker

THE RETRIEVAL OF AFRICAN AMERICAN POETRY was a primary goal for Dudley Randall's Broadside Press. Publishing well-known poets with significant standing and distinctive voices in the literary annals, as exemplified in the first broadsides, solidified the identity of the press. Randall expanded this premise by soliciting manuscripts from some of the same poets published in *The Broadside Series*. Most of them had already achieved considerable and even international literary fame, but despite their previous accomplishments and obvious talent, many of them watched their earlier books go out of print and their more recent writings patiently awaiting publication. Randall said, "The popular poets of today may be forgotten tomorrow."

Since value and substance are not necessarily constants in the measure of art by audiences or in literary criticism, Randall included an expansive range of styles and perspectives, which accorded Broadside a complicated, and possibly contradictory, profile. Indeed, Randall's editorial depth and capacity to recognize well-crafted poetry with memorable themes was what grounded the press in solid literary standards representative of the tradition. Publications by established writers with distinct styles appeared alongside works by the younger poets, whose voices melded with the politics of the moment; hence, a synergistic effect conferred an immediate impact and assured the long-term cultural value of Broadside productions.

This editorial vision is best reflected in Randall's relationship with Robert Hayden. By maintaining contact with Hayden, Randall used their long-standing friendship to connect Hayden to Broadside despite the other poet's disgruntled attitude about the cultural movement and reluctance to be associated with the reputation of some of the new and younger poets. Randall's diplomacy elevated their mutual interest in poetry above ideological warfare for a larger purpose and to the benefit of cultural longevity.

Hayden was the editor of *Kaleidoscope: Poems by American Negro Poets*, which was published in 1967, one year after the famed Fisk University Writers Conference, when he had refused to retreat from his position on racial politics and poetry. His aesthetic attitude was reflected in the canon of *Kaleidoscope*, which demonstrated which poets, including which Black Arts poets, he felt merited notice. Dudley Randall's letter to Hayden about *Kaleidoscope* included praise for the jacket cover, the printing features, the selection of poets, and the insightful introductory essay. But he warned Hayden to anticipate some hostile responses:

> By accident I saw an approval copy of *Kaleidoscope* at my library, and of course took it home. It's a beautiful book. I like the black jacket & the sparkling letters of the title, & I like the title too, instead of one of those prosy ones—Poetry of the N—etc. I'd have preferred for the book to be the same color as the jacket, but the pale blue isn't bad, & the gold letters give it sparkle.
>
> The bold type is large & easy to read, & you're generous with white space, allotting a full page to 4-line poems. Mostly, you avoid the anthology warhorses. Refreshingly, Tolson wasn't represented by his "Chicago Ode." Two of my poems had never been anthologized before, and, as every anthologist seems to be expected to do, you introduced new voices. I knew of Julius Lester, as he was in my *For Malcolm* bibliography, but I didn't know he was a poet, & I had no inkling that he was black. I'd never heard of Barrax, & I see you corralled Bob Kaufman, Gloria Oden, & Moses Holman, & Jean Toomer.
>
> Your criticism had probing insight. You defined both the strengths & weaknesses of poets in a brief compass. In that it was like Johnson's anthology, while it was like *Caroling Dusk* in being a poet's choice & a poet's title.
>
> It's not too weighty with scholarly appendages—indexes of poets, titles. School kids will like it, & the price, $3.95, is surprisingly low. Your stand on Negro poetry might earn you some blows—it'll be interesting to read the reviews. Fuller said its appearance was awaited with interest. Some new Black poets are out—Knight, Neal, Hamilton, Fabio, Snellings, but it's not intended to be all-inclusive. In all, an excellent bk. & thanks for including me. I'm proud to be in it.

You're established as anthologist now, along with Johnson, Cullen, Bontemps & Hughes. Thanks for the mention of the Broadsides. Perhaps I'll get some orders from that. I was thinking of giving them up. Wish you'd mentioned *For Malcolm* & *Poem Counterpoem*, as that might have brought in orders. See what being a publisher has done to me? Changed me from a poet to a businessman. Ugh! My best to Erma & Maia.[1]

In the introduction to *Kaleidoscope*, Hayden ridicules his opposition by referring to them as "poets of the *Negro* revolution" (emphasis added), which was considered an affront during the semantic debate over "Negro" and "Black":

Those who presently avow themselves "poets of the Negro revolution" argue that they do indeed constitute a separate group or school, since the purpose of their writing is to give Negroes a sense of human dignity and provide them with ideological weapons. A belligerent race pride moves these celebrants of Black Power to declare themselves not simply "poets," but "Negro Poets." However, Countee Cullen, the brilliant lyricist of the Harlem Renaissance in the 1920's, insisted that he be considered a "poet," not a "Negro poet," for he did not want to be restricted to racial themes nor have his poetry judged solely on the basis of its relevance to the Negro struggle.[2]

Hayden's vocabulary and stance instigated an antagonistic response from Don L. Lee, whose review of the anthology in the *Negro Digest* provided an opportunity to showcase his polemics by attacking Hayden's critique of Black Arts. Lee's rebuke enlisted the opinion of LeRoi Jones to support his argument, and their ideological alignment constituted a key opposition to Hayden:

In all likelihood, those very words "poems by American Negro Poets," and not the book's title, will sell this anthology. However, in Mr. Hayden's introduction one can't get past the first page without encountering the editor's persistent efforts at apologizing for not only being a "negro" poet but for writing "negro" poetry. For those poets who purposely write poetry directed toward and for the "negro," Mr. Hayden says that its aim is "to give Negroes a sense of human dignity and provide them with *ideological weapons*."[3]

Whereas Lee privileges politics as the purpose of black poetry, Hayden explains the political aesthete as the consequence of historical circumstances and makes a distinction between contextual awareness and preconceived content:

Protest has been a recurring element in the writing of American Negroes, a fact hardly to be wondered at given the social conditions under which they have been forced to live. And the Negro poet's devotion to the cause of freedom is not in any way reprehensible, for throughout history poets have often been champions of human liberty. But bad poetry is another matter, and there is no denying that a great deal of "race poetry" is poor, because its content seems ready-made and art is displaced by argument.[4]

Even more so, the inclusion and exception given to the poetry of Melvin B. Tolson and LeRoi Jones demonstrates that Hayden's editorial decisions were not solely based on philosophical differences. However, Don L. Lee's confrontational critique of *Kaleidoscope* contributed to the ongoing tension; meanwhile, Hayden's national literary prominence thrived and even rivaled that of Jones. In 1969, Hayden was invited to be the poet-in-residence at the Library of Congress and assumed a professorship at the University of Michigan.

On occasion, Randall taught courses in Afro-American literature as an adjunct professor at the University of Michigan. Russell Fraser, who was then the chair of the Department of English at the University of Michigan, recognized the need for a revision in the presentation of American literature. He suggested an editorial collaboration between Randall and Hayden that would produce an anthology specifically for classroom use. Randall thought it was a great opportunity for Broadside:

Russell Fraser wrote me a letter, of which you [Hayden] have a copy, suggesting that you and I collaborate on an anthology of black poetry to supplement the one used in the introduction to poetry courses in the U. of Mich. English department to be about 30 pages long, to sell for about 95 cents, and to be ready for the fall semester, and to be published by Broadside Press. I told him that I would be willing to do so, but the last time I talked to him, he had received no reply from you. I would be very glad to work with you on this project. I remember years ago in Detroit you used to suggest that we collaborate on something. Would you let me know whether you'd be willing to do this? If so, I could send you my ideas on the subject.

I'm in Chicago this week to read in the high schools. Saw Gwen. Don Lee told me he was going to read at Louisville. I asked him to say hello to you. I'm thinking of starting a Broadside Critics series, like the Minnesota or Columbia pamphlets. Would you like to write one on Countee Cullen? Your *Heartshape* is now in the public domain, unless you've renewed the copyright? Could I reprint some of the poems?[5]

Interestingly, Randall suggested that Lee speak to Hayden at the reading despite the tension between the two poets. Though courtesy may have encouraged Hayden to engage Lee in a professional setting, Hayden's view of Lee's poetry remained negative. The book, which Randall edited alone, was entitled *Black Poetry: A Supplement To Anthologies Which Exclude Black Poets*, but after reviewing the manuscript, Hayden was unable to reconcile his steadfast position on some of the new poetry:

> I think you have done a good job with the little anthology. I am enclosing some notes on the selections, but feel free to do as you like with the booklet.
>
> I think we can be completely candid with each other about most things. And I feel constrained to say that, although I recognize the necessity for separate anthologies, having brought out one myself, I am nevertheless more than a little repelled by the concept of "black poetry." And by the abusive chauvinism—this more than anything else—displayed in the work of most of the newer poets you are including.
>
> For this reason, I wish to withdraw from the project. I haven't had time to do much with it anyway, as you know. But so much of the work included is blatantly separatist, blatantly *non-poetry*, that I'm out of sympathy with it and it would therefore be hypocritical of me to let my name be used as one of the editors.
>
> You may use the poems of mine you've chosen—but again, not "Gabriel"—and I'll do what I can to get October House to reduce the permissions fee.[6]

Despite their various attempts, Randall and Hayden never accomplished a poetry project together. They agreed to disagree and continued to publish each other in their respective works, and Hayden's poetry appeared in the contested *Black Poetry* anthology. Even when Hayden insisted that Randall not reprint "Gabriel," he eventually relented and it appeared in *The Broadside Series*. Moreover, the ongoing disputes during the Black Arts Movement did not distract Randall, who focused on the need for historical consistency within the context of historical change. While the Black Power Movement dominated the vocabulary of the cultural movement and militant poets like Don L. Lee and LeRoi Jones, the leadership responsible for the institutions that provided forums for literary militancy was grounded in the expertise and experience of writers from the previous generation.

In the Midwest, Chicago and Detroit were key cities during the Black Arts Movement because they contained large and industrious African American populations and housed major cultural institutions. The Du Sable Museum of African American History and Art, the Kuumba Workshop, the Organization of Black Art and Culture, and *The Negro Digest* operated in Chicago by a Detroiter, while Broadside Press, Rappa House, Concept East, the Museum of African American History and the Shrine of the Black Madonna were the foci of much activity in Detroit. Sustained through collective interests and burgeoning activities, interaction between writers in the two cities was largely the result of proximity and personal histories.

For some undetermined reason, prominent cultural leaders of the time were often poets. Perhaps as prophets and visionaries they were particularly suited for the role of institutional directors. At any rate, women poets were as critical to the era as their male counterparts and counterpoints. To a large extent, Dudley Randall was able to make Broadside Press a viable institution because of his relationships with Margaret Danner, Margaret Burroughs, Gwendolyn Brooks, and Margaret Walker. All of them, at one time or another, lived in Chicago, and, for a very brief period, Margaret Danner lived in Detroit. They all frequented Detroit, however, throughout their careers. Broadside Press published their poetry during the late 1960s and early 1970s, and they gave readings to enthusiastic crowds in Detroit and Chicago during the Black Arts Movement.

But inasmuch as a romantic revisionism of literary history might be more satisfying for the "racial" identity, a closer examination of these interpersonal relationships revealed the differences and difficulties within the camp. Just as the confrontations between some of the younger writers and Robert Hayden illustrated ideological conflict between generations, the politics of personalities sometimes strained friendships and created tension within literary generations. Hence, it was a challenging and colorful period when the pretense of racial solidarity was the reigning rhetoric, but not necessarily the practice.

The aesthetic activism of Gwendolyn Brooks, Margaret Walker, Margaret Danner, and Margaret Burroughs greatly influenced the consciousness of younger poets. Although these women writers embraced the goal of African American freedom and their poetry articulated race pride in imagery configured to counter inhumane stereotypes of black people, there was also a class-consciousness that permeated their poetry. Because of their historical development during the Great Depression (1930s) and the Labor Movement (1930–40s), they encouraged a deeper understanding of the socioeconomics of discrimination.

As individual artists, Margaret Danner, Margaret Burroughs, Margaret Walker, and Gwendolyn Brooks had already achieved considerable artistic acclaim during the Post Renaissance period (the 1930s–1950s). But collectively, their distinct styles and variegated politics sometimes converged and sometimes clashed, as cultural nationalism turned the community inside-out in an attempt to define the new black aesthetic. Despite the ins and outs of these four women writers, they exerted considerable influence on Randall and the Black Arts Movement as artists and as institution builders.

MARGARET DANNER

Margaret Esse Danner Cunningham was born in Kentucky but spent most of her adult years in Chicago, where she attended Loyola and Northwestern Universities. Danner achieved national recognition as a poet when she was awarded the John Hay Whitney Fellowship for "Far From Africa: Four Poems," which was published in the premier journal *Poetry* in 1951. Of the four women poets discussed here, only Margaret Danner lived for some time in Detroit (1962–1964). During this period, she was the poet-in-residence at Wayne State University and the founder of Boone House for the Arts, which placed her at the center of literary activity.

Boone House provided an institutional locus for black Detroit artists for the first time. From humble beginnings, these connections became even more manifest during the Black Arts Movement a few years later. Dudley Randall and Naomi Long Madgett, who first met at Boone House, forged a lasting friendship and a cooperative association that benefited the national poetry community. Randall founded Broadside Press, and Madgett founded Lotus Press shortly thereafter. They published each other's poetry and developed poetry presses that altered the perception and reception of black poetry for the next thirty years.

Contrary to the congenial relationship between Madgett and Randall, the Randall-Danner connection essentially began to mirror the contentious structure of *Poem Counterpoem* when Danner circumvented their joint publishing venture to publish *To Flower*, her solo collection of poetry, through Robert Hayden's Counterpoise Series. Randall resolved to transcend this transgression by focusing on the poetry and thereby managed to sustain a prickly friendship and finally get their book out.

But when Danner returned to Chicago in 1966, she was deeply disturbed by the political climate of the cultural community and imagined that she was being shunned by the black writers there. She wrote unsettling letters to Hayden, which claimed there was a conspiracy to discredit her work and her reputation. She viewed herself and Hayden as outsiders and as kindred spirits because they disagreed with the racial dynamics emphasized by the movement and because they were both members of the Baha'i faith. Hayden and Danner's isolation fostered their perception of a hostile literary community, a conclusion that was not totally unfounded. But rather than there being a conspiracy designed to destroy their particular literary reputations, the tension and the talk was more the consequence of an ideological warfare that was larger than any one or two writers. In her letter to Hayden about a poetry reading that Langston Hughes gave in Chicago, Danner conveyed her fears about the gossip, her version of ongoing conflict, and a defense of Dudley Randall's individuality and integrity:

> You have such a kind heart and are so sensitive that it bothers you to think they have him [Dudley Randall]. They don't. And when the other day here in Chicago (the home of all devilish activity) Margaret Burroughs had a "thing" for Langston Hughes and Gwen invited Dudley and Don Lee, in order to keep in with them and show Margaret up as not inviting them and the auditorium was filled to capacity which was about 3,000 people . . . after they had done all that they could to take advantage of everything to push themselves, Dudley Randall, who Gwen had invited, got up and told the people how I had struggled at Boone House and how I had been maligned and lied on. I had not mentioned him at all when I read my poem to Langston and so Gwen who thought she had hurt me and Margaret in reality only opened the door for someone to say something good about me and Dudley WILL BE THE SAME WAY ABOUT YOU IF HE THINKS PEOPLE ARE WRONGING YOU.[7]

The belief in intrigue expressed in Danner's correspondence to Hayden persisted, and her obsessive impressions of her contemporaries contributed to the subterfuge and friction between writers.

In 1968, Randall published *Impressions of African Art Forms* by Danner, a chapbook that contained poetic responses to various forms of African imagery in artistic expression and black life. This book acknowledges Hoyt Fuller as her friend. Even though Danner was opposed to most of the new black attitude, her earliest poetry converges with Africanity in Black Arts aesthetics. Danner's themes in this collection (some of which had been published as early as 1950) confront issues of ignorance and converge with the new enlightenment regarding the underrated and distorted interpretations of African imagery in art and culture. Despite her opposition to the impetus of the Black Arts Movement, her expertise and exploration in this area anticipated subsequent attempts by other black writers to adapt authentic African aesthetics into the features of African American poetry and identity.

MARGARET BURROUGHS

Margaret Taylor Goss Burroughs's reputation as a writer pales by comparison to her fame as a visual artist. Her commitment to cultural revolution was grounded in her leftist politics; hence, she engaged the Black Arts Movement within a broader political framework, enlisting her socialist ideals to expand the cultural nationalism that dominated the era. As an artist, Burroughs recognized the necessity of bringing artists of color together in order to accommodate their special aesthetic and career considerations. The marginalization of black artists made a Black Arts Movement inevitable, and the need to establish community-based arts organizations was another logical progression. Burroughs was an artist with the historical vision and the tenacity to build something tangible.

Her institutions made her a beacon for the black arts community in Chicago. In particular, she was one of the founders of the National Conference of Artists (NCA) in 1959, which predates the Black Arts Movement. She was also the primary force behind the founding of the Du Sable Museum of African American History and Art in 1961, whereby she had already assumed the responsibility of institution building, a major tenet of the Black Arts philosophy. The National Conference of Artists, which ultimately developed chapters throughout the nation (thirteen different states within ten years), became a thriving organization that sponsored conferences, forums, educational programs, and galleries for developing and mature visual artists.

Likewise, the founding of the Du Sable Museum of African American History and Art facilitated even broader concerns. By combining history with art, this institution linked artistic expression to documentation, thereby demonstrating that cultural memory is a critical aspect of African American aesthetics, deriving its subjects and thought from metaphors grounded in historical narrative. The museum's holdings include literature, visual art, audio recordings, and biographical and bibliographical resources—materials from various facets of black life and culture.

As a writer, Burroughs entered the genre as a children's author. *Jasper, The Drummin' Boy* was published in 1947 (Viking Press). She developed an interest in children's rhymes and poems, which she collected and published. For the most part, her poetry did not surface until the Black Arts Movement. In a 1957 article about her that appeared in *The Milwaukee Journal*, Burroughs revealed that, "she had at least twenty manuscripts that had been rejected."[8] As a major cultural force, she attracted the attention of the younger, aspiring poets, especially Don L. Lee (Haki Madhubuti) who was employed by the museum. It was at the museum that Lee met Randall, who became Lee's primary publisher during the Black Arts Movement. Many of the young Chicago writers who were members of the Organization of Black American Culture (OBAC) benefited from the institutional vision of Burroughs and the creative support of Gwendolyn Brooks, who sponsored OBAC.

But even before the founding of the museum and the NCA, Burroughs's home was known as a center for intellectuals and artists in Chicago. In her autobiography, Gwendolyn Brooks relates how central these parties were to intellectual life:

> Margaret Goss lived above a Michigan Avenue barn. Triumphantly, Margaret and her second husband later originated what was at first the Ebony Museum in the Quincy Club, the ancient mansion that fronted the barn. Her home supplied the South Side artist contingent with its most fascinating parties. Parties? But it was always open house at Margaret's. Three people would "fall in." Then three more. Before evening deepened there might be twelve. There would be your "party." You might meet any Personality there, white or black. You might meet Paul Robeson. You might meet Peter Pollock. On any night you might meet Frank Marshall Davis, the poet, Robert A. Davis, the actor, artists Eldzier Corto, Hughie Lee-Smith, Charles White, Elizabeth Catlett; sculptor Marion Perkins (father of the enterprising young poet Eugene Perkins); once every couple of years one might get lucky enough to run into Margaret Walker.[9]

Burroughs and Brooks had been life-long friends. According to Brooks, she met her husband, Henry Blakely, through Margaret Burroughs. But this friendship was marred by an accusation of plagiarism when Burroughs published the poem, in 1968, "What Shall I Tell My Children Who Are Black?" which begins:

> What shall I tell my children who are black?
> Of what it means to be a captive in this skin?
> What shall I tell my dear one fruit of this dark womb
> When everywhere they turn, they are filled with
> Abhorrence of black.
> (Cited in Strong, "Margaret Taylor Goss Burroughs," 161)

Burroughs felt the title and theme had arisen so naturally that it might have been derived from a poem she had encountered elsewhere. She phoned Brooks and asked her if she had written a poem by that title. "Mrs. Brooks immediately assured her that she did not and had never used such a title nor would she."[10] According to Burroughs, this was the beginning of a serious breakdown in their relationship: "unfortunately, after the work had been presented publicly and had gained fame, her friend [Brooks] called and accused Mrs. Burroughs of stealing the title from her."[11] Perhaps the discrepancy was related to a line from one of Brooks's more famous sonnets, "What Shall I Give My Children?" which opens with the line: "What shall I give my children who are poor?" Whatever the case, "What Shall I Tell My Children Who Are Black" was later published with a parenthetical epigraph, "(With apologies to Gwendolyn Brooks)." The tension from this dispute manifested itself in the Chicago arts community in subtle and undoubtedly painful ways, as reflected in Margaret Danner's accounts of encounters between Danner and Brooks and between Brooks and Burroughs at the party for Langston Hughes.

At the Du Sable Museum, Burroughs functioned both as curator and publisher. She would send out subscription forms for proposed book projects. With the subscriptions she received, she would finance the publication of the books. Impressed by Burroughs's ingenuity and tenacity, Randall enlisted her as his co-editor for *For Malcolm X*. Subsequent to the appearance of this work, which includes Burroughs's "Brother Freedom," poetry by Burroughs began to appear in noted anthologies, including that of the Detroit native Woodie King, *The Forerunners: Black Poets in America* (1975).

Although situated squarely on the political left, Burroughs was also capable of cutting across political lines. To some extent, the poems in *For Malcolm* displayed these ambivalent ideological stances, including the poem by Danner. While Burroughs supported and interacted with the more nationalist tendencies of the movement, she also organized the delegation of black artists that visited the Soviet Union in 1966. Moreover, the inclusion of a poem by the African American Russian poet James Patterson in *For Malcolm* represented the internationalist politics of Burroughs and Randall.

Similarly, Randall was quite capable of working with black leftists or black nationalists, and in his unique way he resolved the need to attend to nationalist issues while maintaining an appreciation of folk culture and class-consciousness. But these resolutions are more readily observed in his poetry and in his working relationships than in any espousals or articulated doctrine. Resistance to ideological restraints provided the philosophical freedom he needed to configure his own politics. Moreover, the debate about race and class was common discussion during the labor movement of the 1930s, a period that influenced the creative perspectives of Randall, Hayden, Burroughs, Brooks, and Walker, as well as other writers of that time.

Because Burroughs's institutions were so critical to the developing arts community, she maintained contact with Danner and Brooks, no matter how strained the encounters became. A similar bittersweet ambiguity registered with Burroughs's publishing efforts, for most of her poetry remained in manuscript form in her private collection: "Some had been published, some written for special presentations, then filed away. The creations located at this site alone filled six file containers."[12]

GWENDOLYN BROOKS AND BROADSIDE PRESS

Gwendolyn Brooks Blakely and Margaret Burroughs were both Chicagoans, and to a large extent they were emblematic of black artistic accomplishment. Like Burroughs, Brooks hosted writers and intellectuals in her home:

As for my husband and myself, our own best parties were given at East 623 Street, our most exciting kitchenette. 623 was right on the corner, the corner of 63rd and Champlain, above a real estate agency. If you wanted a poem, you had only to look out of a window. There was material always, walking or running, fighting or screaming or singing."[13]

We squeezed perhaps a hundred people into our Langston Hughes two-room kitchenette party. Langston was the merriest and the most colloquial of them all. "Best party I've ever been given!" He enjoyed everyone; he enjoyed all the talk, all the phonograph blues, all the festivity in the crowded air. And—I remember him dropping in unexpectedly some years later. His dignified presence decorated our droll little quarters. We asked him to share our dinner of mustard greens, ham hocks and candied sweet potatoes, and he accepted. "Just what I want!" exclaimed the noble poet, the efficient essayist, the adventurous dramatist."[14]

When the Black Arts Movement began to take everyone's attention, Brooks embraced the dramatic shift and the liberating possibilities of the movement:

I—who have "gone the gamut" from an almost angry rejection of my dark skin by some of my brainwashed brothers and sisters to a surprised queen-hood in the new black sun—am qualified to enter at least the kindergarten of new consciousness now. New consciousness and trudge-toward-progress.

I have hopes for myself.[15]

Because of her involvement with Broadside, she and Dudley became good friends:

**1974-75
BROADSIDE PRESS CATALOGUE**

23. Some Broadside Press books.

I first met Gwendolyn Brooks in 1966. I had long read and admired her poetry. I had read about her in *Negro Digest* where Hoyt Fuller referred to her as a shy and retiring lady. When the Metropolitan Detroit English Club invited her to read at Oakland University, I inquired whether they planned to have any one meet her, or to entertain her. When I learned there were no such plans, I asked several English teachers to pick her up at the train station, and arranged for her to appear at [Ed] Vaughn's Book Store and afterward to meet a small group at my home. Harold Lawrence [Kofi Wangara] and Joyce Whitsitt [Malaika Wangara] met and drove her first to Joyce's home and then to the college. At the luncheon she read "Negro Hero," which was a daring poem for those days. At the conclusion of Gwen's reading I went forward to meet her, uncertain how this shy lady would greet me. To my surprise, she held out her hand, smiled, and said, "You're Dudley Randall. I thought you were terrible, but you're all right." Later she told me that from reading my book reviews in *Negro Digest*, she had thought I was fierce, but my "pleasant expression and mild manner" had seemed to say otherwise. I regarded my reviews as mild, but because I used simple declarative sentences they perhaps had seemed forthright.

We took her to Vaughn's Book Store, but instead of reading her own poems she said (of a poet present), "this young man has said something very interesting. Instead of reading my poems I'd like to listen to what he has to say."

Her modesty was further shown at my house after dinner, where instead of making herself the center of attraction she sat quietly by the fireplace like Cinderella, while the other guests pontificated on the state of the world. We took snapshots, and in a moment of ebullience, she threw her arms around my shoulders and those of Joyce Whitsitt.

When I started the Broadside Series and asked her for a poem, she said,

"You can use any poem I have." We used her poem "We Real Cool" in our first group of Broadsides. After the assassination of Martin Luther King, she told me she was doing a little book and wished to donate it to Broadside Press. Titled *Riot*, it was published in 1969. All proceeds from the book went to Broadside. It was followed by *Family Pictures*, and *Aloneness*, a children's book.[16]

Regarding the need to sign "major" writers, Gwendolyn Brooks has demonstrated how that is done. She simply decided to leave Harper, although they had been fair to her, because she saw the need to help a Black publisher. I remonstrated with her, warned her that she'd lose money, told her that Broadside Press could give her neither the advances nor the pro-

motion that Harper could, but she insisted on giving a major work, her autobiography, *Report From Part One*, to Broadside Press. When I saw that
she was determined, and that if Broadside Press didn't take the book she
would give it to another Black publisher, I gratefully accepted it.[17]

Randall appealed to Brooks to help him edit the poetry selections for his
first solo publication, *Cities Burning*. In a letter to poet James A. Emanuel,
Randall explained the need "to whittle down to 16 pages," and that "Gwen
Brooks (bless her) is tearing the poems apart, and she'll help to throw out the
weak ones."[18] When Randall published *Cities Burning*, Brooks gave a book
signing party for him at her Chicago home where he also presented her with
her broadside "We Real Cool":

> I met all the Chicago brains—Lerone Bennett; Sterling Stuckey; Ellis,
> who runs a Negro bookstore; a young sociologist from the U of Chicago.
> Hoyt Fuller, whom I knew in college, and the novelist Ronald Fair whom
> I met at Margaret Burroughs', were also there. I met her husband, Henry
> Blakely, a witty and charming host, and her fifteen-year-old daughter
> Nora. Nora was shy and embarrassed. She said, "Are you really DUDLEY
> RANDALL?" And I was embarrassed too, at anyone thinking that Dudley
> Randall was anybody. We were both tongue-tied. Anyway, the brains
> talked about some article in the New York Times, which I hadn't read,
> and all I could do was listen. Gwen Brooks is a charming hostess, a real,
> nice person.
>
> I was surprised that anyone would be in doubt about the line "We jazz
> June." But I guess I shouldn't be. When I picked up the original broadside
> from the artist (which incidentally I presented to Gwen), her minister was
> there & she said he didn't understand what "jazz" meant. From the first I
> thought of it as the salacious term "screw." Even school children get it &
> giggle. The other interpretation is interesting though, & I'm sure that Gwen
> would be interested in hearing it. It shows the richness of poetry.[19]

These gatherings became characteristic, as Brooks hosted most of the
Broadside poets whenever they were in her city. The press also published two
poetry anthologies edited by Brooks, *Jump Bad* (1971), which promoted the
young Chicago writers, and *Broadside Treasury* (1971), which contained selected works by Broadside authors only. Brooks often forwarded manuscripts for Randall to consider, and he often consulted her with editorial
concerns. She worked diligently as an advocate of the younger writers, giving
book parties and writing generous introductions.

Brooks became the queen of the Chicago poets. But even at her most generous, Randall recalled how disagreements and differences emerged:

At a meeting of her Workshop of militant young writers, Gwen read a statement setting forth what she would and would not believe. Don stood up and said, "I believe I don't belong here." And left the house. After two or three meetings, he quietly returned. (And Gwen, on the other hand, realized that much of her former conviction had been mistaken.)[20]

Brooks's artist to activist shift was a major statement to the literary world, which now had to consider black cultural power a factor when negotiating and determining which writers and which literature would be credited, and her association with Broadside distinguished its position as a new literary power broker. Brooks not only changed her publisher, she also changed her vocabulary. Under the influence of the younger writers, she began writing in a style more in sync with a black-consciousness audience. As an institution builder, she gave her reputation, her poetry, her skill, and her home in the service of the cultural struggle. The epigraph for the poem, "The Sermon on the Warpland," reiterates her stance with a quote from Ron Karenga: "The fact that we are black is our ultimate reality" (in Randall, ed., *The Black Poets*, 170) Her more conventional sonnets, intricate metaphors, and subtle understatements were abandoned for free verse conversions bursting with proud, bold words advocating change:

> Build with lithe love. With love like lion-eyes.
> With love like morning rise.
> With love like black, our black—
> luminously indiscreet;
> complete; continuous.
>
> (In Randall, ed., *The Black Poets*, 170)

MARGARET WALKER

After graduating from Northwestern University (B.A., 1935), Margaret Walker Alexander became active in politically conscious writing circles in Chicago. As critic Jerry Ward Jr. explains: "In the years between 1936 and 1939, she benefited from her friendships with the novelists Nelson Algren and Frank Yerby, poets Arna Bontemps and Frank Marshall Davis, the artist Margaret Taylor Goss Burroughs and the playwright Theodore Ward."[21] However, the foremost contemporary influence on Walker's writing was Richard Wright. Walker relayed her frustration as an isolated, struggling writer to Langston Hughes, who then introduced her to Wright: "I tried to press my manuscripts on Langston, but when I admitted I had no copies he would not take them. Instead, he turned to Wright, who was standing nearby, listening to the conversation and smiling at my desperation. Langston said, 'If you people really get a group together, don't forget to include this girl.'"[22] A few months later, Wright formed the Southside Writers Project in the spring of 1936. According to critic Jerry Ward Jr., "It was under Wright's influence that Walker made the decision to be a writer for the people."[23] It was during this period that Walker began work on what would become the novel *Jubilee*: "I felt hopeless about my novel manuscript which became *Jubilee* and of which I had 300 pages in first draft written at that time. We [Wright and Walker] both decided I should put it away until another time."[24]

In 1939, her experience with the Federal Writers Project was terminated and she enrolled in the Writers' Workshop at the University of Iowa. The poetry that was the text for her master's degree, *For My People*, received the Yale University Younger Poets Award in 1942, and she became a noted poet of national and international fame. However, in 1943 she married and returned to the South to teach and raise a family. It was not until 1966, with the publication of *Jubilee* (Houghton-Mifflin), that Walker was returned to the forefront of black literature. This was the same year of the Fisk Writers' Conference, where she encountered Danner, Burroughs, Brooks, and Randall. Because Walker's home was in Mississippi, her social interactions with writers in other parts of the country were limited. To some extent, this removed her from the sharp, competitive edges of interpersonal politics in the North, but it also reconfirmed the rich resources of black southern life for her poetry. In his essay about the writers of the 1930s, 1940s, and 1950s, Randall comments on Walker's particular contribution to African American literature through her innovative poetics and subjects derived from folk culture:

> In her only volume of poetry, *For My People*, published in 1942 in the Yale University Series of Younger Poets, there are ballads or rural southern folktales of the witch Molly Means, of "Bad-man Stagolee" and "Big John Henry." The most famous of these is the title poem, "For My People." This poem gains its force not by tropes—turns of language or thought— or logical development of a theme, but by the sheer overpowering accumulation of a mass of details delivered in rhythmical parallel phrases. "We Have Been Believers" is another powerful poem in a similar form and on a racial theme.[25]

"For My People," with its terse imagery, riveting, rhythmical phrasing, and thematic embrace of the black masses, anticipated the aesthetics of the Black Arts Movement. Although a mainstream New York press published her novel, the poetry movement was happening in the black community. In addition to the broadsides, two books, *Prophets for a New Day* (1970) and *October Journey* (1973), constituted major contributions to Randall's Broadside Press. These works reiterated the significance of mature poets such as Walker, whose breadth and depth illustrated the substance and consistency of a literary legacy that undergirded the cultural revolution. With uncanny skill, Walker's powerful civil rights poems, such as "For Andy Goodman—Michael Schwerner—and James Chaney (Three Civil Rights Workers Murdered in Mississippi on June 21, 1964)," exalted this historic moment in the freedom struggle and provided aesthetic direction for aspiring poets:

> Three faces turn their ears and eyes
> sensitive
> intense
> impassive
> to see the solemn sky of summer
> to hear the brooding cry
> of the mourning dove
>
> Mississippi bird of sorrow
> O mourning bird of death
> Sing their sorrow
> Mourn their pain
> And teach us death,
> To love and live with them again!
>
> (In Randall, ed., *The Black Poets*, 160)

Other poems, such as "Street Demonstration" and "Girl Held Without Bail," focused on the activities of the Civil Rights Movement in Mississippi and the South. "Prophets for a New Day" and "Malcolm X" illuminated the radical shift in political thought and action as the Black Liberation Movement took hold in the North.

The Broadside Press publications by Margaret Walker were another display of Randall's deliberate effort to build a strong and complex identity for the press. At the same time, as she reported to critic Maryemma Graham, Walker appreciated Randall's publishing industry because Broadside brought her poetry back into print, twenty-six years since the appearance of

For My People in 1942. As an institution builder, Walker made a lasting impression on the establishment of the Institute for the Study of the History, Life, and Culture of Black People at Jackson State University (renamed the Margaret Walker Alexander National Research Center). In 1973, she organized the Phillis Wheatley Festival, which was a provocative pronouncement in support of an eighteenth-century poet whose poetry came under fire by many of the younger, more militant poets and critics.

THE LEGACY

The leftist politics of the 1930s and 1940s and the Civil Rights Movement of the 1950s and 1960s directly or indirectly influenced Robert Hayden, Margaret Danner, Margaret Burroughs, Gwendolyn Brooks, and Margaret Walker. The interconnectedness of the decades was personified by the interactions and activities of Langston Hughes (1902–1967), whose career spanned the Harlem Renaissance of the 1920s and the Black Arts Movement of the late 1960s. Hughes was a symbol of affirmation for the Second Renaissance as he published with Randall's Broadside Press and collected the poetry of the upcoming era in *New Negro Poets: USA* (1964). Likewise, a sense of cultural community was first nurtured in house parties, where personalities mingled and cultural thought flourished. Institutions conceived in these settings captured the enthusiasm of poets who laid the foundation for successful cultural enterprises that followed.

Randall's sense of independence reflected a progressive consciousness that preceded the dogma of the Black Arts Movement. Although he and his contemporaries advocated a strong sense of community responsibility, their various cultural activities benefited them individually and collectively. As writers, editors, and directors, they made significant contributions to an explosive cultural movement that enhanced their visibility and broadened their audiences. Although the green-eyed monster found much fodder in the competitive field of contentious personalities and ideological warfare, to some extent this internal adversity was constrained by their collective interest in artistic and cultural progress. *For Malcolm* was inspired by Walker's poem, edited by Burroughs and Randall, and contained the poetry of Hayden, Danner, Burroughs, and Walker. This book was emblematic of a new era of synergism emanating from a divided camp.

12

THE NEW BLACK POETS

I have not locked myself in any rigid ideology in managing Broadside Press, but I suppose certain inclinations or directions appear in my actual activities. As clearly as I can see by looking at myself (which is not very clearly, because of the closeness) I restrict the publications to poetry (which I think I understand and can judge not too badly). . . . I reserved the press for black poets (except in *For Malcolm*), as I think the vigor and beauty of our black poets should be better known and should have an outlet. I try to publish a wide variety of poetry, including all viewpoints and styles (viewpoints as opposed as Marvin X's and Beatrice Murphy's, styles as diverse as James Emanuel's and Don L. Lee's). I deplore incestuous little cliques where poets of a narrow school or ideology band together, cry themselves up, and deride all others. I believe that in the house of poetry there are many mansions, and that we can enjoy different poets for the variety and uniqueness of their poetry, not because they are all of a sameness.[1]

Just as Dudley Randall's quiet and unassuming manner accommodated the zeal of the new black voices, his nonpartisan editorial style facilitated the individuality of their work. From production to public appearance, *For Malcolm* became a vortex for many of the new poets, and Broadside Press, in turn, became the most productive publisher of Black Arts poetry. Don L. Lee (Haki Madhubuti), Etheridge Knight, Sonia Sanchez, Nikki Giovanni, James A. Emanuel, and James Randall were some of the first to benefit from Dudley Randall's cultural venture. For the most part, the circumstances that directed their poetry to Broadside illustrated their collective condition as well as the spirit of the times.

THE POPULAR POETS

Don L. Lee and Nikki Giovanni were the two most popular poets of Broadside Press. They were also two of the most ambitious. During a visit to Chicago to meet with his co-editor Margaret Burroughs after the first shipment of *For Malcolm*, Randall met Don L. Lee (Haki Madhubuti), who was an intern curator at Burroughs's Du Sable Museum of African American History. Lee showed Randall a copy of a self-published collection of poems, *Think Black*, and explained that he sold a printing of seven hundred in one week by simply peddling them on street corners on Chicago's Southside:

> His style was unformed, varying between rimed verse and free verse. I commented on his poems, and he asked me to publish his second book, *Black Pride*, and to write an introduction. I told him that his second book showed a distinct advance over his first one, and Don replaced the preface of his first book, took out some poems and added new ones, and asked me to publish it too. Initially there were no contracts. We shook hands and spit over our shoulders. . . .[2]
>
> Every time Don came to Detroit he would stop at my house and help me to ship books in my upstairs bedroom. All agreements we made were verbal. "Brother, you do this, and I'll do that." Then we would shake hands and observe all commitments scrupulously. It was only with later poets that I had to have written contracts. Once Random House offered to distribute Don's books, but Don refused emphatically, although he had no signed contract with Broadside.

Don L. Lee's *Black Pride* (1968) followed the publication of *Poem Counterpoem* and *For Malcolm*.[3] In a letter to Etheridge Knight, who was writing a review of the upcoming book, Randall relayed Lee's exuberance and impatience: "Don was in such a hurry to get his book out that he didn't send me the galleys until his book was at the printer's, and I suppose you noticed numerous errors."[4] Lee's capacity to adapt street imagery and language into riveting, rhythmic poems quickly identified his distinct style. In many ways, poems such as "Re-Act for Action," which thematically indicts black people who submit to oppressive circumstances and the status quo, were favorably received because the tone reiterated the confrontational militancy of the times:

> re-act to yr/self:
>> or are u too busy tryen to be cool
>> like tony curtis & twiggy?
> re-act to whi-te actors:
>>> understand their actions:
>>> faggot actions & actions against yr/dreams
> re-act to yr/brothers & sisters:
>>> love.
> re-act to whi-te actions:
>>> with real acts of blk/action.
>>> BAM BAM BAM
>> (Lee, *Think Black*, 16)

In the introduction to Lee's third book, *Don't Cry, Scream* (1969), Gwendolyn Brooks promotes his style and states that:

> Don Lee knows that nothing human is elegant. He is not interested in modes of writing that aspire to elegance. He is well acquainted with "elegant" literature (what hasn't he read?) but, while certainly respecting the advantages and influence of good workmanship, he is not interested in supplying the needs of the English Departments at Harvard and Oxford nor the editors of *Partisan Review*, although he could mightily serve as fact factory for these. He speaks to blacks hungry for what they themselves refer to as "*real* poetry." These blacks find themselves and the stuff of their existence in his healthy, lithe, lusty reaches of free verse. The last thing these people crave is elegance. It is very hard to enchant, with elegant song, the ears of a fellow whose stomach is growling. He can't hear you. The more interesting noise is too loud.

As his popularity soared, Lee read his poetry on college campuses and at political conferences. When he read his poetry at Western Michigan University in the spring of 1970, students crowded into an auditorium that rarely showcased black speakers or writers. The audience was amazed at his spitfire, confrontational style and taken aback by the way he chastised higher education as cultural brainwashing. Between poems, he exclaimed that the students were being processed into want-to-be white people, an accusation that echoed the charges of H. Rap Brown, who had addressed the black students in a similar voice and manner on the eve of King's assassination. The general sentiment of Lee and Brown was that the real education and revolution was in "the streets" and not in the confines of the ivory tower. It felt like someone had been playing the dozens behind your back, and now the word was out.

Lee's *We Walk the Way of the New World* appeared in 1970; in 1971, the Pulitzer Prize–winning poet Gwendolyn Brooks exclaimed in the introduction to *Jump Bad: A New Chicago Anthology* (Broadside Press) that Don Lee "is now the most significant, inventive, and influential black poet in this country." By virtue of enthusiastic backing from Brooks, the publishing resources accorded him from Randall's Broadside Press, and the visibility of his poetry and reviews in Hoyt Fuller's *Negro Digest*, Lee's career catapulted him to center stage on the black literary scene. Though he did not have a bachelor's degree, he secured visiting lectureships as black studies programs emerged on campuses at various universities, including the position of writer-in-residence at Cornell University. He became a close associate of LeRoi Jones, who assumed a new persona as Imamu Amiri Baraka, and Lee served on the executive council of the Congress of African People, a political organization headed by Baraka. Similarly, in 1974, *The Book of Life* appeared with Lee's African name, Haki R. Madhubuti (Justice Awakening Strong).

Although Brooks proclaimed Lee the "most influential of the new poets," Nikki Giovanni was undoubtedly the most popular of the new poets. An article in *Encore Magazine* deemed her "the princess of black poetry," and this declaration was repeated time and again in the media and in the community. Randall's initial encounter with Nikki Giovanni was similar to his first meeting with Lee, but their first contact occurred when she reviewed *For Malcolm* for a Cincinnati newspaper. She was a graduate of Fisk University and Randall remembered seeing her at the Fisk University Writers Conference in 1966. While living in New York, she self-published *Black Feeling Black Talk* and *Black Judgment* and edited *Night Comes Softly: Black Female Voices*, which she hauled in a wagon from bookstore to bookstore. "Nikki writes rapidly, and sometimes carelessly. If you point out bad spelling and grammar to her, she'll say defensively, 'Let it stay.'" She wrote a letter and submitted her first works to Broadside for republication:

> The first printing of *Black Feeling, Black Talk* disappeared quickly. I have been looking for a first printing of the little green book, but even Nikki doesn't have a copy. She included a poem to me called "For Dudley Randle." I told Nikki she didn't write the poem for me, because my name was Randall. When she asked Broadside to distribute the book, I told her she'd have to spell my name correctly in the new printing, and she did.[5]

Giovanni was the first to benefit from Broadside on a large scale. Her poetry became popular because it was daring and dramatic. The philosophy of "passive resistance" was ironically undermined by the assassination of Martin Luther King, and angry responses from a frustrated generation informed verbal violence and the formation of organizations devoted to self-defense. As Randall noted, many of Giovanni's poems "were touchstones in the turbulent 1960's," in particular, "The True Import of Current Dialogue: Black vs. Negro," which calls for a violent response to racism:

> Can you kill huh? Nigger
> Can you kill?
> Can you run down a protestant with your
> '68 El Dorado
> (that's all they're good for anyway)
> Can you kill
> Can you piss on a blond head
> Can you cut it off
> Can you kill
>
> (In Randall, ed. *The Black Poets*, 318–19)

But in his *Memoirs*, Randall focuses on Giovanni's gentler attributes:

> While some poets raised angry and individualistic voices against Negroes, Greek letter organizations, and older people, Nikki thought there were strengths in tradition, organization, and experience, and joined Delta Sigma Theta, the National Council of Negro Women, and praised older people in her poetry. She has gone through many changes and probably will go through many more, meantime enriching Black poetry.[6]

Giovanni's "Nikki-Rosa," a poem that has been quoted and anthologized often, voices this tenderness:

> I really hope no white person ever has cause to
> write about me because they never understand Black love
> is Black wealth and they'll probably talk about my hard
> childhood and never understand that all the while I was
> quite happy
>
> (Giovanni, *Black Feeling, Black Talk*, 16)

Giovanni cleverly marketed her work on the gospel albums "Truth Will Find Its Way" and "Like A Ripple on a Pond." These recordings were immensely successful and surpassed Lee's recordings, *Rappin' and Readin'* and *Tough Poems for Tough People*. She reached a mass audience and in a short time became the most famous of the younger poets. Her albums were played on stereos in homes and on college campuses. Wrapped in the familiarity of black church music, her poetry delivered a critical message within the comforting sounds of renewal. Lines from "Ego Tripping" became a part of everyday conversation because the poetry instigated a strong sense of race pride and a "bodacious" attitude about blackness:

> I was born in the congo
> I walked to the fertile crescent and built
> the sphinx
> I designed a pyramid so tough that a star
> that only glows every one hundred years falls
> into the center giving divine perfect light
> I am bad

> (Giovanni, *Re:creation*, 37)

Giovanni's popularity contributed to Broadside's visibility, and her three chapbooks, *Black Judgment, Black Feeling, Black Talk*, and *Re:Creation*, were very profitable. At the same time, she parlayed this popularity to her own benefit and signed a book contract with Morrow, the New York publisher, in 1970. *Black Feeling, Black Talk/Black Judgement* appeared the same year that she published *Re:Creation* with Broadside. Randall supported a poet's right to choose where to publish his or her poetry whenever the opportunity surfaced, and he did not advocate literary segregation, a position that Robert Hayden also espoused. Randall related this opinion about black writers and publishing to Etheridge Knight when Donald Hall, a white poet and editor, asked for permission to publish some of Knight's poems:

> I suppose I'd better tell you that Hall wrote to LeRoi Jones asking for poems, and one Larry Miller wrote back, "Our answer is NO." My own feeling is that I believe my poems are good enough to go anywhere they can go. I've never believed in segregated anthologies anyway, although I've been constrained to be in them. I sent poems to Jones' anthology *Black Fire*, and they were not accepted. Now when somebody else wants my poems, I'm not going to refuse them just because Jones said NO. But make up your own mind.[7]

ETHERIDGE KNIGHT AND SONIA SANCHEZ

When the Black Arts Movement began, Etheridge Knight was in an Indiana state prison reciting poetry in the form of toasts for his fellow inmates. After attempts at transforming his oral renditions onto the page, he initiated correspondence with Brooks and Randall, and when Knight submitted poems for consideration in the *For Malcolm* anthology, Randall replied:

> Thanks for your poems for the Malcolm anthology. I'm going to Chicago this weekend to make final selections with Mrs. Burroughs, and I'm sure that you will be included. I'd like to use some lines from "For Malcolm, A Year After" in a folder describing the book. In line 4 of your poem you wrote "damn." Do you mean dam?[8]

Randall's investment in Knight's poetry resulted in several trips to the Indiana State Prison. Of all the Broadside poets, Knight benefited most from Randall's editorial guidance, and Knight eagerly responded to Randall's incisive directions. His correspondence with Knight was frequent and consistent, covering a range of topics from writer's block to poetics:

> Don't worry about your seeming barrenness. One always comes back, and often even more strongly. Perhaps the subconscious is all the while working on something. And everyone needs some time to lie fallow and be enriched again—like a field. [9]
>
> I hesitated about returning the poems, but finally decided you wanted me to level with you. You are capable of writing better poems. Don't forget your grandmother's terms. That's a rich heritage, and can be very effective if used in the right place. [10]
>
> Well, getting sleepy. Messed up some typing I had to do. Things here are a mess. Desk overflowing with mail, some containing checks not taken out, orders not filled. It's getting too much for one man. Looked for a letter from University of Michigan asking for book list for class I'll teach in January. Can't find it. A mess. [11]

About Randall's impact on his writing and the significance of Broadside to his career, Knight said:

> I already had an audience in the prisons, but I wanted to extend my voice over the walls. . . . He oriented me towards the page more; I was more oral, oriented more towards the audience and would depend on the audience to

fill in what I would leave out. When you write a poem for an unseen audience, you can't assume they are going to fill in what you've left out. He taught me the formal aspects of the craft. If anybody reads my poetry and reads Dudley's and Gwen's [Brooks], it's clear they are my major influences. It's almost plagiarism to some point, I knew they were the best out there. Robert Bly made a statement once: "Minor poets imitate. Major poets steal outright." I think I picked the best. [12]

While serving in the U.S. Army during the Korean War, Knight was wounded and became addicted to morphine while recovering in the infirmary. His return to America was a familiar and sordid tale of an addict robbing to support his habit. But in prison he acquired a reputation as a toaster, sharing his poetry with other inmates for entertainment. Voracious reading and attempts to translate his oral poetry into written works ultimately paid off, and to a large extent, transformed his future.

The appearance of Knight's poetry in *For Malcolm* attracted attention from other poets and editors. In contrast to Lee and Giovanni, who approached Randall about publication, Randall recruited Knight to Broadside: "Your poems seem to be making quite an impression. I liked your Langston [Hughes] poem. Could you get a batch of poems together? I'd like to see them."[13] After Randall read the collection, he expressed his enthusiasm and explained the details of the publishing process, from manuscript to print:

Your book is great! Even if I have to beg, borrow, or steal the money to publish it! . . . After studying the poems some more, I'll send you the titles of my selections, plus suggestions for revision. There'll be time for making every poem perfect.[14]

I'm not a big publisher. I started by publishing broadsides. Even now I can't publish full-sized books. What I planned was 16-page paperback pamphlets, but you fecund poets keep on sending me more good poems.

I'd like to start cautiously with a small edition, 500, and see how it goes. If it sells out, we can reprint it. It should be priced so the brothers can afford it—$1.00. You'll get royalties of 10% of the list price; I'm afraid you won't get rich. Copyright will be in your name. All reprint rights will be yours. . . . What do you want to call the book? I've thought of Poems from Prison, slightly changing a phrase of yours. What's your idea?

Don Lee's book comes out in January. Three months will be time enough to work on that, so yours can come out in April. There are some changes in grammar & spelling I'd like you to consider.[15]

24. Etheridge Knight, ca. 1970.

Randall consulted with Gwendolyn Brooks for her critique of Knight's manuscript and arranged for Knight to write a review of Lee's book for *Negro Digest*:

> Hoyt Fuller has given the go-ahead to your reviewing Don's book. Feel free to say whatever you like, either pro or con. I think the book is such as to evoke a definite response from you, so read it, feel it, think about it, and write what you feel and think.
>
> Good luck with your hearing. I showed some of your poems to Gwendolyn Brooks, and she said she was happy, because reading good poetry made her feel that way. I asked her about various revisions, but she said

your poetry was such that one could sit back and relax, knowing the poet knew what he was doing. So there won't be so many revisions after all.[16]

In the spring of 1968, *Poems from Prison* appeared with an introduction by Brooks, and by the end of November Knight was released from prison. Just as his talent caught the attention of Gwendolyn Brooks and Dudley Randall, Knight's originality and amazing blues rhythms captured the imagination of the reading public. His imagery, uniquely rooted in painful personal awareness, is also steeped in black cultural thought and folk wisdom. While other poets wrote about "the streets" for the "man in the streets," Knight was a product of the "streets." In contrast to many other poets, Randall observed that Knight "does not pose as self-righteous, but admits his vulnerability like ours, and his poems about black prisoners and himself are powerful and moving."[17] Hence, his poetry attracted a complex and racially diverse audience, appearing in *Black World* and *American Poetry Review*. "The Idea of Ancestry," first published in *Poems from Prison*, one of his most often anthologized poems, exhibits his uniqueness and the nuances of literary genius:

> Each fall the graves of my grandfathers call me, the brown
> hills and red gullies of Mississippi send out their electric
> messages, galvanizing my genes. Last yr / like a salmon quitting
> the cold ocean-leaping and bucking up his birthstream / I
> hitchhiked my way from L.A. with 16 caps in my pocket and a
> monkey on my back. And I almost kicked it with the kin folks
>
> (Knight, *Poems from Prison*, 13)

As with Giovanni, Randall not only published Knight's work, but also supported his second book with another publisher:

> After a publisher has invested in an author's first book, he feels he should have first chance on his second, with whatever fame or skill he's gained from the first. I, alone, am the exception. After I've published your first book, you're free to fly upward and onward, and God bless you, man. [18]

Randall secured a translator so Knight could understand the contractual terms of the Italian publisher of the collection, *Black Voices From Prison* (1968), which included Knight's essays, short stories, and poetry, as well as works by some of Knight's fellow inmates. Shortly thereafter, in 1970, Pathfinder Press published *Black Voices From Prison* in its original English with an introduction by Roberto Giammanco, who was responsible for the

Italian edition of Knight's work and the Italian translations of the writings of Malcolm X.[19]

Knight's courtship of Sonia Sanchez began when she wrote him about his poetry. When Sanchez's mail was returned because her name was not on Knight's approved list, Randall forwarded her letters and a parcel of books to Knight, and then encouraged romantic intrigue with the possibility of Broadside publishing a book of poetry by Sanchez:

> I got a long distance call from Sonia tonight. Since she asked me how your voice was, I'll tell you how she sounded. Her voice was very soft, sweet, & melodious. It made one instantly feel protective, & like calling her "lil sis." She who writes so many 4-letter words used only a couple, "hell" & "shit," I think. She often used the locution of "like this," "like that." She called because there was some confusion about her book. It seems that you have had it, & now Don has, & once she told me that she wasn't going to publish it, & I asked Sarah Webster Fabio about her, & Sarah called her when she got back to California.
>
> I told her I wanted to publish it, & Don had it & was writing an introduction, & would send it to me when he finished writing it. May I pick your brains? What do you think of the book, since you've read it? Please send me Sonia's pictures for her book. I'll return them.[20]

Enjoying his role as Cupid, Randall instigated the romance as a part of poetry business:

> Talked with Sonia long distance the other night. She has a lovely, melodious, liquid voice which comes in breathless little bursts, & she uses the same language as in her letters: "like," "beautiful," "the warriors," etc. I asked if she had a message for you. She said to give you her love, but you know all that's going on, as she writes you every day. (Man, how do you do it? And she's never even seen you!).[21]

In another letter, Randall told Knight, "it's definite about the book. She says you helped her. What's happening?"[22] Correspondence concerning poetry production built a supportive network for Broadside poets and their publications. Just as Knight wrote a review for Don L. Lee's book, Lee reviewed Knight's book and wrote an introduction for Sanchez's first book. Lee's interplay with militant overtures and nationalist cultural values was characteristic of his vocabulary and of the times and a militancy that popularized his poetry: "Her ABC's were learned in alleys & corner bars; she knows what motivates her blk/sisters & she understands the hurt of the blackman." Lee continues: "She doesn't have time to indulge in meaningless poetics. She need not talk about the aesthetics of a tree; they're no trees in Harlem or on the Westside of Chicago. The use/beauty she/we see in a tree, at this time in space, is the number of rifle butts it will produce." [23]

The more established poets also interacted with these budding careers. Randall contacted the San Francisco poet Sarah Webster Fabio concerning Sanchez, and he consulted Brooks with regard to Knight. These relationships affected publishing decisions and personal entanglements. In 1969, Sanchez's first book, *Home Coming*, was published, and she and Knight announced their plans to marry. Randall queried, "What about the wedding, man. Gwendolyn wants to come, but ain't got no invite & all I have is a verbal invite. What time is it, etc.? What's a good hotel or motel in Indianapolis, & do they discriminate?"[24]

At the time, Randall described them as "one of the strongest writing teams in black poetry,"[25] but the Knight-Sanchez merger was short-lived because Knight had difficulty adjusting to life outside of prison. Though he had secured a teaching position at the University of Pittsburgh, his addiction to drugs resurfaced, and his marriage to Sanchez disintegrated. During this destructive cycle, Vivian and Dudley Randall were supportive friends encouraging a positive resolution. But as Knight's poem "Feeling Fucked/Up" portrays, he and Sanchez separated, and Knight's addiction spiraled downward even as his poetry career soared:

> Lord she's gone done left me done packed/up and split
> and i with no way to make her
> come back and everywhere the world is bare
> bright bone white crystal sand glistens
> dope death dead dying and jiving drove
> her away made her take her laughter and her smiles
> and her softness and her midnight sighs—
>
> (Knight, *Belly Song and Other Poems*, 31)

In a letter dated 9 December 1970 from the Bridgeport Correctional Center, after an arrest for possession of heroin, Knight appealed to Randall for $100 in an attempt to raise a $2,500 bond: "I got busted on my way to Hartford from New York. It's nothing serious, unless I'm unable to get out on bond." [26] But according to an article in *The Hartford Courant*, the arrest was serious enough to warrant a trial and judgment. Anthony S. Keller, executive director of the Commission on the Arts, appealed to the court on

Knight's behalf. He described Knight's prose and poetry as "the work of a pre-eminent writer." But the journalist who wrote the article derisively characterized Knight's poetry: "The works deal primarily with ghetto and prison life."[27]

Ironically, it was prison poetry that got Knight out of jail, kept him out, and helped to rehabilitate him again. The judge placed Knight on probation and in a drug rehabilitation program. Randall suggested that perhaps Knight could prepare a second book of poems while at Daytop Rehabilitation Center. Moreover, Brooks offered to finance a hardcover edition of *Poems from Prison*. Randall's suggestion was critical to Knight's writing career, and the title poem, "Belly Song," dated "June 1971, Seymour, Connecticut, dedicated to the Daytop Family," conveys intense self-study and revelation:

> This poem/is/
> a death/chant
> and a grave/stone
> and a prayer for the dead:
> for young Jackie Robinson
> a moving Blk/warrior who walked
> among us
> with a wide/ stride—and heavy heels
> moving moving moving
> thru the blood and mud and shit of Vietnam
> moving moving moving
> thru the blood and mud and dope of America
> for Jackie/ who was/
>
> a song
> and a stone
> and a Feather of feeling
> now dead
> and/ gone/ in this month of love

After Etheridge Knight's *Belly Song* appeared (1973), Randall received a letter from his classmate and a previous member of the Miles Poetry Workshop, Philip Levine:

I was recently informed that Etheridge Knight has published a new book. I believe you should inform the National Book Committee of this fact so that the book might be considered for the National Book Award. On the basis of *Poems from Prison* & other publications I've seen, I believe Mr. Knight is one of our best poets. It's true that the NBA has paid little or no attention to both small presses & Black poets, but I happen to be one of the judges this year, & I'd like to do what I can to remedy that.[28]

In the introduction to Sanchez's second book of poetry, *We a BaddDDD People* (1970), Randall alludes to Sanchez's difficult dealings with Knight and his drug addiction:

Sonia Sanchez is one of these revolutionaries. This tiny woman with the infant's face attacks the demons of this world with the fury of a sparrow defending her fledglings in the nest. She hurls obscenities at things that are obscene. She writes directly, ignoring metaphors, similes, ambiguity, and other poetic devices. But her bare passionate speech can be very effective.

Some of her poems are political, but I think the most moving are those in which she talks of man and woman, of women, and of drug addiction. It is apparent that she has suffered during the writing of this book. Her suffering has moved her to song, sometimes to inarticulate screams. [29]

In particular, the abrupt pacing and scattered spacing in "hospital/poem (for etheridge. 9/26/69)" reveals the suffering of both poets:

> they have sed
> u will die in
> this nite room
> of tubes/
>   red/death/screams.
>   how do
> they ima
>   gine death?

(In Randall, ed., *The Black Poets*, 236–37)

After the separation, Sanchez joined the Nation of Islam, and her 1971 book, *It's a New Day*, a childrens book that opens with "As-Salaam-Alaikum," is full of Islamic allusions and illustrations. Sanchez dedicated her second book of poetry, *Blues Book for Blue Black Magical Women* (1974) to her natural father, Wilson Driver, and her spiritual father, Elijah Muhammad. She quotes the Koran at the beginning of the book, and the Islamic allusions and the absence of four letter expletives in the poetry outlined a new direction in her creative vision and vocabulary.

JAMES A. EMANUEL

In contrast to the high-profile poetry of Lee, Giovanni, Knight, and Sanchez, James A. Emanuel's more sedate literary style appeared during the 1960s in periodicals and journals such as *Negro Digest*, as well as in Hughes's *New Negro Poets: U.S.A.* and Hayden's *Kaleidoscope*. Randall was unable to publish Emanuel's submission to the *Malcolm X* anthology because it arrived too late, but Randall's appreciation of Emanuel's poetry resulted in Broadside's 1968 publication of *Tree House and Other Poems*. In a letter to Emanuel, Randall shares the peculiar irony of the black writer's aesthetic politics and the interracial composition of the reading audience:

> We've discussed terms, haven't we? Royalties are 10% of list price, payable twice a year in January and July. I'm trying to develop a black market for poetry, and the paper-bound will sell for $1.00. Poets don't get rich on poetry, do they? That's why David Slavitt wrote The Exhibitionist. He said he was tired royalty checks for $2.00. But, our reading habits being what they are, the book will probably be bought by more whites than blacks. The poem "A Negro Author" will probably be attacked. But let it. It'll make people talk about the book. Possibly even buy it.[30]

Emanuel's *Tree House* is almost the antithesis of the confrontational vocabulary typically identified with the new black poets. With a Ph.D. from Columbia University and a previous military career during which he was confidential secretary to General Benjamin O. Davis, Emanuel's professional training and military experiences influenced a literary voice that is introspective, exploratory, and a source for imaginative fulfillment. One of the early Broadside Press chapbooks (1968), *Tree House and Other Poems* appeared the same year as his anthology (co-edited with Theodore L. Gross), *Dark Symphony: Negro Literature in America*, when Emanuel was an assistant professor at City College of New York. *Dark Symphony* became a major curricular contribution for the teaching of black literature. Randall's "Perspectives," "Booker T. and W. E. B.," "To the Mercy Killers," and "The Southern Road" were selected for this anthology.

Emanuel's earlier meditative poetry conveys both personal and public themes, and in many respects reflects the regimen and control of his advanced studies in literature. However, just as Emanuel eventually expatriated to live in Paris, his later poetry, influenced by blues, jazz, and asymmetrical free verse, departs from measured formal structures. Prevalent and influential, Emanuel's poetry spans the Second Renaissance and the Black

Arts Movement. Hence, his black-consciousness themes resonate stylistically between Randall's generation and Emanuel's younger contemporaries. From this unusual position, a more mature voice with vibrant undertones offers an interesting contrast to the didactic diction, the macho bravado, and the unseasoned zeal of the younger writers. From "The Treehouse":

> To every man
> His treehouse,
> A green splice in the humping years,
> Spartan with narrow cot
> And prickly door.

or from "Negritude":

> Black is waiting in the darkness;
> Black the ground where hoods have lain.
> Black is the sorrow-misted story;
> Black the brotherhood of pain.
>
> Black is a quiet iron door;
> Black the path that leads behind.
>
> (In Randall, ed., *The Black Poets*, 190)

In 1970, *Panther Man*, a second Broadside collection by Emanuel, was published, and he consented to be the editor for the newly initiated *Broadside Critics Series*. The critics series contributed support to scholarly activities in black poetry and provided publishing opportunities for Houston A. Baker, Bernard Bell, William H. Robinson, and others. These works covered subjects ranging from Phillis Wheatley to the new black aesthetic. Emanuel's work as poet and scholar is similar to the work of Dudley Randall, Sterling Brown, and other black writers, wherein the poet engages variegated roles in the institutional dynamics that affect the evolution of the literature.

JAMES A. RANDALL JR.

From the closer reaches of Randall's world, James Andrew Randall Jr., the son of Dudley Randall's oldest brother James, joined the Broadside Press roster. James Jr., who has lived in New York City since 1967, was the first black journalist at *Time* magazine. His recollections of his uncle go back as far as

World War II, when Dudley and his father returned to Detroit on an army furlough:

> I remember Uncle Dudley as a handsome, dark man in a pressed uniform going off somewhere and the adults not being very happy about it. But I was impressed with the way he looked. . . .
>
> It always seemed to me that Uncle Dudley was the typical image of a poet: rumpled and chain-smoking cigarettes. Poetry and writing seemed to consume him. I don't mean that pejoratively, but positively. Uncle Dudley was the one who was going to be the next great poet. He realized a lot of that dream.
>
> This poet image and kind of keen seriousness always struck me about Uncle Dudley. He was very, very serious about his poetry. With me, poetry was okay. It was nice to be able to write, but I could take it or leave it. But Dudley was a poet, is a poet, and every aspect of his personality was pushing in that direction. For many years he was a librarian, so were a lot of other poets and that too was a help.
>
> He was helpful to me and Jon Randall, my brother [*Indigoes*, Broadside, 1974] with our poetry. Every time I saw Uncle Dudley, the first question was "Jim, what are you writing? Show me some poetry," or worse, he'd say, "Recite some." That made me shake in my boots because I've never been the kind of poet who could stand up and exclaim a couple hundred lines of verse. So, I would be frantically digging around, trying to find something; hopefully, one of the books Uncle Dudley had been kind enough to publish for me, either *Cities and Other Disasters* or *Don't Ask Me Who I Am*.
>
> As an editor, Dudley was very easy and supportive of my poetry. I don't remember his ever desiring to change my poetry. On the other hand, Donald Hall, who was my creative writing professor at the University of Michigan, was very critical of my poetry and wouldn't write an endorsement for my book, even though I had won a Hopwood Award for it in 1960. A few years after this, Dudley came to see me and asked to publish the poetry, but I had this nagging thought that it was nepotism, and was afraid my poetry wasn't that good. However, I'm still being published. In fact, some of the Broadside poetry has been translated and published in Hebrew, Dutch and Spanish.
>
> I remember meeting Sonia Sanchez and Don L. Lee with some trepidation, wondering why Uncle Dudley was publishing my poetry because it was so different from the more popular styles of the times. One thing Uncle Dudley wanted to do was a book of poetry by members of the family; Jon, Dudley, and me. But he never did it.[31]

In the "many mansions in the house of poetry," James Randall's voice is distinct from that of his contemporaries because his carefully arranged vocabulary contrasted sophisticated and abstract allusions against the harsh, gritty reality of black life as well as other themes. At the same time, his capacity to transcend his anger distinguishes his voice. Despite the doubts that Donald Hall had about James Randall's poetry, Dudley Randall published two collections of poems derived from his nephew's award-winning Hopwood manuscript and other poems. James Randall's formal training in poetics confers a density and a similar meditative sensibility and intensity to that found in the poetry of James Emanuel and Dudley Randall:

> Somewhere in the flesh mirror
> I saw myself.
> And after the silent promise,
> I, feeling something heavier
> Than the tortured face,
> Felt the bewilderment of one
> Who has recalled his murdering.

(James A. Randall Jr., "Jew," in Dudley Randall, ed., *The Black Poets*, 278)

While the incendiary vocabulary and revolutionary bravado of the new black poets broke down cultural barriers between poetry and black folks "in the streets," the measured reflection and skillful poetics of the newly "college-educated" black poets split the yoke of caucasian literary supremacy. Collectivity, the new black poets brought an excitement that attracted a broader audience, black and white. By 1970, it was apparent that a literature that had been marginalized and nearly rendered invisible had transformed American literature. Black poetry broadsided libraries, literary discussions, and the racial boundaries of American cultural imperialism. To a large extent, "the many mansions in the house" of Broadside Press were responsible for this revolution. In 1971, when Bantam Press, a mainstream, New York house published *The Black Poets*, a seminal anthology of black poetry, Dudley Randall, who edited the volume, gave political protest and cultural liberation as the reasons for the shift from indifference to enthusiasm for black poetry:

In 1962 Rosey E. Pool published *Beyond the Blues* in England, a book which was the first comprehensive anthology of black poetry since Langston Hughes's and Arna Bontemps's *The Poetry of the Negro 1746–1949*. Because the United States would have been its greatest market, she tried to find a publisher or a jobber to distribute the book here. Everyone she queried said the book was too special and declined to handle it. Now, in 1970, after Watts and Detroit, and the Black Arts Movement, there are so many anthologies of black poetry that each editor must justify the publication of a new one. . . .

The turning away from white models and returning to their roots has freed black poets to create a new poetry. This book records their progress. They no longer imitate white models, strain toward white magazines, defer to white critics, or court white readers. They are in the process of creating a new literature. Whatever the outcome, they are taking care of business.[32]

13

DUDLEY RANDALL'S POETIC DIALECTICS
AND THE BLACK ARTS MOVEMENT

I don't know whether you would call me a full-time revolutionary poet. I write about the struggle when I am moved to write about it. My poem, "Roses and Revolutions," which I consider as prophetic, was written as long ago as 1948. But I don't consider this my whole expression. I would say, "Nothing human is alien to me," quoting the Roman African writer, Terence. I write about the whole gamut of human experience, which includes liberation. I don't believe, however, that the poet is programmatic. He may be programmatic in his outside life, but, in poetry, you cannot lay down a blueprint or a program for revolution. This is something, which requires careful planning, organization, discipline, and hard, humdrum, routine work. I don't think that poetry should bore people by preaching to them. Being a preacher's son, I've heard too many sermons. I write poetry in order to move people—to give them the emotions and the ideas, which could perhaps lead to a better life. I also believe that poetry is something which gives pleasure—something which people enjoy.[1]

In the midst of the Black Arts Movement, Dudley Randall referenced an African Roman writer, which reflects the depth of his literary knowledge of black writers throughout the ages and reiterates his creative freedom to express any theme. And in 1989, Naomi Long Madgett concurred: "Dudley doesn't write the kind of poetry he published."[2] This statement refers to some of the more popular Broadside Press poets who emerged during the

Black Arts Movement and whose poetry has come to typify that era. Randall's publishing activity brought attention and recognition to these writers, while his own poetry assumed a less prominent position. Ironically, the founding of this Detroit poetry press ensured that the rights to his poetry stayed with him and provided a venue for his first book with Margaret Danner, but the timbre of his verse was not received with the same enthusiasm as the works of others that he published.

Randall engaged this literary period (1965–1977) with poetry that complemented, countered, and satirized prevailing themes and political attitudes; in many instances, Randall's themes contradicted the rhetorical dogmatism and ideological rigidity that typified the Black Power Movement. Even when imbued with nationalist sentiments, the predilection of his Black Arts poetry maintains internationalist integrity with class consciousness and a humanist critique. Although many of the younger generation of writers obscured or misunderstood his meaning, his poetry argued for reason and challenged irrational rhetoric with insight and wit. It also appeared as if these poets were reluctant to publicly disagree with him or confront him, possibly because they relied on his press to project their poetry into prominence. As previously discussed, there were strong personal and philosophical similarities between Randall and Robert Hayden, but while Hayden was the target of Black Nationalist attacks, Randall's perspective was tolerated, especially in his hometown.[3]

Detroit is a production-oriented city. The attitude of the cultural community, whether nationalist or Marxist, was more focused on what one does rather than on what one says, which provided an ideological flexibility compatible with Randall's independence. At the time, Detroit nationalists had a sense of class consciousness because of the impact of a radicalized labor movement; likewise, Detroit Marxists incorporated race issues as a critical component within their class struggle while dealing with racism in the labor unions. But this broader dialectic did not necessarily extend to the national debate.

Hayden, who no longer lived in Detroit, may have escaped aesthetic assault if he would have sidestepped a futile and circular argument: Are you black first or a writer first? When the question was posed at the 1966 Fisk University Writers Conference, Hayden said he was a poet first. Hayden's view dismissed the nationalist attitude out of hand, while Randall responded, "I'm Black."[4] He approached this rhetorical mine field with poems that raised questions and challenged the premise of this essentialist argument. He embraced the movement and positioned himself in the middle of it. Instead of becoming a target, he became a force to be reckoned. When Randall compared the aesthetic attitudes of the preceding era with the Black Arts Movement of the 1960s, he projected literary growth and a positive outcome from this aesthetic formation by inserting his own opinions:

> There was no consciously formulated Black Aesthetic. Black poets considered themselves as part of American literature, although most of them were excluded from textbooks, anthologies, and, to a great extent, from magazines. It remains to be seen whether, in our time, the Black Aesthetic will stimulate superior poetry. The proof will have to be in the poems produced.
>
> However, I will not hedge in caution, but will be imprudent enough to weigh the historical facts, note the trends, and make a prediction.
>
> In the forties, black poets absorbed the innovations of white poets. In future years, they will not only absorb them, but will transcend them, and create their own innovations. All that I can foresee is a poetry of increasing power and richness, which will make a glorious contribution to the world.[5]

It was this patient, progressive attitude that endeared Randall to the younger poets. His enthusiasm about the possibilities for change engaged their needs and facilitated their aspirations. In an interview by *Negro Digest* in 1968, Randall appraised cultural demands and criticized the black bourgeoisie for their cultural indifference, as he identified the exuberance of the common folk:

> We're a nation of 22,000,000 and should be able to nourish a flourishing literature. As a writer and publisher, I'm concerned about this. Where do we find our audience? I advertised *For Malcolm*, which won fine reviews, through the mail to Negro dentists of Detroit, Negro colleges, and Negro poets (not in the book). From the dentists I received no response, from the 120 colleges three responses, from the black poets one response. If the rich dentists with their leisured lives, the Negro colleges with their "Negro collections," and the black poets don't buy books, where are you going to find your audience? Perhaps the answer lies in the orders I do get, often on ruled paper torn from a notebook, once on the top of a paper bag—in short, from the people, the man in the street. It's to them we should address our work, and voice their hopes and fears and dreams.[6]

But while preparing his second book, *Cities Burning* (1968), Randall confided in Etheridge Knight that he was ambivalent about self-publishing. This reticence is very telling because it reflected a desire to be endorsed by a book publisher other than himself, and, perhaps on a subliminal level, it suggested how writers internalize persistent rejection. In Randall's own words, Knight countered Randall's doubts:

> Dig, Man—about publishing your own book—That wouldn't be vain at all—and anybody who knows you wouldn't even think in that direction. Plus, you have been published enough by other people to erase any doubts as to whether you're publishable or not. On top of that, Black readers have a right to hear your songs, and you have an obligation to publish where your work will be best handled. End of lecture! Dig, why don't you send your manuscript to me and Sonia, and let us choose the ones to go in your book, and then you publish it. Okay?[7]

Indeed, by 1968, Randall's poetry had appeared in many journals and anthologies, especially in *Negro Digest*, where key political and cultural perspectives and some of the most influential debates were outlined in pages edited by Hoyt Fuller. The December 1969 issue of *Negro Digest* carried a review of Randall's *Cities Burning* by Ron Welburn. Welburn's observations reflect respect and consideration for Randall as an elder statesman, and many passages in the review praise Randall's skill and insight. But the irony and complex literary influences in Randall's poetry escaped Welburn's critical reading and the perception of many others.

Welburn concluded that "Randall has brought to this first volume a good heart, ear and eye for sensitive observation, all which enhance his lyricism. Young black poets who read him should be influenced by him to some degree, for his voice alone is infectious; more so, he is contributing something to black literature that has a lasting value." And he predicted that "black readers will respect these statements by Dudley Randall as near monuments along the way toward the liberation of black poetics." Welburn interpreted the poem "Primitives" as an attempt on Randall's part to change his style: "Try as he might, any poet endowed with a sense of music cannot easily escape it for it is a natural asset."[8]

Randall's "Primitives" cunningly approaches the literary attitude of the day using language as its metaphor and infusing this metaphor with personified verbs that speak to the inherent difficulty of this aesthetic quest. "Primitives" points out the futility of senseless destruction, and the language is not an attempt at adherence, but at mockery. The word "little" in the last line is a twist that demonstrates the volatile character and dangerous consequences of poetry crafted to exalt oppression to justify "hate deified":

Paintings with stiff
homuncules, flat in iron
draperies, with distorted
bodies against spaceless
landscapes.
Poems of old
poets in stiff
meters whose harsh
syllables
drag like
dogs with
crushed
backs.

We go back to
them, spurn difficult
grace and
symmetry,
paint tri-faced
monsters,
write lines that
do not sing, or
even croak, but that
bump,
jolt, and are hacked
off in the mid-
dle, as if by these dis-
tortions, this
magic, we can
exorcise
horror, which we
have seen and fear to
see again:
hate deified,
fears and
guilt conquering,
turning cities to
gas, powder and a
little rubble.

Randall used the pronoun "we" to include himself in this critique, which conversely encourages receptivity in his audience. But this technique had a limited effect on that audience. Moreover, the poem "recalls, in phrasing and metric, some of the lyrics in Pound's *Hugh Selwyn Mauberly*."[9] The complex influences that emerge in Randall's poetry are not recognizable via a narrow critical perspective. Similarly, Randall observed that the unlearned poetic utterances of the younger generation of poets illuminated this cultural arrogance:

> There is something ironic in it, too. By refusing to read or to study the older poets, oftentimes they unwittingly repeat the things that the older poets have already done. When you discard punctuation, for example, you are really going back to something very old because the oldest printing was done without punctuation. Words were just run together on the line, and the reader had to supply his own separations and pauses. Punctuation was invented— not because people wanted to make rules of grammar—but to make it easier to read. Many of the innovations in punctuation and division of words come from e. e. cummings. Although some young Black poets have not read cummings, they have been influenced by his unique style of writing which has been filtered down to them through secondary sources. Of course, they would be quite shocked if you told them that they were, in fact, imitating a white poet. When poets use the slash (/), for example, they may think it's new and revolutionary, but in actuality, this method was taken from white business reports that read, "He/she must do this" or, "This sum should be paid to him/her." Young Black poets adopted this method thinking that it was a "Black thang" when, in reality, it was a "white thing." . . .
>
> Recently, there was a writer's conference at the University of Wisconsin, and there were some Black students there from Yale University who were very brilliant and articulate. I said then what I am saying now, and one of them got so angry that he almost jumped out of his skin. Nevertheless, it is true that ideas filter down through secondary sources, and one may be following a white innovator and not know it.[10]

Randall made a similar observation about a poetry reading by Amer Rashid and Ahmad Malik Shabazz in a report on "The Second Annual Black Arts Convention" for *Negro Digest*: "Shabazz said a new breed of poet was coming out who went deeper than surfaces and caused the reader to go deeper. They used the art of LeRoi Jones [Baraka]—images, symbols, rhythms without rimes, line endings and split lines to suggest their meanings instead of direct presentation.[11] The point of their aesthetics was to produce poems that "exorcise/horror," as exemplified in Baraka's "Black Art": "We want 'poems that kill'" (in Randall, ed., *The Black Poets*, 223).

This aesthetic charge became the lexicon of this generation of writers and their literary identity. One of the most dramatic of these expressions was articulated in Nikki Giovanni's famous line, "Can you kill, nigger?" In a complimentary review of Randall's *Cities Burning*, Giovanni characterizes Randall's poetry as being on the "long black train of poets from Wheatley to the dudes we don't even know puffing the same ole tune . . . get off my back," and notes that "Dudley Randall, author of *Cities Burning* (Broadside, $1.00), is an important link in the total hook-up that we are needing."[12] On the surface, her comments appear to make sense, as she recognizes his criticisms of her generation, especially in the poem "Rites"; however, her conclusion misses the mark, at least in terms of Randall's feelings about cities burning: "Check it out. CITIES are BURNING and he thinks that's a good good thing. So do I."[13]

Contrary to Giovanni's conclusion, the last poem in *Cities Burning*, "Augury For An Infant (For Venita Sherron)," written upon the birth of his first grandchild, illuminates the irony in the title of the book and in Randall's literary vision. The poem and the collection are full of questions about promise and what his granddaughter's new life might bring the world. He enlisted the names of heroes and heroines of the race and ends the last poem with: "In you, babe, I see infinite possibility." Most of the poems in *Cities Burning* were composed during the 1960s, but "Roses and Revolutions," the opening poem, was written in 1948, twenty years prior to publication. He also included "Ballad of Birmingham" (also published in *Poem Counterpoem*) and "Dressed All In Pink." (Both were first printed as broadsides.) The collection ends with a poem about birth and renewal in a book published in 1968, a year of assassinations, destruction, and civic disappointment. It is also the year his sister Esther died from cancer.

Randall's "The Rite," which was first published in *Negro Digest* (September 1964), identifies regressive historical cycles as a key flaw in human experience. In the pursuit of power and fame, the son proclaims self-importance by displacing the prestige of the father. The previous generation is supplanted in a destructive manner; however, the poem explains that this action is a learned value. The poet is confronted in the opening lines with:

> "Now you must die," the young one said,
> and all your art be overthrown."
> The old one only bowed his head
> as if those words had been his own.
>
> (*Cities Burning*, 7)

The poem reveals the viciousness of this cultural attitude, which in some respects typified the aesthetic aggressiveness of many younger writers. But the poem does not attempt to mirror a particular case, such as the attack on Robert Hayden at the Fisk University Writers Conference in 1966; rather, it acts more as a catalyst for the poem's subject than as an interpretation of the confrontation. The purpose of the poem is to reach into the heart of the behavior as typically displayed to bring attention to its core meaning, as "the young man acted out his part." The ritual of sacrifice is no less savage when it occurs in cultural wars, as the new poet "drank his blood and ate his heart." As a cunning structural comment, Randall uses traditional form and terminal rhyme, a closed format with a circular structure.

Another issue during the cultural wars was what to name the people. While Don L. Lee (Haki Madhubuti) attacked Robert Hayden for referring to "us" as "Negroes" in Hayden's anthology *Kaleidoscope*,[14] in a section of "The Rite," Randall composed a sardonic response to the popular debate about naming in "An Answer to Lerone Bennett's Questionnaire On a Name for Black Americans" in 1968 that ridicules the debate:

> Discarding the Spanish word for black
> and taking the Anglo-Saxon word for Negro,
> discarding the names of English slave masters
> and taking the names of Arabian Slave-traders
> won't put a single
> bean in your belly
> or an inch of steel
> in your spine.
>
> (Collected in *More to Remember*, 67)

In this poem, the syndrome of name changes for the race is related to an identity crisis in the intellectual community. The identification of various imperialist slave traders illustrates the futility of escape from historical experience, and of an unnecessary obsession with it. He reduces the abstract distance from such thinking and material reality as a "bean in your belly" or "an inch of steel / in your spine." This leveling is further extrapolated in a satirical manner with familiar imagery drawn from Shakespeare and mingled with contemporary references in the theme: "a rose by any other name is just as sweet" is humorously inverted by Call a skunk a rose, / and he'll still stink," and then reversed with "Call a rose a skunk and it'll still smell sweet." Even more emphatically, it will "even sweeten the name."

Randall alternates vocabulary in this poem in order to mock the circular debate, and he executes this by probing into the nature and function of language as well as into its epistemology. In order to demonstrate the need to reach past this cycle and the superficial associations of labels and into the power of truth and deeds, he informs his imagery with concrete issues. Direct in imagery and matter-of-fact in tone, the ending does not leave room for excuses:

> If the white man took the name Negro
> and you took the name Caucasian,
> he'd still kick your ass,
> as long as you let him.

For the most part the poems in *Cities Burning* are free verse, which relates to the attitude of the content. Most poetry written during the Black Arts Movement was written in free verse, and for Randall, this selection of form was dictated by the themes. It was an era of freedom. The quest for new expressions and new ways of thinking required a language that broke with the forms of conventional poetics and themes that challenged cultural imperialism. Though his poems often challenged the limited vision of the younger generation, Randall was still critical of the status quo. His ultimate challenge was to push the rhetoric to substance and to transform the language into action.

"Black Poet, White Critic" faces "The Rite" on the opposite page like a counterpoem. Whereas "The Rite" criticizes the overthrow of tradition, "Black Poet, White Critic," which was first published in *Negro Digest* (September 1965), pokes fun at the imposition of tradition. This poem relays the cultural conflict between a colonized culture in the face of oppressive literary values. The simplicity of the poem affirms the profundity of the rhetorical response in the last line of the one line stanza: "A white unicorn?" The bold-face black print of the word "white" emphasizes and contradicts simultaneously. The poem outlines the limitations of traditional Western literature by focusing on key areas of concern for black writers, for example, "freedom," and "murder." This poem articulates Randall's ridicule of critical censorship. It is also the frontispiece for the section in the seminal anthology *The Black Poets* (Bantam, 1971), which Randall edited.

On a related topic, Randall published an essay whose title was the poem's inverse: "White Poet, Black Critic." It is an essay about cultural identity and poetic expression that discusses the interactions between Robert Frost, William Stanley Braithwaite, and Claude McKay: "He [Braithwaite] advised McKay, because of the overwhelming prejudice against anything Negro, to write and send to the magazine only such poems as did not reveal his race."[15] Meanwhile, Braithwaite engaged Frost and suffered insult and literary injury. "Thus in spite of Braithwaite's fostering of American poetry, his promotion of Frost, and his determination to avoid anything that smacks of Negro, he is referred to as polluting the letter so that Frost breaks off and starts over on a fresh sheet." Randall concluded that "young Negro writers, who are pondering the question of identity, can learn from Braithwaite's experience."[16]

"The Melting Pot" (*Negro Digest*, 1968) extends Randall's suspicion of the nation's racial intolerance and insincerity in iambic rhythm, end rhyme, and standard verse that mocks the myth of the melting pot. Sam, a persona symbolic of all black people, consistently attempts to integrate with the European mix but is rejected. Reflecting the attitude of the 1960s, he rejects his rejecters and says, "I don't give a damn." By repudiating the system, Sam accepts himself and his blackness as the poem plays on the old adage, "you can take it and shove it," with "Shove your old pot."

AFRICA

Although Randall maintained his eclectic perspective on poetry and race, the times directly influenced and impacted his muse, as Africa became central to the aesthetics of the Black Arts Movement. Randall decided to go to West Africa, rather than blindly subscribing to a romantic invention of an unrealized space in another time, four hundred years ago and across the Middle Passage. In 1970, Dudley and Vivian Randall visited Ghana and the Ivory Coast. While in Africa, Randall attended seminars at the University of Ghana and made a serious study of the history and the heritage. His initial response was: "Like Richard Wright, when I was in Africa, I felt like an American." This was not the popular or the appropriate response during a time when nearly everyone was aspiring to be an African. Amiri Baraka had given the treatise, and only those who were independent or mischievous, like Ishmael Reed for instance, broke rank and declared themselves to be Americans. In an interview shortly after his return, Randall made some contradictory observations about his sojourn to Africa:

> Africa is a very big place. It is very hard to try to sum it up. . . . I think, moreover, that it is very unwise for a person to talk as if he knows a country after visiting it for only a short time and getting only superficial impressions. An instant expert? There were some contradictions. One of them, for example, was being part of an audience that was two-thirds Black, and the African speaker referred to us as "you white folks," which may give you some ideas of how . . . this person looked upon Black Americans. Yet I wouldn't generalize and say that every African had this attitude. In the village that we vis-

25. Dudley Randall and Vivian Randall in Ghana, West Africa, 1970.

ited, for example, they said: "We know that you are our brothers who were taken away from us, and now you are coming back to see the land where your fathers lived, and we welcome you back."[17]

In "Slave Castle (Elmina, Ghana)" Randall interpreted his encounter with a relic of the slave trade by infusing the poem with the vocabulary, lyrical form, and "call and response" pattern of the Negro spiritual "Crucifixion." This adaptation simultaneously reminisces and activates the African American consciousness that connects memory to source and force of that suffering: "Many people who were not well educated and who knew few books beyond the Bible, yet were able to speak and write with eloquence because hey had absorbed some of the beauty of that Book. Think of the songs of the slave singers."[18]

I took movies of black American students coming out of the dungeons of the former slave castle in Elmina, Ghana. The tour of the castle was a profoundly moving experience for us. Probably all of us thought, "Long ago our mothers and fathers passed through just such a place as this. People like us suffered and died here." Our emotional upheaval was evident in facial expressions, gestures, words, tears.

> Some were crying
>   and some were cursing
> Some were dry-eyed
>   and some said never a
>   mumbalin word
>
>   when we stooped in the dark dungeons
>   felt the chains and manacles
>   stared at the cold grey waters
>   tossing to frightful shores
>
> Some were crying
> some were cursing
> some were dry-eyed
> some said never a
> mumbalin word

There were also white American students in the group, but perhaps they were not so deeply affected. Perhaps they reflected on man's inhumanity to man, but doubtless some of them thought, "I was a slave here, long ago." As all of us looked over the parapets at the cold gray Atlantic and thought of America far away, our thoughts of our ancestors who crossed those waters had to be different. The ancestors of the white students probably had some foreboding of a strange land, of physical hardships, of natives who might resent having their land taken from them, but mostly they had a sense of freedom—freedom from religious and political persecution, freedom from famine, from debt, from jail, freedom to achieve a new and prosperous life. On the other hand, the ancestors of the black students were kidnapped from their traditional culture to a land which they could consider only with horror and fright.[19]

Africa was the symbolic center of the new aesthetic, but Randall's poetry reflected the perspective of an empathetic descendant respectful of his African past, critical of current neocolonial exploitation of the continent, but mindful of his American historical reality and identity. He did not change his name or exchange his native perspective. "Hotel Continental (Accra, Ghana)" condemns imperialist racism, and "Hotel Ivoire (Abidjan, Ivory

Coast)" mocks the preference given to foreigners over the Africans. These critiques reflect a radicalized perspective in conflict with his privileged position as a Western tourist.

> Africa's
> not considered
> a continent
> here.
>
> While Europeans,
> Americans,
> Asians
> dine,
> the only Africans
> in the room
> are waiters.

("Hotel Continental (Accra, Ghana)," in *After the Killing*, 6)

And:

> Outside the hotel
> a beautiful black girl
> in a white bikini
> lolls
> in a billboard.
>
> If she should step out of the billboard
> to swim in the hotel pool,
> she would gash her feet
> on the broken glass
> set in the concrete fence
> the French erected
> to keep the Africans
> OUT.

("Hotel Ivoire (Abidjan, Ivory Coast)," in *After the Killing*, 5)

"A Different Image" reflects Randall's most pronounced identification with an African heritage, and it suggests a transformation via this cultural alternative. The poem harkens back to Paul Laurence Dunbar's "We Wear the Mask," which coincides with Du Bois's concept of "doubled consciousness."

Randall exchanges this mask and model for collusion and internalized oppression with the "classic bronze of Benin." As the old mask is replaced with the new, the reconstruction will "shatter the icons of slavery and fear" by doing rather than impersonating. Again, the contrast is also articulated in free verse form, but includes end rhyme for an alternative closure:

> The age
> requires this task:
> create
> a different image;
> re-animate
> the mask.
>
> (In Randall, ed., *The Black Poets*, 142)

For Randall, the poem, like the cultural attitude, should address doing. The words "task" and "create" are central to Randall's beliefs about change. Indeed, his muse was inspired by the Black Arts Movement to devise art capable of liberating the black American imagination, but without violent rage being a part of this transformation and without constraints imposed by any aesthetic authority—black or white.

IN LOVE, IN WAR

In a similar, albeit more understated act of aesthetic independence, Dudley Randall remained true to what motivated his muse to write in the first place, "a young girl with hazel eyes." The publication of *Love You* (1970) by Paul Bremen's Heritage Series in London made for an interesting contrast with the backdrop of militant poetry that pervaded the historical moment in black America. Baraka expressed defiantly in his poem "Black Art" that:

> Let there be no love poems written
> until love can exist freely
> and cleanly. Let Black People understand
> that they are the lovers and the sons
> of lovers and warriors and sons
> of warriors Are poems & poets &
> all the loveliness here in the world
>
> (In Randall, ed., *The Black Poets*, 224)

In his own way, Randall executed another poetry revolution. The publication of a collection of love poems during the Black Arts Movement (dedicated to Gwendolyn Brooks, "an inspiration to us all") articulated a softer literary mood in an atmosphere of aesthetic anger. Despite the urgency of cultural conflict and political confrontation, Randall's interest in love poetry illuminated a special angle in his creative current and a position he supported on race and writing:

> How else can a black writer write than out of his black experience? Yet, what we tend to overlook is that our common humanity makes it possible to write a love poem, for instance, without a word of race, or to write a nationalistic poem that will be valid for all humanity, such as "By the Waters of Babylon, there we sat down, yea, we wept, when we remembered Zion."[20]

To reiterate this point, he submitted "Four Love Poems" ("Love Poem," "And Why the Softness In A Lover's Eyes," "Profile on the Pillow," and "Goddess of Love") to the September 1970 issue of *Black World*, devoted to poetry: an obvious statement about aesthetic freedom. In particular, Randall expanded his premise of love poetry during the 1960s by connecting it to the volatile imagery of the times. This poetry offers love as a kind of spiritual self-defense from the onslaught of cultural deconstruction and social devastation. These poems also reflect the influence of the Russian poet K. M. Simonov, who wrote love poetry in warlike settings.[21]

"The Profile on the Pillow," the premiere poem in *Love You*, parallels the last poem in the collection, "Sanctuary." "The Profile on the Pillow" is Randall's best-known love poem, has been reprinted in several anthologies, is often associated with Randall's literary profile. Written in 1968 ("the year of the fire and the whirlwind"), when Martin Luther King and Robert Kennedy were assassinated, the theme intertwines romantic love with turmoil. The Vietnam War loomed in the distance and on television screens while college campuses and city ghettos became battlefields for social change. About the poem, Randall said:

> "The Profile on the Pillow" was written in the late 1960s, in a time when cities were burning and there were rumors that the government was preparing concentration camps for black Americans, like the camps for Japanese-Americans in World War II. I tried to make it powerful by enclosing conflicting emotions in the same poem—love and fear, tenderness and terror. The tension of the times made writing that poem a powerful experience.[22]

Sexual tension converges with historical uncertainty as the imagery reclines into shadows and half tones, "dark against the white," or black against the white. The poem pivots between hot and cold, life and death, and love and hate. But the mood is soft, relaying the joy of life and love as life in the same way that sexual attraction hinges on uncertainty:

> Perhaps
> you will cease to love me,
> or we may be consumed in the holocaust,
> but I keep, against the ice and the fire,
> the memory of your profile on the pillow.
>
> (*Love You*, 3)

Love You is a slender volume, a chapbook of only sixteen pages. Broadside Press was the distributor for the Heritage Series in the United States, which was a cooperative agreement with a nonblack publisher. (This is yet another indicator of Randall's resistance to dealing within strict boundaries outlined by race politics.) Other poems in the collection have no political designations and were written during the previous decades, such as "And Why the Softness," a short poem with only a single point, to love, to explain the title. The perspective is the inner glow reflected in the lover's eyes. Her beauty is compared to the radiance of the sun or the moon, relating this attraction to a central and natural force, which finally resolves sexual desire, the reason for this softness. Likewise, "Goddess of Love" is also a short poem containing a similar complete focus and romantic devotion as the subject of the poem is worshipped and associated with heavenly powers.

The more explicit "Good To Be in You" opens with this line, and sex is the center of the poem. As the poem progresses, the circular construction of the imagery broadens with the refrain "good," "but from" in you to "near you." Levels of intimacy are conveyed in subtle, suggestive images of shoulder "touching mine," "side by side," and "about the room." Using refrain and repetition, the second stanza in "good to be in you" imitates the format of the first three lines. The first line repeats the first line of the poem, and the second line recalls the refrain, "good," with slight variation in the phrasing, "with you." The imagery changes the position and perspective: "To sit, look into your eyes," and "see feelings." He relates her feelings to natural images and to the mundane by a basic sharing of personal histories. The second stanza is one line longer than the first, moving the poem into closure with a phrase that implicitly connects with the first line. The imagery is not unique, and in this respect the familiarity affirms awareness, as the last line connects with the first line: "Good to be in you . . . and know our souls have touched." The poem relates "good" as the essence of sexual intimacy and its ascending values in the building of a relationship. The sound employed in the poem creates a circular and sexual rhythm that foreshadows his bawdy poetry of the 1980s.

"The Gift" is also dependent on sound to construct meaning, but with comparisons, point and counterpoint. This poem emphasizes feelings and values of love by repeating phrases, constructing the point and the counterpoint. In subtle and skillful use of phrasing, Randall ends a line with the preposition "of," to effect a sense of longing, a feature of romantic love.

"Thunderstorm" is impressionistic and reflective of the imagist poets of the 1930s and 1940s, a stylistic shift that occurred while Randall was a student at the University of Michigan (1949–1951). Single words separated by periods and spacing construct a setting and a terse rhythm to simulate passionate lovemaking. Randall merges love making with the inherent elements of the setting. Sound contrasted against silence effects a sense of anticipation in the first line, which is, in turn, contrasted against a fragment in the second line, that rushes into the abstract image of "together" at the period. This poem and "Black Magic" echo William Carlos Williams's scant phrasing and E. E. Cummings's employment of spacing to affect sound patterns. "Black Magic" uses no punctuation. The poem was formed by the arrangement of words into lines contrasted against the background of the blank page. "That old black magic," which is a line from a popular song with a similar title, takes on positive racial symmetry in this interpretation. The last line alludes to a folk saying, "the blacker the berry, the sweeter the juice" and the novel by Wallace Thurman, *The Blacker the Berry* (1929). "Black Magic" reached its largest audience when it was published in *Ebony Magazine* in August 1977.

"Faces" uses the forces of nature to describe the contour of the various "portraits" in the poem. Randall employed alliteration and repetition to configure an onslaught of abstract images separated by commas that control the rhythm of the poem. The insertion of a dash after a comma following the one word line "antiphonies" separates the preceding lines as definitive and focuses on the subsequent lines for emphasis. Characteristic of the spirituals and work songs, Randall developed the "call and response" pattern with the repetition of the word "faces." The scope of time is connoted by variations on this pattern: "crocus faces," symbolic of spring, and "fresh-snowfall faces," symbolic of winter. These seasonal images are stationary, while the motion of the poem emanates descriptions of "driftwood faces," which "grooved," "gnarled," "chiseled," and "molded," respond to the rugged forces of life. These faces "resound" or respond to the call.

"Meeting" comprises of one-word sentences contrasted against fragments. Similar to "Thunderstorm," the poem pivots on time and distance as point and counterpoint. "The Brightness Moved Us Softly" and "At the Post House" are impressionistic poems. The former poem has a conventional *ababcc* rhyme scheme, but the rhythmic flow of the lines obscures the end rhyme in a manner that privileges the imagery. The supple phrasing contributes to the emphasis on nuance and mood, which builds into the final line, "the brightness moved us softly to a kiss." Whereas the imagery in "The Brightness Moves Us Softly" weaves the ambiance of dawn with the afterglow of lovemaking, "At the Post House" pivots on perspective to determine the meaning of the imagery, as ambiguity conveys the concept of oneness. "At the Post House" shifts from the third-person plural to the first-person plural in the second, one-line stanza, and then moves to the third person plural in the last line. This shifting broadens perspective and thematic meaning as the initial imagery infuses emotional interplay with a description of two lovers. From the perimeter, "We smile toward them." The gesture of the line emanates from the words "smile toward," and reflects approval and proximity between the lovers and the omnipotent insight in the perspective of the last line: "Love gives understanding to the eyes."

"Love You," the title poem of the collection, is energized by word play and the absence of punctuation, and the effect is as overwhelming as the emotion. The last seven lines reflect how the poem flips, turns, adds, subtracts, and moves the words inside out until it resolves: "love you." "My second birth," on the other hand, metaphorically correlates love with life by declaring the beginning of the relationship as this "rebirth" through love is "christened" by a kiss. This religious imagery is similar to "Goddess of love" and avoids pretension, showing a consistency in Randall's view of romantic love as a vibrant force that exhilarates life. Hence, the end of this relationship carries the power of spiritual demise. In "My second birth," the development of the single metaphor conforms to the simplicity of the ballad form. With alternating lines of eight and six meters and an *abacb* rhyme scheme, it appeals to a lyrical imitation of song.

"Sanctuary" begins with an allusion to Gwendolyn Brooks and to "The Profile on the Pillow" in the opening line, "This is the time of the whirlwind and the fire."Both poems propose love as a force of deliverance during the intense, confrontational 1960s. "Sanctuary" uses its opening line to define and contrast chaos in a historical moment of "turbulence" with the momentary peace that love provides.

> you may find peace and tenderness,
> even in the center of the fiery winds.

This poem transcribes the imagery of the whirlwind with circular and encompassing language. In "Sanctuary," Randall hyphenates the cycle of time, "of nation-death-and birth," to compress and connect these concepts. By contrasting this circle of "turbulence" with "the circle of love's arms," he contours a sanctuary inside the eye of the storm, "in that little space."

As a cultural activist, Randall's voice often uses contrasting themes. While he advocated civil disobedience and self-determination, his audience is reminded that love is stronger than hate and is the strength that holds the spirit of a people together, even in "the center of the fiery winds." Turning to the inner sanctum of fiery passion, the last stanza invites his lover to embrace him and the whirlwind as an act of defiance and courage:

> So step into the circle of my arms
> while we are hurled, with the other doomed spirits
> around and around in the fury of the whirlwind.
>
> (*Love You*, 16)

The appearance of *Love You* in the middle of the Black Arts Movement conveyed the balance of "Roses and Revolutions"; that is, all radical actions should emanate from love; otherwise "hate deified" will overwhelm and distort any just cause or revolutionary purpose. Whether in love or war, Randall's muse engaged a romantic vision to enthrall, inspire, or resolve a passionate purpose for poetry and life. Despite the proliferation of anger and violence raging in the books he published, he envisioned a revolution that would transcend the contradictions of the era. Dudley Randall's editorial policy promoted diversity and tolerance in literary expression, and with that liberated vision, his own poetry engaged the cultural terrain. He waged aesthetic and civil arguments about freedom, expanded the debate about identity, and advocated the freedom to write whatever moved his muse.

> Perhaps
> you may cease to love me,
> or we may be consumed in the holocaust,
> but I keep, against the ice and the fire,
> the memory of your profile on the pillow.
>
> (*Love You*, 3)

14

"AFTER THE KILLING":
DUDLEY RANDALL'S BLACK ARTS POETRY

I N 1971, THIRD WORLD PRESS PUBLISHED *More to Remember: Poems of Four Decades* by Dudley Randall. Dedicated to Don L. Lee, it represents Randall's first comprehensive poetry collection. Lee founded Third World Press in Chicago and published poetry and other genres related to the black experience, including Randall's *More to Remember* and *After the Killing* (1973). Since Lee modeled the poetry books after Broadside productions, and in many instances used the same Detroit printer, Randall maintained creative control over the text and the presentation. *More to Remember* represents a broad spectrum of styles and themes reflective of the poet's development since the 1930s. This juxtaposition of his earlier structured lyrics and tempered tones with his later direct free verse provides a clearer measure of his artistic range. In the preface, he explains the purpose of this retrospective:

> Because of the nature of my two previous books, many poems had to be omitted. *Poem Counterpoem* included only poems which could be paired with Margaret Danner's. *Cities Burning* was limited to poems about this disintegrating era. This book is inclusive, containing poems selected from those written from the 1930's through the 1960's.
>
> > Here are the ways I was. Warts and all.
> > Now I feel free to strike off in other directions.[1]

Finally, "Vacant Lot," "Ghetto Girls" (formerly "Hastings Street Girls"), "Pacific Epitaphs," "The Ascent," "Coral Atoll," "Hymn," "Poet," and many other poems from the past were collected. Although there is some overlapping, the first section of the book includes poetry written during the 1930s, the second section reflects writing activity during the 1940s, and the third section includes poetry from the 1950s. For the most part, this collection is contemplative, intricate, and conscious of traditional poetics. With regard to these literary features, Randall expected an educated, "cultured" audience would read these poems. His Black Arts poetry, on the other hand, is directed at contemporary black poets and everyday black folks. Consequently, he simplified his vocabulary, abandoned complex poetic forms and a preponderance of Western literary allusions. The fourth section of *More to Remember* contains poems written during the 1960s and, for the most part, reflects this radical shift in poetics. His next book, *After the Killing*, demonstrates an even more explicit departure from his literary past. He articulated the reason for this transformation:

> In my own poetry, I no longer strive for the intricate, sonorous stanzas of "The Southern Road." I try for a looser form, a more colloquial diction, as in "Frederick Douglass and the Slave Breaker." I want my poems to be read and understood by children, students, farmers, factory workers, professors. I seek directness and lucidity, but also a richness so that the reader will find added meanings on each new reading. I avoid eccentricities and grotesqueries.[2]

The fourth section of *More to Remember* reflects the issues of the times and provides a connecting point between Randall and the aesthetics dominating the 1960s. He enters the scene with direct language and cutting lines, which contrast sharply against the backdrop of his earlier, more sedate and soft-spoken expressions. At the same time, Randall believed that a poet should master the craft, and the regimen requires knowledge and practice of all poetic traditions:

> Those poets who ridicule traditional verse by saying it goes monotonously "da-dum, da-dum, da-dum" either have wooden ears or do not know how to read aloud. Because of the different weights of vowels and the easy-to-pronounce and hard-to-pronounce combinations of consonants in the English language, there are immense variations in the speed, quantity, tone color, and pitch of lines, to say nothing of the variations in volume, pitch, pause, tempo dictated by meaning. The "da-dum" is only an understood

pattern, like the 4/4 beat in music, against which you can play innumerable variations. The best writers of free verse are those skilled in traditional verse, but many writers write bad free verse because they never learned to write traditional verse.[3]

Randall's free-verse poems join the Black Arts aesthetic, but they also reiterate his particular brand of radicalism and his critique of political and cultural activities. This poetry is more rhetorical and is reflective of the black oral tradition. Since he rarely engaged in oral arguments, his poetry was his rebuttal, his response to the verbal posturing of others. Randall viewed his voice as being in the moment, and although his poetry argues against the opinions of many of the militant poets, he considers his poetry to be a part of the new black aesthetic. A case in point is "The Militant Black Poet." Drawn from a personal experience, it demonstrates Randall's identification with the radicalism of the poetry movement as he mocks himself and the irony of audience receptivity:

> I read at Grosse Ile, which is an island past southwest Detroit [a suburban area], near the Detroit River. These people may not be wealthy, but it's an isolated community with a bridge, and they have their lovely homes there. And I guess it was in the sixties when a Black poet was a curiosity. I worked at the Wayne County Library, and Isabella Swann, our assistant librarian, had a home out there, and I think it was through her I was invited to read to this Tuesday Club—genteel, white-haired women. And I read some poems, and a little old white-haired lady, who was more militant than I was, said: "Yes, that's right!" So, I said, "What am I doing here?" to myself. "I should be reading this poem to Black folks, not to these wealthy white folks." That's what I thought. I exaggerated that. I said the poet went home and hanged himself.[4]

> A militant black poet
> read his scariest poems
> to a literary club
> of suburban white women.

> After the reading
> a white-haired lady commented
> what a nice man he was,
> and that in his place
> she'd be much more bitter.

The militant black poet
went home
and hanged himself.

(*More to Remember*, 74)

Randall devised humor from the setting and the characters in a reversal that usurps expectation, as the last line exaggerates the travesty of aesthetic failure. In much of his poetry, Randall's uses humor to engage and to lighten the seriousness of literary attitudes, and he also confronts misguided hostility in the Black Power generation that alienated many of their elders with political arrogance and historical ignorance. "Seeds of Revolution" critiques young militants who assume they are the first to protest or to shake a fist at the white world. The poem opens and closes with the same two stanzas:

The Revolution
did not begin in 1966
when Stokely raised his fist
and shouted, Black Power.

Nor did it begin last year
when you read Fanon
and discovered you were black.

The interior stanzas are historical and propose different acts of rebellion and resistance, as a black on a slave ship leaping overboard or as an "Uncle Tom" outsmarting the white-supremacist arrogance of the slave master. The reference to "father" and "mother" as domestic and menial workers is parenthetically followed with attitudes of shame and resentment for forefathers and foremothers who endured so that the militants-to-be, the descendants, "could go to school / and read Fanon." There is also a class analysis embedded in this image, and an accusation of a misreading of Fanon as well. The structure of the poem is cyclical, as the connection to Fanon reflects on the beginning and the ending of the poem to demonstrate that revolution is also cyclical, and this level of political perspective requires historical clarity and a keener political analysis. As the title suggests, "Seeds of Revolution" were planted in our cultural consciousness through anonymous acts of sacrifice and humble, strategic maneuvers. This poem is also thematically reflective of Randall's 1962 short story, "Shoe Shine Boy."[5]

"Straight Talk from a Patriot" and "Daily News Report" are antiwar poems that intersect with the Black Power Movement, the Civil Rights Movement and the peace movement of the 1960s and 1970s. "Straight Talk" is crafted in four short lines: a rhyming couplet followed by an oblique rhyme. The ending rhyme is slightly off because the thinking, expressed in the voice of the patriot, is distorted. Full of racism, aggression, and destruction, the perspective of the "patriot" contains an ironic and frightening honesty.

"Daily News Report" is constructed around the word play of one line from a news report: "We killed 250 men to day." The matter-of-fact delivery of the news report is transformed into deliberations on the meaning of "killed"; who must assume responsibility, and how many people died? 250. Visually constructed to force the audience to linger in reflection on each word in the report, the poem reverses the pattern by repeating "today" and interchanging "living" and "were living" to emphasize that what is in the past is now obscured in the present and in its true meaning. "Today" is used as counterpoint in the third pivot, as the poem focuses on the word "killed" and emphasizes and reiterates it in italics and capital letters. The poem builds into a printed protest, shouts from the page, but ends with small letters and single-word lines with no punctuation, which extends the thought into a quiet sadness:

> Now they are dead
> We killed them
> We killed
> KILLED
> KILLED
> them
> today
>
> (More to Remember, 65)

"Nationalist," "Put Your Muzzle Where Your Mouth Is (Or Shut Up)," "Informer," "F.B.I. Memo" and "Abu" are satirical and critical observances about the political climate of the era. They are clever quips, which provide contradictions and warnings. The "Nationalist" reveals the romantic preferences of a so-called race-lover by coining the popular phrase in a typical setting:

> "Black
> is beautiful,"
> he said,
> as he stroked
> her white
> breasts.
>
> (More to Remember, 69)

"Put Your Muzzle Where Your Mouth Is (Or Shut Up)" exposes the hypocrisy of many "militant" rhetoricians who advocate violent assaults against "whites" or "representatives of the establishment," but are not willing to risk their own necks:

> Kill, Kill, Kill, he screamed.
> But when I asked him
> (naively, I suppose)
> how many
> *he*
> had killed,
> he said,
> Not
> 1.

(*More to Remember*, 70)

The visual design of the poem moves from the extended clamor of the militant's call for killing into short lines, which deescalate to the pronoun "he" italicized for emphasis and progressing toward the one-word final lines: "Not / 1." The same technique is used in "Informer," which features a character shouting "Black Power," as a militant cover for an FBI agent.

"F.B.I. Memo" parallels these themes, as the "Informer" or the perfect FBI spy can be spotted in appropriate black nationalist garb, speaking Swahili and inciting violence. Even though the poem is serious, it mocks these incredible characters by using one-word rhyming lines: "tiki," "dashiki," "Swahili," and the rhetoric "Kill the honkies." "Put a Muzzle Where Your Mouth Is" could also be a response to Giovanni's "The True Import of Present Dialogue: Black vs. Negro."

"Abu" is longer than the aforementioned poems, but it is thematically related because it exposes the lack of insight and depth in such characters and their macho grandstanding. The poem mimics the language of some of the new poets, as exemplified in "Primitives," as it makes fun of the intelligence of "Abu," who perceives of himself as "a stone black revolutionary." Not only does Abu publicly publish his "inten/ shun" to "blow up City Hall," but he does not recognize the FBI spies who have infiltrated his organization when he reveals his assassination plans. Moreover, Randall reveals the absurd logic of a "militant," who attacks liberals with perverse reactionary reasoning that conversely excuses fascists for extreme racist practices. The persona is made to appear ridiculous, someone who should not be considered a leader. To what extent his audience recognized this warning at the time is questionable. Randall did not argue with persons who exemplified the behavior reflected in these poems, but the poems enact argument.

"The Trouble with Intellectuals" and "The Intellectuals" are direct criticisms about verbosity and inaction:

> The trouble with intellectuals
> Is that they talk
> To o
> Mu c h.
>
> (*More to Remember*, 58)

Not being much of a talker, the economy of Randall's speaking and writing vocabularies are directly related to his personality. From his earliest irritations with his father's preaching and his avoidance of debate, his intolerance for too much talk in social and political settings was clear. This civility was not silent acquiescence. These poems reveal a real disagreement with the interference of excessive language with actual living. In the first poem, he accuses intellectuals of not knowing when to shut up, even during the most primal arrangements, such as making love. Their lives have been overwhelmed by talk.

Similarly, "The Intellectuals" ridicules this excessive talking as their enemies attack them. The talkers are metaphorically eliminated:

> Meanwhile the others,
> Who believed in action,
> And that they should be up and all the rest down,
> Stormed the hall, shot the leaders and arrested the remainder.
> Who they later hanged.
>
> (*More to Remember*, 59)

In contrast to these satirical poems about intellectuals and false militancy, "Sniper" rings like a shot in the dark:

> Somewhere
> On a rooftop
> You fight for me.
>
> (*More to Remember*, 75)

In this poem, Randall's radical clarity distinguishes rhetorical clamor from actual self-defense. During the 1967 Detroit Race Rebellion, there were snipers who fought back when the police and National Guard shot up neighborhoods without warning or consideration for the consequences. Forty-five people died, but many believed that if snipers had not retaliated the tally would have been higher because the police and the soldiers would have felt invincible. These instances of self-defense are not equated with the senseless, merciless violence advocated by rhetorical revolutionaries, as in the case of "Abu" or "Put Your Muzzle Where Your Mouth Is."

"Mainly by the Music" is another, albeit subtler lesson about language, especially for poets. Randall offered his insight into the effects of sound in poetry at a time when rhetoric ruled supreme. In short rhymed verses, this quiet poem is a stark contrast to boisterous tone of other Black Arts poetry:

> And mainly by the music
> That feelings subtly play
> Upon these instruments of air
> Does meaning find its way.
>
> (*More to Remember*, 62)

As in "Seeds of Revolution," in "Ancestors" Randall poses a question to black nationalists that challenged their lack of class consciousness and historical clarity:

During the sixties, people boasted about their African ancestry. They would say that their ancestors were kings and queens. But if we are all descendants of royalty, what happened to all the other people? Obviously, there were more common people than there were kings and queens.

> Why are our ancestors
> always kings or princes
> and never the common people?

It is important to note the male gender in these lines, which subtextually suggests the patriarchal nature of the nationalist political orientation:

> Was the Old Country a democracy
> where every man was a king?

The answer appears as a question, which confirms a truth that deflates a false premise for the freedom movement and the invention of an identity based in romantic illusions:

> Or did the slave catchers
> steal only the aristocrats
> and leave the field hands
> laborers
> street cleaners
> garbage collectors
> dishwashers
> cooks
> and maids
> behind?

In the third stanza, the image of humble origins shifts the perspective back to the poet, who uses hyperbole to lighten a rhetorical engagement that might offend some cultural nationalists:

> My own ancestor
> (research reveals)
> was a swineherd,
> who tended the pigs
> in the Royal Pigsty
> and slept in the mud
> among the hogs.

The symbolic use of pigs is also an inside joke because there was so much fuss made about no longer eating pork, especially survival cuisine developed during slavery, such as chitterlings. It could also be a subtextual suggestion that royalty in Africa was greedy and repressive, just like it was in Europe, Asia, and elsewhere. Randall's Detroit-based class consciousness tempered his nationalist concerns and challenged the racial arrogance emerging in the devout espousals of some black nationalists. The final lines define and separate him from the ruling class and confirm his working class identity and heritage:

> Yet I'm as proud of him
> as of any king or prince
> dreamed up in fantasies
> of bygone glory.
> (*More to Remember*, 76)

"On Getting a Natural (For Gwendolyn Brooks)" (1969) was first a broadside published as a poster, and it is clearly a tribute to someone Randall deeply admired. The soft language and the gentle flow of the rhythmic structure are designed to conform to Brooks's congeniality and unobtrusive style.[6] More importantly, this tribute to Gwendolyn Brooks reflects the admiration and awe Randall felt for her. Her literary contributions to his efforts at Broadside brought prestige to the press, which elevated the prominence of the roster of poets. What was truly "Black and Beautiful" about this era were the selfless contributions of persons like Brooks, and this poem speaks to that.

"For Gwendolyn Brooks, Teacher" is also a tribute, but in this instance Randall emulates the terse style of Brooks's "We Real Cool," which was also published as a broadside. Randall's poem corresponds with Brooks's two line stanzas, but instead of rhyme, he uses a repetitive rhythm structure in the first line of each stanza:

> You teach
> without talk.
>
> Your life
> is lesson.
>
> We give
> because you do,
>
> are kind
> because you are.
>
> Just live.
> We will learn.
> (*More to Remember*, 77)

Imitation is again employed in a poem written upon the death of Langston Hughes (1967). In "Langston Blues" Randall emulates the blues form that Hughes made famous:

> Your lips were so laughing
> Langston man
> Your lips were so singing
> Minstrel man
> How death could touch them
> Hard to understand

Your lips that laughed
And sang so well
Your lips that brought
Laughter from hell
Are silent now
No more to tell

So let us sing
A Langston blues
Sing a lost
Langston blues
Long-gone song
For Langston Hughes

(*More to Remember*, 63)

This poem hearkens to Randall's first blues poem, found in the second section of *More to Remember*, "Jailhouse Blues," which adapts the blues format to lament an inmate's regret and to mock his ironic sense of "right." Written during the forties, the poem does not indict the persona, but it brings attention to a condition that may be the cause of his anguish and symptomatic of an unfortunate syndrome in the black male experience—womanizing.

I got three women
to love me day and night,
black, brown and yellow
to love me day and night.
When I leave this jailhouse,
I'm sure gonna treat 'em right.

(*More to Remember*, 29)

This poem is printed facing "The Line Up," which complements its theme. In iambic tetrameter, the poem mocks the documentation of the prisoner in the police station after the arrest. What's interesting about these two poems is that the relationship between black males and the criminal-justice system has become increasingly commonplace because of the economic and social repression that intensified during the 1960s and thereafter.

Although "Souvenirs" does not appear in his fourth book of poetry, *More to Remember*, the book's title is derived from a line in the love poem. The few love poems that are collected in *More to Remember* reflect Randall's past work and his careful study of classical forms and traditional views on romantic love. For example, "Love Song" (from the 1950s; initially published in *Negro Digest*, September 1969) imitates a melody with simple, picturesque language that compares the gentle spirit of love to "a doe / upon the mountain tops." The end rhyme and the repetition of meter reinforce the songlike pattern, and the repetition of the first stanza is rearranged by a break in the stanza to interrupt the regularity of the rhythm with visual spacing. His mastery of vocabulary shows in the poem's diction, as the rhyming pattern demands monosyllabic and two-syllable words to affect precise pitching and sound duration. Like a single chord on a keyboard, the word "copse" is finely tuned with the word "tops."

In a similar regard, Randall's interest in the sonnet coincides with the origin and evolution of the form initially conceived by Sicilian love poets in the thirteenth century and made famous by the Petrarch's "Canzoniere," a poem written in adoration for his great love, Laura. Randall's "April Mood" (also written sometime during the 1950s) is a Spenserian sonnet, which resembles the Italian sonnet and also has a difficult, interlinking rhyme scheme: *abab bcbc cdcd ee*. The speaker takes chivalry as his theme. He reflects on "Young knights" and the tales of how they would "rescue damsels from magicians' charms" to "win eternal glory and a dame," in a playful tone and a fanciful iambic rhythm. He compares these mythic conditions to his own modern neighborhood, which rarely renders opportunities for grand acts of heroism.

"Anniversary Words," written for Vivian Randall, combines a rush of images that run together like the habitual years of marriage, emphasizing his disruptive messiness and her irritated tolerance as the words reflect the couple's minor daily adjustments. Randall craftily improvises on the Spenserian sonnet: *abba abbba cdcd cc*, with the structural distinction of the Elizabethan sonnet, which comprises two stanzas, an octave and a sextet. Randall further improvises the form by ending all but two of the lines with a comma, thereby running the sound pattern and the imagery of the octave into the sextet. The poem illustrates the intimacy of nonverbal exchange between partners and the emotional convergence that binds and centers them as a couple.

Randall displays his personal shortcomings in the fluid line endings separated only by commas: "carelessness," "forgetfulness," "genial neglect of practicality," and, foremost, "for leaving rooms in great disorderliness," and the ending accentuates his wife's counterpoint and complement, "which when I entered were as neat as they could be." The comma also posits a pivot in perspective that departs and yet conforms to convention, as the last six lines resolve the tension in the first stanza. The second stanza continues with "despite the absent-mindedness of my ways," which characterizes his behavior with her frustrated responses in the "acerbity" of her "tone." But

the tension resolves into confirmation that transcends these minor aggrava-
tions that occasion everyday living:

> I sometimes catch a softness in your gaze
> which tells me after all I am your own

The last lines regard the profundity and depth of their bonding and emphatically confirm this in the final two rhyming lines, which both end in periods:

> and that you love me in no little way.
> But I know best by the things you never say.

AFTER THE KILLING

After the Killing is "dedicated To the Memory of Ruth Whitsitt Fondren,
One of the builders of Broadside Press." Ruth Fondren, who died in 1972,
was one of the first volunteers in the press office. She was also the sister of
Bill Whitsitt, who was the office manager of the press. The book's cover is
the artwork of John Dobroczynski, who was a typesetter at Harlo Printing,
the company that printed Broadside books and books by Randall published with Third World Press. The overall theme of this collection is clearly antiviolence, as it contains perspectives parallel to those elicited in *Cities
Burning* (1968) and in the poems from the 1960s in *More to Remember*
(1971). In a review for *Black World* (formerly *Negro Digest*), the poet Frank
Marshall Davis stated: "In his brief but potent new book, *After the Killing*,
Dudley Randall again offers visual proof of why he should be ranked in the
front echelon of Black poets. His words are the distinctive reaction of a
sensitive Afro-American to the world he has come to know, both at home
and abroad."[7]

The collection opens with a section titled "African Suite," which includes
"Slave Castle," "Hotel Continental," "Hotel Ivoire," and "Village Girl." The
title poem, "After the Killing," demonstrates the cyclical nature of violence
as vengeance overtakes the quest for peace.

> "We will kill,"
> said the blood-thirster,
> "and after the killing
> there will be peace."

But after the killing
their sons
killed his sons,
and his sons
killed their sons,
and their sons
killed his sons

until
at last
a blood-thirster said,
"We will kill.
And after the killing
there will be
peace."

(*After the Killing*, 9)

"Courage" is a reminder of Randall's concerns in "To The Mercy Killers" and an answer to certain macho assumptions, which ignore context and circumstance. "Courage" posits a solution for "After the Killing" or to end the deadly syndrome of violence:

There are degrees of courage.
One man is not afraid to die.
A second is not afraid to kill.
A third is not afraid to be merciful.

(*After the Killing*, 11)

As in "News Report," Randall uses spacing for temporal control and thematic emphasis in "Beasts," which criticizes the savagery of human killing by listing the excuses for it on an angle. The visual form of poem, the use of indentation, gestures at the inhumanity of the reasoning:

Beasts kill
to live.

Men kill
for sport
for love

for honor
for bro-ther-hood
for God
for red
white
and blue.

To praise a man
call him bestial.
To slander beast
cry, Human!

(*After the Killing*, 9)

"To the Mercy Killers" is far more intricate than the other poems about killing. Possibly an antieuthanasia position, it is reminiscent of Emily Dickinson's "Because I Could Not Stop For Death." The graphic imagery in this sonnet is imposing and disturbing, which is biographically interesting when one considers that Randall subsequently contemplated suicide. He told an interviewer that "I was hospital librarian to the patients at Eloise, the Wayne County General Hospital. Out of that experience I wrote 'To the Mercy Killers.'"[8]

If ever mercy moves you to murder me,
I pray you, kindly killers, let me live.
Never conspire with death to set me free,
but let me know such life as pain can give.
Even though I be a clot, an aching clench,
a stub, a stump, a butt, a scab, a knob,
a screaming pain, a putrefying stench,
still let me live, so long as life shall throb.

In the more pensive construction of the sonnet, the humility embedded in these lines provides an alternative approach to contemplating the end of life:

Even though I seem not human, a mute shelf
of glucose, bottled blood, machinery
to swell the lung and pump the heart—even so,
do not put out my life. Let me still glow.

(*After the Killing*, 10)

About these poems Davis states that "although we react to stimuli mainly as Blacks, we can and should be turned on by other unforgettable phenomena, and if the written results are worthwhile, they should be available to and appreciated by all. For instance, the title poem, "After the Killing," along with "Beasts," "The Mercy Killers" and "Courage" stand by themselves as fine, perceptive poems with no racial designation."[9] But at the same time, these themes are responses to a period fraught with violent proposals and reprisals espoused in political rhetoric in the black community.

"Tell It Like It Is" and "Words Words Words" are parallel poems addressing ambiguity in language and contradiction in the practice of rhetoric. In "Words, Words, Words," Randall engages the popular slogan "Black Is Beautiful," which brothers proclaimed even as they excluded dark-skinned women from their romantic choices:

> but almost never
> a black one,
> although they say
> that black
> is beautiful.

The second stanza considers the pervasive appearance of the homophobic word "faggot," and the excessive use of the expression "motherfucker." When the poet is told these words have another meaning in their revised lexicon, the poem concludes:

> so maybe black
> doesn't mean black,
> but white.

Randall understood context; but the poem demonstrates inconsistency. Similarly, "Tell It Like It Is" is an appeal for some semblance of the truth and an argument against posturing and grandstanding:

> Tell it like it is.
> Lies won't get it.
> Foaming at the mouth won't get it.
> Defamation of character won't get it.

The poem calls out machismo in the young men and their propensity to insult the virility of white males as a reason to criticize the system. Such insults are useless and are based on an abuse of language, as reflected in "Words Words Words." At the end of "Tell It Like it Is," he advises:

> If you want to be virile,
> be virile,
> but you ain't gonna get virile
> by saying somebody else ain't virile.
> And if the white boys are all faggots,
> like you say,
> how come we got all these black poets
> with yellow skin?
>
> (*After the Killing*, 7)

This daring reference to miscegenation is also a historical reminder about racial identity and heritage, which he never forgot even when he visited and wrote about Africa. Davis reiterates Randall's perspective: "He has an African Suite composed of impressions received in Ghana and the Ivory Coast, and in such poems as 'Words, Words, Words' and 'Tell It Like It Is,' he comes down hard on some of the sham current in today's world of American Blacks. And there is plenty."[10]

With the exception of "I Loved You Once," a translation of Alexander Pushkin's "Ya Vas Lyubil," the love poems in *After the Killing* (1973) are in free verse. Even in a book whose title suggests themes of violence, the inclusion of love poetry provides a dialectical balance in the aesthetic sensibility of the collection. "Miracle" is (three lines, and one sentence long) thematically structured to make a small, but lingering statement:

> Always
> there is the wonder
> that you should love me.
>
> (*After the Killing*, 13)

"The Flight" is also one sentence long, but in contrast to the momentary emphasis affected in the short three lines in "Miracle," "The Flight" has unpunctuated, longer lines that move the imagery to simulate the flight portrayed in the poem. It begins with the word, "Out," which immediately evokes an urgent need to escape. No subject appears until the fifth line, the middle of the poem, and it is conveyed within the rush out of the "banquet room," through "halls crowded with laughing guests," "down empty stairs," and "through crowded lobby" as "our way." The pace of the poem slows with shorter lines and a shift in setting, "into the still night street," "hand in hand." But the poem returns to a faster pace and with definition in the repetition of "running" in a longer line juxtaposed with the word "isolated" and halted in the following line, announcing the landing "into each other's arms."

"Marriage" is structured around simplicity and symmetry. As the monetary value of the man's gifts to his wife increases, the essence of his love decreases. The first and third stanzas each comprise three short lines, which encase the contrasting five lines in the second and middle stanza. The "rosebud" is the primary image and acts as metaphor for the couple's love at the beginning of the marriage. The shift in verb from "brought" to "send" indicates emotional and spatial distance. Moreover, it demonstrates how materialism can kill love in a marriage, a kind of silent violence. These three poems, in particular, illustrate how Randall translates the metaphysical into spatial and temporal constructions in language, whereas "Sniper," composed in 1967, is concrete and immensely clear.

Initially published in *The Broadside Series*, "Green Apples" was very popular and soon sold out its print run in that format. A young woman is compared to a "green apple" that is "raw, unformed, without the mellowness of maturity," "who talks and talks and talks about herself," lacking in "the experience of intimate, sensitive silences." He further chastises young women because, according to him, they don't know how to make love:

> Panting, they pursue their own pleasure,
> forgetting to please their partner, as an older woman does.

The poem is more a humorous criticism of the inadequacies of youth than it is a serious statement about gender. The last line confirms this view of immaturity and is likewise consistent with Randall's reliance on structural balance and humor as teaching strategies:

> It's only just that young women get what they deserve.
> A young man.
>
> (*After the Killing*, 15)

The sound devices in this poem are internal. Alliteration, repetition, and internal vowel sounds craft a subtle system that undergirds the imagery. The first stanza consists of three lines; the second and third stanzas balance the body of the poem with five lines each. A question is posed in the first line of each stanza, which is then answered in the subsequent lines, a pattern of call and response. A twist at the end of the poem shifts the critique of women to a critique of youth, as the poem ends with a fragment for contrast and emphasis: "A young man."

"Frederick Douglass and the Slave Breaker" (see appendix 2 for draft versions of this poem) returns the audience to their African American roots in a poem that revives racial memory. Randall derived the poetic experience from a portrait and a story from Douglass's autobiography, *The Life and Times of Frederick Douglass* (1881):

> I enjoyed writing "Frederick Douglass and the Slavebreaker" because it was a commissioned poem and because it took its place in the poetic tradition. I was asked to write a poem for the dedication of the murals in the Frederick Douglass Branch library in Detroit. I knew that two other poets, Robert Hayden and Langston Hughes, had already written two famous poems about Douglass, so I was treading on hallowed ground. One day I was in the studio of the painter, LeRoy Foster, and saw his painting for the mural. It was not the familiar Frederick Douglass, with a long beard. It was a bare torso of a beardless boy. At once I said, That's the teen-age Douglass when he fought old Cosey, the black slave-breaker. I knew I had found my subject. It was enjoyable to join the company of two fine poets like Hughes and Hayden.[11]

> So all day long we battled,
> the man and the boy, sweating,
> bruising, bleeding . . .
> till at last the slave breaker said,
> "Go home, boy. I done whupped you enough.
> Reckon you done learned your lesson."
>
> But I knew who it was that was whipped.
> And the lesson I learned
> I'll never forget.
>
> (*After the Killing*, 11)

In this poem, Douglass resists a whipping from the slave breaker, who is black, and decides to risk his life in order to save his self-respect. What's interesting about Randall's vocabulary in this poem is that words such as "horse," "dog," and "man" and "boy" define the parameters of thought and the struggle between chattel slavery and manhood (or humanhood). The second and third stanzas convey a sense of this energy and tension.

"Frederick Douglass and the Slave Breaker," as historical subject, is similar to "Booker T. and W. E. B." and "Blood Precious Blood," which was initially composed after the assassination of Martin Luther King Jr. in 1968 and commemorates Medgar Evers, Malcolm X, and King in a poem about sacrifice. As does "Slave Castle," "Blood Precious Blood" emulates the chant found in Negro spirituals, as the names of the heroes of the age are called, and the refrain, "blood precious blood," reflects the refrain in the gospel "Precious Lord":

> What can wash cleanse purify redeem this land
> stained
> with your blood,
> your precious blood?
>
> (*After the Killing*, 77)

Dudley Randall's poetry occupied a pivotal position in the Black Arts Movement. Because he honed his craft prior to the cultural excitement, his poetry did not offer the pangs of rebellion as violent words, but embellished the moment with an honest acceptance of blackness in all its wonderful ambiguities. The wisdom of his muse confronts unpleasant truths, brings joy to the pain of realization and humor to an angry audience. Randall's lyricism, poetic balance, temperament, and radicalism were a force within the new black aesthetic, which was struggling for sense and sensibility:

The press of business and the tendency to abstract keeps us from really seeing the world, makes us reduce it to cliched abstractions. We see a white man, a Negro, a Jew, a woman. Instantly there springs to mind some abstract stereotype, instead of our scrutinizing the person and trying to understand a unique individual different from all the three billion other individuals on earth. This is the virtue of poetry, that it goes back to the primitive radical roots of language, and makes us live in the poem, not move abstract counters, such as honkie, nigger, Jew, broad. If we could feel how even a pin prick hurts, then we would not be so apt to consign whole populations to death: "the final solution," "drive them into the sea," "the yellow peril," "put the nigger in his place," "the only good Indian is a dead Indian."[12]

As Frank Marshall Davis concluded, "Mr. Randall knows how to intelligent ly use Black lingo without it becoming annotated graffiti. He also has a gift for irony. The poems in this brief collection are militant and memorable."[13]

15

POETRY AS INDUSTRY

Broadside Press did not grow from a blueprint. I did not, like Joe Goncalves when he planned *The Journal of Black Poetry*, save money in advance to finance the press. Broadside Press began without capital, from the twelve dollars I took out of my paycheck to pay for the first Broadside, and has grown by hunches, intuitions, trials and error. Our first publication was the Broadside "Ballad of Birmingham." Folk singer Jerry Moore of New York had it set to music, and I wanted to protect the rights to the poem by getting it copyrighted. Learning that a leaflet could be copyrighted, I published it as a broadside in 1965. Jerry Moore also set the ballad "Dressed All in Pink" to music, and in order to copyright it I printed this poem also as a broadside. Being a librarian, accustomed to organizing and classifying material, I grouped the two poems into a *Broadside Series*, and called them Broadside number one and number two. Since Broadsides, at the time, were the company's sole product, I gave it the name Broadside Press.[1]

Once Gwendolyn Brooks asked me what title to call me by. I replied that since I, in my spare time and in my spare bedroom, do all the work, from sweeping floors, washing windows, licking stamps and envelopes, and packing books, to reading manuscripts, writing ads, and planning and designing books, that she just say that Dudley Randall equals Broadside Press.[2]

For the first five years, Broadside Press was largely a one-man operation. But despite the limitations of the developmental period, within a few short

years, the press grew beyond Dudley Randall's wildest dreams. In a similar regard, several interviews with Randall were published to determine this man's
vision and energy. To a large extent, these narratives outline the essence and
the day-to-day determinations that turned a solo act into an industry:

The press started in my house. *For Malcolm* was stored in the basement, and
they sold out. I didn't know how, but gradually the books disappeared and
one day there were no more. We made several reprintings of *For Malcolm X.*
But, as we got other poets and other books, the basement became too crowded and my study became too cramped, so we moved to a little office space
across the alley. When that office got too small, we moved to a larger space
further north on Livernois near Fenkell. Soon that office became too small,
and we moved back to our original place, but occupied more office space. The
exterminator who owned the building had retired, so we took over the whole
building. (He went to Florida and died; that happens when you retire.)

I remember a fellow came to the office, and he told me he was surprised
to find that Broadside Press was in this little hole in the wall. He thought it
would be in some big building, like a big company. I think it's easy to get
the wrong impression. I remember I used to receive orders from a "bookstore" in Chicago, and I thought it would be a flourishing operation, but
when I went there, it was a little storefront with one glass counter and with
a curtain across the door, behind there in that room was a bed where the
man slept. The owner had a half-a-dozen Broadside books and some racing
forms on the counter.

At one time I tried to contain the publication schedule to four books a
year. I think when Jill Witherspoon, Naomi Madgett's daughter, started
working at Broadside, she wrote down a list of the books that were to come
up, and I was amazed. I didn't know that I had promised to publish so
many books. I got scared. I said, We can't afford to put out so many books.
So then I set out trying to keep it down to four books a year, but we weren't
able to maintain that limit.

When you begin, you might have one poet, well, you publish the one
poet. Then you have two poets. Maybe, three or four. Then they each have
a second book, and that makes eight. Then here are other new poets appearing. So you add their work to the eight titles. It increased like that, year
after year. Broadside began publishing more and more poets, and there
were so many that we had to have contracts. I believe labor is worthy of
hire. In these contracts, the poets got royalties at the rate of 10 percent.

I tried two or three different printers before I settled on Harlo Printing.
Some people said that he was expensive, but I liked him because he did

26. Dudley Randall at Broadside Press office with John Walthal and Lottie Butler, ca. 1970.

good work, was dependable, and would give you advice. So even though it might have cost a little more, I stayed with him, because I had confidence in his work. We had a friendly relationship. If I wanted to do something that was not practical or not good, he would advise me against it.

Because of printer's delays, *For Malcolm* was not published until June 1967. In the meantime, *Poem Counterpoem*, by Margaret Danner and myself, was published in December 1966. The next book to be published by Broadside Press was one of our bestselling books, *Black Pride*, by the popular young poet, Don L. Lee. We published *Black Pride* in 1968 and took over *Think Black*. In 1969, we published his *Don't Cry, Scream*, in both paperback and cloth editions. The cloth edition of *Don't Cry, Scream* was the first hard cover with Broadside Press, but shortly afterward we put out our second hard cover book, the second edition of *For Malcolm*.

At this writing, *Think Black* has had twelve printings, and there are twenty-five thousand copies in print. *Black Pride* is in its seventh printing, and *Don't Cry, Scream*, just out in March 1969, had its third printing (5,000 copies) the following September. It is only lack of money, which prevents these printings from being 10,0000 instead of 5,000, as they sell rapidly and it is hard to keep bookstores in supply. All together, there are about 55,000 copies of Don Lee's books in print at this time. This has occurred without book reviews in the mass media. The only reviews of Lee's books have appeared in small black and underground magazines. In March 1969 there was an article on Lee by David Llorens in *Ebony*, a widely circulated magazine, but the article appeared after, not before, Lee had attained his popularity.[3]

Another poet who has been warmly praised is Etheridge Knight. He contributed three poems to *For Malcolm*, and I corresponded with him in Indiana State Prison. I asked him to do a book for Broadside Press, and we published his *Poems from Prison* in 1968, which is now in its third printing. While living in Indianapolis, he completed his second book of poetry, *Belly Song*.

James Emanuel's first book of poetry, *The Treehouse and Other Poems*, was also published in 1968, as was my second book of verse, *Cities Burning*. The same year we became distributors for Nikki Giovanni's second book, *Black Judgment*, and published Margaret Danner's *Impressions of African Art*. This book, which is a facsimile of the original edition privately printed in 1960, has the distinction of being the only volume of poetry completely devoted to the vivid, varied, sophisticated arts of Black Africa. Among books that were promised to us were two by Pulitzer Prize–winner Gwendolyn Brooks and Margaret Walker, winner of the Yale University Younger Poets Award.[4]

In a different dimension is *Broadside Voices*, which is a series of poets reading their own books on tape. So far, James Emanuel, Dudley Randall, Etheridge Knight, Sonia Sanchez, Jon Eckels, Beatrice Murphy and Nancy Arnez, Marvin X, Willie Kgositsile, Don Lee, and Stephany have taped their books. James Emanuel was the first to complete a tape, and he read so well that Etheridge Knight, to whom I sent Emanuel's tape as a model, said that Emanuel gave him an inferiority complex with regard to his own reading. Knight made four tapes before he produced one which was satisfactory.

There are interesting sound effects in some of the tapes. An explosive sound which occurs at a dramatic moment in Emanuel's tape near the end of "A View from the White Helmet" is the sound of an automobile backfiring. The percussive sounds at the beginning of Sonia Sanchez's tape, which she recorded in my home, are the tapping of her shoes as she walked back and forth while reading. When I played back the first few poems, I detected the noise, and asked her to pull off her shoes.

In 1969, books by Jon Eckels, Beatrice Murphy, Nancy Arnez, Sonia Sanchez, Marvin X, Keorapetse Kgositsile, and Stephany were published. Our list had expanded considerably from the two Broadsides with which we began in 1965. By 1970, we had sixteen books and thirty-two Broadsides.

Some of the books that were scheduled to be published were books by Lance Jeffers, Doughtry Long, and John Raven.

In 1968 Broadside Press began United States distribution of Paul Breman's *Heritage Series*, imported from England, which includes Conrad Kent Rivers' posthumous *The Still Voice of Harlem* and Russell Atkin's *Heretofore*. The series eventually included books by Lloyd Addison, Ray Durem, Owen Dodson, Audre Lorde, Dudley Randall, Ishmael Reed, and other poets. We also distributed an anthology of poetry, *Black Creations*, edited by Ahmed Alhamisi and Harun Kofi Wangara, published in 1969 by Alhamisi's Black Arts Publications.

We were reviewed by *Library Journal*, but we didn't get reviewed in the big periodicals, except for one book, Gwendolyn Brooks' autobiography, *Report from Part One*. *The New York Times* published a review of it. I also advertised in magazines and through mailing lists. We also sent out a newsletter and press releases on upcoming titles. The black journals, such as *Black World*, reviewed many of our books.[5] Probably, the one thing that helped us was that our books were inexpensive and were ordered for college courses. The Black Studies courses in colleges and universities would order many of our titles.[6]

Randall's relationship with Don L. Lee evolved into a poetry business exchange. Lee's popularity drew attention to Broadside while Randall's credentials brought credibility to Third World Press. But when Lee proposed that Broadside Press and Third World Press merge, Randall disclosed to his assistant editors that Lee was young and ambitious and that it was better to keep Broadside independent. While Lee wanted to join forces with Randall, Nikki Giovanni switched publishers and signed a contract with the William Morrow publishing house in New York. Her rationale was that Morrow serviced a different audience, but this business decision was a far cry from the suggested militancy of the times. Many in the Black Arts Movement regarded this shift as a defection, trading commitment for mainstream fame. Although Broadside's business manager, Bill Whitsitt, explained that Giovanni's Morrow publications adversely affected Broadside sales because it was a compilation of two of her three Broadside chapbooks, Randall expressed no disapproval of Giovanni's decision or any poet's decision to publish with mainstream publishers:

> Since Black publishers can't publish all Black writers, perhaps it's the writers who have the courage to pioneer, experiment, cooperate, and perhaps sacrifice in determining who should publish with Black publishers. I don't

think that Black writers should feel any guilt about publishing with a white publisher. There are more than enough authors to go around.[7]

In retrospect, Randall elaborated on the popularity of black poetry, its universal appeal, and the marketplace for Broadside books:

There was something in the air the '60s, and the poetry was new too. People today are not as enthusiastic about poetry as they were then. The political climate, the sit-ins and the civil demonstrations focused attention on the black revolt. Poetry is more emotional than prose, and it was a time of emotions.

During the 60s, I would go to Vaughn's Bookstore and observe the people. He wouldn't even have to try to sell a book. I remember a time when all he had to do was stand behind the cash register and ring up sales. People have told me they have spent hundred of dollars there because when the big bookstores wouldn't stock black books, it was the main place to go to get them.

I think it was sales that also helped to change the publishing of black literature. Then, blacks were in the public eye. Major publishers even went back and reprinted works from the Harlem Renaissance. They reprinted DuBois's Souls of Black Folk, *originally published in 1903, because they wanted to get into the money. Black books would sell, if for no other reason than curiosity. The public questioned: What do these people want?*

When Bantam first published The Black Poets, *which I edited, the cost was $1.65. It was a two-or three-hundred-page book. We couldn't afford to do that. Our first books sold for $1.00 and were sixteen pages. During the sixties and early seventies, there was a proliferation of black publishers. Don Lee for instance, followed my example and founded Third World Press, and then there was another press founded in New York. There was Amiri Baraka's Jihad Press in Newark, and there were presses in the West, in San Francisco.*

I think Broadside set the precedent and we were well known across the country. I have a niece in New York, Marilyn Randall, who's a television actress, and she says she knows a lot of actors and writers and they know my name; as soon as she tells them she's Marilyn Randall, they say, are you any relation to Dudley Randall? I said that to say that I think Broadside Press was partly responsible because people knew the books all over the country. We also sold books in Europe, Africa, Australia, New Zealand, New Guinea, South America, and elsewhere.

Reprints were very popular then. There was a company that bought all of our books, and I think they were hoping that we would go out of business like a lot of small publishers. Then, they could reprint our books and sell them at a profit. We tried to keep Broadside prices low. Most of our books were printed *in soft covers because we wanted students, young people, and poor people to be able to afford them. But we would also publish the same titles in hard covers and sell them for $5 or $6 dollars.*

One of the influences on me was the Great Depression. The depression, I think bred in my generation a distrust of businessmen, and I'm afraid I was not a good businessman because I looked on making a profit as a bad thing. Looking back, I see that was not the right attitude because if you want to stay in business your income must at least equal or should exceed your expenses. But I didn't care about making money. I wasn't interested in profit. I just cared about publishing good poetry.

Some people are better working with their hands than I, and they would type their manuscripts and mimeograph their books, but we never had a book like that. Because I worked in the library, I handled books. I liked good, clear type. All the Broadside books were letter pressed in sharp, offset letter type. I would choose the type to harmonize with the book, and I would design the cover to harmonize with the contents of the book. We engaged Detroit artists to help us, like Shirley Woodson-Reid and Cledie Taylor. Some of the poets had their own artists, such as Sonia Sanchez had an artist who designed some of her books.

Many of the Broadsides were designed by artists. There is a famous poem of Gwendolyn Brooks, "We Real Cool," that's been anthologized maybe hundreds of times. It was designed as a broadside by Cledie Taylor. Cledie designed it like a scroll on a blackboard. I had a young assistant editor, and I designed the Broadside, "To Darnell and Johnny" by Melba Joyce Boyd in the black nationalist colors: red, black, and green. The top is red, the body of the poem is black, and the bibliographical information is in green.

We published a Broadside by Jean Toomer, who was one of the best poets of the Harlem Renaissance and one of my favorite poets. He's been called a poet's poet, because it is poets who especially admire his work. We published a broadside by Etheridge Knight, which was illustrated by Juanita Long, who is the wife of the Broadside poet Doc Long.

It was either fate or a coincidence that the preacher who performed my first marriage was Rev. William Whitsitt Sr., who is the father of Bill Whitsitt Jr., who became the office manager of Broadside Press in 1971 until 1977. Reverend Whitsitt is also the father of Ruth Whitsitt Fondren and Joyce Whitsitt, aka Malaika Wangara, both of whom were office managers for Broadside Press before Bill. I met Joyce in 1962 when Margaret Danner directed Boone House, and Joyce came to one of the poetry readings. When I found out her name was Whitsitt, and I realized it was her father who had performed the marriage ceremony, I brought photographs of the wedding to Boone House to show her. She was not even born in 1935, but that was how I became friends with the

27. William Whitsitt, office manager of Broadside Press, 1972.

Whitsitt family, and years later she, her sister, and her brother worked for Broadside.

At one time, there were as many as eight people working at the press, mostly part-time. Jill became the editor of The Broadside Annual. *William Whitsitt, Melba Joyce Boyd, Deirdre Honore, Lisa Fondren (daughter of Ruth Whitsitt Fondren), Deborah McAfee, Gayle Harris, and Ricky Roberts. While writing her master's thesis on Broadside Press, poet Frenchy Hodges worked at Broadside. Sandra Boyd and John Clore, Melba's sister and brother, worked for Broadside as well.*

Situated directly across the alley from Randall's home, the third Broadside Press office, like the others before it, had no sign on the door or marquee extending from the building. Only the mailman, a myriad of poets, relatives of the staff, and friends from the community found the path to the side door. The harsh overhead lighting rebounded against drab, beige walls that divided the tiny offices into spaces where boxed books were shelved. Chairs were arranged at heavy, wooden desks covered by paper, order forms, and hopeful manuscripts awaiting examination or galleys anticipating the printer's final directions for production.

Like the obscure rafters of a poet's imagination, the Broadside staff worked in isolation. In the rustic quarters of an office initially constructed to exterminate vermin from homes and businesses, they made beautiful books full of energy and light and posted them for destinations around the world. Detroit was a big city, a population of approximately 1,600,000 during this time. But in other ways, it was still a small town, where families intersected and worked together.

The poets, more often than not, were absent. Sometimes their voices came through the telephone, but their image was the imagery of words and their visages were single portraits on book covers. The staff assessed the poets by their telephone manners and measured their value inside the vortex of their poetry. In these modest quarters—shipping, filing, packing, and editing were weight of work—they processed literary products.

An artistic sensibility characterized Broadside publications. The chapbooks are sixteen pages in length, with offset type, and printed on heavy stock paper. With the longer books, the pages warranted perfect binding instead of staples, which could stress the pages, or glued binding, which hardens and dissipates over time. Printings of five thousand and ten thousand contributed to affordability without sacrificing quality. Broadside Press books rivaled those produced by large publishers with comparable production standards because of Randall's deep regard for "the feel and the heft of books." The properties of presentation were as important as the poetic expressions they illuminated.

As a gift for Don L. Lee's thirtieth birthday, Gwendolyn Brooks financed the publication of *Directionscore: Selected and New Poems* in 1972. This evergreen, hardcover, limited-edition book with gold trimmed pages celebrated Lee's prolific and successful career. In the case of George Barlow's *Gabriel*, Randall selected distinctive materials for the soft- and hardcover editions. Believing the audience should be able to see the poet, Randall placed photographs on the back of most of the books. Barlow's black and white photograph was imprinted on the front of the antique gold paperback, but the hard cover sports a rich, scarlet red with gold lettering for the title.

A monthly newsletter, prepared by the staff, reported on the number of books sold, the reissue of printings or editions, as well as notices of book reviews. Press releases were drafted and sent to all viable patrons, periodicals, journals, and critics, and review copies were sent out in considerable number. The *Negro Digest* (later *Black World*) noted information from the newsletters in nearly every edition. *Library Journal* was also responsive to the press releases, which prompted considerable library orders of books and broadsides from a press run by a librarian. African American poetry published by Broadside was circulated nationally and internationally throughout bookstores, libraries, and by personal orders.

Without the economic resources available to large-scale businesses, persistent financial difficulties plagued the press and constituted real problems. But as the press grew and drew attention from the commercial establishment, appeals to co-opt publishing initiatives were extended to Broadside and other small presses. Randall insisted on remaining independent:

> Several years ago a publisher's organization invited Black publishers to hearings, where they could unfold their plans in order to obtain financial or technical help from white publishers or financial institutions. I talked it over with other writers, whose consensus was that it was like standing upon the slave auction block, and I did not attend the hearings. When Rosyln Targ, a literary agent, suggested that I arrange to have Broadside books distributed by a large publisher, I told her no.[8]
>
> About delays in publication, again lack of funds of under-capitalized Black publishers is the probable cause. The publisher may owe his printer, and may be loath to get deeper into debt, or perhaps the printer holds up his copy until his debt is reduced. I think the writer should understand this, and be willing to wait. Amos Tutuola had to wait six years after acceptance before his best-selling *The Palm Wine Drunkard* [*sic*] was published, and he had a wealthy white publisher. Some authors have a reassuring confidence in their publisher. When I questioned Larry Neal about the delay in publishing his *Black Boogaloo*, he smiled and said, "Joe Goncalves has it, and I know Joe will publish it in good time."[9]

BROADSIDE CRITICS SERIES

In the service of black literary criticism, Randall wrote several reviews for *Negro Digest*, on the poetry of Gwendolyn Brooks, Margaret Danner, Robert Hayden, June Jordan, Audre Lorde, Naomi Long Madgett, Carolyn Rodgers, and Margaret Walker, among others, as well as articles on a number of anthologies of black poetry. In "Ubi Sunt and Hic Sum," Randall identifies parallels in technique and historical circumstances between the "Ballad of Dead Ladies," by the fifteenth-century French poet François Villon, and "Harlem Gallery," by Melvin B. Tolson, demonstrating his extensive knowledge of poetry and the collective unconscious. In the same issue of *Negro Digest* (September 1965) he published reviews of the poetry of Derek Walcott, Kath Walker (an Australian aboriginal poet), and *Ik ben de nieuwe Neger* (I am the new negro), an anthology of black poetry edited by Rosey E. Pool.

In a letter to James A. Emanuel, Randall expressed his frustration with the dearth of literary criticism on black poets:

> When I was writing a paper about the late Melvin B. Tolson, I was surprised to find so little about him. There were many critical articles about poets to whom he had been compared—T. S. Eliot, Ezra Pound, and others, but almost nothing about him. I had the usual reaction of labeling this neglect "white discrimination"; but when I reflected, "Why do we have to wait for whites to study our writers? Why don't we do it ourselves? We have plenty of professors, poets, critics, writers. Why don't we write our own criticism?"[10]

Randall wanted Broadside's series on criticism to be a comprehensive overview of black poetry. Without a historical appreciation of the genre, the poetry would not be understood within its unique context or within the nuances of its cultural experience. Moreover, his observations about this pervasive literary ignorance instigated the decision to develop a critical series so the poetry audience could be more sophisticated in its readings, if it so desired.

In a review for *Negro Digest*, Randall praised James Emanuel's book of criticism on Langston Hughes for the Twayne Series of American Literature. So, when he decided to initiate the series, he contacted Emanuel. In 1970, Emanuel became the chief editor of *The Broadside Critics Series*. Randall and Emanuel devised the concept for the series, identified poets to be reviewed, and considered literary subjects for the series. Topics ranged from the eighteenth-century poet Phillis Wheatley to the militant poets of the 1960s. *The Broadside Critic Series* was a rather ambitious project and was far more difficult to negotiate than the poetry publications. However, due to an overextended publishing schedule in 1973, Randall explained in a letter to Emanuel that the publishing plans for the series had to be modified:

> Bill and I went over the list of books we're committed to in 1974 and there were 20! I'd hoped to cut down to 4 (our ideal number) in 1975 and perhaps keep down to 6 in 1974. I guess my left hand didn't know what my right hand was doing. So we can go easy on the series for now. You're a painstaking worker and I guess you've worked over-hard on the editing. This will give you a respite. There are still some things we can keep in mind for when the pressure eases. My study of Gwendolyn Brooks and our history of Black American literature. The work on Gwen I don't know when I can find time

28. James A. Emanuel with Dudley Randall in New York, 1968.

to write. I want it to be definitive, with an exhaustive bibliography and a careful examination of her major poems and evaluation of previous criticism, all in 48 pages. That's something I think you'll have to insist on.

I've seen the Columbia and Minnesota series and they keep to 48 pages even though they treat major writers such as Frost and Hemingway. You can still be working on the history. It will require much reading, thinking, and weighing. You'll have to sift out the less important writers and weigh your words carefully to give just estimates. In a way, it's harder to write a short book than a long one. Melba, my assistant editor, wants to do a criticism, and I suggested Hayden. She said she couldn't do it now and I said, Fine!, and explained the situation. Your proposed book of excerpts is much like my idea—"Black Poets on Black Poetry." But since we'd have to pay for excerpts, I think the history would take precedence.[11]

Randall and Emanuel developed an ideal roster of critics that included Larry Neal on Amiri Baraka; Stephen Henderson on Don L. Lee; Sarah Webster Fabio on Margaret Walker; William Robinson on Phillis Wheatley; Addison Gayle on Claude McKay; Lance Jeffers on the Negro Spirituals as poetry; Dudley Randall on Gwendolyn Brooks; James A. Emanuel on Langston Hughes and a historical overview of black poetry.

They were unable to secure Neal, Henderson, or Fabio for the series, but aspiring young academics who also needed publishing opportunities submitted manuscripts to the series. A manuscript on Jean Toomer by Houston A. Baker was rejected because it was not sufficiently focused on the language of Toomer's poetry, but his book on Countee Cullen, *A Many Colored Coat*, was subsequently accepted for publication. William Robinson's *Phillis Wheatley in the Black American Beginnings* and Addison Gayle Jr.'s *Claude McKay: The Poet at War* were very popular titles. Other critics included Bernard Bell, who authored *The Folk Roots of Afro-American Poetry*, and Don L. Lee wrote a collection of essays on contemporary poets entitled *Dynamite Voices*.

Although the problems of small press publishing persisted, the accomplishments of Broadside Press in only eight years were astounding. In a 1974 interview, Randall proudly exclaimed that "Haki Madhubuti has made history by selling more than 100,000 books, not once depending on white publishers."[12] By the time *Broadside Authors and Artists,* a bio-bibliographic publication, appeared in 1974, the press had published one hundred and ninety-two authors either in individual books, in the eight anthologies, or in the eighty-nine broadsides.[13] Randall's liberated editorial perspective was a contributing factor to the growth of the press and the diversity in the publications.

In 1975, Broadside Press published *The Last Ride of Wild Bill* by Sterling Brown, a Harlem Renaissance poet whose *Southern Road* (1932) had been out of print for a decade. Randall explained in his essay "The Black Aesthetic of the Thirties, Forties, and Fifties" that

> like Langston Hughes, [Brwon] brings the blues stanza into formal verse. He has the unusual and valuable quality of humor, which permeates his ballads of Slim Greer, a picaresque adventurer. There are ballads of John Henry and of the chain gang, and poems of sharecroppers and southern rural life. These are poems of Negro life written out of black experience grounded in folk poetry which he intensifies with his art.
>
> (Randall, "The Black Aesthetic," 40)

In the preface to Brown's book, Randall recalls the occasion when Brown announced that he had consented to publish a book with Broadside Press:

April 18, 1973 was an important date for Broadside Press. That night some of us attending the Gwedolyn Brooks seminar at Howard University—Gwedolyn Brooks, Carl Carter, Mari Evans, Hoyt Fuller, Don Lee, and I were invited to Sterling Brown's home. There, we literally sat at the feet of the venerated poet while he showed us his rare books and entertained us with anecdotes ("lies," he called them) of W. E. B. Du Bois, Walter White, and other outstanding men he had known.[14]

Randall's ambition to address the invisibility of black poetry was comprehensive, and his belief in economic independence for this enterprise was steadfast.

I believe poetry should cover a broad range. I didn't want to censor the poets. I may have disagreed with some of the things they said in their poetry, but I would let it go because I don't believe in censorship.

I believe that a poet has the right to write as he or she wants to write and not as they are told. As long as the poetry moved me or other people, it could be published. I would accept poets on whether I liked the poetry, not so much on their political stances but on what I thought was their ability as poets.

Broadside Press has not been subsidized or funded by any individual, organization, foundation, or government agency. It is, has been, and always will be, free and independent. It is a free, black institution. Support for the Press has come from the grassroots, from poets who donated their poems to the anthology *For Malcolm* in honor of Malcolm; from the poets in the first group of *The Broadside Series*, who steadfastly refused payment for their poems; from the many persons who subscribed in advance for *The Broadside Series* and the anthologies, so that they could be printed; and from others who donated sums above their subscriptions. It is the poets and the people who have supported Broadside Press.

I've declined partnerships, mergers, and incorporation, as I want freedom and flexibility of action; want to devote the press to poetry; and am afraid that stockholders in a corporation would demand profits and would lower quality or go into prose in order to obtain profits. Income from the press goes into publishing new books in an attractive and inexpensive format. I pay royalties to other poets, but royalties on my own books go back into the press. I'm not against royalties for myself, or profits for the company, if they ever come, but I'm more interested in publishing good poetry. . . .

In a broader sense, however, Broadside Press is, in embryo, one of the institutions that black people are creating by trial and error out of necessity for self-determination and independence. I don't think it's necessary to belabor the importance of poetry. Poetry has always been with us. It has always been sustenance, a teacher, an inspiration, and a joy. In the present circumstances it helps in the search for black identity, reinforces black pride and black unity, and is helping to create the soul, the consciousness, and the conscience of black folk. . . .

I admit that I am not well qualified to operate in a capitalistic society. I came of age during the Great Depression, and my attitude toward business is one of dislike and suspicion. Writers who send me manuscripts and speak of "making a buck" turn me off.

Capitalistic writers praise the profit motive as a powerful incentive. I think they are liars. I have to confess that I seldom think of profits. My strongest motivations have been to get good black poets published, to produce beautiful books, help create and define the soul of black folk, and to know the joy of discovering new poets. I guess you could call it production for use instead of for profit.

We are a nation of twenty-two million souls, larger than Athens in the Age of Pericles or England in the Age of Elizabeth. There is no reason why we should not create and support a literature which will be to our own nation, and to the world, what those literatures were to theirs.[15]

16

"SHAPE OF THE INVISIBLE":
THE RISE AND FALL OF BROADSIDE PRESS

Light has laid down its chisel.
Only a staring, mutilated moon
Crawls over the dim meadows of the mind
Where my love lies irrevocably lost,
Beyond the clasp of pity or desire.

—From "Nocturne," by Dudley Randall

WHEN I CAME TO WORK AT BROADSIDE PRESS IN THE SUMMER OF 1972, the company was approaching its peak period. Forty-five of the eighty-one books published between 1966 and 1975 were printed in the last three years of that period. The office was bursting at the seams from boxes of books piled on floors, shelves, and under tables. Stacks of paper crowded desktops—manuscripts, correspondence, galleys, schedules, newsletters—publishing matter in various forms and stages of development commandeered any available space. In kind, my life was as densely packed as Broadside Press operations. In the midst of an antagonistic political climate, my editorial work at the press, my teaching responsibilities, and my emergence into literary culture intensified my return home from the university. The city bristled with cultural fervor and radical politics.

Entry into the cultural community via Broadside positioned me in the middle of literary activity. In a very short period of time, I knew almost all of the black writers in the city. I hung out at Concept East and spent considerable time with Ron Milner and Bill Harris. Milner discouraged my interest in literary criticism and insisted writing poetry was more important. But the activity that best focused my creative energy was a writing workshop organized by Mary Helen Washington that included myself, Jill Witherspoon Boyer, Frenchy Hodges, Paulette Childress White, Toni Watts Eubanks, and Betty De Ramus. Initially, Dudley Randall and Naomi Madgett attended the sessions, but eventually our meetings serviced the developing literary styles and philosophical concerns of young women writers

The times were changing. The machismo nationalism that characterized the Black Power Movement and campus politics was challenged by the Women's Movement and complicated by Marxist radicalism. In Detroit, these debates emanated throughout the campuses of Wayne State University and the University of Detroit and in political organizations in the community. Emotionalism was not an effective offering in a debate about an actual event that involved duplicitous actions on the part of black and white politicians. Unlike the ranting and rhetorical rage of cultural nationalism, which held few answers, unreliable strategies, and too much ego worship, scientific socialism used logic and analyses based on material reality. Being black and proud was a slogan best expressed in the refrains of James Brown, and it wasn't long before the illusion of self-promotion required serious self-criticism that could not be excused by simply blaming "the white man." Moreover, the dialectic was broadened to include gender. In turn, these complications surfaced in the poetry.

AUDRE LORDE

Born in Grenada, Audre Lorde developed a poetry that affected the stylistic and thematic concerns of upcoming writers of the 1970s. This New York–based poet's first contact with Dudley Randall occurred through a review he wrote for *Negro Digest* of her first book, *The First Cities* (The Poet's Press, Inc. 1968):

Audre Lorde's *The First Cities* is a quiet, introspective book. You first notice the striking phrases: "the crash of passing sun," "a browning laughter," "the oyster world." Then you notice the images, most of them drawn from nature, a source unusual in this age of urban poets who write of concrete and machines.

But Audre Lorde is not a nature poet. Her focus is not on nature, but on feelings and relationships. The nature images, many of them pertaining to the seasons, illustrate inner weather, the changes of love or feelings. . . . She does not wave a black flag, but her blackness is there, implicit, in the bone, in "Suffer the Children."

Audre Lorde, for the most part, writes in a rhythmic, sparsely punctuated free verse. Sometimes, as in "To a Girl Who Knew What Side Her Bread Was Buttered On," she uses rime, and we notice the emphasis and the richness of sound which rime imparts. Audre Lorde's poems are not strident, and do not grab you by the collar and drag you in, but they attract you by their fresh phrasing, which draws you to return to them and to discover new evocations.[1]

As a consequence of this review, Lorde submitted *From A Land Where Other People Live* to Broadside. Randall almost rejected it because: "I had already over published my schedule, but Gwendolyn Brooks anxiously urged that I publish it."[2]

> Audre Lorde's style is unique among contemporary Black women poets. Her lines are long, Homeric, full breathed. They are full of images drawn from nature. Yet the subjects and book titles, *The First Cities*, *Cables to Rage*, *From a Land*, *The New York Head Shop*, are urban. Her approach is indirect, metaphorical, symbolic. Even her manner of reading aloud is different. She reads slowly, enunciating each word distinctly, hearing herself as she reads, not in the rapid, machine gun style of many Black women poets.[3]

In 1973, Audre Lorde's *From A Land Where Other People Live* was nominated for a National Book Award. Poems such as "New Year's Day" demonstrate Lorde's enigmatic and distinctive imagery:

> Rain falls like tar on my skin
> my son picks up a chicken heart at dinner
> asking
> does this thing love?
> Deft unmalicious fingers of ghosts
> pluck over my dreaming
> hiding whatever it is of sorrow
> that would profit me
>
> I am deliberate
> and afraid
> of nothing.

The distinction of the nomination identified Lorde as a major American poet. Randall went to New York for the awards dinner and their first face-to-face meeting:

> Audre and I excitedly attended the ceremonies in New York, where Audre was to meet Adrienne Rich to make a joint statement of the women poets nominated, including Alice Walker with *Revolutionary Petunias*. After the ceremonies—enlivened by a streaker—Audre and I went downstairs where we were to meet Ms. Rich backstage. As I paused at the breast-high stage,

wondering how I was to get on it and lift Audre upon it, Audre nimbly scrambled up and gave me a hand saying, "How's that for a fat old lady?"

We found Adrienne back stage with her publisher's representative, who took us in a long black limousine to the cocktail party at the Biltmore Hotel. (I wondered when Broadside would be able to afford a limousine.) Audre had promised to take me on the Staten Island ferry and show me her house in Staten Island, but we celebrated so late that we didn't have time the next morning.[4]

Lorde's poetry complicated the political and social perspectives of race and gender and disrupted the popular values of nationalist aesthetics. About her gender, Lorde said Randall "never accepted or approved of my being a Lesbian, but he did publish the work and supported it—altho it was only on the insistence and with the financial support of Gwendolyn Brooks that he accepted the manuscript of *From a Land Where Other People Live* for publication."[5]

Unbeknownst to Lorde, Randall's initial decision against publication was financial. Regarding the lesbian content, he explained that he suggested the exclusion of poems that were explicitly homosexual to protect her. His paternalism anticipated a negative critical response, but it was precisely her feminism and her lesbianism that distinguished her literary prominence in the upcoming decade and illuminated the narrow homophobic values inherent in nationalism. In sync with the rise of the Women's Movement, Broadside published a second book by Audre Lorde, *New York Head Shop* (1975). Lorde's Bremen Press publication, *Cables to Rage*, was also distributed by Broadside. Lorde's voice was fast becoming a critical and consulted source for black feminist issues and lesbian concerns.

In the face of more definitive ideological discussions and shifting political positions, the Black Arts Movement began to dissipate. Black women writers challenged black male chauvinism, and the right and the left sides of issues turned into battles that ultimately exposed the fragility of race unity. Two short years after the Black Political Caucus in Gary, Indiana, Imamu Baraka rejected cultural nationalism and embraced Marxism as his political doctrine. He had effectively gone full circle, and he and Don L. Lee (Haki Madhubuti) parted ways. Poet and scholar Lorenzo Thomas, who was a member of Umbra during the 1960s, discusses Baraka's conversion in *Extraordinary Measures*:

He's been quite straightforward about it. His own earlier militant poems, Baraka said, "came from an enraptured patriotism that screamed against whites as the eternal enemies of Black people, as the sole cause of our disorder + oppression. The same subjective mystification led to mysticism,

29. Audre Lorde, ca. 1973.

metaphysics, spookism, etc., rather than dealing with reality." Reality he feels, would have been the recognition of his movement's innocent adherence to "an ultimately reactionary nationalism that served no interests but our newly emerging Black bureaucratic elite and petit bourgeois, so that they could have control over their Black market."[6]

Inside the eye of the storm, poetry and Broadside Press persisted, as the boundaries of the press were expanded to include African and Latino poets.

Jose-Angel Figueroa's *East 110th Street* (1973) was our first publication by a Puerto Rican poet, and the decision to publish Richard Carr's translation of *Tengo* (1974) by Cuban poet Nicolas Guillen expanded Broadside's identity and its mission. Although we could not afford to publish it as a bilingual edition, Dudley and I felt it was an important book to bring to our audience. Jill Boyer further demonstrated this direction with *The Broadside Annual*. The 1973 edition was international in scope, including Black American, African, Puerto Rican, and Brazilian poets. The diasporic perspective infused our editorial decisions. We were as aware of the dynamics of international literary developments as we were attuned to the historical consciousness of our national literature. That same year, we published *Betcha Ain't: Poems from Attica*, edited by Celes Tisdale, who conducted a poetry workshop following the prison demonstration and crisis of September 9–13, 1971.

The list of poets was legion and legendary. By 1975, in addition to the poets already discussed, those poets who had published single collections included: Ahmed Alhamisi, Nancy Arnez, Alvin Aubert, George Barlow, Henry Blakely, Jill Witherspoon Boyer, Arthur Boze, Linda Bragg, Sterling Brown, Charles Cannon, Gene Drafts, Jon Eckels, Jose-Angel Figueroa, Nicholas Guillen, Everett Hoagland, Frenchy Hodges, Mae Jackson, Lance Jeffers, Keorapetse Kgositsile, Lyn Levy, Pearl Cleage Lomax, Doughtry Long, Clarence Major, Beatrice Murphy, Marion Nichols, Arthur Pfister, Jon Randall, John Raven, Judy Simmons, William Thigpen Jr., and Habte Wolde. Poets published in the *Broadside Series*, ninety-five by December 1975, became even more representative of our literary diversity. Many new poets were introduced in the series as Randall shifted the focus from classic and well-known poems to previously unpublished poets. In this regard, he brought attention to neophyte poets, but he also published practically every noted poet at this time, including: Robert Hayden, Gwendolyn Brooks, Melvin B. Tolson, Jean Toomer, Margaret Walker, Naomi Long Madgett, Margaret Danner, Lucille Clifton, June Jordan, Sterling Plump, Sarah Webster Fabio, Eugenia Collier, Charles H. Rowell, Melvin Dixon, Michael Harper, Alice Walker, Pinkie Gordon Lane, Johari Amini, Bobb Hamilton, Stephanie Fuller, Carolyn Rodgers, Askia Muhammad Toure, Sterling Plumpp, Herbert Martin, Charles Rowell, Sterling Brown, Walter Cox, and others.

The chapbooks, the anthologies, and *The Broadside Series* claimed nearly two hundred poets, a spectrum that spans the twentieth century, since and including the Harlem Renaissance. To accommodate the growing demand for biographical and bibliographical information on the writers, Randall recruited a fellow librarian at the University of Detroit, Leonead Bailey, to edit a resource book, *Broadside Authors and Artists* (1974). Randall's comprehensive view for the needs of black poetry and black poets were reiterated by this project:

> There are 192 persons included in this book. Out of a total of 183 entries for Americans, 169, or 94 per cent, are not listed in *Who's Who in America* 1972–73. Out of a total of 184 entries for authors, 166, or 90 per cent, are not listed in *Contemporary Authors*. These inclusions, I believe, make *Broadside Authors and Artists* a needed supplement to these and other biographical reference books.[7]

Other books published by Broadside outside the realm of poetry included an autobiography of a Tuskegee airman, *Who Is Chauncey Spencer?* Randall was particularly interested in publishing the book because the author was the son of the poet Anne Spencer. Broadside also published a cookbook, *A Safari of African Cooking*. Randall published *Broadside Memories: Poets I Have Known* in anticipation of the tenth anniversary celebration.

Within a cultural context that advocated the aesthetics of resistance, the range of Broadside Press publications illustrated the diversity of discontent and the beauty of poetic dissonance. About Jon C. Randall's *Indigoes*, Dudley wrote that the poetry "is enriched by sudden startling phrases and images which upon reflection are seen to be appropriate." To Jill Witherspoon Boyer's *Dream Farmer*, he conferred "'sunken' images, that is, images which do not present a sharp sensuous picture, but gain their power through the suggestiveness of relationships, as in the phrase, 'learning her.' Such images recur in contemplative or philosophical poetry, and though the following poem about relationships is mostly stark, such images do occur."[8]

The subtlety and introspection that emerged in the poetry of the 1970s was a logical response to the volatile didacticism of the 1960s. Perhaps this shift occurred because the next generation of poets benefited from the wealth of resurrected black literature. Black Arts poetry was constrained by an urban linguistic landscape that was dominated by the black male perspective. The emerging literary demands engaged the challenges of the Women's Movement and connected with global, human struggles within the context of world literature. This new poetry claimed the recently liberated literary space and infused it with more diffuse imagery and ecliptic reflections that challenged Black Arts poetics. Audre Lorde's poetry, in particular, was a direct link to this rethinking of aesthetics, as history and politics demanded a new vocabulary for another conversation.

My sojourn to Tanzania in the summer of 1975 was in accord with this design to expand my own vocabulary. I encountered an undefined colony of

African American expatriates composed of Vietnam War draft resistors, disillusioned civil-rights activists, and optimistic Pan Africanists exploring an alternative socioeconomic system in Dar Es Salaam. I befriended some of the most fascinating personalities negotiating blackness in a poor, socialist country. The depths of the cultural differences affirmed my American identity, and yet this short visit extended my personal capacities into deeper regions of consideration because the experience was so unique. The gentleness of the people in the desert and in the mountain town of Arusha revealed a serene and uncontaminated humanity. Generosity was offered with such effortless grace, that I was convinced that "progress" in our "advanced" lifestyle was largely responsible for the killing of kindness.

But in the city I was appalled by the aggressive male chauvinism, shunned by people with a narrow perception of black identity, and criticized by British-educated African men for being American and an educated woman. Despite its possibilities and the striking beauty of the land, the repression of women triggered my rebellious nature. Because of my physical ambiguity, I was often mistaken for a white person, a Portuguese, and treated rudely because of my fair complexion. Once, when waiting for a fellow American in the desert town of Singhita at the bus station, a drunk started harassing me because he thought I was a defenseless woman traveling alone. Because of his unstable condition and his small frame, I surmised I could handle the situation. I was annoyed but unafraid.

Then Kaijucha, an African American from Chicago, appeared and told the Tanzanian to leave me alone. The man asked him why did he care about this white woman. He was then told, "She is not a white woman, but the daughter of the woman you sold for a bottle of beer." A look of deep shame sobered the man's expression. He walked over to the concession stand and purchased a bottle of beer, promptly set it on the table in front of me, bowed his head and apologized profusely for his disrespect. The apology was both personal and historical. It was the first time and only time that anyone, black or white, had ever apologized to me for slavery.

My return trip to the United States included a five-day layover in Paris. The hassles in customs presented me with racism from the other side of the black/white prism. (I was the only person of color to disembark.) Skin color was a global signifier for international mistreatment of others. I pretended not to understand a word of French and promptly produced my American passport. After they realized that I was not a dark-skinned immigrant from one of their previous colonies, I was politely excused from any further scrutiny. In this situation, being an American overshadowed my racial difference.

The contrast of Paris against the backdrop of weeks spent in East Africa was startling. The artistic sensibility of the city—the architecture, the shops, the museums, the cafes, the attention to detail in every aspect and nuance of cultural expression—whetted my appetite and aroused my jealousy. But as in Africa, the social disappointments countered much of the charm. The discrimination against Africans from the former colonies was evident in the social stratification. During my brief stay in Paris, I walked effortlessly and anonymously throughout the city. I walked for miles through narrow side streets into curio shops, into bookstores, into museums, and into the campus of the Université de la Sorbonne. I wondered at this place that had inspired Alexander Dumas, Charles Baudelaire, and Victor Hugo. I searched for sites where Richard Wright and Chester Himes cavorted and Josephine Baker and Duke Ellington dazzled. I saw copies of Broadside books in American literature sections of bookstores and felt gratified. Then, I bought a great pair of brown leather boots to wear on the flight crossing the Atlantic Ocean.

BROADSIDE PRESS TENTH-ANNIVERSARY CELEBRATION

When I got home, I cast myself into preparations for the upcoming anniversary celebration for the press. The trip to Africa interrupted my duties, and I discovered that some of our volunteers had been less than responsible to their commitments. Nevertheless, the press staff and a supportive Detroit network, including writers, family, and close friends, effectively came together and organized the final arrangements. On the weekend of 26–28 September 1975, Broadside Press celebrated its tenth anniversary. The initial planning, however, did not anticipate the overwhelming response of about 1,000 participants at a range of events. The audiences comprised poets, would-be poets, cultural advocates, and poetry lovers who poured into Detroit from all over the country.

The autumn weather was serene. An Indian summer ushered in a reversal of cool temperatures on warm winds and a reception given by Coleman A. Young at the Manoogian Mansion on the Detroit River. In his usual fashion, the mayor charmed the poets, the staff, and the guests by interrelating stories about politics and culture with his characteristic wry wit. Dudley Randall told Madhubuti at the mansion that "you never heard of Mayor Daley giving a reception for poets. This demonstrates the cultural advancement of Detroit over Chicago."

"Later, over 300 people packed the Faculty Club room of the University of Detroit at a 'meet-the-authors' party hosted by the school's Center for

Black Studies Director, Mary Helen Washington."[9] A poetry reading arranged by Washington included the Broadside poets Henry Blakely, Stella Crews, Etheridge Knight, Frenchy Jolene Hodges, Audre Lorde, Don L. Lee (Haki Madhubuti), Arthur Pfister, Charles Rowell, Sonia Sanchez (aka Laila Mannan), Eileen Tann, Celes Tisdale, Jill Witherspoon Boyer, Dudley, and me.

Saturday morning writing workshops were held at the Detroit Public Library for poetry, fiction, journalism, and drama. In addition to the featured Broadside writers as workshop leaders, playwright Ron Milner and children's author Toni Watts Eubanks completed the roster. An open-mike reading in the auditorium of the main building of the Detroit Public Library for the attendants and workshop participants funneled a rush of creativity into performance.

Organized by the Delta Sigma Theta Sorority, the $30-a-plate sit-down dinner at Cobo Hall offset some of the cost of the celebration. Val Gray Ward of Chicago, the mistress of ceremonies, introduced the lineup as salutations and congratulations were exchanged in the form of testimonials, testifyin' and lyin', as well as the usual resolutions from municipal, county, and state officials. Councilwoman Erma Henderson proclaimed the dates of that weekend "Broadside Press Days" in the city of Detroit and Gwendolyn Brooks pledged to underwrite the cost of two new Broadside books and read her poem in honor of the occasion:

> —And when I told you,
> meeting you somewhere close
> to the heat and youth of the road,
> liking my loyalty, liking belief,
> you smiled and you thanked me but little believed me.
>
> Here is some sun!
>> (Brooks, "On the Tenth Anniversary of Broadside Press,"
>> *Negro Digest* 25, no. 3 [January 1976]: 91)

While dining on turkey, dressing, baked potato, and green beans almondine, the program proceeded with Randall's reading "The Six," a special broadside composed and printed for the celebration. Then, five of the six, Brooks, Knight, Lee, Lorde, and Sanchez read their poetry (Giovanni was not there). Etheridge Knight was the hit of the evening with a recitation of his sassy folk poem, "I Sing of Shine."

30. Dudley Randall, Sonia Sanchez, and Mayor Coleman A. Young at the Manoogian Mansion during the Broadside Press tenth-anniversary celebration.
Photo: Kwado Akpan. Courtesy Laura Mosley Collection.

31. Arthur Pfister, Don L. Lee (Haki Madhubuti), and Dudley Randall at the Manoogian Mansion during the Broadside Press tenth-anniversary celebration.
Photo: Kwado Akpan. Courtesy Laura Mosley Collection.

32. Gwendolyn Brooks at the Writers Workshop,
Broadside Press tenth-anniversary celebration.
Photo: Kwado Akpan. Courtesy Laura Mosley Collection.

33. Naomi Long Madgett at the Broadside Press tenth-anniversary celebration.
Photo: Kwado Akpan. Courtesy Laura Mosley Collection.

34. Frenchy Hodges in performance at the Broadside Press
tenth-anniversary celebration.
Photo: Kwado Akpan. Courtesy Laura Mosley Collection.

On Sunday in the Community Arts auditorium at Wayne State University, poetry readings by Jo Ann Anderson, Alvin Aubert, Linda Bragg, Jim Cunningham, C. Gene Drafts, Sarah Webster Fabio, Dennis Folly, Glenda Gracia, Pinkie Gordon Lane, Naomi Long Madgett, Herbert Martin, James A. Randall, Jon Randall, Ruth Steed, Eleanora Tate, and Reginald Wilson brought the weekend to an end. About forty Broadside poets attended the celebration that reinforced the reach and spirit of the press and Randall's belief in his work. For the first time since its founding, Broadside's budget was in the black, and all indications pointed toward creative prosperity and posterity. Or so it appeared.

THE FALL

Less than two months after the tenth anniversary celebration of Broadside Press, Bill Whitsitt announced to the staff that the press was in dire financial straits. The figure was in excess of $30,000, which was the outstanding amount owed to Harlo Printing Company. Most businesses would not have balked at this amount, but the press was inextricably woven into the finances of Vivian and Dudley Randall. The fall of the press could have meant financial ruin for the Randalls. Bookstores and poets alike owed Broadside significant sums, and over the long haul, Randall's generosity had become the undoing of the press.

When Sandra Boyd drafted a letter to send to debtors, Randall was reluctant to sign it because the letter stated that the debt would be turned over to a collection agency if the overdue bill was not paid. He said, since he had no intention to do that, why would he make such a threat? The staff persuaded him that this was merely a tactic that might render some payments. Besides, the staff felt engaging a bill collector was not such a bad idea. There was actually some response to the well-crafted "threat." Shortly thereafter, the Dun and Bradstreet company was engaged as our collector. However, the reason most businesses had not paid was because the national economy was slipping into a recession. Many of the small bookstores had gone out of business. Black studies courses were cut back or eliminated. Higher printing costs, as well as the tax on books in storage, had altered the economics of small press publishing.

To add insult to injury, the Internal Revenue Service audited the press. The books that remained in stock over a specified period of time were considered taxable revenue. The press was better off giving the books away than keeping them. We strategized to sell first edition collections of Broadside books and to offer substantial discounts in bulk sales to authors. At first, these appeals brought in some returns, but incessant bills and a dismal outlook far outdistanced the scant checks that trickled into the office with the daily mail.

Distressed and dismayed, Randall took an early retirement from the University of Detroit when he turned sixty-two on 14 January 1976 in order to work full time in an attempt to save the press. Etheridge Knight attempted to surmise the situation in a letter to Dudley:

I "heard" somewhere-someplace that you were "retiring." Any truth to that? What's happening?—Hope you are well. In any case, you are the best knower 'bout Dudley Randall. I don't mind telling you (as the ol folk say) I was mighty upset—still am when I "heard" it. You're such an important man/brother/poet to me. So. I'm selfish. But it's true to a lot of us. Guess I'll be seeing you if I come to Univ. of Detroit in mid-February. . . . Take care of yourself.[10]

Historical forces and economic circumstances undermined our efforts to save the press, but Dudley's response to our situation was personal. He was very fragile, more fragile than we imagined. In a short note to Etheridge Knight several months later, Randall hinted at his dire financial and emotional condition: "Book sales have fallen off, and I'm somewhat depressed. I hope things get better."[11]

In a letter to James Emanuel, Randall regretfully explained why he could not publish another book of poetry or any new selection for the *Broadside Critics Series*:

> I'm quite discouraged. It seems Broadside Press will have to go out of business. So don't plan on our doing another book for you. We owe the printer $31,000, besides other debts. I don't think we'll put out another critics book either.
>
> Sorry to give you this bad news, but that's the way things are here.[12]

Because Emanuel was in Warsaw, Poland, as a Fulbright professor and touring elsewhere as well, two months passed before he answered the letter:

> I was sorry to learn, from your letter of 10 February, that the press is in bad financial shape. Everywhere I went in Romania, Hungary, and Austria, I showed audiences copies of about a dozen Broadside Press books of poetry that I carried with me (some by Madhubuti, Sanchez, Knight, Lorde, you, and others). They were always interested. What a shame that some plan cannot be devised to put BP back on its feet (like investment-contributions from a number of Black writers—which I would surely join). But I suppose that you have considered a number of alternatives already.[13]

When Johnson announced the end of *Black World Magazine*, the press incurred another serious blow. Fuller's periodical served as the main source for announcements and provided critical space for poets and book reviews of their works. But unlike many writers, who stormed to an emergency meeting with the executives of Johnson publications to declare cultural treachery, Randall's response was that Johnson was a businessman and was invested in publishing to make a profit. Suffering his own peculiar conundrum, Randall cast no stones at Johnson's reconciliation with the inevitable.

In the fall of 1976, Bill Whitsitt started his own business venture. His time was divided between the press and this neighborhood bar. Although I was no longer teaching (having been fired from my position at a local college for union organizing), my time was divided between Ann Arbor, where I was a full-time doctoral student in English at the University of Michigan, and Broadside, now working only as a part-time editor. Broadside had once been our collective priority. As the workload declined, individual aspirations intervened, and we assumed disparate paths. Less than a year after the tenth anniversary celebration, Randall sold the press to the Alexander Crummell Center, a church-based organization.

As a poet, Dudley Randall viewed each facet of life as an opportunity to develop his poetic vision and vocabulary. As an assembly line worker, he developed an understanding of the power of labor. As a librarian, he recognized the resources of cultural production. He translated all of his life experiences and expertise into publishing. The sale of the press devastated Dudley, and his self-image was severely distorted by a sense of catastrophic failure. I expressed my disbelief at his self-deprecation and scolded him for dismissing the accomplishments of the past twelve years. Standing atop a library of Broadside books, I could not understand how he could consider this low period in Broadside Press history as failure, or, given the economic circumstances, view the decline as his fault.

But for Dudley, this was the death of a dream. His self-recriminations were subjective and psychological, and in my immaturity, I could not guess the depths of his emotional despair. In conversations with Naomi Madgett, I tried to grasp what was happening to Dudley. But his identity and his muse were more deeply invested in Broadside than any of us imagined. For when he stopped publishing, he also stopped writing. Even after the word went out, and his authors clamored to his side, neither Knight, Brooks, Lee (Madhubuti), Lorde, nor Sanchez could derail his depression. His voice receded, and conversations became one-sided echoes ringing in resolute silence. He declined reading invitations, ignored the mail, and turned a deaf ear to telephone calls.

In contrast to all the other appeals, he did respond to Robert Hayden, who was the poet-in-residence at the Library of Congress at the time (1976–78). The director of the Library of Congress invited Randall to give a poetry reading, but he never opened the letter. After much prodding on the phone, Hayden managed to convince Randall to come to Washington, D.C., for the reading. Hayden scheduled some private time with Dudley during a day filled with activities, including a luncheon in Randall's honor and an 8:00 P.M reading. Seeing his old friend and reading at the Library of Congress momentarily lifted Dudley's spirits. But even this honor failed to reassure him; as he told many of us, he had come to doubt the value of his poetry. Upon his return from the premier library of the United States and his birthplace, he told Ron Milner, "I'm not a poet. Gwen Brooks is a poet. Robert Hayden is a poet. My poetry is nothing."

Although he was a reticent participant, we convinced Dudley to attend our workshops. Our meetings were lively, and Dudley was comfortable in and comforted by a room full of women writers. We appealed to his knowledge and experience in our deliberations as we considered the aesthetic demands of popularity and the link between audience appeal and the intensity of protest. When poetry confirmed the anger and popular perceptions about our historical and racial circumstances, it generated interest and attracted a large audience. But when social movements declined and the times became more repressive and dismal, the audience became disinterested and distracted, and the poetry seemed to become disembodied words without a realizable context. To a large extent, this was what had undermined Broadside Press. Paradoxically, the poetry of the Black Power Movement, characterized by clever and cutting attacks against "the white man" and merciless berating of the masses with a big, black poetry stick, generated excitement and enthusiasm.

But these times motivated more complex aspirations. There was no mass movement to attach our poems to, and yet our internationalism and class issues intersected with the generation of writers that bridged the Harlem Renaissance and the Black Arts Movement. Moreover, our feminism complicated our racial concerns, and our creative vision pushed the aesthetic boundaries beyond the didacticism of protest. Our challenge, as we saw it, was to construct a vocabulary that could speak to black people, contemplate the intersection of race, gender, and class, engage the conversations of an international literary community, and address artistic demands with a transcendent vision. These were the kinds of conversations and conclusions that confounded our workshop and the next generation of writers.

Dudley had received a Michigan Council of the Arts Individual Artist Award. He was working on his autobiography. But his writing was very slow, and he was obviously uninspired. Mary Helen Washington completed the work for *Black-Eyed Susans* and, through her academic activities, shared information and contacts that helped the rest of us to get published. In particular, she sent short stories by Betty De Ramus and Paulette Childress and some of my poetry to the editors of *Sturdy Black Bridges* (Doubleday, 1979), a creative and critical anthology of works by and about black women. Paulette was working on a collection of poetry, *The Watermelon Dress*, that was eventually published by Naomi's Lotus Press, and Betty secured a column at the

Detroit Free Press. Toni Eubanks moved to New York and became a successful author of children's books.

Since I was one of the few people Dudley would let in the door, I visited him frequently, sharing new poems and personal traumas from my own life. While I was revising my doctoral dissertation, I was completing the manuscript for my first book of poetry, *Cat Eyes and Dead Wood* (1978), to be published by Fallen Angel Press. I asked Dudley to write the introduction. Initially, he refused, saying he could not write anything, anything at all. He had stopped working on his autobiography, as the personal reflections had become too painful. But I insisted, and reminded him that he was the only one who should write it since he was my mentor and the first to publish my poetry. He relented after I explained he only needed to write a short presentation:

> With the publication of her first book, Melba Joyce Boyd joins the roster of noteworthy young Black women poets. She has been an assistant editor of Broadside Press and has been published in *Broadside Series* and *First World*.
>
> Some exemplary lines illustrated his observations about the poetry, and the introduction ends with:
>
> She has moved from the direct emotional statements of her earlier poems to a more subtle evocative style. Her poems are introspective, but project a wide range of emotions and disturbing images of the city and its people. We are touched by her tensions, and can watch her development with interest, as she moves among shock and conflict.[14]

The publisher, Leonard Kniffel, was a librarian and an acquaintance of Dudley's. Capable and meticulous, Leonard acquired publishing grants from the National Endowment of the Arts and the Michigan Council for the Arts for the publication. Artist and activist Michelle Gibbs provided the drawings. The book appeared in December, the same month Dudley's older brother, James Andrew Peabody Randall, died of a heart attack (12 December 1978). Dudley was the sole surviving child of Arthur and Ada Randall. This chilling reality sealed his sense of desolation. He began wearing a long mustache in the style of his dead brother and receded further into a dark void.

THE RETREAT

In 1977, the attorney Ken Cockrel was elected to the Detroit City Council, and Mayor Young seemed to have the police under control. But the end of the Vietnam War adversely affected a national economy that had thrived on wartime profits. Automobile factories were shut down, jobs were exported to nonunion states or south of the border, and businesses and the middle class fled to suburban enclaves. In the broader context, the Civil Rights Movement was fading like a shadow from a previous life, and deadly drugs became the haven for despair and desperation. Although the Democrats had regained the White House, runaway inflation had thrown the nation into a state of flux, and the black community was conflicted by ambivalence and internal strife.

Like the end of the glorious Second Renaissance overwhelmed by financial collapse, or like the Harlem Renaissance overwhelmed by the devastation of the Great Depression, Dudley's depression was a metaphor for our cultural and social malaise. Almost without a pulse, we awaited change in what appeared to be more like a plague than a failed promise.

> knowing all that
> and a poem
> cannot repair yesterday
> or place the moon,
> i still suck in my sadness,
> sifting these words,
> trying to catch your smile
> before it slips
> below us,
> and the little life
> we have
> left.[15]

17

"IN THE MOURNING TIME": THE RETURN

For Vivian who snatched the shotgun out of my mouth,
Who walked by my side into the black pit and came out holding my hand,
Who shouted and scolded, cursed and wept, was patient and puzzled,
silent and smiling until she led me out the dark depths.

—Dudley Randall, from "A Litany of Friends"

DESPITE EVERYBODY'S PROTESTATIONS, Dudley repeatedly said to me, "My poetry is not that good." He turned a deaf ear to the counsel of his psychiatrist, and his refusal to write sealed his mental coffin. He sank deeper and deeper into the "black pit," until he resolved to kill himself.

> To my sleep at night there comes a constant guest.
> His eyes, deeper than any woman's eyes
> that ever burned in mine, destroy my rest.
> His voice. knifing and vibrant as the cries
> of lovers at the summit of delight,
> calls out my name with more than lovers' passion,
> while his pale hands, that drip blood in the night,
> reach to embrace me in forgiving fashion.
>
> ("Apparition," *More to Remember*, 20)

"Apparition," which was conceived after his first divorce and possibly marks when the first signs of his depression appeared, best reflects his spiritual desperation, his desire to ecape his torment. This was Dudley's mental condition when Vivian found her husband sitting on the side of their bed with the barrel of a shotgun pointed at his head. She quickly snatched the gun from his hands, grabbed him, and held onto his fragile, desperate utterances, reeling him out of the depths of despair.

This happened in winter, a few days after his birthday, 14 January, when the days are frozen and dark, and clouds threaten snowstorms and ice. A few weeks later, death revisited Dudley to claim the life of Robert Hayden. A tribute to honor Hayden was organized by the Department of English at the University of Michigan, but he was bedridden, dying from cancer. Dudley attended the program, but Hayden was unable to appear. Before Dudley left Ann Arbor, he went to see him at his home. Hayden complained that he did not have a copy of his Bremen publication, *Night Blooming Cereus*. He told Dudley, "Odd, I don't know how that happened. I don't have a single copy." The next day, Dudley returned with the book. This would be their last meeting. It had been a long journey since their first meetings in Black Bottom, a space that now lived only in stories, memories, and poetry. Hayden encouraged Dudley to appreciate the importance of his own existence, to abandon this gloom and regret. He praised Dudley's poetry and encouraged him to write, to carry on:

> We must not be frightened or cajoled
> into accepting evil as deliverance from evil.
> We must go on struggling to be human,
> though monsters of abstraction
> police and threaten us.
>
> (Hayden, "In the Mourning Time,"
> in *The Black Poets*, ed. Randall, 138)

Late that evening, Randall received a phone call announcing Hayden's death on 25 February 1980. A few weeks later, Dudley began writing again: "It started the fourth of April, when I wrote 'The Mini Skirt.' That was my first poem in five years. . . . And I followed two days later on Easter Sunday with 'To an Old Man.'"[1] He drafted a will and outlined his funeral program:

At my funeral there shall be no words except announcements. Father Charles Granger will preside. A skilled pianist will play the following pieces, to be printed on the program. My daughter, Phyllis Ada Randall Sherron and my wife, Vivian Barnett Spencer Randall, will write the obituary.

Funeral Service: (or program)

Processional: First movement of Chopin's Marche Funèbre, from Sonata No. 2, B Flat Minor, Op. 35.

Priest: "Our brother who lies here wishes that we close our eyes, listen to this music, and recall his life, his hopes and dreams, his struggles, failures, and achievements."

Pianist plays Beethoven's "Appassionata Sonata," Sonata No. 23, in F Minor, Opus 57.

At conclusion, Priest: "Let us rise and sing the first stanza of the Black National Anthem, "Lift Every Voice And Sing."

At conclusion, Recessional, while pianist plays, second, lyric movement of Chopin's Marche Funèbre, from Sonata #2, B Flat Minor, Op. 35.

When casket reaches door, pianist plays Schubert's joyous "Impromptu. . . . [Not discernible] and Priest says: "Our brother's final message is: Life is beautiful and wonderful. Sing. Laugh. Dance. Rejoice. AMEN."

Pall Bearers: Don Lee, Alvin Aubert, Hoyt Fuller,[2] Gwendolyn Brooks, Sonia Sanchez, Melba Boyd, Phillip Randall and Shirley Randall Ware.

Flower Bearers: Women of Delta Sigma Theta and Alpha Kappa Alpha.

As part of this resurrection, he traced his death walk by approaching the subject as a finite and measurable conclusion. When Dudley gave me a copy of his funeral program, he said, "According to the Bible, a man is only promised three score and ten and so I have only four more years left on my calendar."

"Okay," I said, "but you may live longer than that."

"In that case, it'll be extra time. I've also named you my official biographer in my will, but I don't want it to be published until after I'm dead."

It was a pretty bizarre conversation, but I was glad that he was out of the depression. All this discussion about funerals and life spans appeared to be his way of dealing with his attempted suicide and the inevitability of death. Oddly enough, despite his resistance to religion, he had turned to the Bible to reconcile his anxieties about death and dying. It provided a finite conclusion to his fears, and from this perspective he realized that he should continue writing. His rebound rendered unusual responses typical of a manic-depressive. On this opposite end of the scale, he entered an ethereal high that celebrated life, acknowledged death and life as intricately intertwined realities. He entered the space where poet greets self, and, without excuses, wrestles with the muse.

His first poems were for and about women, a return to his first muse, "to impress a girl with light-colored eyes." "The Mini Skirt" and "The New Women" are humorous poems that tease and defend his poetry against feminist critiques. "A Leader of the People," on the other hand, is a political and personal poem for Roy Wilkins that criticizes an ungrateful, ravenous public. In the first case, the poems are playful, like a teenage boy flirting with the opposite sex for attention, but "A Leader of the People"[3] reflects an attitude of distrust toward the masses. "To An Old Man" portrays the decline of his dying father-in-law, from his wife's perspective, and a deliberate confrontation with death. All of these poems were written in the month of April, the

35. Dudley Randall in his home library, ca. 1981.
Photo: Hugh Grannum, *The Detroit Free Press.*

month of Easter, and they cover an array of subjects that reflect his aesthetic independence and a radical shift in Dudley Randall's oeuvre.

He also took a temporary job with the U.S. Census Bureau, which brought him into direct contact with people through daily interviews. This job also provided him with a new writing philosophy:

> I think I used to be very shy and self-centered. I would think about myself.
> If I met a new person, I would think about myself. But do you know what
> I do now? I meet somebody on the street, and I look at that person, and I
> think about that person instead of myself. . . . So I start talking about that,
> and I don't think about myself. I'd be riding around for the Census, and I'd
> see a man walking on the street. I'd wave to him, and he'd wave back. And
> because I go out of myself—and I use a census term. You know the circle
> that you're supposed to blacken? And if you don't blacken it all the way,
> then it doesn't register on the computer.

So instead of saying, "Be universal," which is fraught with emotion—you make some guys angry if you say anything about universality—I just say, "Blacken the FOSDIC circle." The FOSDIC circle is the other person or the object. It may be a bird, it may be a sparrow. And you forget about yourself. You obliterate your ego and your personality, and you go out to the other person, to the other person's mind. Forget about yourself.[4]

This FOSDIC circle philosophy is reflective of poet John Keats's theory of "negative capability," which had served Randall's earlier aesthetic values. Because Randall said "blacken," he conveys racial concerns, a kind of opposition to "whiteness" and the subliminal cultural dominance associated with "universality." But the FOSDIC approach provides additional insight into his creative vision. It challenged Randall to be more outgoing, to take more personal risks with people he encountered. Similarly, he took more risks with his writing, exposing some of his innermost secrets by writing bawdy poetry. Despite protestations from some of his literary colleagues, especially Gwendolyn Brooks, this trend continued through October of 1980.

Within a thirteen-month period, April 1980–May 1981, Randall composed twenty-nine poems. Like a dam breaking during a flood, a profusion of poems portraying painful recollections and intimate revelations ushered in his return. The themes he pursued in May, June, and July are romantic and erotic. Many of these poems are daring and counter previous assumptions about Dudley Randall and his poetry. "On Wooing a Woman: Probing the Circle" is one of the most controversial of his later poems:

> First, propinquity,
> The nearness of the probing male cell
> And the rounded receptive female cell,
> Second, the subtle chemistry by which only one mixture of eyes, hair,
> Voice, face, and figure sets off the mystical response,
> Then the dance toward, the magnetic attraction

The poem celebrates the subtleties of romance—aspects of desire, illusion, and confusion that create a structural tension with experiential details leading up to sexual climax:

> And all the while you hot and throbbing,
> Your penis tingling and hardening,
> A glow suffusing your loins rising to your chest

Making your heart beat faster your lungs breathe deeper
your eyes burn brighter
And all the world beautiful and new.

Against the backdrop of an elaborate, intense portrayal of sex and romance, the poem ends with a startling twist in the last two lines:

Today, with jet flights and rockets to the moon, courtship is faster:

"Hello. Let's fuck."

The directness of this shocking ending reiterates the theme of the poem, which celebrates sexual love and bemoans the death of romance in a contemporary technologically driven society. Time, in its various forms, mediates the pace of the poem and distinguishes the difference between romance and sex. This is the most sexually explicit of his later poems and the energy and the vocabulary released provide a stark contrast to the earlier, constrained lyrics of "The Profile on the Pillow" and "Souvenirs." But the tone in "Wooing" is typical of the later poems, and the perspective intersects with the themes he engaged during 1980, especially "My Verse That Once Was Tender," To Be In Love," "The Erotic Poetry of Sir Isaac Newton," and "A Warning." These poems parallel Dudley's psychological profile at the time and serve as vessels for the release of pent-up emotions and suppressed sexual anxiety contained during his depression.

Unlike the love poems that acknowledge his personal presence, many of the later poems are less focused on Dudley Randall as subject and are more in tandem with themes found in his earlier works, even in "The Ones I Love" and "Women and Poets," wherein his point-of-view is more philosophical. "A Litany of Friends," for example, begins with his depression and his transcendence and is primarily a tribute to others. Randall's interest in bawdy poetry did not repel the aesthetic judgment of all poets and editors. He asked me what I thought about it, and I told him, "You should write whatever you feel like writing." I was so glad to see him out the den of despair; I felt if this was the remedy, "Write on." Ron Milner concurred. He thought this was an important shift in Dudley's writing, and that it was liberating. He told me that Dudley promised to show him some of the poetry, but the occasion never occurred. When Conyus, the poetry editor for *The Black Scholar* (1977–1985) heard about the rejection of Dudley's bawdy poetry by the Chicago contingent, his immediate response was, "I'll publish it. Tell Dudley to send them to me."

Conyus was originally from Detroit, but he was living in San Francisco. He appeared on the Detroit literary scene around the spring of 1978, when he returned to attend to his ailing father. I met him at a poetry reading where I was reading with John Sinclair. Subsequently, the three of us read together at a jazz/poetry concert at the Band Shell on Belle Isle Park to a curious audience whose literary enthusiasm was encouraged by a considerable consumption of beer. That year, I introduced Conyus to Dudley on a summer afternoon in Dudley's living room. Dudley had invited some poets over to share their work, and Conyus read "The People Are Disappearing." The amazing energy and sardonic imagery of this poem was both frightening and prophetic. During this informal reading, Dudley shared some of his risqué poetry, and Conyus subsequently published "A Leader of the People" and "On Wooing a Woman: Probing the Circle" in *The Black Scholar*.[5]

Dudley Randall's renewed writing activity generated another reconnection. He resumed his affiliation with the press, then renamed Broadside/Crummell Press. As a consulting editor, he launched the Broadside Theater and solicited new manuscripts for publication. Due to a clause in the contract with Crummell that stipulated the possible return of the press to Randall, he regained control of Broadside in 1981. In the first *Broadside Newsletter* (August 1980) since his departure, he announced his return and a flurry of activity on the horizon in an article headlined "Dudley Randall Ends Retirement":

Another item, with the headline "Broadside Press Launches Broadside Poets Theater," demonstrated the new energy and ideas that Randall had brought back to the press:

Using the slogan, "Poetry is the greatest entertainment," Broadside Press presented Act 1 in its new Broadside Poets Theater Sunday August 3, 1980 at Alexander Crummell Center in Highland Park, Michigan. Dudley Randall, founder, editor, publisher of Broadside Press, came out of retirement to read old and new poems. Two of his poems, set to music by folk singer Jerry Moore and composer Ed Nelson, and a third poem which Randall wrote for Chopin's Prelude No. 7, in A major, were sung by Maaiah Toney, formerly a song writer for Motown, now a free lance songwriter and performer. Both Randall and Sister Toney received standing ovations.

Each month Broadside Theater will present a poetry reading by a Broadside poet. Admission is $2.00. Seating is informal coffee house style. Coffee, tea, fruit juices, and refreshments are available. Books will be available, and the featured poets will autograph their books.

For a schedule of future acts read this newsletter, the Detroit and Highland Park newspapers, Poetry Resource Center NEWSLETTER, and Detroit Council of the Arts PROMENADE.

With renewed vigor, Dudley Randall responded to a letter from Etheridge Knight, congratulating his new poetry publication by Houghton-Mifflin and inviting him to read in the program series:

Good to hear from you, man. I'm a little worried, tho, to learn you're in hospital. Don't know what to do with you. When things are bad, you booze; then when things are better, with a new book favorably received & money coming in, you booze again. Don't know what to do with you, man.

I bought your book at the Book End Bookstore in Northland, but you can bring me another, if you wish. It's a good book, and it'll be widely read and will enhance your reputation. What were you trying to do on the cover photograph—establish yourself as the best-dressed contemporary poet, in the tradition of the poet dandy like Byron, Dunbar, De Musset, and Baudelaire?

Broadside Press is trying to make a comeback. Our Poets Theater is exciting. My rationale is that if a supreme poet like Shakespeare could use theatrical hoopla to make his poems more exciting, like gorgeous costumes, songs, music, dancing, masques, and stage props, we lesser poets could also use the same devices to make our poems exciting. I was thrilled to hear my poems sung. The music expanded & intensified the emotion.

We can offer you $100 plus transportation costs to come, but we don't have much money, still owe the printer thousands, who just upped his monthly usury this June, so if you could tell me when you'll be in Detroit, we could schedule you then & save transportation costs, or maybe H-M [Houghton-Mifflin] could pay for a book party trip for you here. You could read at the Poets Theater & I could arrange at least two other autograph parties for you. Send me your editor's ad & I'll ask him to send you here.[7]

Dudley Randall's return coincided with Lines, a poetry series started by Detroit poet George Tysh at the Detroit Institute of Arts. This high-profile literary series identified national and Michigan writers to read at the art institute. This multicultural, multiethnic series attracted attention and brought in some of the most interesting writers of the times. It also brought the broader Detroit writing community together in an institutional setting for the first time. Baraka was one of the writers featured in the fall of 1980. He gave an afternoon lecture and an evening poetry reading. Speaking from his new Marxist stance, he lectured about how writers are not artists but are workers. His comments had an odd resonance for an audience of largely unemployed writers and workers that had a pretty clear and impoverished understanding of the politics of cultural work. During the question-and-answer period, Xavier Nicholas asked Baraka what he thought about Dudley Randall. Baraka stated simply that, "I have only the utmost respect for Dudley Randall."

George Tysh asked me to interview Baraka for an article for *The Metro Times*, the Detroit cultural newspaper that I sometimes freelanced for, but Baraka was unresponsive to my questions over dinner. Not only was he indifferent to my questions, he seemed uncomfortable in the company of the rest of the Detroit poets. After all, Marxism was neither a new language in our political libraries or in Detroit poetry. Baraka's reading that evening included much shouting and fist shaking at the racism and classism that plagued American society, and he set the audience off. They applauded in agreement with his acidic words and chilling anger.

This new enthusiasm for poetry was also felt as audiences crowded into the church basement to see the mainstays of Broadside Press read their poetry. To some extent, the project was successful. The initial lineup consisted of the top-name Broadside poets and the turnout was impressive. The most memorable occasion was the weekend Sterling Brown came to Detroit by invitation of Dr. Walter Evans and the Phylon Society at Wayne State University. Brown's visit was highlighted by Mayor Young's ceremony endowing Dudley Randall as the Poet Laureate of Detroit on 5 November 1981. Within the context of a dual tribute, Mayor Young identified the perfect occasion to recognize Dudley Randall. Dudley admired Sterling Brown and had returned Brown's poetry to print with the publication of *The Last Ride of Wild Bill* in 1974, a publishing activity that was praised by the mayor. Young's eloquent remarks about the power of poetry revealed his appreciation of Randall's work and black literary culture. His heartfelt recitation of Brown's "Strong Men" from memory rekindled images and reflections from the Labor Movement of the 1930s and 1940s:

> They cooped you in their kitchens,
> They penned you in their factories,
> They gave you the jobs that they were too good for,
> They tried to guarantee happiness to themselves
> By shunting dirt and misery to you.
>
> You sang:
>   Me an' muh baby gonna shine, shine
>   Me an' muh baby gonna shine.
>   The strong men keep a-comin' on
>   The strong men gitten stronger . . .
>
> They brought off some of your leaders
> You stumbled, as blind men will . . .

36. Dudley Randall reading his poetry as poet laureate of Detroit, ca. 1981.
Photo: Leni Sinclair

They coaxed you, unwontedly soft-voiced . . .
You followed a way.
Then laughed as usual.

They heard the laugh and wondered;
Uncomfortable;

> Unadmitting a deeper terror . . .
> The strong men keep a comin' on
> Gittin' stronger . . .
>> (Brown, "Strong Men," in Randall, ed. *Tha Black Poets*, 113)

The audience, comprising the old guard of the labor struggle and the cultural community, was glassy-eyed with memory and camaraderie. Brown, charming and comfortable in Detroit, proudly reiterated his 1930s socialist politics, complemented by his radical Christianity. Similar and familiar company surrounded Brown. Detroit poets, black, brown, and white followed him from reading to reception, mesmerized by his countenance and mastery of words. He told personal stories about W. E. B. Du Bois's affected Harvard accent and lies about famous folk characters with similar dramatic affects. Brown was the quintessential black poet-scholar, capable of making the profound sound matter-of-fact and of transforming the most common place by revealing its hidden beauty.

His presence at Randall's confirmation as the Poet Laureate of Detroit made the occasion even more memorable. Undoubtedly, when Coleman Young claimed Dudley Randall as the city's special poet, it was the highlight of his writing career. "Detroit Renaissance," a poem he had written for Coleman Young, was printed as a poster-broadside, framed and prominently displayed in the reception area of the mayor's downtown office:

> Cities have died, have burned,
> yet phoenix-like returned
> to soar up livelier, lovelier than before.
> Detroit has felt the fire
> yet each time left the pyre
> as if the flames had power to restore.

It ends with allusions to Langston Hughes's famous poem "Harlem," from the line "a dream deferred," and Aldous Huxley's novel, *Brave New World*:

> Together we will build
> a city that will yield
> to all their hopes and dreams so long deferred,
> new faces will appear
> too long neglected here;
> new minds, new means will build a brave new world.

As the poet laureate, Dudley was readily available to do poetry readings in the city and accepted invitations to read in New York, Chicago, Cleveland, and elsewhere. I invited him to give a reading at a program for an integration project for gifted and talented school children in the Inkster Pubic Schools and the Cherry Hill School District in Dearborn Heights. Inkster is a predominantly black suburban area adjacent to Henry Ford's Dearborn, which at that time was still predominantly white. As the creative writing teacher, I had published the children's writings for presentation at the program and for them to share with their fellow students. Rosa Parks was the other distinguished speaker that evening. At the time, she worked in Congressman John Conyers's office, and during my family's confrontation with Detroit police, she called my mother often to tell her she was praying for us. The audience was spellbound as she spoke about the great potential of the nation and the need for compassion and cultural understanding. Dudley followed her presentation with praise for the children and their poetry books. He marveled over Ronnie Wilson's novel, *The Runaway*, and then read some of his own poetry.

Dudley had reclaimed the press, was reading his poetry, and was writing with a renewed sense of purpose. So, when Naomi Madgett suggested that it was time for him to publish a new collection of poems, it affirmed his new zeal. *A Litany of Friends: New and Selected Poems* appeared the same year that he was named poet laureate. The book contains new and selected poems, and a substantial display of Randall's work since the publication of *More to Remember* in 1971. *Litany* reflects the lyrical range and reach of Randall's previous work while presenting innovative patterns in his resurrected muse, as unanticipated paths surfaced in this last creative leap. But because the imagery in "Wooing A Woman: Probing the Circle" is explicit in its signification of sexual activity, Naomi Madgett, excluded it from the collection.

But the jubilation of 1981 was marred by the sudden death of another lifelong friend, Hoyt Fuller. Dudley's response was to edit an anthology *Homage to Hoyt*, comprising works published during Fuller's editorship of *Negro Digest* (later *Black World*). Despite Dudley's renewed enthusiasm for life and literature, Fuller's death was the final blow to a literary era. A somber mood hung over the black community as the hostile politics of the right and the reactionary attitude in the country at large adversely affected material conditions. Dudley reentered writing and public life during a regressive political period, a time when affirmative action was under attack and unemployment, poverty, homelessness, and the illegal drug trade were symptomatic of the economic devastation of the city:

The physical traces of this catastrophe were etched in Detroit's crisis-pocked landscape. In nearly every neighborhood of the city and its blue-collar suburbs, there was at least one abandoned factory—a single or multi-story shell vacated within the last year or the last decade. From each abandoned workplace, the ripple effect of its closing left shuttered restaurants, deserted gas stations, half-empty bars, "for-sale" signs, and boarded-up homes.[8]

The election of the conservative Republican Ronald Reagan to the office of President of the United States in 1980 had devastating consequences for predominantly black and Democratic Detroit. Mayor Coleman A. Young and his administration encountered economic indifference and political hostility from the federal government and its agencies. Additionally, the historical shift from an industrial society to a technocratic one disrupted the automobile industry. Chrysler, Ford, and General Motors found it more profitable to build new factories in nonunion states or in nonunion countries. International competition also dwarfed Detroit's Big Three, and "by 1980 imports had taken nearly 30 percent of the U.S. market, and for the first time in postwar history, Japan's production of cars and trucks surpassed America's faltering output."[9]

Dudley Randall's poetry reflected the decay of the city and his advanced years. In comparison to his earlier poems that contain a hopeful romanticism, a broad social outlook, and that celebrate or bemoan love as universal pleasure or pain, his later poems contemplate love, death, and community in more immediate and tragic terms. Inside the sanity of silence, a poet envisions a perfect world, but reality can sabotage that dream. Reentry into reality required reconciliation with self and with others. This meant engaging forbidden realms of expression, which was a direct challenge to being an aesthetically correct black poet. Rebuked by prominent personalities of a once adoring black literati, Dudley's honest engagement with his muse resulted in severe criticism. Soon, the pathways that once protected his feelings and his sense of an ideal place vanished.

18

A POET IS NOT A JUKEBOX

THE FIRST PART OF THE TITLE FOR DUDLEY RANDALL'S *A Litany of Friends: New and Selected Poems* is also the name of the opening poem, initially drafted on 1 April 1980 after he came out of his depression and began to write again.[1] He later transformed those lines, on 17 December 1980, into a form for publication. The shocking first lines outline the horror of his depression years and provide the crux of the poem, as he identifies his wife as the stalwart who rescued him from suicide and the depths of despair. Like notes from his diary (the entries are dated 1 April 1980 and 17 December 1980), he entrusts the public with the naked truth about himself and gives thanks to a list of family, poets, and friends. It is a dedication to camaraderie in his defeat over depression:

For Vivian who snatched the shotgun out of my mouth,
Who walked by my side into the black pit and came out holding my hand,
Who shouted and scolded, cursed and wept, was patient and puzzled,
silent and smiling until she led me out of the dark depths,

For Gwendolyn, my friend for ever, who remembered me and wrote me
    and sent gifts on Christmas and birthdays,
Who asked my friends to call me and write me and invited me to read and
    assured me that I was somebody,
For Don whose satire slashes but who was gentle and kind and opened his
    home to me,

For Safisha and Laini and Bomari, three beautiful loving people, who
   welcomed with tenderness and trust,
For Hoyt who accepted and respected me as I was and not the hero I
   ought to be,
For Audre who wrote to me and sent donations from her readings,
For Sonia who called me and sent herbs and tea and scolded me for
   smoking and laughed and joked when I was glum,
For June who sent me her book at a time when I needed reassurance,
For Etheridge who told me to live my pain and transcend it,
For Shirley who urged me to live and not to die,
For Lance who had faith in me and gave me his royalties and praised me,
For Naomi who assured me that my work was worthwhile
For Robert who honored me with his friendship and confidence,
For Leonard who listened, and talked when I was silent,
For James and Marguerite who gave me the sanctuary of their home
   where for a while I could forget,
For Jim who sent advice and for Jon who was kind and soft-spoken,
For Clyde who did not forget me and invited me to return,
For Melba whose faith in me gave me faith in myself,
For Arthur and Sarah who invited me to speak and argued and laughed
   with me,
For Todd who covered my class when I was afraid to appear before them,
For Joyce who wrote about me with empathy and invited me when I
   thought I was forgotten,
For Judy who called me and sobbed when I couldn't remember her name,
For Mildred who listened and talked to me when I was alone and afraid to
   go home to an empty house,
For Susie lover of dolphins who sent me a card and a note
   every Christmas,
For Carolyn who seldom wrote me, but who surprised me with an
   unexpected Christmas card,
For Walter, brother poet, who called me with concern and sent me
   a letter,
For Jean and Louise and Val who asked me to write a poem for them
   because they believed I would write again and for whom I wrote my
   first poem in five years,
For Malaika who invited me to live and work in Africa,
For Billy and Venita who asked to visit me and to spend the night
   with me,
For Phyllis and Ruby who called me when they needed help or advice,

For Evelyn who always kissed me when we met
   (A touch, a hug, a kiss can save a life)
For Xavier who often called me and asked "What's going on?"
For Clifford who helped me recall my childhood,
For John who invited me to bowl and golf;
For all these ropes which pulled me to shore,
For these roots which anchored me against the wind and fed me
   from the past,
For the ties and integuments which bound me to them and them to me
   and fastened me to life,
For those who unfroze my tears and my laughter so that for the first
   time they flowed freely,
For all those who touched and hugged and kissed me
(A touch, a hug, a kiss can save a life),

For these, my thanks, my love.

Naomi Madgett explained her decision to publish *A Litany of Friends* (1981): "He [Dudley] had published a number of chapbooks, but I thought it was time for him to do a collection of new and selected poems." The book contains a number of his classic poems including: "George," "For Pharish Pinkney," "Old Witherington," "Langston Blues," "For Gwendolyn Brooks," "Anniversary Words," "The Profile on the Pillow," "I Loved You Once," the World War II poems, "Ancestors," "Frederick Douglass and the Slave Breaker," "Memorial Wreath," "The Southern Road," "Roses and Revolutions," "Legacy: My South," "Ancestors," "A Different Image," "In Africa," and "Poet."

The new poetry displays a bold excitement that the more sedate and genteel Randall would not have permitted to surface. Although his acumen is as skillful and deliberate as it was in his earlier works when precision balanced the tension of opposites and the polarity generated an implosive dynamism within the poetic structure, his departure from conscious inhibitions during the composition process released a more intuitive, subconscious vocabulary from the repressed realms of his imagination. As R. Baxter Miller points out in his essay "Endowing the World and Time: The Life and Work of Dudley Randall," the collection "demonstrates an intellectual depth of themes used and technical mastery of the poetic form. Of the eighty-two poems collected, twenty-four are reprints, and forty-eight are new."[2] The poems written from 1980 to 1981 illustrate much of Dudley Randall's conscious and subconscious thoughts during this period.

But it was the urging of Jean Ellison, Louise Wallace, and Val Gray Ward that resulted in the first poem he had written in nearly three years. "The Mini Skirt" (4 April 1980) is a wild and zany piece that is the antithesis of the severe, serious side that led to his depression. What also comes with this burst of passion is a more risqué sense of humor.[3] The poem addresses the irony of honesty as a consequence of physical exposure but does not configure images of sensuality, instead:

> greatest invention of the 20th century
>
> no mask hiding pimples & warts
> no long skirt stirring up dirt
> hiding bow legs knock knees
> & fat thighs that rub together
>
> here it is jack
> what you see is what you get
> knobby knees skinny shanks
> or would you rather
>
> lola falana legs
> tina turner thighs
>
> whatever I have or you want
> it's all there in open air
>
> maybe small modesty
> but total honesty
> & no hypocrisy
>
> (*A Litany of Friends*, 36)

This poem motivated a flurry of love poems focused on various aspects of love—romance, friendship, marriage, and heartbreak. In contrast to his earlier love poems, wherein romantic love is idealized, exalted, and revered in highly structured verse, the romantic poems from this period are full of uncertainty, difficulty, and sexual anxiety in spontaneous, unpredictable free verse. Love also takes on broader thematic dimensions during this later stage in his life, as he contemplated friendship and his attraction to the opposite sex in more philosophical terms. In many ways, these last poems reflect an oblique perspective that reproached the balance and serenity that permeated his early love lyrics.

Similar humor can be found in "The New Woman" (13 April 1981), dedicated to "M. H. W. and D. H. M., who said my poem "Women [1975] was sexist." The poems appear on opposite pages, and thereby function like a poem/counterpoem. The initials in the dedication refer to Mary Helen Washington and D. H. Melhem.[4] The freewheeling language in the response poem, "The New Woman," would not have appeared during any other period in his writing. As a parody of the earlier poem "Women,"[5] the first lines of "The New Woman" contrast and parallel the opening lines of the earlier poem:

> I like women they're so hard & tough & strong
> Feel their muscle it's hard & hairy as a coconut
> doctors lawyers lumberjacks truck drivers wrestlers weightlifters
>   bank robbers

"Women" exalts the physical attributes of females and employs fruit metaphors to describe breasts, which is especially characteristic of male objectification of female sexuality. In Randall's view, these romantic images glorify woman's sexuality as wonderful; in his own defense, he drafted a series of hard-line images to exaggerate his point:

> Their fingers are quick as whips their lips rip out quips
> Their brains are steel traps their mouths volley raps
> They swear smoke pot & chew tobacco
> Hawk & spit & collect art deco

The poem continues with male-macho lines such as, "They do all the lousy things lousy males used to do." His poem bemoans the demise of "traditional behaviors" and characteristics he preferred over certain changes since women's liberation, which threatened a familiar female identity. From his point of view, the emulation of male behavior contributes more to the problem than a solution. The poem poses a reprieve for the poet's male distinction through his sex organs, an adolecent, pubescent obsession:

> Only two things a man can be a woman cannot be
> One is the dad of a large familee
> Number two is with all their care

> They cannot piss six feet straight up in the air.

The frustration is summed up in the last line: "Where have all the women gone" (A Litany of Friends, 49). This complaint represents the confrontational tone of many of these new poems and responds to Randall's initial conclusion in "Women," which reflects not only his attraction to the opposite sex, but also identifies God's gender as female and pledges his preference for them as the superior gender:

> God made man first then woman correcting Her mistakes
> And put her on earth to aspire and achieve and rejoice.

In these poems, Randall challenges the Women's movement in a similar manner that he critiqued the Black Liberation Movement. His opinion runs contrary to the political grain and represents the resistance of a male from a previous generation who, despite his complaints in this poem, was a genuine supporter of gender equity before it was fashionable. Randall retrieved fruit imagery from "Women" to create lush impressions in "Sweet Breathed Celia" (9 June 1980), a passionate piece that corresponds with the flood of love poems:

> Her mouth is sweet
> not from medicinal washes
> perfumed discs
> or Sen Sen,
> but from juice pulp peel of oranges
> warm green red purple grapes
> cold crisp apples,
> making it clean for kisses
> and tongue's caresses.
>
> (*A Litany of Friends*, 31)

By comparison, the two poems that precede and follow it in the book illustrate a contrast in vocabulary. The imagery in "Sweet Breathed Celia" is tangible, whereas the words in "A Marriage" and "The Profile on the Pillow" are illusory, allusive, and contemplative. Moreover, the language in the later love poems is immediate and active, a key distinction.

Similarly, "The Erotic Poetry of Sir Isaac Newton" (a found poem copied from Newton's *The Motion of Bodies* in volume 34 of *Great Books of the Western World*) was translated into verse on 16 May 1980 from the original text written in 1687. Randall's fixation on the subject of love saw this law of physics—"to every action there is also imposed an equal reaction"—as a function of physical dynamics translatable into love poetry by interrelating psychological impressions within sexual imagery:

> The face of a screw to press a body
> Is to the force of the hand by which it is moved
> As the circular velocity of the hand
> Is to the progressive velocity of the screw
> Towards the pressed body.

It is a very long poem (100 lines) that parallels romantic love with this particular law of physics. It is a clever arrangement of lines abstracted from scientific text, and it is suggestive of Randall's preoccupation with the subject, or at least his interest in relating the subject as a natural, physical property in the universe. The poem ends with this conclusion:

> The qualities of bodies
> Which admit neither intensification nor remission of degrees,
> And which are found to belong to all bodies
> Within the reach of our experiments,
> Are to be esteemed the universal qualities
> Of all bodies whatsoever.
>
> (*A Litany of Friends*, 51)

"Translation from Chopin (Prelude Number 7 in A Major, Opus 28)" (30 June 1980) is an adaptation of one of Randall's favorite musical compositions. Chopin's melancholic composition becomes a sad love poem that laments an unbalanced and failed romance:

> If I had loved you less,
> Or you had cared for me,
> I never would have wept,
> My pain would never be.
>
> (*A Litany of Friends*, 47)

The words are simple and precise and arranged like song lyrics. The thematic interpretation is determined by the somber mood of the music and the poet.[6]

"May and December: A Song" determines the contrast of seasons as incompatible in nature as it is in relationships, but within that contrast, contradictions can reverse expectations and capacity. Since "May and December" was set to music, the balance of the imagery and the symmetry of the rhythm conform to the pattern of song lyrics. The poem is highly dependent on rhyme, but the inversion of experience generates the unanticipated explanation of a common theme. The question is: Is the poet discussing actual experience, or is he relaying how common assumptions are of little value when the variables of possibilities are evidenced in nature, as in human behavior, or both?

In some ways the appeal of "May and December" is that it appears as the thoughts of an aging man who reverses the fires of passion. Just as "My Verse That Once Was Tender" (29 June 1980) alters the gentle, loving gesture of previous poetry, as in the case of a relationship, into a voice that "now is fierce." This poem reflects the more aggressive and even angry tone that could not be detected in Randall's "tender" verse of the past, though the craft is clearly reflective of an artist in complete control of his pen.[7]

Angered by the suggestion that the speaker was only interested in having sex, the poem addresses the woman with outrage, insulted by the game that was played:

> You thought I was a dunce, a dolt, a child,
> To avoid, evade, fool, foil, con, be by lies beguiled.
> But I am not. I'm a thinking, bleeding human.
> Needing dignity and love like any man or woman.

The second stanza is quite "fierce," as the poem explains that there are alternatives to the woman's shortcomings available with the convenience of love purchased by mail, which will not assault or assail honest feelings. This rejection includes cruel rebuttals justified by weighing them against the injuries of the experience:

> Who cannot lie, be sullen, obstinate,
> And cannot make, postpone, and break a date.
> Of course she cannot think about another,
> But that's an act which never gave you bother.
> And, what is best of all, she'll last for years,
> Without, on lip and chin, those darkling hairs.
>
> (*A Litany of Friends*, 45)

Randall's sharp tone appears repeatedly throughout these last poems, spoken from repressed anger that was banished from previous expression because it would not have been in accord with his shy and self-sacrificing demeanor. However, such control and repression in language and actions possibly contributed to his ultimate fall into depression. In the same regard, this effusion of love poems, which gushed forth when he resurfaced, includes the range, depth, and content indicative of unresolved issues festering beneath the tranquillity of a quiet personality.

While "My Verse That Once Was Tender" reflects the same pain of a failed passion and "May and December" details the particular slights and emotional transgressions, "If I Were God I'd" curses to hell all those who "love and will not tell" and "love and will not share." "A Warning" (June 1980) carries a similar theme of "love rebuked," and "A Plea" offers a heart. "To Be in Love" (28 September 1980) praises the state of being in love.

"To Be in Love" is written in rhyming couplets, and the language is predictable and possibly even pedestrian. It appears to represent the simple truth with regards to Randall's essential need at this time:

> To be in love: is to be glad,
> For love converts away from sad,
> Rejoice at splendors of the world,
> Sun, moon, and sky with stars impearled,
> Enjoy birds' dawn and sunset cries,
> And love each creature that's alive,
> Because your love for her extends
> To all the world and never ends.
>
> (*A Litany of Friends*, 39)

These love poems represent a shift in Randall's romantic lyrics, but the more sexually explicit imagery does not appear in this collection because, as his editor and friend, Madgett felt the poems would irreparably damage his literary reputation.

During this period, Randall was excited about life and the poetry of life to the extent that he stressed his system and suffered another heart attack. His wife Vivian became frustrated with this exuberance, and, in the same manner that she ripped him from the stranglehold of suicide, she scolded his carefree and careless adventurism. He told me a story about giving a ride to a woman hitchhiker who pulled a knife and robbed him. A similar dangerous image appears in "My Muse," which may provide insight into his reckless activities and his aesthetic exuberance. "My Muse" (1 October 1980) cannot be classified as a love poem of the flesh, friendship, or lust; rather, it is a poem that reflects the inspiration of his creative core as an encounter with a personality who inspires his pen "in an unending stream." The other love poems written in 1980 are focused on one aspect of affection, either caring or rejection. "Zasha" is compared to the muses of past poets, "Catullus' Lesbia, Shakespeare's Dark Lady, Dante's Beatrice and Poe's Annabel Lee." The range of these allusions also reaffirms the cosmic diversity of Randall's literary influences. As the poem gushes over her sable beauty and graceful movements, the brash and reckless side of the muse is revealed in a startling twist at the end of the poem:

> I never thought I'd have a Muse.
> Then I met you.
> Now poems gush in an unending stream,
> Inspired by you.
>
> Sometimes in tenderness,
> Sometimes in wrath,
> The poems pour forth.
>
> To me you are Catullus's Lesbia,
> Shakespeare's Dark Lady,
> Dante's Beatrice,
> Poe's Annabel Lee,
> My Zasha.
>
> My Zasha.
> Who will live for ever in my poems,
> Who in my poems will be for ever beautiful.
>
> My Zasha,
> Who makes the poems pour forth.
>
> Zasha, of the tall slim dancer's body,
> The dark face,
> The dark voice,
> The narrow, sidelong-glancing eyes.
>
> My Zasha,
> She Devil,
> Who spews forth filth when she is questioned,
> And carries a butchers knife in her purse.
>
> (*A Litany of Friends*, 38)

This contrast between "tenderness" and "wrath" within the dark loveliness that inspires the poet conveys a hidden dimension in Randall's imagination. "Impromptus (Thoughts About Zasha)," a sensual love poem, extends the imagery of Zasha into the realm of desire. But it is a forbidden love, something the poet regards as evil. Sexual intimacy in this context would violate his marriage vows and his Christian upbringing; at the same time, the sexual fantasy invigorates his imagination and inspires him to write. This seven-part poem builds on aspects of her physical being towards sexual fantasy:

> "I'm going to take a bath."
> Said Zasha. How I wish
> I were warm water which caresses her.
> I'd kiss her skin with a million water mouths,
> Massage her legs, knees, thighs,
> Embrace her waist,
> Nuzzle her breasts and nipples,
> And enter every crevice of her brown beauty.
>
> (*A Litany of Friends*, 37)

This fantasy carries the creative passion expressed in "My Muse" into more explicit imagery and perhaps explains the profusion of love poems that dominate his writing in 1980, the year he rebounded from his depression. Whether real or fantasy, her name is Russian and therefore alludes to an interior connection with Pushkin and to Dudley's earliest interest in love poetry.

Despite his publication of poets who represented new feminist perspectives, especially in the case of Audre Lorde, Alice Walker, June Jordan, and my own work, the hypermasculinity expressed in many of these poems suggests that Randall was threatened by the feminist views and gender issues that dominated the contemporary literary terrain. He was certainly aware that he was in discord and even defiance with current trends, and on some level realized this inconsistency in his own behavior. At the same time, this paradox is even more perplexing because despite limitations he placed on sexual identity or gender identity, he valued the intellectual resourcefulness and creative genius of women. This conclusion is based on the fact that in his cultural work he initiated joint publishing projects, reviewed and promoted women's writings, and treated them with respect for their intelligence and talent, something that I experienced firsthand and document in other chapters in this history.

Perhaps Randall's fixation on the subject of sex and gender identity reflected a need to exorcise sexual repression and anxiety related to cultural mores and social conditioning. In the past, his poetry was primarily concerned with race and class; these poems presented opportunities to work through his sexuality, a paradox that vexed his life and perplexed the aesthetic freedom he craved, as he specifically expressed in "A Poet Is Not a Jukebox."

CLASSIC RANDALL

On a more sedate level, the poem, "To An Old Man," dated 6 April 1980 and dedicated to his wife, Vivian, and her father, James Barnett Spencer, was inscribed as an Easter gift. This poem about the cycles of life, death, and resurrection, written from Vivian's perspective is also a reflection of Randall struggle with these incremental issues. Classic Randall, it hinges on tension built on contrast, as in the poem "George." Birth/death and father/daughter are juxtaposed in imagery developed through acts of touch related through fingers, arms, hands—holding, making, caring, protecting, creating, and shaping. But the poem does not linger in nostalgia. Infused with dissipation and decline—"Your shit, piss, snot, sweat, tears I wipe away"—a dutiful daughter embraces these unpleasantries with tenderness and reflection:

> Your hand rigid and still or shaking wild
> once held my hand, restrained when I would stray.

His mastery of detail and vocabulary rendered evocative imagery from commonplace settings:

> There was a girl who cried for a garden pool,
> and your numb fingers nimbly fashioned one.
> Their craft and all their cunning long since gone,
> they balk at buttons, vainly pluck and pull.
> O diapered old man, you're now a child,
> your child your parent. Talk with me a while.
>
> (*A Litany of Friends*, 16)

Configured in his most complex voice, "To An Old Man" resounds with the poetic grace of his earliest work and conveys his deepest reach, an attempt to soothe the suffering of his wife and to understand the encroachment of old age and death with regard to his own existence. Interestingly, this poem is a sonnet, and by theme and style it is reflective of his compositional interests during the 1930s, 1940s, and 1950s.

His interest and appreciation of form is explained in "Verse Forms" (1 October 1980):

> A sonnet is an arrow.
> Pointed and slim, it pierces
> The slit in the armor.

A point of contrast to the free-wheeling free verse, his retrieval of form in many of the new poems is explained in the second stanza of "Verse Forms":

> Free verse is a club.
> If it batters long enough,
> It may crush a breastplate.
>
> (*A Litany of Friends*, 90)

Although Randall writes poems as tributes to famous poets and for those close to him, as in "To An Old Man" and "Poor Dumb Butch,"[8] about his beloved dog, some of his most memorable poems are portraits of anonymous people, neglected, ignored, and misunderstood by society. This interest in these obscure personas reflects sensitivity and an eye for negated humanity. "Bag Woman" and "The Aging Whore" are compacted with empathy and are designed to relieve suffering in the presence of an inevitable ending. These poems are offerings of genuine remorse.

In an interview with Howard Blum of *The New York Times*,[9] Randall explained his engagement with the city as part of his responsiblity as the Detroit's poet laureate:

> I go around the city and write about what I think or feel. Part of a poet's work is to look at people. And it's the people in this town that make it such a poetic place, more than New York, London, even Paris.

Randall explained how he inconspicuously observed people in an obscure downtown luncheonette, as he lit "one of the thin, multi-colored cigarettes from his leather case." He told a story that exemplified "how he uses the city as his muse":

> I was sipping coffee at Lando's when this man comes in and asks for some spare change to get some food. I've got no money to give him, so he goes to the next booth where a man is sitting with fancy clothes and two pretty women.
>
> When this guy turned him down, too, he didn't give up so easy. The beggar just waited till the guy paid his bill, and then he took out a knife and stabbed the guy in the gut. I guess he figured it wasn't right not to help out somebody when you're sitting there in fancy threads with two women. And that's a part of the city I write about too:

> The girls who rest in booths in
> Lando's Superb Food
> Do not play rock 'n roll like
> Other kids.

Not many places where I go do they know I'm a poet—forget about their knowing I'm poet laureate.

But I'm always aware of the title. . . . I don't believe in preaching. Maybe I got enough of that from my father, who was a Congregational minister. But I believe a poet can change things. He can change the way people look and feel about things. And that's what I want to do in Detroit.

During the 1980s, the effects of the economic recession were painfully apparent in Detroit. The homeless are the hobos of this decade, and the imagery in Randall's "Bag Woman" connects with "For Pharish Pinkney, Bindle-Stiff During the Depression." Anonymous and abandoned humanity is revisited in "Bag Woman" as a familiar figure in a devastated cityscape:

> Another stray cat or abandoned dog,
> She sleeps where cats and dogs sleep, in the streets.

The next stanza is the poet's perspective, an inquiry addressed to the bag woman but actually aimed at the audience. Randall created a history or a memory for an indigent who was not cognizant of time, space, or self. This poem presents the bag woman as a person with intimate experiences and human responses and ponders her demise. The poem turns on contrasting imagery, from the sexual intimacy in a loving relationship into the possibility of a violent gang rape. The poem affirms her humanity despite default or individual failings through the offering of simple kindness:

> Sister, I do not know. But I know that I am you.
> I touch your rags, clasp your dumb eyes,
> Talk with you, and drink your fetid breath.
> (*A Litany of Friends*, 81)

From his wanderings on Detroit streets, Dudley Randall salvaged the ravages of human devastation through poems like "Bag Woman" and "The Aging Whore" (21 February 1981). In the latter poem, the focus contours a tragic figure dressed in her sex costume in a camouflage of grotesque makeup, moving to the magical voice of Ella Fitzgerald while an indifferent city ignores her:

White wig askew above black face,
She totters on high heels up Woodward Avenue
Waving her hands above head,
Cutting dance steps to Ella's scatting
Over radio from a McDonald's hamburger palace.

She wears a tan blouse with belly bulging farther than her breasts
Baggy blue pants with rubber bands below the knees
To accentuate her legs. No longer a stripling
In tight skirt slit to the crotch,
Or crisp, hip-hugging slacks, black men ignore her.
They can get younger trim for nothing.

Randall identifies Puritanical subconscious as the reason men view such women only as sex, as "trim"; this devalues sexual intimacy into something "grotesque." She was "praised, petted" and marketed by her pimp until her body was transfigured by age and abuse, her sexuality no longer profitable:

Perhaps some lonely and aging white from the suburbs,
Whom Puritans have taught that sex is grotesque,
Will stop his car and bargain with her.

But no one stops. Tired,
She sinks to the bench outside McDonald's.

As in "Old Withering," dialogue is integrated into the text, parenthetically:

(Don't let no man touch you.
Don't give 'em nothing.)

She commands an audience by spewing her pain and frustration in "accents scabbed with obscenities." Her outrage contrasts with the silence of the "bag woman," which gives her voice, and the poem acts as a warning:

which spatters the shocked faces
Of women and school girls
Stopped at the curb by the red light.

The ending reconnects with the thematic suggestion about men and sex—"trim for nothing." The poem carries a larger statement about immorality and male sexuality. The whore's grotesque appearance is emblematic of the exploitation that ruined her and distorted her body. The poem is a sympathetic portrayal of a victim, but it is underscored with a critical tone regarding the ruthless indifference of the male sexuality that markets and devalues these women. The theme of this poem also echoes one of Randall's first poems, "Hastings Street Girls" (1935) which foreshadows the fate of "the aging whore":

> Lovers and kisses, cruel, careless, light,
> Will you remember down the long, deep night?
>
> (*A Litany of Friends*, 82)

There are many parallels in the later poems with the earlier one, which demonstrates Randall's consistency in themes and skill in subtlety as articulated in "Birth of the Sun":

> Trees swim from dark.
> Hues burst from trees.
> Grass greens.
> Flowers sparkle.
> Dew glistens
> cold.
>
> (*A Litany of Friends*, 91)

Or in "Killing a Bug":

> That little black dot
> Felt fear and panic
> As it shot
> Across the table
> Not
> Able
> To linger
> Before my finger
> Smashed it.

Randall was a master at capturing small moments and elevating them to profound introspection:

> Will I
> Feel such fear and try
> To hide and linger

when I chance to stray
To a place and day
Where some Eye
Will Brush me
And a huge Finger
Crush me?

And will He
Be
As careless and uncaring
As I
In my
Smearing?
(*A Litany of Friends*, 92–93)

A LEAP OF FAITH

No doubt, Randall's last collection is a reconsideration of poetry, poets, and his return to literary life. In some instances, Dudley takes this last leap to complete unfinished poems and unstated thoughts. But the strongest impetus that accompanied the return of his muse in her myriad manifestations was also a return to familiar motivations—love and romance. "Women and Poets" resounds like "Belle Isle" ("Joy and delight, joy and delight, like bells / Or bell-like flowers pealing in memory). The poem lauds the glory and wonder of the feminine mystique as being akin to the nature of the muse:

So when a woman walks,
A miracle in the street.
The poet's heart hallelujahs,
And his lips repeat,

"Women and poets
Are sister and brother
Sorcery and enchantment
They share with one another."
(*A Litany of Friends*, 94)

As Randall stepped beyond the expectations of his audience to reclaim his space in time, he embraced his deepest fears, exposed his sexual vulnerability, exalted his fullest passions, and expressed vestiges of anger to empower his voice. At the same time, he included complex constructions in this last collection of poems to remind his critics that he was as skillful as need be. But when the charge was to upset arrogance, rebuke a cruelty, or challenge aesthetic impositions, he used language like a weapon that "batters the breastplate."

"A Poet Is Not A Jukebox" is one of the last poems in the book and was written in defiance of those of his family, fellow poets, and his friends who attacked the validity of his new risqué love poetry. Randall's more tactful responses to the aesthetic attitudes of certain personalities during the Black Arts Movement were obviously abandoned in this poem. Whereas irony and subtle sarcasm were his linguistic strategies before, in "A Poet Is Not a Jukebox" outright defiance employs didacticism to defend artistic freedom. The poem is a response to a conversation between Randall and Gwendolyn Brooks wherein he shared that he was writing bawdy poetry. She quipped: "So you're in that bag now," and then asked why wasn't he writing about the race riot in Miami?

Randall's retort sarcastically references the mundane daily occurrences of an ordinary job and the distractions of cultural indulgences like music and writing, distancing him from the television, newspapers and the deluge of the information media:[10]

> So it wasn't absence of Black Pride that caused me not to write
>   about Miami,
> But simple ignorance.

The poem builds momentum as it critiques the absurdity of an aesthetic dictatorship by focusing on political poetry in the Soviet Union, which takes on a deeper significance because Randall had more than a curious interest in Russian literature.

> Telling a Black poet what he ought to write
> Is like some Commissar of Culture in Russia telling a poet
> He'd better write about the new steel furnaces in the Novobigorsk region,
> Or the heroic feats of Soviet labor in digging the trans-Caucausus Canal,
> Or the unprecedented achievement of workers in the sugar beet
>   industry who
> Exceeded their quota by 400 per cent (it was later discovered to be a
> typist's error).
> Maybe the Russian poet is watching his mother die of cancer,

Or is bleeding from an unhappy love affair,
Or is bursting with happiness and wants to sing of wine, roses
   and nightingales.

I'll bet that in a hundred years the poems the Russian people will read,
   sing, and love
Will be the poems about his mother's death, his unfaithful mistress, or his
   wine, roses, and nightingales,
Not the poems about steel furnaces, the trans-Caucausus Canal, or the
   sugar beet industry.
A poet writes about what he feels, what agitates his heart and sets his pen
   in motion.
Not what some apparatchik dictates, to promote his own career
   or theories.

The reference to his poem "Ballad of Birmingham" reminds his critics of his
established politics within the black aesthetic and continues his argument as
an advocate for love poetry as a source of power against the fascist and ter-
rorist tendencies of politics gone awry:

If Josephine had given Napoleon more loving, he wouldn't have sown the
   meadows of Europe with skulls.
If Hitler had been happy in love, he wouldn't have baked people in ovens.
So don't tell me it's trivial and a cop-out to write about love and not
   about Miami.

A poet is not a jukebox.
A poet is not a jukebox.
I repeat, A poet is not a jukebox for someone to shove a quarter in his
ear and get the tune they want to hear,
Or to pat on the head and call "a good little Revolutionary."
Or to give a Kuumba Liberation Award.

A poet is not a *juke*box.
A poet is *not* a jukebox.
A *poet* is not a jukebox.

So don't tell me what to write.

(A Litany of Friends, 100–101)

This is one of Randall's longest published poems. In free verse, it rolls from line to line in an assertive tone that reflects his sense of conviction and his adamant position on the issue. As the founder of Broadside Press, he practiced a policy of noncensorship because cultural subordination and discriminatory practices by establishment publishing houses kept black poets out of editorial consideration. In fact, the Federal Bureau of Investigations established a "Red File" on Randall during the 1960s because Broadside Press published poetry that contained controversial themes. Moreover, having rethought his response at the Fisk University Writers Conference to the painful political attacks launched against his close friend Robert Hayden, Randall's angry reaction to a recommendation for aesthetic conformity was intensified. In retrospect, Dudley stated that "even though at the time I agreed and said I was black first and a writer second, I should have said none of your business."

All of these historical factors and dimensions contributed to the fury in this poem, and it should be seriously regarded in any attempt to realize Randall's deepest belief in aesthetic freedom. As the last poem in his last book, it is his last word on the subject. The broader meaning of this poem is that love is revolutionary and the complexity of struggle and the needs of the poet serve and entail not only political resistance, but also human tenderness and compassion. In celebration of the creative spirit, "joy and delight" and "roses and revolutions," Randall reiterated that in poetry these themes are not antithetical.

The confluence of opposites in Randall's poetry reflects the polarity in his inner self. In his earlier, more stable periods, this polarity was balanced, as is the case with most of us, holding life together within an intricately woven web of psychologically familiar and safe havens, with pockets of hidden fears. The construction of a personality given to testimony and exposure through poetry renders the poet privy to public observation and extreme personal scrutiny. To a large extent, the poet strips naked whenever pen is honestly lifted and script emerges—the words offered can be no less than the task, and the possibilities for failure are infinitely clear.

To some extent, Dudley Randall's avoidance of conflict or argument with personal encounters left him vulnerable to his inner disappointments that drove him to despair. His expectations from life could not be realized at the particular moment he wished for and needed them to materialize. Consequently, he did not view the decline of Broadside Press as the consequence of historical and economic dynamics, but rather as personal failure. Like humidity evaporating after a storm, confronting aesthetic judgment without disintegrating between the pages of unprotected poetry created an agonizing dilemma for Dudley because he had to face rejection. In the past, his poetry was rejected because of racial discrimination, but that experience was not personal. As history corrected some of its injustices, his poetry was recognized and collected in major American literary anthologies and textbooks, and requests for permissions to reprint still continue. Ironically, the tables had turned, and rejection from fellow black poets was especially painful.

Dudley Randall's dry period lasted over three years, but when he began to write again, his words burst wide open. Buried under years of repressed anger and sexual anxiety, a flood of issues and concerns were transformed into daring poetry. He confronted these anxieties and his own aesthetic dissidence, and his muse rebounded in both familiar and unexpected language. The rebirth of the poet in a rebellious mood during uncertain times resulted in significant and insightful works about the poet's psyche, but ultimately it was a costly leap. However, the quiet librarian, who had avoided arguments most of his life and tried to seek balance in a peaceful medium of expression, exclaimed in a blues refrain italizcized to emphasize the black ink:

> A poet is not a *juke*box.
> A poet is *not* a jukebox.
> A *poet* is not a jukebox.
>
> So don't tell *me*   what to write.

19

AT PEACE WITH THE MUSE

Good news: Detroit Poet Laureate Dudley Randall is back in the book publishing business at his previous stand, the Broadside Press.

"I was in a deep depression when I sold the Press in 1977, " he says, "and didn't come out until 1980, when I became their editorial consultant. I just didn't remember that under the contract the Press actually would revert back to me after five years."

The five years are up, and Randall's first offering this time around is Melba Joyce Boyd's *Song for Maya*, a cooperative project of Broadside and the Detroit River Press. Ms. Boyd, a native Detroiter and a Ph.D. graduate of the University of Michigan, teaches women's studies at the University of Iowa. She describes her book as "an epic poem that attempts to construct an American mythology that engages the historical and cultural experiences of three races. . . ."

Three more books are planned from Broadside Press this year: in May, *Blood River*, lyric poetry by Gloria House; in November, Randall's editorial collaboration with Gwendolyn Brooks, *A Broadside Treasury, 1971–1975*; and in December, an anthology, *The Best of Black World Magazine*.[1]

On April 4, 1983, *The Detroit News* announced Dudley Randall's return to publishing in a joint venture with poets Dennis Teichman and Glenn Mannisto and their Detroit River Press. I was in San Francisco giving a reading from *Song for Maya* at an event organized by *The Black Scholar*. I did a second reading at the University of Iowa with Paule Marshall, who was a visiting lecturer for the semester in the Writers' Workshop. In August of that same year, I went to West Germany as a Fulbright Scholar to teach at the University of Bremen. Just before I left for Germany via Detroit, Etheridge Knight and I were featured at a Broadside Theatre poetry reading.

There was a great turnout. Old friends like Ron Milner, Naomi Madgett, and Paulette Childress came, as well as new poetry enthusiasts. Dudley was in good humor. He encouraged me to study German poetry and said that I should translate it into English—that it would help my German. From all indications, poetry and Broadside appeared to be having a comeback. Nine months later, after a several poetry readings throughout Germany, I ran out of books. I called Dudley to order more copies of *Song for Maya*. He told me there needed to be another printing, but he would send the fifty or so copies he had left.

He then insisted on calling me back because he wanted to talk about something else and he didn't want me to have to pay the cost for the international telephone call. He was very upset about a conversation he had had with Haki Madhubuti (Don Lee). Haki said he was completing a book of criticism on black poets. Dudley asked him if he was writing about Dudley's poetry. Haki told him no, because he (Dudley) believed that white people were human beings, so he wasn't a black poet. I was shocked by Haki's insensitivity, especially since he had supposedly changed his mind about such rigidity and dedicated his last collection of poetry to Robert Hayden. Dudley was hurt by this categorical dismissal. It was the recurring force of a misguided thought, returning like a bad penny or a marked bill. We thought statements like this had been left behind in the rubble of the previous era. But no matter how remote and ridiculous it sounded, it was still painful.

That June, I presented a paper at the annual conference for the German American Studies Association in West Berlin. Berlin evoked an odd sensation in me, because it was where the United States and the Soviet Union squared off—gun to gun, bomb to bomb. The city was a landlocked island that rocked with popular music all night long. It was documented to have had more bars than any other cosmopolitan city, and I did not doubt it. The possibility of nuclear annihilation generated a tension that was superficially contained by alcohol and loud American music.

Audre Lorde was a visiting professor at the Frei Universität Berlin (Free University) and she gave a poetry reading the opening night of the conference. She introduced herself as a "black woman lesbian activist" to a crowded room of curious and, primarily, German intellectuals. A number of Americans, mostly Fulbright scholars, were also in attendance. Her reading was profound, and her poems explored gender identity and sexuality, challenged racial essentialism, and mocked cultural provincialism. Afterwards, she offered to take questions, but the spectators appeared to be overwhelmed by her raw honesty and provocative stance.

In private conversation, Audre and I chatted about Dudley and the tenuous status of the press as well as my stay in Bremen. I was complemented by her inclusion of my first collection of poetry in her syllabus, and I gave her copy of *Song for Maya*. Audre had made a significant impact on the women's movement in Berlin and on Afro-German women writers. She was conducting a women's workshop, the consequences of which was firmly asserted at the opening session of the conference when a cadre of women students confronted the organization with a petition for a women's studies program at the university. There was resistance from the "Man" in charge of the proceedings in a call for "Order." He insisted that they leave the stage. But a sympathetic audience (the theme of the conference was women's studies) shouted in support, and so they were permitted to speak.

The last day of the conference I gave a poetry reading at the Berlin Amerika Haus, in the same room where Audre read a few days earlier. It was the night before the NATO military parade, a show of force to be broadcast everywhere but the United States (I supposed). Before living in Germany, I thought military parades were only common in communist countries since they were the ones I ususally saw on the news. At any rate, in order to avoid a clash between peace protesters and the military, the peace march was permitted the day before. Hence, the Amerika Haus was barricaded and guarded by German soldiers and German shepherds. This bizarre juxtaposition of international symbols—peace demonstrators, armed soldiers, barking dogs, and black poetry—disrupted the ambiance of the evening and the timbre of my voice. Of course, the military was protecting the property and not my poetry, but by some strange twist of fate I was situated within a dichotomy of political oppositions. In solidarity, I read my anti–nuclear war poem, "False Moonscrape Umbrellas":

> they will never hear
> our words
> gently raving
> in a book.
> scientists don't visit
> poets.
> capitalists don't under
> stand esoteric words

studded with hot ice.
they live inside fortresses
hiding under false
moonscrape umbrellas

As I was sifting through my poems, I paused at "Why They Keep Beating Hayward Brown." I started to read it, but suddenly I was overwhelmed by a deep sense of hollowness. I felt totally disconnected from the audience. I thought to myself, they wouldn't understand, and opted for a less personal piece, one with less biographical baggage.

When I returned to Bremen a few days later, there was a message from home. Hayward had been mysteriously murdered on June 11—the night of the poetry reading.

I returned to Detroit the following autumn, and Dudley had regained some sense of self through his arguments for creative freedom. The day I came to visit he was sitting in his easy chair, intellectually cushioned between piles of books on an end table and a hassock, a familiar arrangement as he referenced his most current library during our conversation. Vivian was working in the den, polishing a gem stone, patiently angling the dull object against the diamond glazed sander until the nuances of shape and color glistened with their own unique beauty. Like found poems, uneven and yet smooth, basic and yet eternal, she gathered these stones from foreign and domestic travels, collecting these ancient earth formations, unclogging the dust of ages embedded in the grooves. Like them, her sensibilities were elemental and earthbound, while her husband's thoughts rose on the lithe currents of words, on the possibility of imagery configured in imaginary space. She was the silver thread that kept the dream maker's flights from disappearing between words or drifting off into the abyss.

"For Vivian" is a self-effacing poem that confesses humble gratitude. There is a sense of finality that goes beyond the immediacy of minor daily irritations and personality adjustments described in "Anniversary Words" and the pledge of commitment in "A Plea." In "For Vivian," his last love poem, dated 26 January 1982, Randall confesses his love and his appreciation for Vivian's enduring him and weathering the trials and tribulations of their marriage.

Me, this snoring, belching
    babbling, semblance of mankind,
What woman
    could refrain from laughing at?

> Or, caring more,
>   quietly take her hat
> And leave?
>   Yet these four and twenty years
> You've stayed. Though not without
>   heart wring and tears.
> For which my thanks.
> And bless your love which binds.

Dudley described the publication of "For Vivian," which was brought out as Broadside No. 93 in February 1982, as a valentine card:

> The new broadside is beautifully hand lettered on fine vellum paper by Calligrapher Oral Carter, is illustrated in red and gold, and bound in a plain white folder of the same stock, encased in a transparent slip. This new poem, unpublished elsewhere, is printed in a limited edition of 100 copies, signed by the poet and calligrapher.[2]

I once asked Vivian what kind of stone do humans become. She laughed and said, "Our remains haven't existed long enough to evolve into another matter. Our bones have to be here a few more million years for us to transform." This information struck me as sad, and yet it made so much sense. It explained so much about our value, our primitive state of existence, our incapacity for transformation. To some extent, Dudley's return to public and poetry activities was derailed by another era, and he lost the flash of excitement and retreated into the safety of private company. But this time, he understood that these affairs illuminated the unfair and unrealistic expectations of others. That day he shared a new hard cover copy of *The Autobiography of Leroi Jones/Amiri Baraka* because he thought it would help me with my work on his biography.

My visits with the Randalls occurred during holiday breaks and summer vacations, interrupted by long winters of teaching at the University of Iowa. Since time moved more slowly for Dudley, my long absences strained our reunions. Our conversations became more and more dependent on my voice; even when I turned on the tape recorder and asked him to talk about himself, I had to fill the long pauses with stories about my children or what was new on the literary scene. He would nod in agreement at my observations or in accordance with the cadence in my speech. Sometimes, he would interject a comment or a subtle query about bad prose broken into lines pretending to be poetry, or about the curious deconstructionist vocabulary dominating contemporary criticism. But at more definite moments, he would retreat from the conversation almost as if he had stepped onto foreign soil, or had encountered a language he did not know.

The disappointment of having to sell Broadside Press a second time cast Dudley into another depression. Even though he acted as a consultant to the new publishers of Broadside, Don and Hilda Vest, and retained a 30 percent interest in the business, Dudley regarded this as the final chapter, just as *A Litany of Friends* would be his last book of his poems to be published in his lifetime. Often, editors would contact him or me about obtaining permission to reprint a poem in an anthology. He always consented, but never offered to publish anything new. Despite his silence, his poetry continued to appear—his voice continued to be heard.

He did not completely lose himself to depression again, but according to Vivian, he was sometimes up and sometimes very, very down. He resigned himself to a delicate heart condition, advancing arthritis, and a less active relationship with cultural affairs in Detroit and elsewhere. This retiring posture also included the return of his shyness. He drew a small circle of friends to enclose and protect his space.

I worried about Dudley's physical and mental health and confided in poet and colleague Marvin Bell, who held the distinguished Flannery O'Connor Chair at the university. He consoled me with a secret that would soon be released. Dudley was to be honored as the 1986 recipient of the National Endowment for the Arts' Life Achievement Award:

We had figured out already that there was a consensus among us. This is an award that can only be gained after nomination. We had been doing a little tentative talking with one another to find out who we might want to give this award to. It was clear; we were unanimous. We wanted to give it to Dudley Randall.

We gave it to him for the whole complex of his efforts over a lifetime of literary work. We gave it to him for his poetry, first of all. We gave it to him for his publishing. We gave it to him for his influence, both as a poet and as an editor. We gave it to him for his spirit. We gave it to him for his standards. We gave it for his stamina.

As a publisher and editor, Dudley's influence has been enormous. One can't overestimate the influence of a good editor. I'm sure his very belief in individual writers and poets gave them the confidence to write about things they might not have written about otherwise, to try styles they might not have tried otherwise.

He had a belief in clarity, if the content was important enough. It was for the poets he has published. He put poetry in the hands of people who would not have seen it otherwise. He gave expression to the voice, a communal voice of a group of poets that would otherwise have been less noticed. He gave them a point on which to focus. Broadside Press had an identity.[3]

This award lifted Dudley's spirits, and he had to respond to a public that would not allow a quiet retreat to his home library. This repose was disrupted by civic and cultural accolades. Both of his alma maters honored him. Wayne State University gave him an Honorary Doctor of Letters in 1986, and the University of Michigan gave him a Distinguished Alumni Award in 1987. Various Detroit public schools gave him awards, usually during Black History Month, including his own Eastern High School, now renamed Martin Luther King, Jr. Senior High School.

Written records and declarations scaled the walls of the den and the living room of the Randall home. The plaques, like broadsides, displayed praise that contradicted any psychological arguments he used against himself. The persistent attention made a serious relapse into depression impossible. Despite himself, he was called on to reveal the secrets of his success and the wisdom acquired through experience. His comments about publishing were almost always intertwined with deliberations about his poetry. The two dynamics, as he presented them, were indelibly imprinted as his life work:

A bit of advice I would give to poetry publishers is be very cautious. If you just put out one book a year, say, just a hundred copies, and you can sell that. At least you can put one book out a year. And you can go on from year to year. A press needs a staff that knows about finances, how to run an office, about marketing and advertising. A press should plan three years in advance. If it is a one-man operation, you must be a businessman as well as a literary person. You have to learn everything.

Broadside took time away from my writing, so in that way it may have interfered with my producing poetry. So much bad poetry was submitted; it discouraged me in my writing and in my publishing. Oftentimes I felt I had lost my sense of judgment in poetry. What is good?

Once I talked to Naomi Madgett's class at Eastern Michigan University, and I mentioned that something was not good poetry. One of her students asked me a question, which stymied me. She said, "Well how can you tell what is good poetry?" I groped around trying to figure how one could define good poetry. About the only definition I could give was it is poetry that you like.

But at different times in my life, there was different poetry that I liked. When I was a teenager, I liked some of the more violent poetry with violent images, but then as I grew older, I liked the more thoughtful poetry. So how can *the same poems change? They seem to be good when you're young and reading them, then they seem to be not so good as you get older. I think it's very hard to define what is good poetry.*

A similar ambiguity occurs in writing. You can write some poems in a day, and sometimes it takes a year to get a poem right, maybe a lifetime.

I write about what moves me. Besides other emotions, I have the heart of a poet, so I write love poems. I've also written about people in my family, like my granddaughter and the girls across the street. The neighbors across the street have a pair of twins, and I've written about them ever since they were born. They are young adults now. One of them said, "Mr. Randall I have a question I would like to ask you." And I said, "What is it?" She wouldn't answer me at first, then finally she got up enough courage and said, "Every time I hear about you, people always say you're so great. But to me you're just an ordinary guy. Just a man who lives across the street." And I said, "Yes, that's all I am."

Dudley Randall's resistance to heroism speaks to his clarity, distinguishing individuality from individualism. He exhibited talent at an early age, but the lesson his life illustrated was that study, sacrifice, tenacity, and industry are the facets and faculties of success. Neither he nor his family tolerated excuses. Racism was an obstacle, a historical factor, but not a finite control of one's destiny. Individual integrity was the measure of character. To the extent that he bemoaned his own existence, his intractable perfectionism became an inflexible yardstick that did not allow any consideration for uncontrollable circumstances, and that nearly broke him.

Just as history afforded the opening for Broadside Press and the emergence of its literature, the end of that era was the eve of another opening that moved the literature further. Today, black poetry no longer aligns the perimeter of the library, but it is incremental to cultural conversations about American literature:

"I got the same satisfaction a gardener gets when he plants seeds and sees flowers growing. I did not publish for money. I enjoyed seeing good poetry, and we published a lot of good poets. Some of the poets have died, or ceased writing, but the poetry has not died." Dudley said this matter-of-factly. But he had been the matter that had created the historical fact.

The 1990s continued the celebration of Dudley Randall. The twenty-fifth anniversary of Broadside Press honored its founder. In the Rackham Auditorium at Wayne State University, poets, family, friends and Mayor Young gave witness to how Dudley Randall had served poetry and the city. A teary-eyed Haki Madhubuti (Don L. Lee) claimed Randall as one of his true heroes, comparing him to Malcolm X, who never gave up on his commitment to the people. Etheridge Knight, then afflicted with lung cancer, read "Ballad of Birmingham," explaining that he always read Dudley's poetry during his readings throughout the country as his way of testifying for all Dudley had done for him as an editor and as a friend. Naomi Madgett provided particular insight into Dudley Randall's literary legacy in her comments about his poetry at the anniversary celebration:

> When Broadside came into being I don't think Dudley had any idea that it was going to grow into the proportions it has grown. I qualify as a Broadside poet because my poem "Sunny (from an old photograph)" was one of the early broadsides. I admire Dudley not only as a friend, a very supportive, a very warm friend, and as a very fine poet, but also as the pioneer of Broadside Press. I don't think if he had realized what he was getting into he would have had the nerve to start it. But he did, and we are all grateful for it. As Haki [Madhubuti] said, it was easier for him with Third World Press and was certainly easier me with Lotus Press to come along in his footsteps because he paved the way for all of us.[4]

When the Chicago contingent, Haki Madhubuti and Gwendolyn Brooks, inducted Dudley into the Hall of Fame for Writers of African Descent, librarian Leonard Kniffel reported this event in a profile for *American Libraries* that included a key quote from fellow Detroit poet and librarian Joan Gartland:

> When we worked together at the University of Detroit, Dudley Randall was the complete professional librarian. He was also poet-in-residence at the time, but he would be on the reference desk like everybody else, and then he would take his lunch hour and get in his car and rush off to Broadside Press, do what he had to do, and rush back. The energy he had, and the concentration—and he was so wonderfully modest about all of it.[5]

On one of my visits to the Randalls, I invited Tony Medina, a young New York poet who had just read his poetry for Black History Month at the University of Michigan—Flint, where I was the director of the African American Studies Program. He got excited, and said, "For real?" Tony, who was usually animated and talkative became as quiet as Dudley after we entered the house. Tony recalls that day in February 1993:

> Dudley's modest home was on a flat, beautiful tree-lined residential street whose front lawns had been blanketed with a pristine carpet of snow. I met

Dudley and his wife and felt like I was living a surreal dream. (He actually had first edition copies of the books he published many years before laying around on end tables!) I couldn't believe I was actually in the home of Dudley Randall! In my mind he was one of the most important figures (leaders) to emerge from the Black Arts/Black Aesthetic '60s. Not only that—I knew that he was the living bridge, along with Margaret Walker and Gwendolyn Brooks, between Langston Hughes' generation and the poets of the 1960s and 1970s. Dudley Randall was not just a great poet, he was a cultural force. It was his selfless dedication to Black people, Black literature and Black writers that distinguished him from all of the other "stars" of his time.[6]

In 1994, I moved back to Detroit after taking a professorial position at Wayne State University, and my son enrolled in Martin Luther King, Jr. Senior High School (Eastern High School), Dudley's alma mater. I began shooting the documentary film about Dudley in 1989 after Coleman Young's office issued a special grant of $10,000 through the Detroit Council of the Arts. At the time, I was on faculty at Ohio State University. I continued working on the project when I assumed the position of Director of African American Studies at the University of Michigan campus in Flint. Funding from the Ohio Arts Council, the Center for New Television, the Michigan Council for the Arts, and the University of Michigan allowed me to complete the project.

Librarians, poets, family and friends convened at the Detroit Institute of Arts for the premiere of the documentary film, *The Black Unicorn: Dudley Randall and the Broadside Press* on 14 January 1996. The occasion was also a celebration for Dudley's eighty-second birthday. In conjunction with the Detroit Film Theatre, the Société of the Culturally Concerned sponsored the event. More than three hundred people converged on the medieval-style Kresge Court as a jazz trio played during the reception in the center of the museum. A brief program preceded the film showing. Poets Murray Jackson, Willie Williams, and Bill Harris gave tribute in verse and in speeches; the Mayor Dennis Archer confirmed recognition of Randall as the Poet Laureate of Detroit via his director of Cultural Affairs, Marilyn Wheaton; and the Detroit City Council and the Michigan State Legislature joined with official proclamations.

The highlight of the evening was eleven-year-old Diarra Kilpatrick's rendition of "Booker T. and W. E. B." During his brief remarks, Dudley said: "It gives me great joy to hear the young lady recite my poem because I know my poetry will live on." A few weeks later he sent a thank-you note, saying how much he liked the film. Since the Randalls didn't own a videotape player, he hadn't seen it before the premiere.

The next year, during Chrysler Corporation's 1997 Black History Month Poetry Program, Dudley Randall was once again honored in high style at the Detroit Institute of Arts. The Chrysler Corporation Fund awarded a $20,000-endowed scholarship to the Department of Africana Studies at Wayne State University. Interested parties at Chrysler were Vice President of Governmental and Community Affairs Frank Fountain and public relations director Alan Miller, who had been a student of Randall's at the University of Detroit. At the affair, Fountain said, "Someone once said, 'Poetry is mankind's mother tongue.' Not English, or French, or Spanish, or Ebonics, but poetry. Well, if that is true, then one man who has contributed mightily to our universal language is our special guest this evening, Mr. Dudley Randall, the patriarch of Detroit poets." In recognition of Black History Month, Randall read "Booker T. and W. E. B."

Two months later, on 11 April, the new building for the Museum of African American History celebrated its grand opening. Founded by Dr. Charles H. Wright in 1965, the same year Dudley Randall founded Broadside Press, this edifice was the manifestation of another man's dream and protracted institutional struggle. The joint effort of the city of Detroit and the corporate community to fund the museum and the elaborate celebration was an ironic twist in black history. It was a moment for pause, especially since Ford Motor Company sponsored the poetry reading scheduled for 13 April as part of the ongoing festivities.

As I drove Vivian and Dudley to the event, I could tell he was invigorated by the occasion. About a block from the museum, a small band of protesters was parading up and down Warren Avenue, displaying a placard that stated "I Am Not A Slave." Dudley grumbled, "What does that mean? I'm not a slave either." He said this with a slight twinge of anger. I explained that the controversy was about the facsimile of a slave ship in the main exhibit. "But why should we be ashamed of our history?" Dudley was proud of Dr. Wright's achievement as the museum founder and as his contemporary, and irritated by this public display of disapproval.

But inside the auditorium, the mood shifted, and the audience was overjoyed to see and hear the poet laureate of Detroit read "Ballad of Birmingham." Unlike the rest of us, who read and were hurried off stage, a standing ovation and enthusiastic applause prompted the emcee to encourage the audience to ask Dudley questions. He was earnest and intense as he encouraged the writers "to write, to read, and if need be, to publish your own work."

As we left the auditorium, he stopped to give his regards to Dr. Charles Wright, who was seated in the audience. We were then directed to view my dedication poem, "This Museum Was Once A Dream," engraved in the museum's bronze dedication plaque at the entrance. Dudley smiled like a proud father. As we signed the poster of the Ford Motor Company Poetry Program for the museum's archives, I jokingly said, "Did you ever expect to do a poetry reading sponsored by Ford?"

Thinking about the sweat-drenched days in the "foundry knockout" during the 1930s, he laughed and said, "No."

"Well," I said, "If you live long enough, you might see anything."

20

"THE ASCENT"

Into the air like a dandelion seed
Or like the spiral of lark into the light
Or fountain into sun. All former sight
from hill or mountain was a mere hint of this.
We gain a new dimension. What had been
Our prison, where we crawled and clung like ants,
We spurn, and vision lying far beneath us.

—Dudley Randall, from "The Ascent"

THE THIRD WEEKEND IN MAY 2000, I attended a conference at the College of William and Mary in Virginia. The French scholar of African American literature, Michel Fabre, asked about Dudley's health. Unknowingly, I said he was fine. But on the day of my return, Naomi Madgett telephoned to tell me Dudley was in the hospital, that he had had surgery for colon cancer. Initially, he had gone into the hospital for a routine procedure when the doctor discovered the disease, and an operation to remove it immediately ensued. She assured me that his heart was strong and that he was doing quite well. So well in fact, that he had been transferred to a semiprivate room for general care. I was relieved and immediately called Vivian.

But within twenty-four hours, Dudley's condition reversed. Perhaps a warning visited his dreams, and so he felt the need to escape. He got out of his bed, insisting he had to get out of the hospital. The nurses had to restrain him by strapping him to the bed frame. By morning, a fever and an infection caused the doctor to transfer Dudley back to the intensive care unit. The signs were dismal, but we were encouraged because his heart was vigilant.

When I arrived at Providence Hospital, Vivian was seated at the foot of the steel hospital bed. She was reading a magazine. The room was cool and white. Sprawling wires and tubes emerged from underneath the bed sheets and from Dudley's mouth and nose like plastic tentacles, connecting flesh to machine. Although I knew this was done to sustain him, he looked trapped by metal contraptions. It seemed so unfeeling, so contrary to life.

Three red roses from Vivian's garden stood in a glass of water on the shelf against the wall. She mused on the fact that Dudley would have to spend Father's Day in the hospital. She assured me he was doing better and then rose to go to his side. She wiped his forehead lightly, and his eyelids opened slightly. She told him to look up, to see who had come to visit. His eyes widened in recognition. I walked to the other side of the bed and stroked his forehead in the same manner. I gave him a kiss on the cheek and told him how glad I was to see him—that I loved him.

I spent that afternoon with Vivian, chatting about this and that while Dudley, suspended by tubes and machines, rested on white sheets. Despite his bouts with depression and his contemplating suicide, Dudley's fighting strength emerged in the hospital. and lines from "To the Mercy Killers" seemed to have prophesied the imagery and finality of that moment:

> Even though I turn such traitor to myself
> As beg to die, do not accomplice me.
> Even though I seem not human, a mute shelf
> Of glucose, bottled blood, machinery
> To swell the lung and pump the heart—even so,
> Do not put out my life. Let me still glow.
>
> (*After the Killing*, 10)

On the drive home, I was afraid. I knew he wasn't coming out of that hospital alive. I thought about the small moments we shared, how he was always there for me, and how he encouraged my children, gave them books. When John graduated from high school, he and Vivian came to the open house in my sister's backyard. It was such a lovely day, a sunny day, and John beamed with pride that Dudley and Vivian had come. He introduced them to his high school friends and felt special. John insisted that I get him an autographed, hardcover copy of Dudley's book, *A Litany of Friends*. That September, Coleman Young died, and I bought the autographed copy Dudley had given to Coleman at the estate auction, and then had Dudley sign it again for my son. I had to bid for the book, and ended up paying two hundred dollars for it.

In a similar setting, I joined the Randall family reunion that was held a year before in Detroit in August 2000. Actually, the site was Windsor, Canada, across the river. I met Phillip Randall's son, Robert, who was a Tuskegee Airman, and who in 1952 became the first black person to pass the National Actuarial Examination. I also met Harry Randall's grandson, who supplied me with the early history of the Randall family. His father, William P. Randall, started a construction business in the 1930s, and when World War II broke out, he got government contracts to build military camps in Georgia. After the war, his business continued to flourish and became one of largest black construction companies in the Southeast.

During the Civil Rights Movement, William P. Randall became active in local politics, and was simultaneously the president of the NAACP and the SCLC. Although his home was riddled by gunshots and members of the Ku Klux Klan tried to run him down in a car chase, he survived. In the 1970s, he was responsible for the installation of an affirmative action hiring program in city government that raised the employment rate of African Americans in civil service in Macon from 15 percent to 40 percent. His son, William C. Randall Jr., served in the Georgia State House of Representatives and, in 1999, was appointed to a federal judgeship in Macon, Georgia.

Dudley's daughter Phyllis asked me to introduce my film and to say a few words about Dudley. I was honored and humbled by this family that had broken down so many social, economic, cultural, and political barriers for African Americans since "freedom came," beginning with Arthur and Missouri Randall during Reconstruction. At eighty-five, Dudley was honored as the oldest living Randall. He had come full circle.

It was Saturday, 5 August 2000. Four years before, on this date, my father had died, so my reflections lingered on him and his passing. My day and night dreams were interrupted by ghosts; refracted images of my father, my brothers, and my cousin appeared as cryptic messages of concern, flashing through my imaginings as distractions.

My sister Sandra arrived in a upbeat mood because we were expecting our younger sister Dorothy from Maryland, and the family's annual escape to our summer cottage in Canada. The sun was bright; humidity was low. It was some of the best seasonal weather the Great Lakes region has to offer, and we intended to take full advantage of it and the rapture of tangerine sunsets on Lake Huron. We were drinking coffee in the kitchen, outlining the upcoming week when the phone rang. My mood had shifted, so I was caught off guard when I answered the phone.

"Melba? It's Naomi. Dudley passed early this morning." I said something, mumbled something else and then hung up the phone. I turned to Sandy and James Kenyon, my partner, and told them Dudley had died. Sandy filled the hole in the air with queries about Dudley's age and illness, seeking verbal anchors to settle the moment, but her voice resounded like empty tin cans rattling inside my head. I tried to respond, but the words felt like cotton caught in my throat. I left the kitchen and sought space to release, so I could breathe.

My daughter Maya followed me. She had just finished painting a portrait of Dudley to be hung in the Africana Studies conference room at Wayne. She had also painted a portrait of Coleman Young, who had donated funds to the department when it was established. She stroked my hair, while I wept on the side of the bed until I could regain my composure. I was always incapable in these moments. I remembered my father's passing, how my son John went with me to his room where we found my father's body slumped over on its side, merged into shadow. My legs weakened, and I fell against him, unable to breathe, unable to receive the finality of my father's death.

James and I had planned to shop for a new desk. It was a bright day, a sunny day, a good day to buy furniture. We left about an hour after Naomi's call. We drove up the Chrysler Freeway to a suburban shopping mall. Along the way, Sonia Sanchez was reading poetry in a radio commercial for Chrysler 300M, a luxury sedan. The Broadside Press poet filled the airwaves, and the irony assuaged my grief. I wondered if Sonia could drive? Had Daimler-Chrysler given her a free automobile for doing the commercial?

The salesman that greeted us at the furniture store started reciting poetry by the English poets Keats and Blake. Fate refused to release the moment. "Are you a poet?" I asked. (Or was this just a novel ploy to sell furniture and entertain himself at the same time, which was what I actually thought.)

"As a matter of fact, I am," he said emphatically.

"So am I," I said.

At that point, he knew he had sold the desk. Besides, it was a decent deal and a perfect fit for the study. Of course, he pretended he wanted to hear some of my verse, and since I wasn't going to commit to a furniture store reading, I directed him to the Detroit Pubic Library and James signed the credit card receipt. All I could think about was that Dudley's muse must be playing a joke on me, and that this salesman was a willing vessel to tease me, to uplift my spirits, even in the banality of this conspiracy with consumerism and our mortal, financial death.

THE RESPONSE

My family left for Canada, and I stayed behind to help with the funeral arrangements. Shahida Mausi, the director of the Detroit Council of the Arts during the Young administration, prepared press releases and sent them out to the media. The Detroit newspapers responded with feature articles and with regular obituaries. Fittingly, the cultural weekly, *The Metro Times*, was the first to respond in the column, "Hot and Bothered," via poet George Tysh:[1]

> After our fierce loving
> In the brief time we found to be together.

So begins the first poem of Dudley Randall's 1970 chapbook, *Love You*, and now the voice which intoned those words is no more. Dudley Randall, founder of Detroit's Broadside Press and a pioneer in the development of an African-American poetics, passed away the morning of Saturday, Aug. 5 at the age of 86, leaving behind him an inspiring body of poems, as well as a tender, courageous legacy of work in the service of writing.

Beginning and ending with poetry, the *Metro Times* article covered the highlights of Dudley's accomplishments, and with a special sensitivity it connected those accomplishments to his creative consciousness:

Randall also edited (with Margaret G. Burroughs) an anthology titled *For Malcolm*, after the murder of Malcolm X. It was this sense of response to and involvement with the world, with the historic events of his time, which infused his own writings. Randall's six collections of poetry . . . have an immediacy and resonance which is totally in and of the world. They will be with us a long time to come.

> And from the turbulence there is no shelter,
> Except within the circle of love's arms.

I promised to meet Vivian at the funeral home to view the body. But I got there a few minutes after she had left. The foyer was crowded with unfamiliar faces. I soon realized by the wailing of young people that some youngster had been murdered. I slipped past the crowd into a small room where a silver casket held Dudley's body dressed in a familiar blue suit. I touched his chest and thought aloud for him to hear my fears about my having to read the obituary and conduct the Remarks portion of the funeral service. "You know how these poets like to go on and on," I told him.

But I was unable to submit to my own grief because the uncontrollable mourning of the teenagers across the hall distracted me. Dudley's body was aged and worn from a productive life, the complete opposite of the immature body of the child lying in the cradle of death. Lines from Dudley's "Roses and Revolutions" echoed in my thoughts:

And I heard the lamentation of a million hearts
Regretting life and crying for the grave

I thought about my brothers and my cousin and their vision of this brutal, internalized attack on life. Their prophetic vision anticipated this genocidal spiral from the drug dealing in our communities long before society realized how deep and depraved the cycle would become.

Cole's Funeral Home was next door to the Hitsville Museum, where Barry Gordy made Motown's legendary music. This funeral home was a familiar site; fallen Motown stars, like The Temptations's David Ruffin, had their corpses laid out for spectacle viewings here. But more often, this funeral home prepared anonymous young bodies for an endless processional to cemeteries, tilled by drug wars and too many guns.

On 11 August, an editorial in *The Detroit Free Press* collected comments from nationally known Broadside poets, but primarily focused on a special quality in Dudley's work as an artist. "'New minds, new means will build a brave new world,' he wrote of Detroit. His words still provide the inspiration":

"Everyone who ever wanted to write knew Dudley Randall," poet Nikki Giovanni said after Detroit's poet laureate died Saturday at age 86.

But few writers—even those who wished to honor him—had Randall's ability to capture the spirit, the soul, the humanity of the people and places he wrote about. He described the heartache of church bombings in Alabama and the potential for renaissance in Detroit with equal poignancy. He created a vision for his home city that people continue to strive toward today.

"I felt since he was helping people who were not accepted by the likes of Harcourt and Harper and Row and others," Gwendolyn Brooks said. "I felt I should not stay safely in the harbor. So I left to join him and I've always been glad that I did."[2]

A few months after Dudley's death, on 3 December 2000, Gwendolyn Brooks also died from cancer.

In the fall of 1997, her last visit to Detroit, Gwendolyn Brooks gave a poetry reading at Wayne State University. I introduced her. Afterwards, there was a luncheon, and I told her I was writing Dudley's biography and that if she had any useful papers or correspondence, I would appreciate them.

Gwen reminded me about the unusual funeral arrangements Dudley mailed to his friends after he recovered from his first bout with depression.

Gwen was not well enough to attend the funeral, but she sent a beautiful, floral arrangement that sat in the middle of the dining room table when the women gathered to plan the service. Vivian presented a photocopy of Dudley's proposed funeral arrangements in his handwriting, with additional comments written in red ink that read: "Vivian: Save & follow Instructions for my funeral, 1984." Most of Dudley's requests were honored, but Vivian made some conventional inclusions.[3] She asked me to write the obituary since I had the historical material. Dudley's daughter Phyllis provided family names and dates. Naomi Madgett edited these materials and prepared the program for printing. Vivian selected a photograph, contacted pallbearers,[4] and approved the final copy before printing.

The funeral was held on Saturday, 12 August 2000 at 11:00 A.M. at Plymouth United Church of Christ, the church Dudley attended while growing up, and the one Naomi belonged to as well. The Reverend Nicholas Hood II, Minister Emeritus, his son Reverend Nicholas Hood III, and associate minister, Reverend Georgia Hill Thomas officiated at the ceremony. Both ministers were involved in city politics and had served as councilmen. Their political careers actualized the vision of Dudley's father, a Congregational minister who advocated the election of black city councilmen when he joined this church, almost eighty years before.

The Washington Post printed an obituary from the press release, but Betty De Ramus, who attended the funeral, wrote a feature article for *The Detroit News*. A photograph of Dudley, circa 1970, working at a manual typewriter covered the top half of the page. The poem "The Profile on the Pillow" was printed underneath the photo and "Booker T. and W. E. B." appears at the end. Dudley's request for the congregation to erupt in jubilation occurred without need for the directions Dudley had left:

When casket reaches door, pianist plays Schubert's joyous "Impromptu. . . . [Not discernible] and Priest says: "Our brother's final message is: Life is beautiful and wonderful. Sing. Laugh. Dance. Rejoice. AMEN."

Somehow the mourners invoked Dudley's wishes. De Ramus's accounting of the event is filled with insightful details and poetic sensibility:

Midway through funeral services for Detroit poet and publisher Dudley Randall, librarian Malaika Wangara leaped up and started singing, "He was a friend of mine." Her strong-willed alto rose and spread its wings, filling Plymouth United Church of Christ with soaring sweetness.

Wangara was not the only person who lifted her voice during Saturday services for Dudley Randall, founder of the nationally known, Detroit-based Broadside Press.

Poets recited Randall's poems, a musician tinkled bells and squeezed fat, wet drops of the blues from his harmonica and Randall's Kappa Alpha Psi brothers sang their fraternity song. Speakers talked about the man who wore a tie, built his own house from the ground up, stayed married to Vivian Barnett Spencer for 43 years and never quit being kind.

They called him a friend, a mentor, an inspiration, a Boy Scout troop leader, a calming influence during the 1967 riot, a Wayne County librarian, a poet-in-residence at University of Detroit and Detroit's poet laureate.[5]

De Ramus compared Dudley Randall to Barry Gordy, but unlike Gordy, who became wealthy and a household name recognizable by millions, Randall, De Ramus aptly explained, "never left the westside of Detroit, never made millions and never became a glitter-sprinkled celebrity. Yet, he too, beamed black voices around the world, receiving a Lifetime Achievement Award from the National Endowment for the Arts." Both men worked hard at the assembly line in the foundry and struggled long and hard to make their dreams come true: "According to the often-told story, Gordy set up Motown with an $800 loan from his family, Randall began his publishing career with $12."

"He was my friend and colleague in the community of poets who flourished during the 1950s and 1960s in Detroit," added Naomi Long Madgett. "Through Lotus Press I followed in his footsteps and brought out his last book. The song may have ended, but the legacy lives on."

We carried Dudley's body to Elmwood Cemetery, the place where he and Margaret Danner used to write poetry and where most of the city's dignitaries are buried, black and white. I recalled the processional of cars that carried Coleman A. Young's casket down Woodward Avenue two years before, and how the citizens lined up along the curb to wave goodbye and pay their respects. For Dudley, the grandeur was transposed into a modest gathering of poets and friends, black and white, who gave their solemnity and their tears in mournful respect.

Poet Terry Blackhawk's poem, "For Dudley Randall, 1914–2000," channels the unspoken thoughts and explosions of emotions that converged that clear day filled with sunshine:

or Ezekiel's wheel, or the sisters
and brothers at the service, their spontaneous
tributes recalling the poet, as mentor,
fighter, seer, friend. Malaika rising
from her pew in *a capella* homage.
Ibn pouring libations on his grave.
What is the difference between will and intent?

Dudley, the dogma I pinned to my chest
Dissolves in songs and stories
And I think of the phoenix you summoned,
How the faith you held in every voice lifts now
Through these dozens of different incantations,
Flashes of hope, like the bird's spangled feathers
Drifting down across this ash-ridden town.[6]

Murray Jackson's "Dudley Randall" reaches into previous lives and unearths the resources of "roses and revolutions" and "green apples":

You find the green moss discover north
tie square knots to hold our world together
press the pressure points to keep u
from bleeding on city streets.

In Paradise Valley, your man
Caruso flashes the ruby stick-pin,
stands on his chair
talks about being colored . . .

You catch the mellow harmony
of their beat
siphon time, bottle it, then
uncork and stick it in our eye.[7]

For the rest of us, with the poet at peace with his muse, Dudley Randall's poem "Happiness" was printed on the last page of the funeral program:

Happiness
is a capricious girl.
Woo her, she flees.

Ignore her, she follows. . . .

When I was young and alone,
Sundays I stayed in my room all day
making poetry on the card table and Tottie,
hearing no sound, would tap on the door and ask,
"Are you all right?" And when I answered,
she'd go down to the kitchen and bring me
sandwiches and milk.

I never thought that I was happy then.
But now when I look back, I know
I was very happy.

EPILOGUE

I'm sitting in a plaza on the perimeter of a medieval castle, the Castello di San Michelle, on the Island of Sardinia, once a Roman outpost in the Mediterranean Sea. The buildings in the distance are pink and yellow and terra cotta brown. The sea and the hills and the clouds meet each other in wavering shades of blue. It is partially sunny, and because of this, it is sometimes cool, sometimes hot.

I've just left an international conference dedicated to the study of African American culture. Everyone there knows who Dudley Randall was and they queried me about the status of the manuscript. Yesterday, at lunch, I met a scholar from Russia. He reminded me of Robert Hayden—his facial contours, the coke-bottle-thick lenses of his glasses, his often tentative mannerisms. I told him about this resemblance and he was complimented. He smiled and told me he had quoted from Hayden's poem "The Middle Passage" in his presentation on the film *Amistad*. We talked about Hayden until a younger American scholar, whose research focused on the Moors, asked about Pushkin. And the conversation returned to Dudley Randall, whose translations and interest in Russian poetry enlivened our conversation. I promised to send the Russian scholar my documentary film on Dudley.

In this ancient space, where armies clashed and merchants exchanged goods and stories with sailors, I can see the crossing routes of humanity in the bronze complexions and black curly hair of the people. As I walk through the narrow, crooked streets, the cracks in the concrete castle evince the ages and a causal indifference for counting time in the face of a joie de vivre. The youth hold very little awe for this history. Graffiti appears in bold letters on the walls and entrances to the castle, and the heavy bass and contemporary poetry of American rap reverberates from their music boxes, leaving impressions like shadows darkening stone.

At this moment, I am thinking about how Dudley once explained the value of anonymity for poets to a *New York Times* reporter.[1] Standing in the cold of winter, he said:

"Not many places where I go do they know I'm a poet—forget about their knowing I'm poet laureate.

"But I'm always aware of the title," he said as he punched at an imaginary target. . . . "But I believe a poet can change things. He can change the way people look and feel about things. And that's what I want to do in Detroit."

Moments later he is behind the wheel of his battered blue Dodge driving downtown along a deserted Woodward Avenue in nighttime Detroit. He tells his passenger:

"Look out your window and what do you see? I bet you see nothing more than a dirty, dingy, empty street.

"But I look out the window and I see memories. I hear things.

"I see myself as a boy walking down that block or coming home from my job at the foundry. I remember how I felt when I came back from the war. I can remember the race riots in 1943 moving up this block, people turning over streetcars. I can hear my daddy calling me."

APPENDIX 1

TRANSLATING POETRY INTO FILM

The Black Unicorn: Dudley Randall and the Broadside Press
54 minutes. Distributed by Cinema Guild, New York.

M Y DECISION to make *The Black Unicorn: Dudley Randall and the Broadside Press* was motivated by a need to document history and culture in a visual and aural medium and to preserve Dudley Randall's image and imagery. Insofar as poetry, especially African American poetry, is as much performance art as it is print art, film provides the optimal means to preserve it by projecting the image of artists reading their own words. Within the broader dynamics of the medium itself, film also affords an opportunity to critically and creatively interact with the presentation of the poet within the visual vortex of the screen through improvisational imagery and a musical score. *The Black Unicorn* is one poet's interpretation of another poet's life and work in another art form, which attempts to provide biographical and historical insight in a manner that enhances the reception of the poetry and the poet's creative perspective.

Documentary film has a particular reach, including public television and the classroom. Accepting the limitations of this cultural reality, it was my intention to prepare a film/video that would appear in educational and social settings for long-term purposes. I wanted to preserve a glimmer of Randall's personality and voice in a form that would more easily attract young people and yet at the same time create an experience that would affirm memory as history.

The initial plan was to make a film that would run approximately twenty-eight minutes, a time frame that would fit easily into classroom schedules with ample room for introductory remarks and follow-up discussion. However, after all the shooting was done and after significant agonizing in the editing room, I soon realized that the story and the concept were too large for the time allotted. If the film were cut to fit the assigned format, the integrity of the project would suffer. Therefore, I decided to break with the original film treatment, expand the narrative, and increase the number of poems included. Rather than let marketing dictate the length and limitations of the film, I opted to let art determine the outcome.

CONCEPTUAL FRAMEWORK

The Black Unicorn has three levels of experience. Randall's poetry is arranged as peaks or apexes, wherein the film begins and ends, rises and falls. The poems are not introduced, nor do they appear in a bibliographical or sequential manner. The poetry presentations provide the creative context for the film and thematic coherence. Poetry is the impetus of Randall's life, and it is the core of his relationship to art and publishing. His profession as a librarian further emphasized his love of books and literature. His awareness of political and social events in African American history, which is conveyed in his narrative, is also reflected in his poetry. The film pivots around the poems as point and counterpoint, thematically and historically. The selection of the poems also represents the range and breadth of Randall's creative reach.

The first scene is the first stanza of the poem, "Black Poet, White Critic." White letters on a black screen literally and figuratively convey the irony of Randall's words and the cultural paradox:

> A critic advises
> not to write on controversial subjects
> like freedom or murder,
> but to treat universal themes
> and timeless symbols
> like the white unicorn.

These lines dissolve into the second stanza, which is only one line in length:

> A **white** unicorn?

This is followed by the author's name, Dudley Randall, then, a fade to black.

The visual contrast of white words on a black screen emphasizes distinctive aesthetic values; it also conversely reflects the title of the film. The cultural conflict between black and white is expressed with subtle sarcasm in a rhetorical question that is answered specifically in the next poem, "Ballad of Birmingham," which is presented with newsreel footage containing images and sounds drawn from history.

The presentation of the poem was crafted in a manner to avoid redundancy in either imagery or sound. Another challenge was to include some of the critical civil-rights imagery reflected in the poem, such as dogs, clubs, and hoses, without simplifying the significance of these historical facts as cliché images associated with the Civil Rights Movement. Hence, the more familiar imagery appears in slow motion before the reading of the poem begins and is later retrieved as quick flashes during the reading. No human voices are heard during the pretextual imagery to suggest a temporal distance in a historical sense, but at the same time, this shift suggests a haunting echo in cultural memory.

The sound of barking dogs and the whir of fire hoses are heard over images of black people being attacked mercilessly. Then, the sound of a siren is heard as an image of the Sixteenth Street Baptist Church appears: 15 September 1963, and Randall's voice begins the poem. The background music is a funeral dirge, but it emerges with an undercurrent of hope. The emotional complexity of the music intersects with the timbre of Randall's voice and the tension of the historical images related to the bombing of the church, which resulted in the deaths of four girls.

The power of the poem hinges on irony. In the larger thematic sense, the bombing of the church and the deaths of the four young girls confirms the violent horror of racism. Their deaths are far more terrifying than murder because they symbolize a deeper hatred of humanity. The church, which should be a sanctuary, is where the mother sends the child for safety. As Randall reads, the image of protesting children appears as the child appeals to join them and the mother explains her restrictions—"No, baby, no. You may not go," which are the words heard as the policeman stops the protesting children. Again, the police dogs are seen barking and biting people and the spray from fire hoses beats the protesters against trees and along the ground is seen as quick flashes at the moment Randall's voice invokes them. It is a recall of the initial, more surreal imagery viewed in the preliminary footage.

The next stanza uses contrast to reflect irony as the poem relays how the mother dresses the little girl to go to church while imagery of a policeman with a gun follows the paddy wagon full of children entering a dark passageway, an allusion to death. This is juxtaposed with images of the child's funeral. As Randall reads, "bathed rose petal sweet," a coffin covered with flowers is being carried to a hearse. The film crosscuts to a crying mother as Randall reads, "the mother smiled." The stanza includes forms of the word "smile" three times, but the corresponding imagery is of weeping and grieving.

The next stanza intersects with the stark reality of the bombing and images of destruction as Randall describes the mother's frantic search through the rubble. The movement of the camera over the devastation parallels Randall's reporting of the mother's futile plea and efforts to find her daughter. Instead, by contrast, crosscutting back to the funeral, the closing of the hearse door, and the wide shot of the crowd swaying to the voice of Randall and the musical score is the answer to the mother's question and the final line of the poem, "And baby, where are you?"

Further irony can be derived from the small American flag being held above the sea of sad and hopeful faces as well as from the billboard in the distance that advertises: "Citizens National Savings." Clearly, as the film is a documentary, the sign was not deliberately planted there, but when I identified it as an oblique statement on the meaning of the Civil Rights Movement's larger purpose, to save its citizens and the country, it was included rather than fading to black before it comes into focus. Unfortunately, this broader spiritual meaning is rarely observed because the nation is too often torn by racial antagonisms and economic competition rather than bonded by national harmony and historical responsibility.

"George" is a poem that uses time as its conceptual basis as it reflects the life of a retired laborer, whom the poet met when he was a young man working in the famous Ford foundry in Dearborn, Michigan. The cinematic strategy for this poem was determined by the challenge to integrate the concrete and the abstract dimensions of the life cycle and the meaning and value of physical labor. In a larger sense, the poem emanates from Randall's upbringing in a pro–labor union church and home.

As in "Ballad of Birmingham," the character in the poem "George" is not identified visually, but his image is reflected in actual footage of workers in a steel foundry that corresponds with the descriptions and activities in the poem. The real and historic imagery is juxtaposed through crosscutting with imagery of the Diego Rivera mural in the Detroit Institute of Arts, which is composed of complex layers of industry, nature, science, and religion. The panning of the camera across, up, down, reverse, and in and out of focus affects the reception of the more abstract dimensions of Randall's poem derived from another art form derived from the actual life experience of workers. The film reenvisions the poem by responding to it. The imagery in the film approaches the ideas and the feeling expressed in the poem, but it does not attempt to duplicate it. Like jazz, it is an interpretation of an experience, which allows space for the audience to interact with the poet's vision and the film.

The opening shot is from the fresco and is a color image focused on the back of a man squatting before a machine, as Randall reads: "When I was a boy desiring the title of man / And toiling to earn it," the camera pulls back and the image expands into a larger view of the factory, containing various levels of industry along with its complement of engineers and laborers. As Randall continues, "In the inferno of the foundry knockout," the image shifts into actual footage of a foundry and workers engaging a fiery furnace.

The next image focuses on the "masks" and the "goggles," and the film shifts back to the mural for still shots of these color images, which then dissolve into the furnace as sparks fly and the fire rages. When the poem refers to "shoulders bright with sweat," the imagery shifts to the mural and images of workers and their rounded shoulders almost merged with the cylindrical blocks and wheels of the factory, Randall relates, "You mastered the monstrous cylinder blocks." The imagery returns to the actual moving footage and the action of the poem intensifies, "with force enough to tear your foot in two, / You calmly stepped aside." The workers move away from the furnace.

In the second stanza, the imagery highlights the power of the factory and the transformation of raw materials into steel. Randall personifies this power with words like "groaning" and "grinding" and a huge roll of steel moves down a track. The action of Randall's "ocean wave" is portrayed as a huge band of steel flexes like a wave, and an "avalanche" of molten liquid is poured from a huge vat. The transition from the foundry to the mural implies the melding of the workers with the elements as these bodies are interpreted in shades of gray and in geometric figures merging with the cylinder blocks: "then braced our heads together / to form an arch / to lift and stack them." Strength is first visually associated with the image of a fist at the end of the stanza, when George is quoted, "You strong as a mule." The symbol recurs throughout the sequence with various images of a fist.

The next stanza requires a shift from a fast-paced rhythm and an intense tone to a slower, reflective rhythm and a sense of melancholic repose, as the poem moves to the present tense and explains that George is in a nursing home. Images from the mural reflect aspects of a hospital, including a doctor in an operating room, as the camera pans down to reveal research. The shift in mood is also related to "a ward where old men wait to die," with gray drawings of men in boats. The camera pans across the river scene in reverse, from right to left, symbolic of the passage of time and impending death as a skull appears directly above the scene.

The words, "You cannot read the books I bring," are juxtaposed with a winding circular shot of a book in the mural. As the shot broadens, one can read the imprint of the inscription that Diego Rivera gave the mural. An abandoned factory, darkly lit with only faint blue light reflected in narrow slits of windows, appears while the poem relates: "And you sit among the senile wrecks, the psychopaths, the incontinent." In this instance, George's death is related to the decline of the automobile industry and end of the industrial revolution.

The final scene reconnects with the mural as the image of a baby in the womb comes into view behind the dissolve of a wrought-iron obstruction, as if looking through a gate:

> One day when you fell from your chair and stared at the air
> With the look of fright which sight of death inspires, . . .

The image of the baby dissolves instantly into a funeral scene from historic footage of a burial of a union member killed during a United Auto Workers strike in the 1930s. The visual scene expands the meaning of George's life and the pride of laborers in the industry. As the poet lifts George "like a cylinder block," a retrieval of the earlier image in the first stanza recurs as the strikers lift the coffin of their fallen comrade, followed by the lifting of their fists in a salute of solidarity. This image is juxtaposed with the meaning and power of life in universal struggle.

The final lines return to the mural as the lifted fists of the strikers are connected to the fists emerging from the earth, grasping the raw materials that industry transforms in the foundry to make cars and trucks. The final image is of a fist, but it is clenched and reflects the power of the worker and George's statement is heard in the poet's tribute to him, "because you're strong as a mule."

"Profile on the Pillow" is the only love poem included in the film, and though the poem is not specifically dedicated to Randall's wife Vivian, it is employed in this instance to underscore the strength of the marriage. The poem was selected because it is his most famous love poem and would be the most useful for reflecting his skill with this theme.

A series of photographs beginning with their wedding pictures are transposed to relate the passage of time and the longevity of the union. Several photographs of the couple relate the closeness and a bond that endures despite internal difficulties and possible external threats. Since this presentation does not include profiles on a pillow, which is the primary image in the poem, the photographs and image of time unfolding portray a profile of the couple's marriage.

"Poet" was presented without the infusion imagery. In this treatment, Randall is identified with and as a poet and not as an external voice or as an observer or interpreter of experience. It was also desirable to show him reading without the intersection of visual effects because the poem is an interior statement about creative values. The close-up shot of his face situates the audience with the direct gaze and delivery of the poem. In contrast, "I Loved You Once" ("Ya Vas Lyubil"), a translation of the Alexander Pushkin poem, is a presentation that emphasizes printed language. Randall's voice is heard while the Russian dissolves into English. In this instance, language is privileged to accentuate Randall's encounter with the poetic experience, first in Russian and then translated into English.

"Roses and Revolutions," on the other hand, combines visual and aural treatments with regards to imagery and sound as well as the interspersion of Randall's face reciting the poem as a critical aspect of perspective. The poem starts with "Musing on roses and revolutions," which is a direct reference to the process of creative reflection and revelation. The poet as muse is a key feature in this poem, and, as the last poem in the film, it draws from earlier visual imagery in "Ballad of Birmingham," "George," and from Randall's reflective narrative.

The initial imagery scans the Detroit cityscape in a bird's-eye shot of burning buildings during the 1967 Race Riot as Randall reads "musing on roses and revolutions." The image shifts to a black bird perched in black tree limbs, which is part of the wrought-iron gate and entrance to the Diego Rivera mural. The poem continues, "I saw night close down on earth like a great dark wing."

The imagery returns to newsreel footage of the riot and converges with "and the lighted cities were like tapers in the night." Flames abound and overwhelm the buildings burning in the night with firemen in the foreground trying to extinguish the fires. The camera pulls back into the darkness, "and I heard the lamentations of a million hearts regretting life and crying for the grave." In the darkness, a national guard searches two black men standing next to their car with their hands behind their heads and their legs spread apart, while another soldier stands on guard with his rifle.

The scene dissolves into a man in a hospital bed with bandages across half his face and body, waving his arm as part of as Randall narrates, "and I saw the Negro lying in the swamp with his face blown off." Then, a stream of black men exit a paddy wagon as soldiers direct them with guns. The scene shifts to four armed soldiers goading two protesting black men to cross the street. A stop sign in the foreground conveys the sentiments of the poem. The images interpret the lines:

> and in northern cities with his manhood maligned and felt the writhing
> of his viscera like that of the hare hunted down or the bear at bay,

The next scene reflects the futility and emptiness of unfulfilled lives as men shovel trash, and Randall relates: "no joy in their work," and "joyless excitement" This image recedes into Randall's face as he reads: "as I groped in darkness and felt the pain of millions," which indicates the poet as source of introspection. "Gradually, like day driving night across the continent," the camera pulls back from a shot of a statue in front of the Detroit Institute of Arts providing a larger view dissolving into "I saw dawn upon them like the sun a vision." The camera moves into the image of an African woman in the Rivera mural.

The vision continues by connecting with the image of the Asian woman in the mural, and the camera pans in reverse movement as a temporal shift and to converge with "of a time when all men walk proudly through the earth." Bones, fossils, and hands clenching raw minerals come into view, an allusion to the sequence in "George" and "the bombs and missiles lie at the bottom of the ocean / like the bones of dinosaurs buried under the shale of eras." The camera ends with the image of the European woman.

The next scene is a negative against the preceding positive vision of humanity. A shot of a military airfield with carrier planes and government bureaucrats in dark suits carrying briefcases rushing across the airfield in unnatural and stiff steps. The accelerated time frame was used to produce a mechanical effect as "men strive with each other not for power or the accumulation of paper."

The next scene returns to Randall's image: "but in joy create for others the house, the poem, the game of athletic beauty." Images appear in sync with words: "a house"—Randall's home; "the poem"—a close up of poetry lines; "athletic beauty"—Joe Louis.

The final stanza returns to the image of a black bird in the wrought-iron gate "washed in the brightness of this vision," which then goes out of focus, and in the distance the image of a Native American woman holding fruit comes into focus: "and benourished." The symbols of insight and life are transformed with a return to raging flame and smoke coming from a building, "suddenly burst into terrible and splendid bloom," as the fire rages. The final lines return to Randall's image and "the blood-red flower of revolution," with a freeze frame after the last word of Randall's downcast gaze. Run credits.

The film begins with "Ballad of Birmingham" and ends with "Roses and Revolutions," Randall's most famous poems. These poems denote high points in his literary career and assure a strong opening and closing for the film. Both poems possess the tension and thematic depth necessary to affirm the point of the poem, "Black Poet, White Critic," the prelude or preface for the film. As stated in that poem, "Ballad of Birmingham" and "Roses and Revolutions" contain controversial subjects, like murder and freedom. The broader point is that these are the universal themes and timeless symbols of the black unicorn.

RANDALL'S NARRATIVE

Just as the poetry sequences serve as passages of creative expression, Randall's narrative provides historical events and personal experience, which are later manifested through artistic expression. The 1989 interview was videotaped at the home of Lotus Press in Detroit, but a previous interview of Randall in 1981 for the "Hastings Street Opera Project" replaced the 1989 interview during editing because the earlier interview was recorded during a period when Randall's responses were more animated, and he displayed the subtle nuances of his personality and a more vibrant spirit.

In his own words, Randall supplies the historical and biographical information that affected his muse, his imagination, and his poetic industry. Randall's biography is filled with Detroit's African American history in particular and African American history in general. He explains the nature and events of his times by discussing the migration of his family to Detroit, growing up during the Great Depression, serving in a racially segregated army during World War II, observing the 1943 Race Riot in Detroit, and developing Broadside Press during the Black Arts Movement.

The film supplies historic photos related to his family, Detroit, culture, and his personal experiences. But the film also supplies imagery of literature. It is a film about a poet, and words are as critical to the visual contour of the cinematic character as the allusions that emanate from those words. In this regard, the words are images, and they appear and dissolve in his handwriting, as lines of poetry or as stanzas or as poems on pages, while Randall reflects them relative to his emerging or diverging vocabulary in the wake of real experience and imagination interacting in the service of art.

To reaffirm this dynamic, these flashes of words and poetic formulas reappear in the presentation of "Roses and Revolution" to remind the audience that words are the imagination and the memory of past and future poems. The narrative demonstrates that poetry melds with the poet. Further introspection reveals Randall's upbringing by educated and religious parents who valued books and respected the human-rights struggle. This background rendered a fertile field for a person possessed by independent creative expression and motivated by progressive social and cultural values. Racial discrimination alienates African Americans and determines a peculiar social construction that, in this instance, contributed to a deeper understanding and a unique consciousness with regards to class issues. Moreover, Randall's early introduction to books and the publication of his first poems in the city's newspapers when he was still a teenager primed a strong sense of confidence in his abilities as a writer despite the pervasive consequences of racial discrimination.

The narrative was crafted in a manner to convey a sense of intimacy with the poet. Against the backdrop of a stone wall, his physical image is framed in a black leather easy chair surrounded by woodcarvings, books, and a colorful African weaving. This is not a prearranged setting, but in fact a favored reading corner in Randall's den. The camera moves in for tighter framing as expressions of personal feelings encourage closer proximity. In order to further capture this relationship, pauses after statements and instances of repose are used to contain his pensive nature. The interruption or interference of this mood with stills would have countered this effect. At other times, the interspersion of family photos and images of Detroit's Black Bottom, the neighborhood where Randall came of age, provide a visual frame of reference as Randall relays history through memory.

About growing up, Randall remembers being a Boy Scout and going to camp in the western part of Michigan where runaway slaves settled and became farmers. A photo by a Detroit historian, Orlin Jones, provides a partially obscured image of Randall peeking above another boy's head. This photo also contains two of his brothers, James, on the left and in full view, and Arthur, standing next to Dudley. Photos of James and Arthur as adults are seen when Randall talks about his induction into the army. Images of Joe Louis and jazz musicians emerging from the radio highlight and simulate the importance of radio during the 1930s.

His discussion of the Great Depression is largely a class-based analysis. As he explains with dry humor, "It was a happy time. We never locked our doors because there wasn't anything to rob." His reporting of the nature of things is a poet's perspective, which penetrates the effects as well as the experience. He offers the example of racial insult in the Penny Kitchen Restaurant when the proprietor refused to serve him and his brother in the dining room. Randall's discussion of the 1943 Race Riot in Detroit considers this event a critical moment in African American memory, while it is merely a footnote in mainstream history. Randall connects that event with racial tension in the labor movement and with housing discrimination. He also extends the consequences of the riot to the increase in the number of black males drafted into the armed services.

Randall's account of the war reveals not only the effect on his poetry, but also on the irony of encountering a Jim Crow South during a time when the United States was fighting a war against fascism. The story about the black troops resisting their removal to a Jim Crow car is highlighted with irony and cryptic humor: "in the dining car, a black cloth separates the whites from the black, so as to not upset the digestion of the white people." It is this wry sense of humor that is a part of Randall's charm and his capacity to rise above racial adversity. It is also his belief in poetry that makes his life special, and it becomes his political contribution to social progress.

Since he did not face military action during the war, he viewed his experience in the army an opportunity that expanded his poetic vocabulary through unique exposures to exotic lands. Randall's exposure to other cultures in the South Pacific during World War II continued after the war, when he studied Russian literature and language during his undergraduate education at Wayne State University. Randall describes his experiences at Wayne State University as an English major, which furthered his formal training with poetry. Photos from the college's 1949 yearbook appear of him alone and with other members of the Miles Poetry Workshop as he explains the founding and the publication of their poetry series.

His 1966 tour of the Soviet Union demonstrates the universal dimension of his poetry and the broad scope of his intellectual interests, which affected the publication of the first Broadside publication, *Poem Counterpoem*. His first collection of poems with Margaret Danner was designed after the format of a book he encountered during his visit to the Soviet Union in 1966. Randall's reflections on the Russian tour reveal his knowledge of the culture and the language. The inclusion of the reading of "I Loved You Once," a translation of a Pushkin poem, articulates the depth of his linguistic and aesthetic knowledge. The emphasis on the reception of poetry and poets by the Russian people illustrates what dynamics affected Randall's decisions as a poet, scholar, and publisher. This is a key view into Randall's identity and the universal dimensions of his poetry and his interest in world culture.

THE SECONDARY PERSPECTIVE

The voice-overs are limited to structural considerations. They provide information for connections, for context, and for clarification. The first commentary occurs after "Ballad of Birmingham," and uses the broadside of the poem to establish the historical connection between its publication and the founding of the press. Randall's achievements are presented by showing his books, and the impressive line-up of Broadside authors are introduced. The camera pans the ninety titles of books to demonstrate the extent of Broadside Press's bibliography, then the image converges with a 1975 photo of Broadside books and me, when I was the assistant editor of the press, to identify the relationship between the filmmaker and the subject. Photos of Randall with poets Gwendolyn Brooks, Sonia Sanchez, Sterling Brown, Haki Madhubuti (Don L. Lee), Etheridge Knight, Paulette White, Hilda Vest, and others facilitate visual associations for future reference.

"Ballad of Birmingham" becomes the founding poem for Broadside Press, as explained in the voice-over and the introduction for the film. What is special about Randall's life is that he was a poet-publisher who made significant sacrifices to open the literary canon to the benefit of writers traditionally discriminated against because they write about "controversial subjects." It is just such a poem that initiates that poetry press, which was an outgrowth of the political impetus of the Civil Rights Movement.

This sequence is followed by images of the twenty-fifth anniversary celebration of Broadside Press in 1990, which was a tribute to Randall, the founder. Randall is introduced, and then Coleman A. Young, who was at that time the mayor of Detroit, pays tribute to him as the poet laureate of the city and to Randall's identity as a vital part of the city. The film returns to the format of its opening, as the ending includes a return to the celebration, a final voice-over, a pan of the hundreds of Broadside poems, and an closing poem. The second voice-over is informational. I explain that in 1951 Randall achieved his master's degree in library science from the University of Michigan, Ann Arbor, after graduating from Wayne State University, and that his first marriage produced a daughter and later a divorce. The bridge also introduces his lasting marriage to Vivian Spencer and the next poem, "Profile on the Pillow."

The interviews with other poets provide testimonials that position Randall's life and work as points of departure and the central focus for these other artists. The sequence on the late Etheridge Knight provides a specific illustration of Randall's impact as an editor and publisher. It begins with Knight reading a poem in a public setting surrounded by white concrete walls. The poem, "The Idea of Ancestry," was written when Knight was in prison, therefore the setting intersects with the concrete cell where the poem was composed. The second half of the poem is read in Randall's home and the transition between settings is an aural one. The inclusion of the poem reiterates poetry as the primary energy in the film, and of course in Knight's relationship with Randall. Knight explains that poetry saved him from a life of crime and that Randall visited the prison to help him develop his craft. The publication of his first book, *Poems from Prison*, which was published by Broadside Press, was a significant factor in his early parole. Knight's poetry has won several awards, including a Guggenheim Fellowship and the National Book Award. He was one of the most prominent Broadside poets, and his talents were largely directed by Randall's tutelage. Historic photos reflect Knight with Randall, as well as in connection with Gwendolyn Brooks. The broadsides of his poems are viewed and scanned by the camera as Knight relays history and fond memories about Randall's gentle presence and personality, his example as a major literary influence, and his dedication as an editor.

Knight was selected to represent the experience of a Broadside poet because his biography is the most dramatic example of achievement and the most intriguing success story. Knight is a clear example of the kind of talent lost or hidden because of the lack of opportunities for African Americans. Therefore, he is the poet who is most capable of influencing a young audience as he explains the power of poetry to transform life, an echo of Randall's statement in the preceding Russian sequence: "Poetry is Power."

The interview with Marvin Bell moves the perspective of the film to commentary on Randall's impact as a poet and publisher and how that legacy is viewed from the broader American artistic community. Bell traces the genius of Randall's poetic gifts and his larger contribution as a poetry publisher as the reasons for his Life Achievement Award from the National Endowment of Arts in 1986. Bell's comments, as a "white" poet juxtaposed with the previous sequence, the reading of the poem "Poet," effect a significant transition.

Naomi Madgett's discussion of Randall is from a closer view as friend, poet, and publisher. As a black American poet and publisher of Randall's last book, *A Litany of Friends*, Madgett exalts the special qualities of "Booker T. and W. E. B.," as images of this and other poems translated into visual art by Shirley Woodson complement the discussion. The setting of the Lotus Press office, framed in such a way that a partial view of a famous print for the first African World Festival in Detroit by visual artist Carl Owens occupies the lower left-hand corner, enhances Madgett's interview. The eye of the figure in the print, who is symbolic of the dual heritage or the "double consciousness" of African Americans, a concept explained by W. E. B. Du Bois, appears to affirm what Madgett relays about the poem "Booker T. and W. E. B." The setting obliquely and graphically conveys the layers of art, history, and culture.

Madgett's sequence changes settings and reconnects with the earlier celebration sequence, wherein she discussed her status as a Broadside poet and Randall as the pioneer in black poetry publishing. This transition moves the film back to the setting of the earlier sequence, when Randall appeared in dynamic footage moving into another temporal framework. With humor and humility, Randall comments on the many years of his cultural service, the people who influenced him, and some of the people who came to pay tribute. He makes reference to Malcolm X in Harlem during remarks about a reading he performed there. This intersects with the film's introductory sequence and the book, *For Malcolm*, the first anthology and the second book published by Broadside Press. His acknowledgment of Chester Cable, his English professor at Wayne State University, also retrieves the importance of that particular segment.

Shahida Mausi, the director of the Detroit Council of the Arts, makes the closing remarks in the celebration sequence: "We want to thank you for what you have done for us and our young people. Thank you for this legacy you have left us," which is interfaced aurally with the concluding voice-over, my poem, "The Black Unicorn":

> Dudley Randall's legacy
> is the deep reach of poetry
> larger than thousands of voices
> disrupting library silence.
> A black unicorn works quietly,
> diligently,
> with ink on paper
> opening the pages of
> history and poetry,
> where freedom dreams
> and roses and revolutions
> bloom.

A still photo of me, working at my desk at Broadside Press, followed by a pan across scores of broadsides accompanies the voice-over. This scene dissolves into a bird's-eye shot of a smoldering fire in the center of 1967 Race Riot, and Randall reads "Roses and Revolutions."

COMPOSITIONAL STRUCTURE

The compositional arrangement provides an external temporal framework for the interviews and Randall's narrative, which takes place in both the immediate past and the distant past. The voice-overs operate outside of the temporal order of the film as introductory, transitional, and concluding remarks by the filmmaker. These sections are related and interrelated to the poetry sequences, but not in a historical order. The film operates in layers, a sequential development, the beginning of the documentary proper, and the ending. These structural units are related and interrelated, forming a pattern that can be likened to a series of interlocking circles, each cycle of narrative connecting to several others in more than one temporal flow. This pattern allows a holistic and multidimensional presentation of the pivot between life and work, providing sight and insight, perspective and introspection, creative expression, collaboration, and interpretation.

A key element in the construction of the imagery in "Ballad of Birmingham," "George," and "Roses and Revolutions" was the timing of the imagery. The aesthetic sensibility of the on-line editor, Mark Yazenchak, was especially important. As the director, I determined the selection and arrangement of the imagery, but he determined the timing and the nuances during the construction of the imagery. The mise-en-scène visually converges with the rhythm and timing of Randall's voice, and Yazenchek's broader talents as a musician and sculptor contribute significantly to his editorial craft. Yazenchak's genius was further executed in the laying of the musical score; as the on-line editor, he intuitively interacted with the aesthetic perspective of the composer. His editing was more like sculpting or playing an instrument than simply manipulating a machine.

THE MUSICAL SCORE

The original score was composed and performed by Kenn Cox, an internationally acclaimed Detroit composer and pianist. He was my first and preferred choice because I knew his talents were boundless. He has a broad cultural reach and a deep appreciation for the work of Dudley Randall. All of the music was performed on the synthesizer, which allowed for an expansive range of simulated instruments.

"The Black Unicorn," the first piece that Cox composed for the project, has a thematic reprise that sonically underscores the film's narrative, which is expanded when performed with "Roses and Revolutions." About the composing process, Cox said, "Dudley is such a great character, it's almost like he wrote the music. The texts of his work and his interviews had a provocative influence on the composing process. To see and hear what he was saying in relation to the cinematic images made it considerably easier than I had anticipated."

"The Ballad of Birmingham," on the other hand, was a serious challenge because of the magnitude of the historical event. In particular, Cox said, "John Coltrane's piece, 'Alabama' was such a benchmark that I didn't want to be influenced by it." Cox extrapolated the music from the rhythmic patterns in the poetry and from the thematic thrust of the poems. In the case of "Ballad of Birmingham," he employed strings, which resulted in more of an organic sound. There is an electronic choir. It delivers a religious and a spiritually heavy sound that is haunting, and yet it is interlaced with a hopeful and uplifting quality. In "George," the pulse of the music stays the same except during the bridge in the middle of the poem, when the poem shifts in tense and in time frame. Cox uses arco strings, which simulate the cello and the bass to affect a masculine quality that relates to the theme of male bonding. The inclusion of the pizzicato provides the lighter strings, which is more feminine and contributes to the spiritual quality of the funeral scenes. There is no resolution to the piece; it fades out.

The sound for the Etheridge Knight sequence was determined by the blues qualities in his poem "The Idea of Ancestry." Cox uses a solo clarinet, an alto range which is plaintive and appropriate for the blues, not only in the rhythm of Knight's poetry, but also in his voice. The solo instrument is also reflective of the solitary existence in prison, where Knight wrote the poem. The music serves as an aural transition as Knight's reading of the poem changes settings. The clarinet solo is retrieved toward the end of the sequence, but it converges with the variations in Knight's speaking rhythm.

The sound track for "Poet" was distanced from the poem itself and plays with the even rhythm and mocking tone Randall employs in the poem. It operates as a complement and as counterpoint to Randall's voice. It is fast and quick, sharp and direct, emulating the attitude of the poem. In contrast, when Naomi Madgett talks about Randall's poetry, the score is in a soprano voice. The xylophone highlights a merry sense of rhythm, which reflects the nature of the poets' camaraderie.

Sometimes Cox takes creative liberty and improvisational leaps. During a moment when Randall reflects on his philosophy of human nature, Cox underscores his statements with the sound of the koto, a small Japanese instrument of thirteen strings. He explains, "The point was to invoke an Eastern philosophical effect, which speaks to the wisdom of the ages and universal truths." In a more traditional reach, Cox uses "The Cake Walk" to represent the description of Randall's reflections when he was growing up during the 1920s because it was the popular African American sound of the times.

When Randall describes his wartime experiences the music races with excitement and dances with the upbeat sound of his voice. This sound is retrieved during the Russian sequence, emitting the same sense of adventure and excitement. Conversely, when he describes the disappointing experience when the Jim Crow law was enforced while his army unit was traveling on a train through the southern states, the sound track at the end of the sequence simulates the churning of train wheels, over and over.

Cox had the most difficulty with "Profile on the Pillow" because originally he tried to apply Chopin's Prelude in C Major, but it was too restrictive. Ultimately, he resolved to derive the first eight bars from Chopin's influence, but he improvised with a twentieth-century bridge. Cox, as a composer and pianist, was strongly influenced by Chopin during his studies and found a sense of kinship with this aspect of Randall's creative psyche. It is a lovely and enduring piano solo.

Kenn Cox undertook the score as a new composing challenge and feels it opened his imagination in new ways because he had not worked in this genre. Relating to both the poetry and the film stimulated his creativity: "The experience was enjoyable and was a challenge that was not frustrating. It was more a matter of I can do this, as opposed to what am I going to do." As the director, I rarely interfered during the composing process, but we did consult when he reached an impasse. And in some instances, we resolved to eliminate music altogether and to use the sound of words or silence as the aural amplifier.

CONCLUDING: MAKING THE FILM

The making of *The Black Unicorn* required many hours of research, writing, and editing. Because of my experience as a worker at Broadside Press and because my own poetry has been influenced by Dudley Randall, I realized that a more objective portrayal of him would be disingenuous and the

the work would be lacking. On the other hand, I did study the relationship between film and literature in graduate school at the University of Michigan, and this training was critical in terms of the drafting and crafting of the film.

One of the most dynamic aspects of this project was the crew. In many ways, it was an experience peculiar to the Detroit attitude about promoting our cultural heroes. I was privy to an excellent set of professionals with strong social and political consciousnesses. They were committed to the integrity of the project, and without their generous spirit the film would never have been completed.

I was the writer, producer, and director, and I also did research and conducted the on-camera interviews. The crew consisted of Terry Kelley, field director; Kenn Cox, musical composer and performer; Rich Weiske, off-line editor and camera operator; Mark Yazenchak, online editor; Robert Handley, camera operator; Bill Bryce, camera operator, Dave McNutt, camera operator; Ron Scott, interviewer; Judy Schonberg, researcher; and Dorothy Donise Clore, Kamala Kempadoo, Robert Matthews, and Denise Swope, production assistants.

My major difficulty was financial. Filmmaking is an expensive enterprise; the cost of equipment rental for recording and editing was often stifling. Acquiring funds for a documentary is a tedious process, and when funds were awarded they were always cut. The crew worked at reduced, proletariat rates, and, thanks to Bill Bryce, I was able to access editing equipment at moments when I did not have funds to pay for the time.

The Arts Foundation of Michigan, the Center for New Television, the Detroit Council of the Arts, the Ohio Arts Council, the Michigan Council for the Arts, the Department of Africana Studies at Wayne State University, and the University of Michigan Rackham Graduate Faculty Research Grant provided funding for the Black Unicorn Film Project. At different junctures, Progressive Artists and Educators Incorporated, the Société of the Culturally Concerned, and the Department of Black Studies at Ohio State University sponsored the film project.

The film served as a blueprint for the larger project, this biography of Randall, and was conceived as a complement to *Wrestling with the Muse: Dudley Randall and the Broadside Press*. The interviews for the film narrative were edited for the limitations of this format, but the extended conversations with Randall are included in the book. The book also provides a more detailed examination of his poetry and the development of Broadside Press. In this regard, the film is an introduction to his poetry and his life's work.

The film reflects Randall's person, voice, and history. It also relays his creativity, personality, and industry in a manner that informs and inspires. The composition not only conveys the substance of Randall's work, it also combines the essence of his biography in a manner that demonstrates how and why he became a dynamic force in American literature by challenging the aesthetic tenets of tradition and by printing words that voice another time and alternate symbols.

APPENDIX 2

WORKSHEETS FOR "FREDERICK DOUGLASS
AND THE SLAVE BREAKER"

The Slave Breaker
Frederick Douglass and the Slave Breaker

I could have let him lash me

      horse
like a ~~mule~~ or a dog,

to break my spirits.

           had never raised a finger
So many of us ~~had suffered passively~~,

         just one more.
I would have been ~~only one of many~~.

But something in me said, "Fight.

            for <u>something</u>
If it's time to die, then die fighting."
And take him along with you

So half the day we battled,

The man and the boy, sweating,

Bruising, bleeding,
~~Grunting, rolling,~~--

Till at last the slave-breaker said,

         whipped
"Go on, boy, I've ~~given~~ you enough.

Reckon now
~~You~~'ve learned your lesson."

But I knew who it was that was whipped,

   what   was.
And the lesson ~~I'd learned~~,

~~Never to forget.~~

Worksheets by Dudley Randall. Version 1.

Frederick Douglass and the Slave Breaker

I could have let him lash me

like a horse or a dog

to break my spirit.

So many of us had never raised a finger;

I would have been just one more.

But something in me said, "Fight.

If it's time to die then die for <u>some</u>thing;

and take him with you."
                    along

So half the day we battled,

the man and the boy, sweating,

bruising, bleeding,

till at last the slave-breaker said,

"Go on, boy, I done whupped you enough.

Reckon now you done learned your lesson."

But I knew who it was that was whipped,

and the lesson I learned

I'll never forget.--Dudley Randall

Worksheets by Dudley Randall. Version 2.

Frederick Douglass and The Slave Breaker

I could have let him lash me
like a horse or a dog
to break my spirit.
None of us ever lifted a finger;
I would have been just one more.

But something in me said, "Fight.
If it's time to die, then die for *something*,
and take him with you."

So all day long we battled,
the man and the boy, sweating,
bruising, bleeding . . .

till at last the slave breaker said,
"Go home, boy. I done whupped you enough.
Reckon you done learned your lesson."

But I knew who it was that was whipped,
and the lesson I learned
I'll never forget.

—DUDLEY RANDALL

Worksheets by Dudley Randall. Version 3, *Black World*, September 1972.

NOTES

INTRODUCTION. WRESTLING WITH THE MUSE

1. All of the quotes in the text of the introduction are from Dudley Randall in *A Capsule Course in Black Poetry Writing* (Detroit: Broadside Press, 1975), 35–64.
2. June Jordan, Review of *After The Killing*, by Dudley Randall, *American Poetry Review* 3, no. 2 (March/April 1974): 32.
3. These numbers were derived from my calculations of documentation of the poets listed in Eugene B. Redmond's exhaustive and comprehensive study, *Drumvoices: The Mission of Afro-American Poetry, A Critical History* (New York: Anchor Press/Doubleday, 1976), and from William L. Andrews, Frances Smith Foster, and Trudier Harris, eds., *The Oxford Companion to African American Literature* (New York: Oxford University Press, 1997).
4. The Melba Joyce Boyd, quoted in Betty DeRamus, "Dudley F. Randall, 1914–2000," *The Detroit News*, 15 August 2000.
5. Tony Medina, personal communication, 1 February 2003.
6. Melba Joyce Boyd and M. L. Liebler, *Abandon Automobile: Detroit City Poetry 2001* (Detroit: Wayne State University Press, 2001), 24.

1. BEGINNINGS AND ENDINGS

1. Dudley Randall, "A Conversation with Dudley Randall," by A. X. Nicholas, *Black World* 21, no. 2 (December 1971): 30.
2. Dan Georgakas and Marvin Surkin, *Detroit: I Do Mind Dying, A Study in Urban Revolution*. Revised edition. (Cambridge, Mass.: South End Press, 1998), 170–71.
3. It has to be noted here that in the accounts reported in Georgakas and Surkin, *Detroit I Do Mind Dying*, that Hayward Brown is described as an former junkie. This is not true. Although Brown admitted to "getting high," he never took drugs intravenously or suffered from the disease of drug addiction. There are no records to sustain this characterization.

4. Arthur Bowman Jr., Paul Curtis, and Conrad Mallet Jr. eventually graduated from law school and became attorneys; in fact, Mallet served on the Michigan Supreme Court as a judge. Tom Williams is a feature writer for the *Port Huron Daily*, and Gene Cunningham became an aid to the Detroit City Council, a real estate agent, and currently the facilitator for the Global Trade Task Force for the City Council.

5. Steve Babson, *Working Detroit* (Detroit: Wayne State University Press, 1984), 174.

6. Ibid, 173.

7. Georgakas and Surkin, *Detroit: I Do Mind Dying*, 20–21.

8. Johnson was placed in a hospital for the criminally insane.

9. For more historical details on this event refer to Georgakas and Surkin, *Detroit: I Do Mind Dying*; and Heather Ann Thompson, *Whose Detroit? Politics, Labor, and Race in a Modern American City* (Ithaca: Cornell University Press, 2001). The Republic of New Africa was a progressive, nationalist organization that advocates a separate black nation in the southern United States.

10. Bennett's goons were Ford's hired muscle, who worked for the so-called Service Department. For more details on this history see Babson's *Working Detroit*. For more information on Coleman's life see his autobiography, Coleman Young and Lonnie Wheeler, *Hard Stuff: The Autobiography of Mayor Coleman Young* (New York: Viking Press, 1994); and Richard C. Wilbur, *Coleman Young and Detroit Politics: From Social Activist to Power Broker* (Detroit: Wayne State University Press, 1988).

11. Young and Wheeler, *Hard Stuff*, 190.

12. Ibid., 175.

2. THE FERTILE BLACK BOTTOM OF PARADISE VALLEY

1. Missouri Hawkins, in Elizabeth McCants, "Memory of Former Slave Now Fading, But She Still Recalls Raid of Yankees," *The Macon Press*, 3 June 1958.

2. William P. Randall, quoted in "Bill Randall: The Man and the Movement," *Macon Magazine* (winter 1987): 23.

3. Missouri told this story to her grandson William C. Randall. It was repeated to the author in an interview via telephone, Detroit, Mich. and Macon, Ga., 24 October 1998.

4. Arnold Rampersad, *Jackie Robinson: A Biography* (New York: Alfred A. Knopf, 1997), 12.

5. A notice in the *Macon Telegraph* newspaper, dated 22 January 1909, announced that "P. J. Clyde Randall, a well known Macon Negro has qualified before Clerk of Court Nesbit to practice law in this state." A description of his education and struggles to get an education are delineated.

6. Steve Babson, *Working Detroit* (Detroit: Wayne State University Press, 1986), 45.

7. Ibid.

8. See a poem by Dudley Randall, "To William T. Patrick, Jr. (On His Leaving Detroit for New York)" in *After the Killing* (Chicago: Third World Press, 1973).

3. POETS OF BLACK BOTTOM:
DUDLEY RANDALL MEETS ROBERT HAYDEN

1. Dudley Randall, "An Interview with Dudley Randall," by Gwendolyn Fowlkes, *The Black Scholar* 6, no. 6 (June 1975): 87.
2. Steve Babson, *Working Detroit* (Detroit: Wayne State University Press, 1986), 93.
3. "Hastings Street Girls" was not published until 1967 as "Ghetto Girls." in *Negro Digest* 16, no. 7 (May 1967): 25. It was collected in *More to Remember* (Chicago: Third World Press, 1971). Even though the poem endured because the imagery persisted, the setting changed. Hastings Street no longer exists, replaced by the Interstate Highway 75, also know as Chrysler Freeway within the Detroit city limits.
4. Robert Hayden, quoted in John Hatcher, *From the Auroral Darkness: The Life and Poetry of Robert Hayden* (Oxford: George Ronald Press, 1984), 6–7.
5. Ibid., 7.
6. For a more detailed discussion on Robert Hayden's life, consult Hatcher's *From the Auroral Darkness*.
7. Dudley Randall, as quoted in D. H. Melhem, *Heroism in the New Black Poetry* (Lexington, Ky.: University Press of Kentucky, 1990), 76.
8. Hatcher reports in his biography of Hayden that Louis O. Martin, who was then an editor for the *Michigan Chronicle*, Detroit's black newspaper, founded Falcon Press to publish Hayden's collection of poetry. Martin printed the book at his press, but Chris Alston and other organizers for the CIO were involved in raising funds for the publication.
9. Dudley Randall, "The Black Aesthetic in the Thirties, Forties, and Fifties," in *The Black Aesthetic*, ed. Addison Gayle Jr., (Garden City, N.Y.: Doubleday, 1971), 235.
10. Ibid.
11. Hatcher, *From the Auroral Darkness*, 13.
12. Chris Alston, interview by author, videotaped, Ann Arbor, Mich., 23 February 1990.
13. Dudley Randall, "Happiness," in *A Litany of Friends* (Detroit: Lotus Press, 1981), 88.

4. WAR AT HOME AND ABROAD

1. Steve Babson, *Working Detroit* (Detroit: Wayne State University Press, 1986), 119.
2. Naomi Madgett married Julian Fields Witherspoon on 31 March 1946 and as a consequence moved to Detroit, where she has since resided. Naomi Madgett, interview, audiotaped, 1 December 1998, Detroit, Mich.
3. This letter is from the personal collection of Phyllis Randall Sherron.

5. THE RETURN: POETRY AND PROPHECY

1. Martin Duberman, *Paul Robeson* (New York: Alfred A. Knopf, 1988), 305.
2. Steve Babson, *Working Detroit* (Detroit: Wayne State University Press, 1986), 156–57.

3. Robert Millender is regarded as one of the city's "black fathers." There is a sky-scraper in downtown Detroit named in his honor.

4. Murray Jackson, interview by author, audiotaped, Detroit, Mich., 1 August 1996.

5. Dudley Randall, "The Black Aesthetic in the Thirties, Forties, and Fifties," in *The Black Aesthetic*, ed. Addison Gayle, Jr., (Garden City, N.Y.: Doubleday, 1971), 224–25.

6. Dudley Randall, "An Interview with Dudley Randall," by Gwendolyn Fowlkes, *The Black Scholar*, 6, no. 6. (June 1975): 88.

7. Dudley Randall, "The Black Aesthetic," 230.

8. Dudley Randall, "Old Witherington," in *A Litany of Friends* (Detroit: Lotus Press, 1981), 13. Originally published in *Negro Digest* 14, no. 111 (September 1965): 62.

9. James A. Emanuel and Theodore L. Gross, eds., *Dark Symphony: Negro Literature in America* (New York: The Free Press, 1968), 489.

10. Dudley Randall, quoted in D. H. Melhem, *Heroism in Black Poetry* (Lexington, Ky.: University Press of Kentucky), 58–60.

11. Ibid., 60.

12. Dudley Randall, "A Conversation with Dudley Randall," by A. X. Nicholas, *Black World*, 21, no. 11 (December 1971): 29.

13. Ibid., 29.

14. The poem was anthologized in Dudley Randall, *The Black Poets* (New York: Bantam, 1971); and collected in *Cities Burning* (Detroit: Broadside, 1968).

15. Dudley Randall, "An Interview with Dudley Randall," by Gwendolyn Fowlkes, *The Black Scholar* 6, no. 6 (June 1975): 88.

16. Dudley Randall, quoted in Emanuel and Gross, eds., *Dark Symphony*, 488.

6. SOJOURN AND RETURN

1. Dudley Randall, "Booker T. and W. E. B.," *Midwest Journal* 5, no. 1 (winter 1952): 77–78; also published in Dudley Randall and Margaret Danner, *Poem Counterpoem* (Detroit: Broadside Press, 1966), 8; and Theodore Gross and James Emanuel, eds., *Dark Symphony* (New York: The Free Press, 1968), 491.

2. Coleman A. Young, interview by the author, Detroit, Mich., 29 September 1996.

3. Steve Babson, *Working Detroit* (Detroit: Wayne State University Press, 1986), 158.

4. Ibid.

5. Phyllis Randall Sherron, interview by author, Detroit, Mich., 15 September 1996.

6. Dudley Randall to Phyllis Randall, ca. 1944, in the personal collection by Phyllis Randall Sherron.

7. Phyllis Randall Sherron, interview by author, Detroit, Mich., 15 September 1996.

8. Vivian Randall, interview by author, Detroit, Mich.

9. Dudley Randall to Etheridge Knight, 15 January 1967, Etheridge Knight Papers, the Ward M. Canaday Center, University of Toledo Library, Toledo, Ohio.

7. THE EMERGENCE OF THE SECOND RENAISSANCE IN DETROIT

1. Dudley Randall, "An Interview with Dudley Randall," by Gwendolyn Fowlkes, *The Black Scholar* 6, no. 6 (June 1975): 88.

2. Ed Simpkins, interview by author, audiotaped, Detroit, Mich., 1 October 1996.

3. Naomi Long Madgett, *Contemporary Authors Series*, vol. 23, ed. Shelly Andrews (Detroit: Gale Research, 1996), 205.

4. "Birmingham Sunday," was composed by Richard Farina and recorded by Joan Baez.

5. "Ballad of Birmingham" was Broadside No. 1, the first publication for Broadside Press, and the opening poem in Randall and Danner's *Poem Counterpoem* (Detroit: Broadside Press, 1966).

6. Randall rearranged the last line when he published the poem in *The Black Poets*, and this alteration retunes the rhythm and tightens the imagery for a better compositional flow. In the first version the phrase, "but where's the foot," ends with a heavy stress and a plosive "t." The second version, "my baby wore," is softer and assists with the repetition of sound. The original reads:

   "O here's a shoe, but where's the foot?
   And, baby, where are you?"

7. The March for Freedom is documented at the Detroit Historical Museum. This information is made available on a Fact Sheet about Detroit History.

8. Rosey E. Pool, ed., *Beyond the Blues: New Poems by American Negroes* (London: The Hand and Flower Press, 1962).

9. Madgett, *Contemporary Authors Series*, 206.

10. John Hatcher, *From the Auroral Darkness: The Life and Poetry of Robert Hayden* (Oxford: George Ronald Press, 1984), 31.

11. Ibid., 32.

12. Ron Milner, interview by author, audiotaped, Detroit, Mich., 3 June 3, 2001.

13. Eurgene Redmond indentifies Russell Atkins and Helen Collins as the founding editors of *Free Lance* in *Drumvoices: The Mission of Afro-American Poetry, A Critical History* (New York: Anchor Press/Doubleday, 1976), but in his article "Stridency and the Sword" (cited below), he states that Casper Jordan and Russell Atkins were the founding editors.

14. Eugene Redmond, "Stridency and the Sword: Literary and Cultural Emphasis in Afro-American Magazines," in *The Little Magazine in America: A Modern Documentary History*, ed. Elliott Anderson and Mary Kinzie (New York: The Pushcart Press, 1978), 544.

15. Ibid.

16. Ibid., 545.

17. Randall's poetry did not appear in *The New Negro Poets: U.S.A.* until after Hughes's death, when Arna Bontemps became the editor in 1970. He omitted some poets and inserted others, including Dudley Randall.

18. Dudley Randall to Langston Hughes, The Langston Hughes Papers, Yale University Library.

19. Dudley Randall to Langston Hughes, 22 January 1964, Langston Hughes Papers.

20. Dudley Randall to Langston Hughes, 2 February 1964, Langston Hughes Papers.

21. Ron Milner, interview by author.

22. Elmwood Cemetery is a historic site where many Detroit dignitaries have been buried for over two hundred years. Mayor Coleman A. Young and Dudley Randall are buried there.

23. Dudley Randall et al., *A Capsule Course in Black Poetry Writing* (Detroit: Broadside Press, 1975), 38.

24. Margaret Danner to Robert Hayden, no date, Robert Hayden Papers, National Baha'i Archives, Box 5, Wilmette, Ill.

25. Margaret Danner to Robert Hayden, no date.

26. Dudley Randall to Robert Hayden, 1 November 1963, Robert Hayden Papers.

27. Margaret Danner to Robert Hayden, no date, Robert Hayden Papers.

28. Dudley Randall to Robert Hayden, 16 March 1964, Robert Hayden Papers.

29. Margaret Danner to Robert Hayden, 22 March 1964, Robert Hayden Papers.

30. This figure is reflected in the bibliographical issue of *Black World* 20, no. 12 (October 1971): 70.

31. Dudley Randall to Etheridge Knight, 1 July 1966, Etheridge Knight Papers, Ward M. Canaday Center, University of Toledo Library, Toledo, Ohio.

32. Naomi Madgett, *Contemporary Authors Series*, 206.

33. Eugene B. Redmond, *Drumvoices*, 178.

34. Hoyt Fuller, "On the Conference Beat," *Negro Digest* 16, no. 5 (March 1966): 91.

35. Edward Simpskins, interview by author, audiotaped, Detroit, Mich., 1 October 1996.

8. "BALLAD OF BIRMINGHAM": THE FOUNDING OF BROADSIDE PRESS AND THE BLACK ARTS MOVEMENT

1. Imamu Amiri Baraka, *The Autobiography of Leroi Jones/Amiri Baraka* (New York: Freundlich Books, 1984), 200–201.

2. Ron Milner, interview by author, audiotaped, Detroit, Mich., 3 June 2001.

3. Betty De Ramus, "Black Power, Black Rebellion," *Negro Digest* 17, no. 1 (November 1967): 41.

4. Dudley Randall, "Black Power," *Negro Digest* 16, no. 1, (November 1966): 95–96.

5. Dudley Randall, "A Report on the Black Arts Convention," *Negro Digest* 15, no. 10 (August 1966): 13.

6. Dudley Randall, *Broadside Memories: Poets I Have Known* (Detroit: Broadside Press, 1975), 24.

7. John Hatcher, *From the Auroral Darkness: The Life and Poetry of Robert Hayden* (Oxford: George Ronald Press, 1984), 37.

8. Gwendolyn Brooks, *Report From Part One* (Detroit: Broadside Press), 70.

9. Dudley Randall, interview by Hoyt Fuller, *Negro Digest* 17, no. 3 (January 1968): 42.

10. Dudley Randall, "The Black Aesthetic in the Thirties, Forties, and Fifties," in *The Black Aesthetic*, ed. Addison Gayle Jr. (Garden City, N.Y.: Doubleday, 1971), 236.

11. Dudley Randall to Robert Hayden, 27 April 1966, Robert Hayden Papers, Box 16, National Baha'i Archives, Wilmette, Ill.

12. Dudley Randall to Robert Hayden, 29 April 1966, Robert Hayden Papers.

13. Ron Milner, interview by author, Detroit, Mich., 3 June 2001.

14. "Victoria," *Negro Digest* 15, no. 7 (May 1966): 64–72; "Shoe Shine Boy," *Negro Digest* 15, no. 11 (September 1966): 53–55.

15. Dudley Randall to Robert Hayden, 29 August 1966, Robert Hayden Papers.

16. Dudley Randall to Robert Hayden, 13 April 1966, Robert Hayden Papers.

17. Dudley Randall to Robert Hayden, 30 May 1966, Robert Hayden Papers.

18. Dan Georgakas, "Young Detroit Radicals, 1955–65," *URGENT Tasks*, no. 12 (summer 1981): 94.

19. For a more expanded discussion on Detroit City poets, consult Melba Joyce Boyd and M. L. Liebler, eds., introduction to *Abandon Automobile: Detroit City Poetry 2001* (Detroit: Wayne State University Press, 2001), 23–34.

20. Dudley Randall, "A Conversation with Dudley Randall," interview by A. X. Nicholas, *Black World* 21, no. 2 (December 1971): 31.

21. Dudley Randall, *Broadside Memories*, 31.

22. The last two lines, both of which were later deleted, read: "Does it believe in integration? / And why not a black unicorn?" Melvin Tolson Papers, Box 1, Dudley Randall file: 1965–1960, Library of Congress.

9. "YA VAS LYUBIL": ALEXANDER PUSHKIN, DUDLEY RANDALL, AND THE BLACK RUSSIAN CONNECTION

1. Dudley Randall, "An Interview with Dudley Randall," by Gwendolyn Fowlkes, *The Black Scholar*, 6, no. 6 (June 1975): 88.

2. Randall to Hayden, postcard, date unclear, Robert Hayden Papers, Box 16, National Baha'i Archives, Wilmette, Ill.

3. Randall to Hayden, 30 May 1966, Robert Hayden Papers.

4. Randall to James A. Emanuel, 13 December 1971, James A. Emanuel Papers, the Collections of the Manuscript Division, Library of Congress, Washington, D.C.

10. CULTURAL WARS AND CIVIL WARS

1. Dudley Randall and Margaret Burroughs, eds., introduction to *For Malcolm: Poems On the Life And Death Of Malcolm X* (Detroit: Broadside Press, 1967), xx.

2. Ibid.

3. Ibid., xxi.

4. Ibid., 110.

5. Dudley Randall, "The Second Annual Black Arts Convention," *Negro Digest* 17, no. 1 (November 1967): 43–45.

6. Dudley Randall to Etheridge Knight, 21 June 1967, Etheridge Knight Papers, Ward M. Canaday Center, University of Toledo, Toledo, Ohio.

7. Imamu Amiri Baraka, *The Autobiography of Leroi Jones/Amiri Baraka* (New York: Freundlich Books, 1984), 194.

8. Dudley Randall, "The Second Annual Black Arts Convention," 43.

9. Ibid., 44.

10. Ibid., 45.

11. Ibid.

12. Ibid.

13. Ibid., 43.

14. Dudley Randall to Etheridge Knight, 9 August 1967, Etheridge Knight Papers.

15. Betty De Ramus, "Black Power, Black Rebellion," *Negro Digest* 16, no. 1, (November 1967): 33.

16. Steve Babson, *Working Detroit* (Detroit: Wayne State University Press, 1986), 171.

17. Ibid.

18. Ron Scott, quoted in Kim D. Hunter, "1967: Detroiters Remember the Rebellion," *Against the Current* 12, no. 4 (1997): 23.

19. Ibid.

20. Ed Vaughn, quoted in ibid., 20

21. Ibid.

22. Betty De Ramus, "Black Power, Black Rebellion," 24–25.

23. Babson, *Working Detroit*, 175.

24. Dudley Randall, *Broadside Memories: Poets I Have Known* (Detroit: Broadside Press, 1975), 28.

25. Ibid., 32.

11. "PROPHETS FOR A NEW DAY": DIVERSITY AND HERITAGE

1. Randall to Hayden, 10 October 1967, Robert Hayden Papers, Box 16, National Baha'i Archives, Wilmette, Ill.

2. Robert Hayden, ed., *Kaleidoscope: Poems by American Negro Poets* (New York: Harcourt, Brace & World, Inc., 1967), xix.

3. Don L. Lee, "On *Kaleidoscope* and Robert Hayden," *Negro Digest* 18, no. 3 (January 1968): 51.

4. Hayden, op. cit., xx.

5. Randall to Hayden, 23 April 1969, Robert Hayden Papers.

6. Hayden to Randall, 7 July 1969, Robert Hayden Papers.

7. Margaret Danner to Robert Hayden, 30 March 1968, Robert Hayden Papers, Box 16, National Baha'i Archives, Wilmette, Ill.

8. Marilyn Gardner, "Author Collects Rhymes, Rejection Slips," *The Milwaukee Journal*, 17 February 1957; quoted in Carline Williams Strong, "Margaret Taylor Goss Burroughs: Educator, Artist, Founder, and Civic Leader," Ph.D. diss., Loyola University of Chicago, 1994, 158.

9. Gwendolyn Brooks, *Report From Part One* (Detroit: Broadside Press, 1974), 69.

10. Strong, "Margaret Taylor Goss Burroughs," 160.

11. Ibid.

12. Ibid., 170

13. Brooks, *Report From Part One*, 70.

14. Ibid., 84.

15. Ibid.

16. Dudley Randall, *Broadside Memories: Poets I Have Known* (Detroit: Broadside Press, 1975), 5.

17. Dudley Randall, "Black Publisher, Black Writer, An Answer," *Negro Digest* 24, no. 5. (March 1975): 35.

18. Dudley Randall to James A. Emanuel, 10 December 1967, James A. Emanuel Papers, Collections of the Manuscript Division, Library of Congress, Washington, D.C.

19. Dudley Randall to Etheridge Knight, 15 January 1967, Etheridge Knight Papers, Ward M. Canaday Center, University of Toledo Library, Toledo, Ohio.

20. Randall, *Broadside Memories*, 16.

21. Jerry Ward Jr., "Margaret Walker," in *The Oxford Companion to African American Literature* (New York: Oxford University Press, 1997), 753.

22. Margaret Walker, *Daemonic Genius* (New York: Amistad Press, 1988) 71.

23. Ward, "Margaret Walker," 753.

24. Walker, *Daemonic Genius*, 76.

25. Dudley Randall, "The Black Aesthetic in the Thirties, Forties, and Fifties, in *The Black Aesthetic*, ed. Addison Gayle Jr. (Garden City N.Y.: Doubleday, 1971), 240–41.

12. THE NEW BLACK POETS

1. Dudley Randall, *Broadside Memories: Poets I Have Known* (Detroit: Broadside Press, 1975), 27.

2. Ibid., 17.

3. A poem by Lee was included in the second edition of *For Malcolm* in 1969.

4. Dudley Randall to Etheridge Knight, 7 April 1968, Etheridge Knight Papers, Ward M. Canaday Center, University of Toledo Library, Toledo, Ohio.

5. Dudly Randall, "An Interview with Dudley Randall," by Gwendolyn Fowlkes, *The Black Scholar* 6, no. 6 (June 1975): 90; Dudley Randall, *Broadside Memories*, 11.

6. Ibid.

7. Randall to Knight, 9 September 1966, Knight Papers.

8. Randall to Knight, 9 September 1966, Knight Papers.

9. Randall to Knight, 15 January 1967, Knight Papers.

10. Randall to Knight, 21 June 1967, Knight Papers.

11. Randall to Knight, 6 November 1968, Knight Papers.

12. Etheridge Knight, quoted in Melba Joyce Boyd, *The Black Unicorn: Dudley Randall and Broadside Press* (New York: Cinema Guild, 1996), documentary film/video, 1996.

13. Randall to Knight, 14 September 1967, Knight Papers.
14. Randall to Knight, 21 October 1967, Knight Papers.
15. Randall to Knight, 31 October 1967, Knight Papers.
16. Randall to Knight, undated, Knight Papers.
17. Dudley Randall, "Black Emotion and Experience: The Literature for Understanding," *American Libraries* 4, no. 2 (February 1971): 32–33.
18. Randall to Knight, 14 December 1967, Knight Papers.
19. Roberto Giammanco is the Italian translator of *The Autobiography of Malcolm X*, *Malcolm X Speaks*, and *The Last Year of Malcolm X*.
20. Randall to Knight, 14 July 1968, Knight Papers.
21. Randall to Knight, 12 September 1968, Knight Papers.
22. Randall to Knight, 16 July 1968, Knight Papers.
23. Don L. Lee, introduction to *Home Coming*, by Sonia Sanchez (Detroit: Broadside Press, 1969), 7–8.
24. Randall to Knight, 27 March 1969, Knight Papers.
25. Dudley Randall, interview by the author, 5 August 1981.
26. Knight to Randall, 9 December 1970, Knight Papers.
27. "Drugs Charges Made Against 2; 1 Sentenced," *The Hartford Courant*, Sunday, 14 March 1971, in Knight Papers.
28. Philip Levine to Dudley Randall, 2 December (year not given), Etheridge Knight Papers.
29. Dudley Randall, introduction to *We A BaddDDD People*, by Sonia Sanchez (Detroit: Broadside Press, 1970), 9–10.
30. Dudley Randall to James A. Emanuel, 10 December 1967, James A. Emanuel Papers, Collections of the Manuscript Division, Library of Congress, Washington, D.C.
31. James A. Randall, interview by the author, by telephone, audiotaped, 27 October 1998.
32. Dudley Randall, ed., introduction to *The Black Poets* (New York: Bantam, 1971), xxiii–xxvi.

13. DUDLEY RANDALL'S POETIC DIALECTICS
AND THE BLACK ARTS MOVEMENT

1. Dudley Randall, "A Conversation with Dudley Randall," interview by A. X. Nicholas, *Black World* 21, no. 2 (December 1971): 33.
2. Naomi Madgett, quoted in Melba Joyce Boyd, *The Black Unicorn: Dudley Randall and the Broadside Press* (New York: Cinema Guild, 1996), documentary film/video.
3. Additional information on the friendship of Randall and Hayden also appears in my essay, "Poetry from Black Bottom: The Tension Between Ideology and Belief in the Poetry of Robert Hayden," in *Robert Hayden: Essays on the Poetry*, ed. Robert Chrisman and Laurence Goldstein (Ann Arbor: University of Michigan Press, 2001), 205–15.

4. John Hatcher, *From The Auroral Darkness: The Life and Poetry of Robert Hayden* (Oxford: George Ronald Press, 1984), 76.

5. Dudley Randall, "The Black Aesthetic of the Thirties, Forties, and Fifties," *The Black Aesthetic*, ed. Addison Gayle Jr. (Garden City, N.Y.: Doubleday, 1971), 42.

6. Dudley Randall, "Black Writers' Views on Literary Lions and Values," interview by *Negro Digest*, *Negro Digest* 17, no. 3 (January 1968): 42, 89.

7. Etheridge Knight to Dudley Randall, 13 January 1970, Etheridge Knight Papers, Ward M. Canaday Center, University of Toledo Library, Toledo, Ohio.

8. Ron Welburn, review of *Cities Burning*, by Dudley Randall, *Negro Digest* 19, no. 2 (December 1969): 94.

9. Quoted from the introductory comments on this poem in *The Norton Anthology of Modern Poetry*, 2d editttion, ed. Richard Ellman and Robert O'Clair (New York: W. W. Norton, 1990), 867.

10. Randall, "A Conversation," 33.

11. Dudley Randall, "The Second Annual Black Arts Convention," *Negro Digest* 17, no. 1 (November 1967): 45.

12. Nikki Giovanni, review of *Cities Burning*, by Dudley Randall, *Negro Digest* 17, no. 11 (September 1968): 95.

13. Ibid., 96.

14. See Don L. Lee, review of *Kaleidoscope*, edited by Robert Hayden, *Negro Digest* 17, no. 3, (January 1968): 88.

15. Dudley Randall, "White Poet, Black Critic," *Negro Digest* 14, no. 4 (February 1965): 47.

16. Ibid., 48.

17. Dudley Randall, "A Conversation," 32–33.

18. Dudley Randall et al., *A Capsule Course in Black Poetry Writing* (Detroit: Broadside Press, 1975), 45.

19. Dudley Randall, "Black Emotion and Experience: The Literature for Understanding," *American Libraries* 4, no. 2 (February 1973): 88.

20. Dudley Randall, "Black Writers' Views," 42.

21. Dudley Randall translated Russian poetry into English. See chapter 9, which discusses his Russian poetry and experiences and explores this subject in more detail.

22. Dudley Randall, "An Interview with Dudley Randall," by Gwendolyn Fowlkes, *The Black Scholar* 6, no. 6, (June 1975): 89.

14. "AFTER THE KILLING":
DUDLEY RANDALL'S BLACK ARTS POETRY

1. Dudley Randall, *More to Remember: Poems of Four Decades* (Chicago: Third World Press, 1971), 11.

2. Dudley Randall, *A Capsule Course in Black Poetry Writing* (Detroit: Broadside Press, 1975), 50.

3. Ibid.

4. Dudley Randall, quoted in D. H. Melhem, *Heroism in the New Black Poetry* (Lexington, Ky.: University Press of Kentucky, 1990) 74–75.

5. For a discussion of "Shoe Shine Boy" (*Negro Digest*, 1966), see chap. 7.

6. Randall describes her charm as "dawn" and "bells" and her beauty as "deep velvet Night," which is also the subtitle for the section where the poem appears in the collection *More to Remember*. As the poem pays tribute to Brooks's internal beauty, reminding that "beauty is as beauty does," a folkism, the last stanza resolves the revelation of real beauty with the crowning of a natural hairstyle, which affirms Brooks's deep inner pride and rejection of white beauty standards.

7. Frank Marshall Davis, Review of *After the Killing*, by Dudley Randall, *Black World* 23, no. 11 (September 1974): 85.

8. Dudley Randall, "An Interview with Dudley Randall," by Gwendolyn Fowlkes, *The Balck Scholar* 6, no. 6 (June 1975): 88.

9. Davis, Review of *After the Killing*, 85.

10. Ibid.

11. Dudley Randall, "An Interview with Dudley Randall," by Gwendolyn Fowlkes, *The Black Scholar* 6, no. 6 (June, 1975): 89.

12. Dudley Randall, *A Capsule Course in Black Poetry Writing*, 38.

13. Davis, 35.

15. POETRY AS INDUSTRY

1. Dudley Randall, *Broadside Memories: Poets I have Known* (Detroit: Braodside Press, 1975), 22–23; initially published as "Broadside Press: A Personal Chronicle," *Black Academy Review* 1, no. 1 (1970): 40–48. Written in 1970, this essay reflected the progress of the press since its inception in 1965. It provides details regarding poetry publications, the Broadside cassette tapes, *The Broadside Series* and the *Broadside Critics Series*.

2. *Broadside Memories*, 28.

3. Ibid, 25.

4. Ibid, 26.

5. In correspondence with Fuller from 1971–1973, Randall concerned himself with policy concerns involving unsolicited reviews by him and for Broadside publications. See the Hoyt W. Fuller Collection, Robert W. Woodruff Library, Archives Department, Atlanta University Center.

6. Randall, *Broadside Memories*, 27.

7. Ibid, 35.

8. Ibid, 34.

9. Ibid, 34–35.

10. Dudley Randall to James A. Emanuel, 17 January 1868, with enclosure of carbon copy of Randall's review of *Langston Hughes*, by James A. Emanuel. James A. Emanuel Papers, Libaray of Congress, Manuscript Division.

11. Randall to Emanuel, 18 January 1973, Emanuel Papers.

12. Dudley Randall, "Black Publisher, Black Writer: An Answer," *Black World* 24, no. 5 (March 1975): 36.
13. Randall, "Broadside Press," 35.
14. Dudley Randall, "The Black Aesthetic of the Thirties, Forties, and Fifties," in *The Black Aesthetic*, ed. Addison Gayle Jr. (Garden City, N.Y.: Doubleday, 1971), 40; Dudley Randall, preface to *The Last Ride of Wild Bill*, by Sterling Brown (Detroit: Broadside Press, 1975), vii.
15. Dudley Randall, *Broadside Memories*, 30–32.

16. "SHAPE OF THE INVISIBLE":
THE RISE AND FALL OF BROADSIDE PRESS

1. Dudley Randall, review of *The First Cities*, by Audre Lorde, *Negro Digest* 17, nos. 11 and 12 (September/October 1968): 13.
2. Dudley Randall, *Broadside Memories: Poets I Have Known* (Detroit: Broadside Press, 1975), 15.
3. Ibid., 16.
4. Ibid., 16.
5. Audre Lorde, quoted in Julius E. Thompson, *Dudley Randall, Broadside Press, and the Black Arts Movement in Detroit, 1960–1995* (Jefferson, N.C., and London: McFarland & Co., 1999), 131.
6. Lorenzo Thomas, *Extraordinary Measures: Afrocentric Modernism and Twentieth-Century American Poetry* (Tuscaloosa and London: University of Alabama Press, 2000), 156.
7. Dudley Randall, preface to *Broadside Authors and Artists: An Illustrated Biographical Directory*, ed. Leonard Pack Bailey (Detroit: Broadside Press, 1974), 9.
8. Randall, *Broadside Memories*, 55–56.
9. Carole A. Parks, "10th Anniversary Celebration in Detroit: The Broadside Story," *Black World* 25, no. 3 (January 1976): 85.
10. Etheridge Knight to Dudley Randall, 1 January 1976, Etheridge Knight Papers, Ward M. Canaday Center, University of Toledo Library, Toledo, Ohio.
11. Randall to Knight, 17 June 1976, Knight Papers.
12. Dudley Randall to James Emanuel, 10 February 1976, Emanuel Papers.
13. Emanuel to Randall, 3 April 1976, Emanuel Papers.
14. Dudley Randall, introduction to *Cat Eyes and Dead Wood*, by Melba Joyce Boyd (Highland Park, Mich.: Fallen Angel Press, 1978), xiii.
15. Melba Joyce Boyd, from "even when the moon don't shine," in *Cat Eyes and Dead Wood*, 2.

17. "IN THE MOURNING TIME": THE RETURN

1. Dudley Randall, quoted in *Heroism in the New Black Poetry*, by D. H. Melhem (Lexington, Ky.: University Press of Kentucky, 1981), 69.

2. The last version of this will is dated 16 October 1980, but Hoyt Fuller's name is crossed out and replaced with William Whitsitt. The change dated 29 May 1981, after Fuller's death.
3. "A Leader of the People" was published in *The Black Scholar* 11, no. 7 (September/October 1980): 91.
4. Randall, in Melhem, *Heroism*, 70.
5. "Wooing a Woman" appeared in *The Black Scholar* 12, no. 5 (September/October 1981): 20–21.
6. *Broadside Newsletter*, no. 34, August 1980.
7. Dudley Randall to Etheridge Knight, no date, Etheridge Knight Papers, Ward M. Canaday Center, University of Toledo Library, Toledo, Ohio.
8. Steve Babson. *Working Detroit* (Detroit: Wayne State University Press, 1984), 212.
9. Ibid.

18. A POET IS NOT A JUKE BOX

1. The following list gives the full names of most of the people named in the poem: Vivian Randall, Gwendolyn Brooks, Don L. Lee (Haki Madhubuti), Safisha, Laini and Bomari Madhubuti, Hoyt Fuller, Audre Lorde, Sonia Sanchez, June Jordan, Etheridge Knight, Shirley Woodson Reid, Lance Jeffers, Naomi Madgett, Robert Hayden, Leonard Andrews, James and Marguerite Randall, James Randall, Melba Joyce Boyd, Todd Duncan, Judy Simmons, Mildred Pinckney Randall, Susan L. West, Walter Cox, Val Gray Ward, Joyce Whitsitt (Malaika Wangara), Billy and Venita Sherron, Phyllis Randall Sherron, Ruby Randall, and Xavier Nicholas.
2. R. Baxter Miller, "Endowing the World and Time: The Life and Work of Dudley Randall, in *Black American Poets Between Worlds, 1940–1960*, ed. R. Baxter Miller (Knoxville, : The University of Tennessee Press, 1986), 89.
3. Randall uses rhyme and short lines to determine a light, humorous tone. The final stanza explains the value of the miniskirt in terms which use contrast to resolve contradiction and possibly to promote liberation.
4. Washington is a friend of Randall's and an important feminist intellectual who taught for some years at the University of Detroit, where Randall was poet-in-residence and reference librarian. Melhem is a poet and literary critic who published an interview and an essay on Randall's work.
5. The poem "Women" opens with the stanza:

   I like women they're so warm & soft & sweet
   Touch one & her skin yields like the flesh of a peach
   Tall & short plump & slim old & young
   they come in fascinating shapes

6. The pitch and timing of the syllables are tautly tuned to the rhythm and meter of the song, similar to the technique Randall employed to translate Russian poetry and other foreign-language verse.

7. In fact, resorting to rhyming couplets and literary language such as "foil," "beguiled" and "strumpet," primarily found in the poetry of past centuries or in literary vocabulary, demonstrates the deliberateness of his choices.

8. "Poor Dumb Butch" is about his conflict at having to put his loyal pet dog to sleep.

9. Howard Blum, "In Detroit, Poet Laureate's Work Is Never Done," *The New York Times*, 29 January 1984.

10. The opening line of the poem becomes the refrain in the last two stanzas, a metaphor for performance and repetition, which is used as rhetorical resistance for a sense of humor, juxtaposed with mounting anger and as his final comment on aesthetic freedom. The use of emphasis for aural inflection also contributes to an improvisational format, a liberating aspect of black expression.

19. AT PEACE WITH THE MUSE

1. Beaufort Cranford, "New Passages," *The Detroit News*, 6 April 1983.

2. Dudley Randall, press release, in Etheridge Kight Papers, Ward M. Canaday Center, University of Toledo Library, Toledo, Ohio.

3. Marvin Bell, quoted in Melba Joyce Boyd, *The Black Unicorn: Dudley Randall and the Broadside Press* (New York: Cinema Guild, 1996), documentary film/video.

4. Naomi Madgett, quoted in ibid.

5. Joan Gartland, quoted in Leonard Kniffel, "New Hall of Fame Honors Writers of African Descent," *American Libraries* 30, no. 2 (February 1999): 52.

6. Tony Medina, unpublished essay, 1 February 2003.

20. "THE ASCENT"

1. George Tysh, "A Poet Passes," *The Metro Times*, 9 August 2000. Although this column is unsigned, George Tysh read the copy to me over the phone before it went to press, and he undoubtedly wrote the it.

2. *The Detroit Free Press*, editorial, "Poetry: Dudley Randall Created a Haven for Writers," 11 August 2000.

3. The order of service was rearranged into:

Organ Prelude[*]

Processional:	"Marche Funebre"—Sonata No. 2, Opus 35 in B Flat Minor (Chopin)[*]
Song:	"Lift Ev'ry Voice and Sing" (Johnson)
Scripture:	Rev. Nicholas Hood, III
Prayer:	Rev. Lee Brown, Jr.
Organ Music:	"My Lord, What a Mourning"[*]
Poems by Dudley Randall:	Alvin Aubert, Naomi Long Madgett, Murray Jackson

Obituary:	Melba Joyce Boyd
Remarks	
Eulogy:	Rev. Nicholas Hood, Sr.
Recessional:	"Appassionata"–Sonata No. 23, Opus 57 in F Minor (Beethoven)
Organ Postlude:	"Largo" (Handel)*

*Elise LaBrew, Organist

4. The list was changed because some of the people had died and others were unable to carry the casket. The pallbearers were Dudley's grandson, William Sherron IV; my son, John Percy Boyd III; Delaney Ellis Jr.; the previous publisher of Broadside Press, Donald Vest; poet Haki R. Madhubuti; Jeffery West; Dudley's son-in-law, William Sherron, III; and poet Willie Williams. An honorary list of pallbearers included many on the original list.

5. Betty De Ramus, "Dudley F. Randall, 1994–2000" *The Detroit News*, 15 August 2000.

6. Terry Blackhawk, "For Dudley Randall, 1914–2000," *Michigan Quarterly Review* 40, no. 2: 313.

7. Murray Jackson, "Dudley Randall," in Melba Joyce Boyd and M. L. Liebler, eds., *Abandon Automobile: Detroit City Poetry 2001* (Detroit: Wayne State University Press, 2001), 186–87.

EPILOGUE

1. Howard Blum, "In Detroit, Poet Laureate's Work Is Never Done," *New York Times*, 29 January 1984.

BIBLIOGRAPHY

WORKS CITED

Andrews, William L., Frances Smith Foster, and Trudier Harris. *The Oxford Companion to African American Literature*. New York: Oxford University Press, 1997.

Bailey, Leaonead Pack, ed. *Broadside Authors and Artists: An Illustrated Biographical Directory*. Detroit: Broadside Press, 1974.

Babson, Steve. *Working Detroit*. Detroit: Wayne State University Press, 1986.

Baraka, Imamu Amiri. *The Autobiography of Leroi Jones/Amiri Baraka*. New York: Freundlich Books, 1984.

Beasley, David. "Bill Randall: The Man and the Movement." *Macon Magazine* (winter 1987): 23.

Blackhawk, Terry. "For Dudley Randall, 1914–2000." *Michigan Quarterly Review* 40, no. 2: 313.

Blum, Howard. "In Detroit, Poet Laureate's Work Is Never Done," *The New York Times*. 29 January 1984.

Boyd, Melba Joyce. *The Black Unicorn: Dudley Randall and the Broadside Press*. New York: Cinema Guild, 1996. Documentary film/video.

——. *Cat Eyes and Dead Wood*. Highland Park, Mich. Fallen Angel Press, 1978.

——. "Out of the Poetry Ghetto: The Life/Art Struggle of Small Black Publishing Houses." *The Black Scholar* 16, no. 4 (July/August 1985): 12–24.

——. "Poetry from Black Bottom: The Tension Between Ideology and Belief in the Poetry of Robert Hayden." In *Robert Hayden: Essays on the Poetry*, ed. Robert Chrisman and Laurence Goldstein, 205–215. Ann Arbor: University of Michigan Press, 2001.

——. "Remembering Dudley Randall." *Against the Current* 15, no. 6 (January/February 2001): 14–15.

——. "'Roses and Revolutions,' Dudley Randall: Poet, Publisher, Critic, and Champion of African American Literature Leaves a Legacy of Immeasurable Value." *The Black Scholar* 31, no.1, (spring 2001): 55–57.

——. *Song for Maya*. Detroit: Broadside Press and Detroit River Press, 1983.

Boyd, Melba Joyce, and M. L. Liebler, eds. *Abandon Automobile: Detroit City Poetry 2001*. Detroit: Wayne State University Press, 2001.

Broadside Press Newsletters. Nos. 24–34. Detroit: Broadside Press, 1972—1976, 1980–1984.

Brooks, Gwendolyn. *Report From Part One.* Detroit: Broadside Press, 1974.

Brown, Sterling. *The Last Ride of Wild Bill.* Detroit: Broadside Press, 1974.

Brown, Sterling A., and Arthur P. Davis, eds. *The Negro Caravan.* New York: The Dryden Press, 1941.

Cranford, Beaufort. "New Passages." *The Detroit News.* 6 April 1983.

Danner, Margaret. *Impressions of African Art Forms.* Detroit: Broadside Press, 1968.

Davis, Frank Marshall. Review of *After the Killing*, by Dudley Randall. *Black World* 23, no. 11 (September 1974): 84–85.

De Ramus, Betty. "Black Power, Black Rebellion." *Negro Digest* 17, no. 1 (November 1967): 24–28.

——. "Dudley F. Randall, 1994–2000: Broadside Press." *The Detroit News.* 15 August 2000.

Detroit Free Press, The. "Poetry: Dudley Randall Created a Haven for Writers." Editorial. 11 August 2000.

Duberman, Martin. *Paul Robeson.* New York: Alfred A. Knopf, 1988.

Emanuel, James A., and Theodore L. Gross, eds. *Dark Symphony: Negro Literature in America.* New York: The Free Press, 1968.

Emanuel, James A. Papers. Collections of the Manuscript Division. Library of Congress, Washington, D.C.

Fuller, Hoyt. "On the Conference Beat." *Negro Digest* 15, no. 5 (March 1966): 88–93.

——. Hoyt W. Fuller Collection. Atlanta University Center. Robert W. Woodruff Collection.

Georgakas, Dan. "Young Detroit Radicals, 1955–65." *URGENT Tasks*, no. 12 (summer 1981): 89–94.

Georgakas, Dan, and Marvin Surkin. *Detroit: I Do Mind Dying.* New York: St. Martin's Press, 1975. Revised edition: *Detroit: I Do Mind Dying A Study in Urban Revolution.* Cambridge, Mass.: South End Press, 1998.

Giovanni, Nikki. *Black Feeling, Black Talk.* Detroit: Broadside Press, 1968.

——. *Black Feeling, Black Talk/Black Judgement.* New York: Morrow, 1970.

——. *Black Judgement.* Detroit: Broadside Press, 1969.

——. *Re:creation.* Detroit: Broadside Press, 1970.

——. Review of *Cities Burning*, by Dudley Randall. *Negro Digest* 28, no. 11 (October 1968): 95–96.

Hatcher, John. *From The Auroral Darkness: The Life and Poetry of Robert Hayden.* Oxford: George Ronald Press, 1984.

Hayden, Robert. *Heart-Shape in the Dust.* Detroit: Falcon Press, 1940.

——. *Night-Blooming Cereus.* London: Paul Bremen, 1972.

——. Papers, National Baha'i Archives, Box 5, Wilmette, Illinois.

——, ed. *Kaleidoscope: Poems by American Negro Poets.* New York: Harcourt, Brace & World, Inc., 1967.

Hodges, Frenchy. "Dudley Randall and the Broadside Press." Master's thesis, Atlanta University, 1974.

Hughes, Langston. Correspondence. Langston Hughes Papers, Yale University Library.

——, ed. *New Negro Poets: U.S.A.* Bloomington: Indiana University Press, 1964.

Hunter, Kim D. "1967: Detroiters Remember the Rebellion." *Against the Current*, 12, no. 4 (1997): 19–25.

Jordan, June. Review of *After The Killing*, by Dudley Randall. *American Poetry Review* 3, no. 2 (March/April 1974): 32–34.

Kniffel, Leonard. "New Hall of Fame Honors Writers of African Descent." *American Libraries* 30, no. 2 (February 1999): 52–53.

Knight, Etheridge. *Belly Song*. Detroit: Broadside Press, 1973.

——. *Born of a Woman: New and Selected Poems*. Boston: Houghton Mifflin, 1980.

——. Papers. The Ward M. Canaday Center. University of Toledo Library, Toledo, Ohio.

——. *Poems from Prison*. Detroit: Broadside Press, 1968.

——, ed. *Voices from Prison*. New York: Pathfinder Press, 1970.

Lee, Don L. Introduction to *Home Coming*, by Sonia Sanchez, 7–8. Detroit: Broadside Press, 1969.

——. "On *Kaleidoscope* and Robert Hayden." *Negro Digest* 17, no. 3 (January 1968): 51–52, 90–94.

——. *Think Black*. Detroit: Broadside Press, 1969.

Lorde, Audre. *Cables to Rage*. London: Paul Breman, 1970.

——. *From a Land Where Other People Live*. Detroit: Broadside Press, 1973.

——. *The New York Head Shop*. Detroit: Broadside Press, 1974.

Madgett, Naomi Long. "Naomi Long Madgett." Vol. 23 of *Contemporary Authors Series*, ed. Shelly Andrews. Detroit: Gale Research, 1996.

——. "Dudley Randall," *The Oxford Companion to African American Literature*. New York: Oxford University Press, 1997, 620–21.

McCants, Elizabeth. "Memory of Former Slave Now Fading, But She Still Recalls Raid of Yankees." *The Macon Press*. 3 June 1958.

Medina, Tony. Unpublished essay. 1 February, 2003.

Medina, Tony, and Louis Reyes Rivera. *Bum Rush the Page: A Def Poetry Jam*. New York: Three Rivers Press, 2001.

Melhem, D. H. *Heroism in the New Black Poetry*. Lexington, Ky.: University Press of Kentucky, 1990.

Miller, R. Baxter. "Endowing the World and Time: The Life and Work of Dudley Randall." In *Black American Poets Between Worlds, 1940–1960*, ed. Miller, 77–92. Knoxville: The University of Tennessee Press, 1986.

Parks, Carole A. "10th Anniversary Celebration in Detroit: The Broadside Story." *Black World* 25, no. 3 (January 1976): 84–90.

Pool, Rosey E., ed. *Beyond the Blues: New Poems by American Negroes*. London: The Hand and Flower Press, 1962.

——, ed. *Ik Ben de Nieuwe Neger*. The Hague, Holland: Bert, Bakker, 1965.

Rampersad, Arnold. *Jackie Robinson: A Biography*. New York: Alfred A. Knopf, 1997.

Redmond, Eugene B. *Drumvoices: The Mission of Afro-American Poetry, A Critical History*. New York: Anchor Press/Doubleday, 1976.

——. "Stridency and the Sword: Literary and Cultural Emphasis in Afro-American Magazines." In *The Little Magazine in America: A Modern Documentary History*, ed. Elliott Anderson and Mary Kinzie, 538–573. New York: The Pushcart Press, 1978.

Sanchez, Sonia. *We A BaddDDD People*. Detroit: Broadside Press, 1970.

Spencer, Chauncey E. *Who Is Chauncey E. Spencer?* Detroit: Broadside Press, 1975.

Strong, Carline Williams. "Margaret Taylor Goss Burroughs: Educator, Artist, Author, Founder, and Civic Leader." Ph.D. diss., Loyola University of Chicago, 1994.

Thomas, Lorenzo. *Extraordinary Measures: Afrocentric Modernism and Twentieth-Century American Poetry*. Tuscaloosa and London: University of Alabama Press, 2000.

Thompson, Heather Ann. *Whose Detroit? Politics, Labor and Race in a Modern American City*. Ithaca: Cornell University Press, 2001.

Thompson, Julius E. *Dudley Randall, Broadside Press, and the Black Arts Movement in Detroit, 1960–1995*. Jefferson, N.C., and London: McFarland & Co., 1999.

Tolson, Melvin B. Collections of the Manuscript Division. Box 1, 1965–1966. Library of Congress.

Tysh, George. "A Poet Passes." *The Metro Times*. 9 August 2000, 30.

Walker, Margaret. *Daemonic Genius*. New York: Amistad Press, 1988.

Ward, Jerry, Jr. "Margaret Walker." In *The Oxford Companion to African American Literature*, 752–53. New York: Oxford University Press, 1997.

Welburn, Ron. Review of *Cities Burning*, by Dudley Randall. *Negro Digest* 19, no. 2 (December 1969): 94–95.

Young, Coleman and Wheeler, Lonnie. *Hard Stuff: The Autobiography of Mayor Coleman Young*. New York: Viking Press, 1994.

SELECTED WORKS BY DUDLEY RANDALL

After the Killing. Chicago: Third World Press, 1973.

"An Answer to Lerone Bennett's Questionnaire." *Negro Digest* 17, no. 3 (January 1968): 41–42.

"Aphorisms." *Negro Digest* 11, no. 11 (September 1962): 45.

"The Black Aesthetic in the Thirties, Forties, and Fifties." In *The Black Aesthetic*, ed. Addison Gayle Jr., 235–45. Garden City, N.Y.: Doubleday, 1971.

"Black Emotion and Experience: The Literature for Understanding." *America Libraries* 4, no. 2 (February 1973): 32–37.

"Black Magic." *Ebony* 32 (August 1977): 30.

"Black Poet, White Critic." *Negro Digest* 14, no. 11 (September 1965): 4.

Black Poetry: A Supplement to Anthologies that Exclude Black Poets. Detroit: Broadside Press, 1969.

"Black Power." *Negro Digest* 16, no. 1 (November 1966): 95–96.

"Black Publisher, Black Writer: An Answer." *Black World* 24, no. 5. (March 1975): 30–37.

"Black Writers' Views on Literary Lions and Values." Interview by *Negro Digest*. *Negro Digest* 17, no. 3 (January 1968): 42, 89.

"Booker T. and W. E. B." *Midwest Journal* 5, no. 1 (winter 1952): 77-78.

Broadside Memories: Poets I Have Known. Detroit: Broadside Press, 1975.

"Broadside Press: A Personal Chronicle." *Black Academy Review* 1, no. 1 (1970): 40–48.

Cities Burning. Detroit: Broadside,1968.

"A Conversation with Dudley Randall." Interview by A. X. Nicholas. *Black World* 21, no. 2 (December 1971): 26–34.

"The Creative Arts." In *Black Expression: Essays By and About Black Americans*, ed. Addison Gayle, Jr. New York: Weybright & Talley, 1969.

"The Cut Throat." *Negro Digest* 13, no. 9 (July 1964): 53–56.

"Games." *Negro Digest* 17, no. 8 (June 1968): 61.

"Ghetto Girls." *Negro Digest* 16, no. 7 (May 1967): 25.

"Incident on a Bus." *Negro Digest* 14, no. 10 (August 1965): 70–71.

"An Interview with Dudley Randall." By Gwendolyn Fowlkes. *The Black Scholar* 6, no. 6 (June 1975): 87–90.

A Litany of Friends. Detroit: Lotus Press, 1981.

"Love Poem," "And Why The Softness In A Lover's Eyes," "The Goddess of Love, "The Profile On The Pillow." *Black World* 19, no. 11 (September 1970): 58–60.

Love You. London: Paul Bremen, 1970.

"Melting Pot." *Negro Digest* 17, no. 3 (January 1968): 53.

"Melvin B. Tolson: Portrait of a Poet as Raconteur." *Negro Digest* 15, no. 3 (January 1966): 54–57.

More to Remember: Poems of Four Decades. Chicago: Third World Press, 1971.

"Mystery Poet: An Interview with Frank Marshall Davis." *Black World* 23, no. 3 (January 1974): 37–48.

"Old Witherington." *Negro Digest* 14, no. 11 (September 1965): 62.

Papers. Collections of the Manuscript Division. Library of Congress, Washington, D.C.

"A Report on the Black Arts Convention." *Negro Digest* 16, no. 10 (August 1966): 13–15.

Review of *Black Poetry in America*, by Blyden Jackson and Louis D. Rubin Jr. *Black World* 24, no. 1 (November 1974): 73–75.

Review of *Exile and Return* by June Jordan. *Black World* 2, no. 8 (March 1975): 81–85.

Review of *The First Cities*, by Audre Lorde. *Negro Digest* 17, nos. 11 and 12 (September/October 1968): 13–14.

Review of *From the Dark Tower* by Arthur P. Davis." *Black World* 24, no. 1 (November 1974): 73–75.

Reviews of *Ik ben de nieuwe Neger* (I am the new negro), ed. Rosey E. Pool, *We Are Going*, by Kath Walker, and *Poems* by Derek Walcott. *Negro Digest* 14, no. 11 (September 1965): 52; 86–88.

Review of *James Baldwin*, ed. Kenneth Kinamon, *Black World* 24, no. 2 (December 1974): 91–92.

Review of *Pink Ladies in the Afternoon*, by Naomi Long Madgett. *Black World* 23, no. 11 (September 1974): 52; 84–85.

Review of *Songs of a Blackbird*. *Black World* 19, no. 10 (August 1970): 52, 82.

Review of *West African Travels*. *Black World* 24, no. 6, (April 1975): 94–95.

"The Rite." *Negro Digest* 13, no. 11 (September 1964): 59.

"The Second Annual Black Arts Convention." *Negro Digest* 17, no. 1 (November 1967): 42–45.

"Shoeshine Boy: A Short Story." *Negro Digest* 15, no. 11 (September 1966): 53–55.

"Song." *Negro Digest* 18, no. 11 (September 1969): 40.

"Souvenirs." *Negro Digest* 13, no. 1 (March 1964): 48.

"Three Poems by Dudley Randall: 'Colonizer,' 'Continental Hotel,' and 'Slave Castle.'" *Black World* 22, no. 11 (September 1973): 23–25.

"To Gwendolyn Brooks, Teacher." *Black World* 22, no. 4 (February 1973): 53.

"To the Mercy Killers." *Negro Digest*, 15, no. 11 (September 1966): 66.

"To the North Star." *Negro Digest* 15, no. 6 (April 1966): 19.

"Ubi Sunt and Hic Sum." *Negro Digest* 14, no. 11 (September 1965): 73–76.

"Victoria." *Negro Digest* 15, no. 7 (May 1966): 64–72.

"When I Think of Russia." *Negro Digest* 16, no. 8 (June 1967): 74.

"White Poet, Black Critic." *Negro Digest* 14, no. 4 (February 1965): 46–48.

"Words of the Poets." *Negro Digest* 14, no. 8 (June 1965): 40–41.

Randall, Dudley, ed. *The Black Poets*. New York: Bantam, 1971.

——, ed. *The Broadside Series*. Nos. 1–94. Detroit: Broadside Press, 1965–1984.

——, ed. *Homage to Hoyt*. Detroit: Broadside Press, 1984.

Randall, Dudley, and Margaret Burroughs, eds.. *For Malcolm: Poems on the Life and the Death of Malcolm X*. Detroit: Broadside Press, 1967.

Randall, Dudley, and Margaret Danner. *Poem Counterpoem*. Detroit: Broadside Press, 1966.

Randall, Dudley, et al. *A Capsule Course in Black Poetry Writing*. Detroit: Broadside Press, 1975.

INTERVIEWS

Alston, Chris. Interview by author. Videotaped. Ann Arbor, Mich. 23 February 1990.

Jackson, Murray. Interview by author. Audiotaped. Detroit, Mich. 1 August 1996.

Milner, Ron. Interview by author. Audiotaped. Detroit, Mich. 3 June 2001.

Randall, Dudley. Interviews by author. Audiotaped and videotaped. Detroit, Mich. 1981–2000.

Randall, James A. Interview by author. Audiotaped. Via telephone. Detroit, Mich. and New York, N.Y. 27 October 1998.

Randall, Robert. Interview by author. Audiotaped. Hartford, Conn., and Detroit, Mich., via telephone. 21 October 1998.

Randall, Vivian. Interviews by author. Detroit, Mich. 1981–2000.

Randall, William. Interview by author. Audiotaped. Via telephone. Detroit, Mich. and Macon, Ga. 24 October 1998.

Sherron, Phyllis Randall. Interview by author. Audiotaped. Detroit, Mich. 15 September 1996.

Simpkins, Edward. Interview by author. Audiotaped. Detroit, Mich. 1 October 1996.

Young, Coleman A. Interview by author. Audiotaped and videotaped. Detroit, Mich. 1 September 1995, 29 September 1996.

BROADSIDE PRESS PUBLICATIONS: 1966–1976, 1983–1984

Arnez, Nancy, and Beatrice Murphy. *The Rocks Cry Out*. 1968.

Aubert, Alvin. *Against the Blues*. 1972.

Alhamisi. Ahmed. *Holy Ghosts*. 1972.

Baker, Houston A., Jr. *A Many Colored Coat of Dreams: The Poetry of Countee Cullen*. 1974.

Bailey, Leaonead Pack, ed. *Broadside Authors and Artists: An Illustrated Biographical Directory*. 1974.

Barlow, George. *Gabriel*. 1974.

Bell, Bernard W. *The Folk Roots of Contemporary Afro-American Poetry*. 1974.

Blakely, Henry. *Windy Place*. 1974.

Boyd, Melba Joyce. *Song for Maya*. With Detroit River Press. 1983.

Boyer, Jill Witherspoon. *The Broadside Annual*. 1972.

——. *The Broadside Annual*. 1973.

——. *Dream Farmer*. 1975.

Boze, Arthur. *Against the Blues*. 1972.

Bragg, Linda. *A Love Song to Black Men*. 1974.

Brooks, Gwendolyn. *Riot*. 1969.

——. *Family Pictures*. 1970.

——. *The Black Position*. Nos. 1 and 2. 1971–3.

——. *Report From Part One*. 1974.

——. *Beckonings*. 1975.

——, ed. *A Broadside Treasury*. 1971.

——, ed. *Jump Bad: A New Chicago Anthology*. 1971.

Brown, Sterling. *The Last Ride of Wild Bill*. 1974.

Cannon, C. E. *St. Nigger*. 1972.

Danner, Margaret. *Impressions of African Art*. 1968.

Drafts, Gene. *Bloodwhispers/Black Song*. 1973.

Eckels, John. *Home Is Where the Soul Is*. 1969.

——. *Our Business Is in the Streets*. 1970.

Emanuel, James A. *Treehouse and Other Poems*. 1968.

——. *Panther Man*. 1970.

Figueroa, Jose-Angel. *East 110th Street*. 1973.

Gayle, Addison, Jr. *Claude McKay: The Black Poet at War*. 1972.

Gibbs, Michelle S. *Sketches from Home*. 1983.

Giovanni, Nikki. *Black Feeling, Black Talk*. 1968.

——. *Black Judgement*. 1969.

——. *Re:creation*. 1970.

Guillen, Nicolas. *Tengo*. Trans. Richard J. Carr. 1974.

Hoagland, Everett. *Black Velvet*. 1970.

Hodges, Frenchy. *Black Wisdom*. 1971.

Jeffers, Lance. *My Blackness Is the Beauty of This Land*. 1970.

——. *When I Know the Power of My Black Hand*. 1974.

Kgositsile, Aneb. *Blood River*. 1983.

Kgositsile, Keorapetse. *Spirits Unchained*. 1969.

Knight, Etheridge. *Poems from Prison*. 1968.

——. *Belly Song*. 1973.

Lee, Don L. *Think Black*. 1967.

——. *Black Pride*. 1968.

——. *Don't Cry, Scream.* 1969.

——. *We Walk the Way of the New World.* 1970.

——. *Directionscore: Selected and New Poems.* 1971.

——. *Dynamite Voices: Black Poets of the 1960s.* 1971.

——. *Book of Life.* 1973.

——. *From Plan to Planet: Life Studies.* With The Institute for Positive Education. 1973

Levy, Lyn. *Singing Sadness Happy.* 1972.

Lomax, Pearl Cleage. *We Don't Need No Music.* 1972.

Long, Doughtry. *Black Love, Black Hope.* 1970.

——. *Song for Nia.* 1971.

Lorde, Audre. *From a Land Where Other People Live.* 1973.

——. *The New York Head Shop.* 1974.

Major, Clarence. *The Cotton Club.* 1972.

Odarty, Bill. *A Safari of African Cooking.* 1971.

O'Neal, Regina. *And Then the Harvest: Three Television Plays.* 1974.

Pfister, Arthur. *Beer Cans, Bullets, Things, and Pieces.* 1972.

Randall, Dudley. *Cities Burning.* 1968.

——. *Black Poetry: A Supplement to Anthologies that Exclude Black Poets.* 1969.

——. *Broadside Memories Poets I Have Known.* 1975.

——, ed. *The Broadside Series.* Nos. 1–94. 1965–1984.

——, ed. *Homage to Hoyt.* 1984.

Randall, Dudley, Gwendolyn Brooks, Haki R. Madhubuti, Keorapetse Kgositsile. *A Capsule Course in Black Poetry Writing.* 1975.

Randall, Dudley, and Margaret Burroughs. *For Malcolm: Poems On The Life And The Death Of Malcolm X..* 1967.

Randall, Dudley, and Margaret Danner. *Poem Counterpoem.* 1966.

Randall, James, Jr. *Don't Ask Me Who I Am.* 1970.

——. *Cities and Other Disasters.* 1973.

Randall, Jon. *Indigoes.* 1975.

Raven, John. *Blues for Momma.* 1970.

Robinson, William. *Phillis Wheatley in the Black American Beginnings.* 1975.

Sanchez, Sonia. *Homecoming.* 1969.

——. *We A BaddDDD People.* 1970.

——. *A Blues Book for Blue Black Magical Women.* 1975.

——. *It's A New Day.* 1983.

Simmons, Judy D. *Judith's Blues.* 1973.

Spencer, Chauncey E. *Who Is Chauncey Spencer?* 1975

Thigpen, William, Jr. *Down Nigger Paved Streets.* 1972.

Thompson, Carolyn. *Frank.* 1970.

Walker, Margaret. *Prophets for a New Day.* 1970.

——. *October Journey.* 1973.

Wolde, Habte. *Enough to Die For.* 1972.

X, Marvin. *Black Man Listen.* 1969.

INDEX

FURTHER ACKNOWLEDGMENTS

SOME OF THE WRITING in this book appeared in slightly different forms in: "*Prophets for a New Day*: The Cultural Activism of Gwendolyn Brooks, Margaret Danner, Margaret Burroughs, and Margaret Walker During the Black Arts Movement," *Revista Caneria de Estudios Ingeles*, Universidad de la Laguna, Spain, vol. 37, November 1998; and "Out of the Poetry Ghetto: The Life/Art Struggle of Small Black Publishers," *The Black Scholar* 15, no. 9 (August/September, 1985).

Works used by permission include: Terry Blackhawk, "For Dudley Randall, 1914–2000," taken from *Michigan Quarterly Review*, reprinted by permission of the author; Murray Jackson, "Dudley Randall," taken from *Abandon Automobile: Detroit City Poetry 2001*, ed. Melba Joyce Boyd and M. L. Liebler (Detroit: Wayne State University Press, 2001), reprinted by permission of Kathryn Lindberg Jackson.

Photos of Wayne State University and of Dudley Randall as a student reprinted by permission of the Walter P. Reuther Labor Library, Wayne State University; photos by Hugh Grannum reprinted by permission of the Detroit Newspapers Association; photos from the Broadside Press tenth-anniversary celebration reprinted by permission of the Laura Mosley Collection; photos from the Orlin Jones Collection reprinted by permission of Orlin Jones; photos of the Randall family and Broadside Press, 1965–77, reprinted by permission of the Dudley Randall estate.